Notable Natural Disasters

Volume 2

Events to 1970

Edited by
Marlene Bradford, Ph.D.
Texas A&M University

Robert S. Carmichael, Ph.D.
University of Iowa

SALEM PRESS, INC.
Pasadena, California   Hackensack, New Jersey

These essays originally appeared in *Natural Disasters* (2001). New essays and other material have been added.

Library of Congress Cataloging-in-Publication Data

Notable natural disasters / edited by Marlene Bradford, Robert S. Carmichael.
p. cm. — (Magill's choice)
Includes bibliographical references and index.
ISBN 978-1-58765-368-1 (set : alk. paper) — ISBN 978-1-58765-369-8 (vol. 1 : alk. paper) — ISBN 978-1-58765-370-4 (vol. 2 : alk. paper) — ISBN 978-1-58765-371-1 (vol. 3 : alk. paper) 1. Natural disasters. I. Bradford, Marlene. II. Carmichael, Robert S.

GB5014.N373 2007
904'.5—dc22

2007001926

CONTENTS

■ **INDEXES**

COMPLETE LIST OF CONTENTS

Volume 1

Volume 2

■ EVENTS

Complete List of Contents

Volume 3

Contents xli
Complete List of Contents xliii

Complete List of Contents

NOTABLE NATURAL DISASTERS

■ C. 65,000,000 B.C.E.: YUCATÁN CRATER

METEORITE

DATE: About 65 million years ago

PLACE: Yucatán Peninsula, Atlantic Ocean

CLASSIFICATION: 10 on the Torino Impact Hazard Scale; energy equivalent to at least 100 million megatons of TNT released

RESULT: Instantly destroyed most life within 621-mile radius and caused worldwide climate changes resulting in the extinction of up to 85 percent of species then living

A team of scientists led by Luis and Walter Alvarez, father and son, were studying the thin clay layer that lies between the rocks of the Cretaceous geological period and the rocks of the following Tertiary period. This boundary is designated the K/T boundary. (By convention, Cretaceous is abbreviated *K*. The letter *C* is used for the earlier Cambrian period.) Knowing that the element iridium is more abundant in meteorites than in earth rocks, and supposing that small meteorites fall at a more or less constant rate, they supposed that the amount of iridium in the clay would be a clue to how long it took to form the clay layer. To their great surprise, they discovered that the iridium concentration in the clay was 300 times that of the rocks above and below it. In 1980, they startled the world with this result and with their theory of what had ended the reign of the dinosaurs 65 million years ago.

According to their theory, now widely accepted, a rocky asteroid 6.2 miles (10 kilometers) or more in diameter hurtled toward Earth at tens of miles per second. Plunging through the atmosphere in a few seconds, its energy of motion was converted into heat as it struck the ground, vaporizing itself along with a great deal of the target rock. The resulting explosion lofted 100 million megatons of dust and rock vapor into the air, much of it out into space. It also produced an earthquake 30,000 times stronger than the San Francisco earthquake of 1906.

Scientist Luis Alvarez, who theorized that a large meteorite destroyed most life on earth in 65,000,000 B.C.E.
(The Nobel Foundation)

There is a huge crater about 112 miles (180 kilometers) across at Chicxulub, Yucatán. It is 65 million years old and is thought to be the impact site of the Alvarez asteroid. Fittingly, Chicxulub (pronounced CHEEK-shoe-lube) means "tail of the devil." Today, the crater is completely covered with surface rock. Further evidence of an impact is that all around the Gulf of Mexico there is a 65-million-year-old layer of tsunami-wave rubble 33 feet (10 meters) thick, including large boulders washed far inland. Shock-fractured crystals found in the K/T boundary layer are another key piece of evidence. While a large impact can form these crystals, volcanic activity cannot.

Shock and heat from the impact killed nearly everything above ground within 621 miles (1,000 kilometers). The vapor that was lofted into space cooled and condensed into rocky globules that reheated as they plunged back into the atmosphere all around the world. Their heat started forest fires worldwide. The amount of soot found in the worldwide K/T boundary layer shows that much of Earth's total biomass burned. Smoke from these fires combined with dust lofted into the stratosphere by the impact formed a worldwide pall that blocked sunlight for months, causing Earth to cool about 40 degrees Fahrenheit and photosynthesis to cease. This has been called "impact winter."

Heat from the fireball caused nitrogen and oxygen in the atmosphere to combine to form nitric oxide, which was lofted into the stratosphere, where it destroyed the ozone layer. Less than 2 percent of Earth's surface is covered with layers of limestone and evaporite 1.2 to 1.9 miles (2 to 3 kilometers) thick, but the Yucatán Peninsula is such a place. Vaporizing these deposits released huge amounts of sulfur dioxide and carbon dioxide. Nitric oxide and sulfur dioxide combined with water vapor in the air to form acid rain. There may not have been enough acid rain worldwide to be a serious problem by itself, but it did add to the environmental insult. As the dust cleared, "impact winter" turned to "impact summer," and the climate warmed about 40 degrees Fahrenheit above normal for thousands of years. These elevated temperatures were possibly due to a greenhouse effect caused by the extra carbon dioxide and water vapor in the atmosphere.

Which species became extinct and exactly when that happened remains somewhat controversial; however, the most complete studies support the hypothesis that the dinosaurs died because of the climate-changing effects of an asteroid impact. The general pattern is that species such as dinosaurs, whose food chain depended upon living plant material, became extinct. Species whose food chain depended upon organic detritus left in logs, soil, or water survived and eventually expanded into niches previously dominated by extinct species. Apparently, mammals survived on insects, arthropods, and worms until the sun began to shine again and plants to grow again.

Charles W. Rogers

c. 65,000,000 B.C.E.*: Yucatán crater*

FOR FURTHER INFORMATION:
Alvarez, Luis W. "Mass Extinctions Caused by Large Bolide Impacts." *Physics Today,* July, 1987, 24-33.
Beatty, J. Kelly. "Killer Crater in the Yucatán?" *Sky and Telescope,* July, 1991, 38-40.
Raup, David M. *The Nemesis Affair: A Story of the Death of Dinosaurs and the Ways of Science.* New York: W. W. Norton, 1986.
Verschuur, Gerrit L. *Impact! The Threat of Comets and Asteroids.* New York: Oxford University Press, 1996.
Zanda, Brigitte, and Monica Rotaru, eds. *Meteorites: Their Impact on Science and History.* Translated by Roger Hewins. New York: Cambridge University Press, 2001.

■ C. 1470 B.C.E.: THERA ERUPTION

VOLCANO

DATE: c. 1470 B.C.E.

PLACE: Aegean Sea

RESULT: Volcanic eruption and caldera collapse, town buried and preserved intact, possible cause of disappearance of Minoan civilization on Crete, alleged location of lost "continent" of Atlantis

The eruption of Thera (now known as Thíra) in 1470 B.C.E. has been compared in severity with the eruption in 5000 B.C.E. that formed Crater Lake in Oregon, but as no written records survive, knowledge of the eruption must be deduced entirely from the geological and archaeological evidence. Judging from the pottery, archaeologists date the eruption to around 1400 B.C.E. Geologists give a date of 1470 B.C.E. based on a radioactive age determination.

The volcano lies in a cluster of islands that used to be known as Santorin or Santorini. These islands form part of a convex arc of recently extinct volcanoes in the Aegean Sea, facing the Mediterranean between Turkey and Greece. Geologists describe this as a firing line where the crustal plate of Africa is plunging down beneath the crustal plate of southeastern Europe.

Prior to the 1470 B.C.E. eruption, Thera had a long and complicated volcanic history, beginning with submarine eruptions from volcanic vents located adjacent to some bedrock islands. When ejecta from these vents reached water level, small volcanic islands appeared, which then grew together with the adjoining bedrock as eruptions continued. Ultimately this complex of overlapping volcanic cones and bedrock masses formed a circular island nearly 10 miles in diameter and with a summit that might have been as much as 1 mile high.

A period of quiescence then followed, which scientists believe lasted for many thousands of years. During this interval, fertile soils developed on the weathered volcanic rocks, lakes and marshes formed in the depressions, and vegetation appeared. Humans colonized Thera from neighboring islands, bringing with them the Bronze Age

culture then prevalent in the eastern Mediterranean. The largest set-tlement appears to have been at ancient Akrotiri on the southern coast, a location that had a natural harbor, shelter from the strong northerly winds, and probably more rainfall than other parts of the is-land.

Excavations begun here in 1967 have unearthed, from beneath the mantle of volcanic debris, the most completely preserved prehis-toric site in Europe. The once-thriving town of several thousand in-habitants had narrow streets; underground sewers to carry away do-mestic effluent; and two-, three-, and four-story homes adorned with frescoes, which are still breathtakingly fresh 3,500 years after they were first painted. In the surrounding fields, the inhabitants of the is-land raised sheep and goats; cultivated grapes for wine; and grew crops of lentils, split peas, and barley, from which they milled flour to make bread. Pottery discovered in the excavation indicates that the residents maintained close trade connections with both Crete and mainland Greece.

Archaeologists have concluded that the first indication of the impending eruption was a large-scale earthquake, which caused major damage to buildings throughout the town. Then came a period of calm—perhaps several months in length—during which people began rebuilding their homes. Repairs were still in progress when the next phase of the eruption struck. This began with a fall of pellets of pumice that eventually built up a layer as much as 15 feet thick over most of the island.

By now the inhabitants of Akrotiri must have fled, taking with

A modern satellite image of Thera. (NASA)

them whatever valuables they could carry and leaving behind the furnishings of their homes, as well as a vast assortment of pottery used for the storing, cooking, and serving of food. The absence of human or animal remains in the ruins indicates that people had time to evacuate safely. After the fall of pumice pellets came a series of minor ash and pumice falls, and then the culminating phase of the eruption: fine, white ash, with scattered basalt boulders, that blanketed the island to a depth of 100 feet or more. The ash is also present beneath the Mediterranean as a layer up to 7 feet thick found in core samples more than 450 miles away.

Following the ashfall—or perhaps simultaneous with it—the central part of the volcano collapsed into the underlying magma chamber, creating a huge depression in the seafloor, known as a caldera. Thera's caldera is 7 miles long and 5 miles wide and has a maximum depth of 1,575 feet. The rim of the old volcano still surrounds it in the form of three ragged islands with rocky cliffs 1,200 feet high, rising toward where the summit used to be. The volume of the collapse has been estimated at 38 cubic miles, which is about the same as the collapse at Crater Lake and more than three times the collapse at Krakatau in Indonesia. Tsunamis (tidal waves) were probably generated at this time, and a pumice deposit found 23 feet above sea level at Tel Aviv in Israel has been attributed to them.

About 70 miles to the south of Thera lies the island of Crete, which was the center of the highly developed Minoan civilization during the Bronze Age. Many archaeologists blame the sudden disappearance of this civilization on the eruption of Thera, citing the destructive earthquakes that accompanied the eruption, the possibility of devastating tsunamis, and the ashfalls from the volcano that could have destroyed the fertility of fields on Crete.

Thera is also cited as a possible location for Plato's famous lost "continent" of Atlantis, which he mentioned in two of his writings. He describes Atlantis as the home of a rich and powerful nation with an advanced civilization. According to him, the end of this civilization came when the island was wracked by violent earthquakes and floods and then, in the space of a single night and day, was swallowed up by the sea. This description would fit the catastrophic end of Thera perfectly.

Donald W. Lovejoy

FOR FURTHER INFORMATION:

Bullard, Fred M. *Volcanoes of the Earth.* 2d rev. ed. Austin: University of Texas Press, 1984.

Doumas, Christos G. *Thera, Pompeii of the Ancient Aegean: Excavations at Akrotiri, 1967-1979.* London: Thames and Hudson, 1983.

Fisher, Richard V., Grant Heiken, and Jeffrey B. Hulen. *Volcanoes: Crucibles of Change.* Princeton, N.J.: Princeton University Press, 1997.

Fouqué, Ferdinand. *Santorini and Its Eruptions.* Translated by Alexander R. McBirney. Baltimore: Johns Hopkins University Press, 1998.

Friedrich, Walter L. *Fire in the Sea: The Santorini Volcano—Natural History and the Legend of Atlantis.* Translated by Alexander R. McBirney. New York: Cambridge University Press, 2000.

■ 430 B.C.E.: THE PLAGUE OF ATHENS
EPIDEMIC

DATE: 430-427 B.C.E.
PLACE: Athens, Greece
RESULT: About 30,000 dead

As the early battles of the Peloponnesian War (431-404 B.C.E.) were being waged between the ancient Greek city-states of Athens and Sparta, urban crowding in several major cities reached an unprecedented level. Perhaps the worst of these over-populated centers was Athens itself. It had been the strategy of the Athenian general and statesman Pericles to protect the entire populace of Attica, the region in which Athens is located, by permitting any resident of this area who wished to do so to take refuge within the Athenian city walls. While this policy won much support because it protected most of the citizenry from Spartan raids, it also caused such intense crowding within central Athens that the city became vulnerable to the swift spread of disease.

The plague that befell Athens in 430 B.C.E. was first observed in Ethiopia, Egypt, Libya, and the island of Lemnos. Scholars assume that it was carried to Athens aboard ship, a theory given credence by the illness's first arrival in mainland Europe at Piraeus, the port of Athens. Because a state of war then existed between Athens and Sparta, initial suspicions fell upon the Spartans. They were accused of poisoning the Athenian water supply in an attempt to win through deceit victories that they could not win on the battlefield. Nevertheless, as the disease spread, ultimately killing as many as a quarter to a third of the entire Athenian population, it became apparent that the cause of the disaster was not an enemy conspiracy but a new form of contagion that had a natural (or, as some thought, a divine) origin.

SYMPTOMS OF THE ATHENIAN PLAGUE. The symptoms of the Athenian plague have been detailed with far greater precision than those of any other ancient epidemic because the Greek historian Thucydides (c. 459-c. 402 B.C.E.) provided a full account of it in his history of the Peloponnesian War. Thucydides himself had suffered from the plague, but, like a number of other fortunate individuals, he survived. The description that Thucydides provided of the plague includes little speculation as to its cause but extensive analysis of its symptoms. Thucydides relates that he provided this information in the hope that future generations would recognize later outbreaks of the disease and understand its prognosis. By taking this approach, Thucydides revealed that he was under the influence of the "father of Greek medicine," Hippocrates of Cos (c. 460-c. 370 B.C.E.), then at the height of his prestige among the Athenian intelligentsia. Hippocrates, too, had stressed diagnosis and prognosis over vain attempts to find cures.

Thucydides notes that the onset of the plague was sudden. During a year that had otherwise been remarkably free of other illnesses, apparently healthy people would unexpectedly develop a high fever. Inflammation of the eyes, throat, and tongue soon followed, turning the victim's breath extremely foul. Several of the plague's initial symptoms resembled those of a severe cold. Patients suffered from sneezing, hoarseness, and coughs. The standard treatments of these symptoms had, however, little effect upon the rapid progress of the plague.

In its second stage, the plague moved from victims' heads to their stomachs. Vomiting and great pain were followed by dry heaves (or, some scholars believe, violent hiccups) and prolonged spasms. Then, as the fever began to subside, the patient's skin turned sensitive. Many victims found that they could not tolerate being touched in any way or even being covered by either clothing or blankets. The patient's skin turned deep red or black-and-blue in spots, with sores breaking out over large areas of the body. Sleep proved to be impossible, both from the pain of the illness and from a general restlessness. Unquenchable thirst caused many victims to throw themselves into public rain basins in their desire to drink as much water as possible.

By this stage in the illness, seven or eight days had elapsed; many of the plague's victims died at this point. Those who survived the plague's initial ravages, however, quickly developed severe diarrhea. The general weakness that resulted from sustained dysentery then caused additional deaths among the very young and very old. Those in the prime of life, however, might begin to regain their health at this point. The severe fevers caused some victims to develop amnesia. Others became blind or lost the use of their extremities.

As the plague lingered in Athens, it increasingly took its toll upon those with weakened immune systems. Thucydides notes that, as the winter continued, nearly any disease that an individual developed eventually turned into the plague. Victims also remained contagious after they died. Thucydides reports that animals did not feed on the corpses of plague victims or, if they did, they died soon after. Human patients who survived appeared to be immune to further attacks of plague. Several of those who repeatedly developed plague symptoms found that subsequent infections were increasingly less severe. In their elation at their restored health, many former victims imagined that they were now immune to illness of any kind. As evidence emerged that this was not true, however, a number of these survivors were plunged into a deep depression.

Subsequent History of the Plague. One unanticipated outcome of the Athenian plague was the emergence of an almost city-wide sense of fatalism. The sudden, indiscriminate death caused by the plague suggested to many individuals that no human action or remedy was useful. Victims died regardless of whether they were ignored or well treated by physicians. Death occurred without respect for a victim's character or individual piety. Diet, exercise, and a person's general state of health had little bearing on the rapid progress of the disease. What was worse in the eyes of many was that the merciful appeared to be dying in even greater numbers than the callous. Compassionate individuals were more likely to treat others suffering from the disease and thus were more likely to be exposed to it themselves. As a result, many Athenians felt that all the virtues they had once cherished—piety, fitness, civic-mindedness, integrity—were of little practical value. In a matter of days, the plague did more to harden the hearts of many Athenians than did all the months of the war against Sparta.

The public disorder caused by the plague, combined with the psychic trauma resulting from daily exposure to victims dying or in intense agony, produced a state of chaos throughout Athens. The law provided no deterrent to citizens who imagined that they would die soon anyway. Crimes of all sorts began to increase. People ceased planning for the future, preferring to direct their efforts toward the satisfaction of immediate pleasures. The worship of the gods declined because many people felt that religion provided no guarantee of health. Even the literature and art of the city was affected by the plague. The god Apollo, until then regarded as a source of inspiration and light in Athenian literature, took on an increasingly negative image in many works, including the tragedies of the playwright Euripides (c. 485-406 B.C.E.). Apollo's oracle at Delphi had promised aid to the Spartans, and, as the Athenians remembered well, Apollo was the god of plagues in Homer's *Iliad* (c. 800 B.C.E.).

When, in the spring of 429 B.C.E., the Spartans again invaded Attica and once more laid waste to the fields, public opinion began to turn against Pericles. The Athenians claimed it was his fault that no crops could be planted for two years and that the city was sufficiently crowded to spread the plague. In part, at least, these criticisms were justified. It had been Pericles' policy to protect behind the city's walls thousands of Athenian citizens who ordinarily would have remained unaffected by the plague in the countryside. As an urban phenomenon, the plague was largely confined to Athens itself and a few other large cities. It did not enter the Peloponnisos, sparing Sparta, a less-populated city than Athens.

Pericles was removed from office as general of Athens. Two of his own sons died in the plague. History, perhaps unreliably, reports that his mistress Aspasia and two of his friends, the philosopher Protagoras and the sculptor Phidias, were placed on trial by the Athenians in an effort to discredit Pericles. Pericles himself was fined for misuse of public funds. Soon, however, public opinion shifted yet again, and Pericles was restored to public office. Nevertheless, by this time, his health was in decline. Calling the plague "the one thing that I did not foresee," Pericles became its most prominent victim. He died in 429 B.C.E. After its initial outbreak in 430 and 429, the plague returned to claim more victims in 427 B.C.E.

In 1994, a mass grave dating to the fifth and fourth centuries B.C.E. was discovered as preparations were being made for a subway station near the ancient Kerameikos cemetery in Athens. Numerous bodies were uncovered, hastily thrown into multiple shafts. One shaft alone contained more than 90 skeletons, 10 of which belonged to children. Because of the date of the burial and the cursory manner in which the interment appeared to have been carried out, many scholars speculated that the site might have been associated with the great Plague of Athens. In his account of the plague, Thucydides had mentioned that the sheer number of casualties had necessitated swift burial in mass graves. Although the date and general location of the burial are appropriate for the Plague of Athens, final identification will never be possible because the site was destroyed as construction continued.

PRECISE CAUSES OF THE ATHENIAN PLAGUE. Historians and epidemiologists cannot agree as to the precise nature of the organism responsible for the Athenian plague. Some scholars believe that the illness was either identical or closely related to various illnesses known in the modern world. Others believe that, because of the rapid evolution of microbes, it was a unique contagion having no parallel in contemporary society. Candidates put forward as possible causes of the Athenian plague have included the Ebola virus, influenza, measles, typhus, ergotism (a disease caused by the ingestion of contaminated grain products), and toxic shock syndrome. The latter two of these possibilities seem unlikely because they would not have been spread in the highly contagious manner attributed to the Athenian plague. The other candidates for the disease all lack at least one of the major symptoms described by Thucydides. Although the precise nature of the Athenian plague will probably never be determined, one thing remains clear: The cause of this disease cannot be identified with that of another famous plague, the Black Death that ravaged Europe during the fourteenth century. Nowhere in Thucydides' account is there any mention of the buboes, those enlarged lymph nodes in the groin or armpits that gave the bubonic plague its name. In the history of epidemics, the Plague of Athens appears to remain unique.

Jeffrey L. Buller

FOR FURTHER INFORMATION:

Bollet, Alfred J. *Plagues and Poxes: The Impact of Human History on Epidemic Disease.* New York: Demos, 2004.

Holladay, A. J., and J. C. F. Poole. "Thucydides and the Plague of Athens." *Classical Quarterly* 29 (1979): 282-300.

Langmuir, A. D. "The Thucydides Syndrome: A New Hypothesis for the Cause of the Plague of Athens." *The New England Journal of Medicine* 313 (October, 1985): 1027-1030.

Morens, D. M., and R. J. Littman. "Epidemiology of the Plague of Athens." *Transactions of the American Philological Association* 122 (1992): 271-304.

_____. "The Thucydides Syndrome Reconsidered: New Thoughts on the Plague of Athens." *American Journal of Epidemiology* 140, no. 62 (1994): 1-7.

Morgan, Thomas E. "Plague or Poetry? Thucydides on the Epidemic at Athens." *Transactions of the American Philological Association* 124 (1994): 197-209.

Page, Denys L. "Thucydides' Description of the Great Plague." *Classical Quarterly*, n.s. 47, no. 3 (1953): 97-119.

Scarrow, G. D. "The Athenian Plague: A Possible Diagnosis." *Ancient History Bulletin* 11 (1988): 4-8.

■ 64 C.E.: THE GREAT FIRE OF ROME

FIRE

DATE: July 19-24, 64 C.E.
PLACE: Rome, Italy
RESULT: Thousands dead (accurate records unavailable), thousands of homes destroyed, more than two-thirds of the city destroyed

In the early morning hours of July 19, 64 C.E., a fire broke out in a slum district south of the Palatine hill. Due to the high density of poorly built and very flammable insulae (tenement houses), the fire quickly burned out of control. During the next several days acre after acre of the city burned up as the fire spread northward. Panic-stricken residents ran through the streets, where many were suffocated or crushed by crowds of people desperately seeking escape. Adding to the confusion were sudden winds that whipped up the flames in different directions. Reportedly, rescuers and soldiers, instead of trying to stop the conflagration, kindled it even more in greedy hopes of obtaining plunder. To make matters worse, after the original fire subsided, a second fire broke out near the Capitoline hill and lasted for three days. The damage was so extensive that many Romans feared the city would never regain its greatness.

By the time the fire was quenched, 3 of the 14 districts of Rome (as originally laid out by Emperor Augustus) were completely destroyed. Only 4 districts were untouched by the fire. The best ancient sources about the fire, historians Cassius Dio Cocceianus, Suetonius, and Cornelius Tacitus, did not record precise numbers of either lives lost or buildings destroyed. Cassius Dio wrote that "countless" people died in the fire, and it seems likely that hundreds of people perished in the disaster. An ancient letter, purportedly from the philosopher Seneca to the Apostle Paul, mentions that 132 domi (private homes) and approximately 4,000 insulae were destroyed in the flames.

Nero was emperor of Rome at the time, and his role in the disaster and its aftermath has been the subject of many debates on the part of scholars. Nero was at Antium, 35 miles from Rome, when the fire broke out, and he rushed back to his palace in Rome. While watching

Emperor Nero sings while Rome burns. (R. S. Peale and J. A. Hill)

the fire from his palace, he composed and sang a song, supposedly called "The Taking of Troy," while playing the lyre. He certainly did not "fiddle as Rome burned," as stated in folklore, because violins had not yet been invented. The fact that Nero was not in Rome when the fire started and that when he returned he graciously opened his palace to shelter many who were made homeless by the blaze has led many historians to conclude that he was not responsible for starting the fire.

On the other hand, Cassius Dio, Pliny the Elder, and Suetonius allege arson by Nero. Nero was known to complain about how Rome was aesthetically displeasing. When he purchased 120 acres in the same area where the fire broke out to build an ostentatious palace, it served to confirm the widespread opinion of Roman citizens that Nero had the fire started in order to rebuild the city according to his own liking. The evidence for implicating Nero in starting the fire is, however, primarily circumstantial, and no firm conclusions can be made in this regard.

After the fire, Nero set about making Rome a safer and more beautiful city. New building codes were established, with an emphasis on the use of fireproof materials, and insulae were constructed with greater access to the public water supply. Wider streets were laid out, and Greek-style colonnaded buildings were erected. Nero also began his famous Golden Palace. This prodigious edifice, had it been finished, would have covered nearly a third of Rome. However, Nero's overly ambitious plans for rebuilding Rome resulted in severe financial strain. The growing economic crisis combined with the lingering opinion that Nero was responsible for the fire jeopardized the stability of Nero's rule. With the likelihood of riots and a revolt against his reign becoming ever more threatening, Nero knew that something had to be done. His solution had a profound impact on a new religious group.

Nero's advisers suggested blaming Christians for the fire in order to distract the public. Nero agreed and made a big display of arresting and executing, often by torturous means, many Christians. One of Nero's more hideous methods of killing Christians was to lash them to stakes, tar them, and then turn them into living torches—a supposed example of the punishment fitting the crime. Making Christians the scapegoats for the fire had its desired effect, and the immediate threat of rioting was diffused. The persecution of Christians, however, resulted in the martyrdom of two of Christendom's greatest leaders, the apostles Peter and Paul. The harrowing circumstances facing Christians during this time is revealed in a letter from Peter to fellow believers (written shortly before Peter's execution), in which he writes about their faith being "tried in fire" (I Peter 1:7).

The Great Fire of Rome continued to influence events in the Roman Empire long after the last flames were extinguished. The persecution of Christians did not turn public opinion in Nero's favor, and within the next four years two plots against his life were made. He was able to foil the Pisonian Conspiracy in 65 c.e., but he succumbed to a second plot in 68 c.e., purportedly committing suicide. Nero succeeded in making Rome a more beautiful city, but his Golden Palace was never finished. Furthermore, his fire-prevention plans did not prevent another major fire that devastated Rome in 191 c.e. Nero's blaming of Christians for the 64 c.e. disaster resulted in the first official Roman persecution of that religious group. Although Nero's actions were restricted to the city of Rome, this persecution did set a precedent that led to larger and more widespread oppressions of Christians by Roman emperors in the succeeding centuries.

Paul J. Chara, Jr.

FOR FURTHER INFORMATION:

Bunson, Matthew. *Encyclopedia of the Roman Empire.* New York: Facts On File, 1994.

Champlin, Edward. *Nero.* Cambridge, Mass.: Belknap Press of Harvard University Press, 2003.

Millar, Fergus. *A Study of Cassius Dio.* New York: Oxford University Press, 1964.

Tacitus, Cornelius. *The Annals and the Histories.* Translated by Alfred John Church and William Jackson Brodribb. New York: Modern Library, 2003.

Tranquillus, Gaius Suetonius. *The Twelve Caesars.* Translated by Robert Graves. Baltimore: Penguin Books, 1957.

Warmington, H. B. *Nero: Reality and Legend.* Edited by M. I. Finley. New York: W. W. Norton, 1969.

■ 79 C.E.: VESUVIUS ERUPTION

VOLCANO

DATE: August 24, 79 C.E.

PLACE: West coast of Italy

RESULT: More than 13,000 dead, 4 cities completely buried, 270 square miles (700 square kilometers) devastated

Vesuvius is a large stratovolcano, having a height of 4,203 feet (1,281 meters). Prior to the 79 C.E. eruption the estimated height was about 6,562 feet (2,000 meters). Mount Vesuvius is located about 93 miles south of Rome, and 4.4 miles inland from the Mediterranean coast off the Gulf of Naples. The gulf is a thriving port, being well protected by surrounding peninsulas and islands. The city of Naples was a major port of call, lying on the northern side of the gulf with the Misenum promontory making up the northern peninsula. Naples was located 7.5 miles northwest from Vesuvius. The cities of Herculaneum and Pompeii (population 20,000), which were located 4.4 and 6.2 miles, respectively, to the southwest and southeast of Vesuvius, were completely buried by the eruption. The southern side of the gulf was formed by the Sorrento Peninsula and the island of Capri, with the city of Stabiae (now known as Castellammare di Stabia) located at the tip of the southern peninsula. Stabiae, which was abandoned during the eruption, lies 9.3 miles south of Vesuvius on the coast.

The eruption of Mount Vesuvius is generally regarded as the most violent eruption in Europe during historic times. Typically, a very violent eruption of a stratovolcano only occurs after centuries of quiescence. This appears to be so for Vesuvius because the historic record of the ancient peoples in the region did not recognize Mount Vesuvius as an active volcano. The first indication of the awakening of Vesuvius was an earthquake on February 5, 63 C.E. This earthquake destroyed a portion of Pompeii and damaged the cities of Herculaneum and Naples. For the following sixteen years the area experienced intermittent earth tremors until the actual volcanic eruption began on August 24, 79 C.E.

EYEWITNESS ACCOUNTS. A vivid and detailed account of the eruption of Vesuvius was recorded by Pliny the Younger, who was almost eighteen years old at the time of the eruption. His account takes the form of letters to a prominent historian, and it chronicles two excursions during the eruption. The first excursion is that of his uncle, Pliny the Elder, who sailed across the bay during the early stages of the eruption. The second account chronicles Pliny the Younger's flight north from Misenum away from the eruption. Pliny the Youn-

ger and his widowed mother lived with Pliny the Elder in Misenum. Pliny the Elder was a scientist, the author of a well-known treatise on natural history, and the commander of the Roman Fleet.

At approximately 1:00 in the afternoon of August 24, Pliny the Younger's mother noticed an unusual cloud in the sky. The cloud that she observed rose in a vertical plume for several thousand feet before spreading out laterally, like a Roman pine tree spreads its branches, into the sky. The cloud was sometimes illuminated by flashes of brightness and then would turn completely dark or become lightly spotted. She brought the strange cloud to the attention of Pliny the Elder.

Pliny the Elder decided to conduct a scientific investigation of the cloud and had his crew get a light boat ready for him to sail to the source of this cloud. Just as he was ready to depart he received a message from a friend who lived in Resina at the foot of Vesuvius. The friend realized that Vesuvius was erupting and that her only chance of escape from the volcano was by sea. Pliny began receiving additional requests for help from other inhabitants on the coastline, and he set off to sea with a fleet of ships to rescue the frightened citizens.

As Pliny's ship drew near Resina, cinders, pieces of pumice, and fragments of burned rock from the exploding volcano fell onto the deck of the ships. Pliny observed that the shore was inaccessible, as fragments of rock and cinders were piling up on the beach, making it impossible to reach the citizens of Resina. Pliny was forced to turn southeast to the coastal town of Stabiae, where his friend Pomponianus lived. He found his friend anxious and frantic to escape Stabiae, but the onshore winds made escape by ship impossible at that time. Pliny felt that Stabiae was far enough away from the volcano to be safe, and he assured Pomponianus of their safety and that they would have ample time to escape if danger was imminent. Pliny then decided to bathe, eat dinner, and to sleep.

As night came the citizens of Stabiae could see tall, broad flames flare out from several locations near the top of Vesuvius. During the night, conditions on Stabiae worsened, with a heavy fall of ash and pumice. When the building began to sway and shake from the eruption tremors, Pomponianus and his companions felt that the time had come to abandon the city. They decided to flee to the beach and attempt to escape by sea. They woke Pliny and tied pillows on their heads with napkins in order to protect themselves from falling volcanic debris as they made their way to the shore. They arrived at the shore, having found their way in the blackness with lit torches. Even though it was well after sunrise, the dark ash clouds continued to block all light from the sun. When they reached the shore they found that the wind was still blowing from the north, continuing to make leaving by sea impossible.

Pliny the Elder, who was overweight, began to feel ill. He lay down on a sheet that had been spread on the beach. Shortly thereafter, strong winds and flames appeared nearby, accompanied by a strong odor of sulfur. Pliny's companion began to flee in panic southward down the beach, and as Pliny the Elder struggled to get up he collapsed and died. It is clear in his letters that Pliny the Younger assumed the sulfurous fumes from the volcano overcame his uncle.

Pliny the Younger also chronicled the ordeal that he and his mother went though at Misenum. Misenum was located on the opposite side of the Bay of Naples from Stabiae, placing it upwind from the volcano and thereby less affected by it. Earthquakes shook the city of Misenum all night, and by 6 A.M. the volcanic ash was so thick that it partially obstructed the sun.

Pliny and his mother decided to flee the city in chariots. They were joined by chaotic mobs of frightened people. Pliny the Younger and his mother took solace in the open country, feeling that they were safe from the falling buildings in the city. However, around 8:30 A.M. the land was ravaged by a series of strong earthquakes. The tremors were so bad that the shaking kept moving the chariots, which they tried to stabilize with stones against the wheels on the level ground. They observed frequent flashes of light in the dark, ash-laden cloud that was sweeping toward them. The sea became very turbulent and receded so much that sea creatures were stranded on the beaches; then, minutes later, the sea would crash forcefully back over the beach.

Pliny the Younger and his mother moved farther into the open country as the black sky seemed to reach down and envelop the sea. The island of Capri and the promontory of Misenum were no longer visible. Frightened for her son's safety and knowing that he could move faster without her, Pliny the Younger's mother urged him to go ahead without her. Pliny refused to leave her, and they traveled on slowly in the thick darkness. As visibility became worse, they heard the panicked screams of men, women, and children who had lost sight of their loved ones; other people were praying or crying in fear. The ash began to snow upon the people so thickly that they had to stand up and shake it off in order to not be buried by it.

Many hours later, daylight began to show though the ash clouds. As the air began to clear and Pliny could once again see across the bay to Vesuvius, he noticed that the smooth cone had become merely a stump. Fields that had been formerly lush with green trees and farmlands were now a gray sea of ash.

SCIENTIFIC ANALYSIS AND PLINY'S NARRATIVE. Pliny the Younger's account of the eruption of Mount Vesuvius proved to be so clear and concise that all similar eruptions are now classified as "Plinian" in honor of him and his uncle. The normal sequence of events in a Plinian (violently explosive) eruption are now well understood and correlate well with aspects of Pliny's narrative.

Plinian eruptions are preceded by a slightly less violent explosion that clears the vent and allows the Plinian eruption to proceed. The eruption of Vesuvius began when the rising magma encountered water and exploded early in the morning of August 24. It was this initial explosion that frightened Pliny's friend at Resina. She sent word to Pliny some 5 miles away via a messenger, who arrived shortly after Pliny the Younger's mother saw the eruption cloud for the Plinian eruption, which began at 1:00 in the afternoon.

A Plinian eruption typically produces three types of deposits, which can be expelled multiple times. The first to form is usually an air-fall deposit that rains down from the initial explosion column. The individual particles fall independently of the other particles around them. The deposit produced, surprisingly, has the smaller particles on the bottom with larger particles occurring higher in the deposit. The larger fragments of pumice and accidental rock are often blown higher in the initial blast. The thickness of an air-fall deposit is largely controlled by the local winds. After three days, the Vesuvius eruption of 79 C.E. produced nine different air-fall layers.

The second type of deposit in a Plinian eruption is ash flow. An ash flow begins with an initial blast called a base surge. This base surge moves at hurricane velocities (usually greater than 108 feet per second) and often will defoliate trees without charring the branches.

Two victims at Pompeii are immortalized in plaster almost 2,000 years after being covered by volcanic ash from the eruption of Vesuvius in 79 C.E. (Library of Congress)

The deposit left by this surge is surprisingly thin, usually only an inch thick. Although thin, this material is distinct because it displays ripple marks and dune structures. The Vesuvius eruption produced seven surge layers. When one of the later surges reached Pompeii the buildings that were not already buried were knocked flat.

Overlying the surge layer are the main deposits of the ash flow, which can be tens of feet thick. Ash flows can result from either avalanching of near-vent material because of explosion tremors or gravitational collapse of the eruptive ash column above the vent. An ash flow usually follows an initial air-fall eruption, when the radius of the vent has been enlarged or some of the pent-up gas has been released. Pliny's description corresponds to ash flows formed by both avalanches and cloud collapse. Six ash-flow layers were generated during the three days of the eruption of Vesuvius.

Ash flows can move incredibly fast, at speeds of 197 feet (60 meters) per second or 124 miles (200 kilometers) per hour. They can reach distances of 1,242 miles (100 kilometers) from the vent. They have sufficient momentum that they can cross ridges that are 2,297 feet (700 meters) high at a distance of 181 miles (50 kilometers) from the volcano. The great distance of travel is due to the particles still dissolving gas. Although the explosion at the vent releases the pent-up gas, the droplets of liquid take longer to release their dissolved gases.

Once moving, the flows trap and heat surrounding air as they glide down the slope. The high gas content in the flow makes the mixture behave like a fluid, and it flows with virtually no internal friction and, often, little, if any, ground friction—it flows on its own carpet of gas. It can reach speeds that approximate the velocity of free-falling objects, when the slope is taken into consideration. An ash flow that contains larger blocks of incandescent volcanic fragments (often with a diameter of a few feet or more) is called a glowing avalanche, or nuée ardente.

A cloud of ash and steam usually rises and expands above the glowing avalanche. The flow itself closely follows canyons and valleys as it moves downslope, similar in behavior to a snow avalanche. The cloud, however, is not deflected by topography, and it rolls onward over ridges and valleys, following a considerable distance behind the flow. The description that Pliny the Younger gives of the cloud overtaking the chariots near Misenum is a classic description of the ash-steam cloud of a glowing avalanche. An ash flow must have moved out across the water in the Gulf of Naples; because they ride on their own carpet of gas they do not need to have a solid surface beneath them.

Volcanic tremors (earthquakes) that displace the seafloor can cause tidal waves, or tsunamis. When ground displacement occurs a considerable distance off the coast, the water at the shoreline will recede entirely from the beach before coming back on the land as an enormous wave. Pliny's description of the Misenum sequence of an earthquake, followed by a tsunami, followed by the engulfing cloud of ash, corresponds to the normal sequence of explosive base surge and ash flow with an accompanying ash-steam cloud.

Accounts vary as to the destructive nature of the ash-steam cloud that hovers over the ash flow. In one historical case, the cloud was so hot and violent that the cloud alone destroyed an entire town and killed all the residents, while the ash flow followed a nearby stream valley and entirely missed the town. In another well-documented account, a geologist on a high ridge reported watching an ash flow sweep down the valley below him before the cloud enveloped him. He reported that there was an enormous thickness of ash in the swirling air and a very strong, almost overpowering odor of sulfur. This corresponds well to the events that are associated with the death of Pliny the Elder.

Most of the ash flows in the Vesuvius eruption were probably generated by the repeated thrusting and collapsing of the eruption column. Pliny's mother described the form of an eruption column that is classic in a Plinian eruption. The lower part is a straight vertical column, while the upper part branches out horizontally in gradually increasing distances with increasing height. The upper portion of the cloud has the appearance of an inverted cone. The lower column is propelled by gas thrusts as the gases are released from the volcanic vent. The upper cloud is propelled by convective thrusts due to the heating and rising of the air above the volcano.

A cloud's height can be calculated easily after the eruption by looking at the deposits of the ash flows. A sloping energy line exists that starts at the boundary between the upper and lower clouds and descends at a 30-degree angle to the ground. The energy line touches the ground at the distant end of the longest ash flow. Calculations based upon the ash flows from Vesuvius indicate that the eruption column was about 18.6 miles (30 kilometers) high.

Another interesting aspect of a Plinian eruption is the gradual change of color in pumice (a volcanic glass) erupting from the vent; starting out white, the pumice gradually grows darker in color as the eruption goes on. Prior to the eruption the magma in a chamber will change its composition slowly, over long periods of time. The upper regions of the chamber become very low in the element iron; the higher the content of iron, the darker the magma's color. When an eruption occurs the first lava erupted is from the upper regions of the chamber and is white in color, whereas after the eruption has gone on for some time the magma comes from lower in the chamber and is gray from the higher iron content.

At Mount Vesuvius white pumice erupted from the vent at a rate of 5,000 to 80,000 tons every second. The white pumice eruption is thought to have lasted seven hours. The white pumice, which erupted first, came from magma at the top of the chamber. It was followed by gray pumice, which originated further down in the chamber. Some scientists feel that the gray pumice, which fell on the evening of August 24, erupted from the volcano at 150,000 tons per second.

Last, it is common for a Plinian eruption to conclude with the collapse of the summit region. When sufficient magma is expelled from the chamber a large void will exist below ground, and the overlying rocks of the volcano are not sufficiently strong to support the weight of the summit area. The collapse can invert the topography around the top of the volcano. The eruption of Vesuvius expelled 247,202 cubic feet (7 cubic kilometers) of magma, and after the eruption had concluded, Pliny reported that the mountain was merely a "stump" of its former shape.

GEOLOGICAL AND ARCHAEOLOGICAL ANALYSES. Quarries and construction in the region of Mount Vesuvius have exposed more than a dozen areas where the deposits of the eruption can be studied in detail. Geological and archaeological research have allowed the history of the region to be determined to a minute-by-minute level of accuracy.

The city hit hardest by the eruption was Pompeii, which was founded in 600 B.C.E. Distribution patterns of the air-fall deposits show that northwesterly winds prevailed during the eruption. These winds blew ash and pumice directly onto the city of Pompeii for almost eighteen hours, burying it under 9.8 feet (3 meters) of volcanic fragments. Some of the townspeople began to leave their homes when the heavy weight of the ash, cinders, and bombs from the eruption caused the collapse of numerous roofs and killed some of the inhabitants. Making matters worse, an ash flow spewing clouds of pumice and dust collapsed downward from the eruption column and flowed into the town at about 7:30 A.M. on August 25 (almost twenty-four hours after the eruption began). The surge flattened most of the second stories of the taller buildings (the air-fall deposits already covered the ground to a depth that covered the first floor).

Survival in the violent surge was impossible; all the residents perished in the hot blast of gas and dust. It is estimated that 2,000 people were still alive in the town when the surge hit. They were all killed within a minute. This was the fourth of six surge deposits that came from the volcano. Another surge deposit swept over the town only five minutes later. This fifth surge and ash flow carried all the way to the outskirts of Stabiae.

The sixth and last surge and ash flow was released at 8 A.M. on August 25. It was the largest and was caused by widening of the vent at the summit of the volcano. As the vent increased its diameter the eruption lost some of it force, and the existing cloud collapsed down toward the volcano. This ash flow reached Stabiae and was probably responsible for the death of Pliny the Elder. Another branch of the same ash flow swept across the waters of the Gulf toward Misenum, 20 miles away, and was recorded by Pliny the Younger.

After the eruption, the town of Pompeii and the surrounding region was a wasteland of ash. It was so devastated that there seemed to be no option but to abandon the area. The tephra, or volcanic debris, from the eruption covered hundreds of square miles, and it buried several small settlements near Pompeii, which remain buried today.

It was not until 1595 that some of the remains of Pompeii were found during construction of an aqueduct. Some coins and pieces of a marble tablet, which contained some writings about Pompeii, were found at that time. This led to the rediscovery of the forgotten city. In the seventeenth and eighteenth centuries wealthy post-Renaissance families in Europe became interested in ancient objects of art, and Pompeii became a favorite site for uncovering statues, jewelry, and other ancient treasures. The diggings took place haphazardly, without any thought to the preservation of the city or its culture. Ravaging and pillaging took place all through the excavated areas. In the nineteenth century people realized the historical and cultural significance of Pompeii, and more coordinated and scientific methods were used in excavating the abandoned city. Many acres of the town have been excavated and are open to the public.

The archaeological excavation found uneaten food laid out on tables in some of the Pompeiian homes, leading scientists to believe that normal life continued in Pompeii until the very last second. The bodies of people killed in the disaster are quite unique, as they were quickly buried in the accumulating ash and cinders from the eruption; when rain fell on the ash, the substance formed a cement around the bodies, making molds. Some of these molds perfectly preserved facial expressions and the patterns and textures of the clothing. Nineteenth century excavators poured plaster of Paris into the molds and were able to produce three-dimensional casts of the people and animals killed. Almost 2,000 skeletons were found with their hands or cloths over their mouths, trying to protect themselves from searing, lethal gases of the surge or from breathing the ash and dust particles of the air-fall deposits.

The city of Herculaneum was located closer to Vesuvius on its western flank and had a population of about 5,000. Unlike Pompeii, which was destroyed mostly by the accumulation of air-fall tephra over a two-day period, Herculaneum was obliterated in minutes by a surge and ash flow at 1:00 in the morning of the 25th. The town had been spared from the thick fallout of the white pumice because the wind had blown the air-fall deposits to the south, toward Pompeii. However, the very first of Mount Vesuvius's six ash flows hit Herculaneum and buried it under more than 65.6 feet (20 meters) of volcanic material. Some buildings were demolished by the force of the surge; others were simply buried in ash and pumice from the ash flow.

In addition, an avalanche of mud passed over Herculaneum, filling every crack and crevice in the buildings and sealing the city so completely that it became a lost city. When this material became impacted and hardened it became a true volcanic rock, making it very difficult to excavate. Excavation of Herculaneum has uncovered approximately eight city blocks. At first it appeared that many of the townspeople had escaped because very few bodies were uncovered. However, further exploration in what was an area of the beach during Roman times has yielded hundreds of skeletons, found huddled in buildings supported by arched chambers, which were opened to the beach and housed boats and fishing tackle. It appears that the townspeople fled to the beach, thinking that the arched chamber would protect them from the volcano.

In summary, the 79 C.E. eruption of Vesuvius was the first volcanic eruption ever to be described in detail. The eruption lasted about twenty-five hours, the last nineteen of these hours being a sustained highly explosive eruption. About 141,258 cubic feet of volcanic material was erupted and blanketed 116 square miles around the volcano. Vesuvius lost 2,297 feet of its summit area to the final collapse. More than 13,000 people were killed, and most of the farms, villages, towns, and cities in the vicinity vanished. Modern archaeological excavation of the towns of Pompeii and Herculaneum continue to reveal details of the last few minutes of life for the residents of this region.

Dion C. Stewart and Toby R. Stewart

FOR FURTHER INFORMATION:

De Carolis, Ernesto, and Giovanni Patricelli. *Vesuvius, A.D. 79: The Destruction of Pompeii and Herculaneum.* Los Angeles: J. Paul Getty Museum, 2003.

Francis, Peter, and Clive Oppenheimer. *Volcanoes.* 2d ed. New York: Oxford University Press, 2004.

Pellegrino, Charles. *Ghosts of Vesuvius: A New Look at the Last Days of Pompeii, How Towers Fall, and Other Strange Connections.* New York: William Morrow, 2004.

Scarth, Alwyn. *Volcanoes: An Introduction.* London: University College of London Press, 1994.

_____. *Vulcan's Fury: Man Against the Volcano.* New ed. New Haven, Conn.: Yale University Press, 2001.

Sigurdsson, H., S. Carey, W. Cornell, and T. Pescatore. "The Eruption of Vesuvius in A.D. 79." *National Geographic Research* 1, no. 3 (1985): 332-387.

■ 526: The Antioch earthquake

Earthquake

Date: May 29, 526
Place: Antioch, Syria (now Antakya, Turkey)
Magnitude: 9.0 (estimated)
Result: About 250,000 dead

Antioch was founded around 300 B.C.E. by the Syrian emperor Seleucus I. Rome captured Antioch in 25 B.C.E., making it into a colony called Caesarea Antiochia. Antioch quickly became a political center for Rome, and Saul of Tarsus (Saint Paul) selected it as the center of his mission in the Roman province of Galatia around 50 C.E. Antioch subsequently became an important, wealthy city of the eastern Roman (Byzantine) Empire, surrounded by olive plantations and home to a silk industry. Located on the Orontes River about 20 miles (32 kilometers) from the northeastern shore of the Mediterranean Sea, Antioch also prospered in trade.

Prominent in Christian worship during the sixth century was the feast of the Ascension, a celebration of Jesus Christ's final rise into heaven that conventionally took place forty days after Easter. A holiday on the same scale as Easter or Christmas, Ascension came on May 30 in the year 526. Antioch, home to thousands of people, swelled with thousands of visitors who had come to worship in its many magnificent churches and to eat, drink, and celebrate in its many inns the night before Ascension.

On the evening of May 29, at a time when most of the people in Antioch were inside buildings, the earthquake struck. Many buildings collapsed or caved in instantly, killing thousands of people. To escape the crushing walls, many fled to marketplaces and other open spaces within the city. One such person was Patriarch Euphrasius, religious leader of Antioch, who reportedly fled to the open space of the Circus (a circular, outdoor arena), only to be killed by a falling obelisk. Bishop Asclepius of Edessa and other prominent members of the Christian Church were also killed.

Some buildings withstood the initial shock but were destroyed by great fires caused by the earthquake. Rain following the earthquake further weakened structures, causing them to collapse days later. John Malalas, an eyewitness to the earthquake, reported that Antioch's Great Church, built under the direction of Constantine the Great, survived for five days after the earthquake, then caught fire and burned to the ground. According to eyewitness accounts, eventually the entire city was destroyed, except for a few buildings on the nearby slope of Mount Silpius. On Ascension Day, according to authors reporting from eyewitness accounts, the survivors gathered at the Church of the Kerateion for a service of Intercession, indicating that the region south of the inner city might have survived the initial damage. In all, an estimated 250,000 people were killed by the earthquake, fires, and aftershocks. Miraculous escapes from the crushing debris were reported. Pregnant women, who had been buried underneath the debris for twenty-one days, were excavated still alive and healthy. Some of these women had even given birth while buried but were still rescued in good condition. Another reported miracle occurred three days after the earthquake, on a Sunday. Above the northern part of the city, a vision of the Holy Cross appeared in the sky and hovered for more than an hour. The survivors of the earthquake who witnessed this vision reportedly fell to their knees, wept, and prayed. Mount Silpius, which stood underneath the manifestation, was thenceforth called Mount Staurin in its honor. ("Staurin" was colloquial Greek for "cross.")

After the earthquake, many survivors gathered whatever possessions they could and fled the city. Many of these refugees were killed by people in the country. A number of robbers were reported entering the city to strip corpses of jewelry and other valuable goods and to gather up the gold and silver coins that the earthquake had scattered about. Accounts of this period tell of the robbers meeting divine justice after molesting corpses. One story tells of a Roman official called Thomas the Hebrew who, after the earthquake, stationed himself and his servants 3 miles away from Antioch at the Gate of Saint Julian. Thomas, with his band of obedient robbers, successfully gathered together a large amount of money and luxurious goods over a period of four days. Apparently healthy with no signs of ailment, Thomas then suddenly collapsed and died as a divine punishment for his bad deeds, and all that he had amassed was distributed among needy survivors.

News of the Antioch earthquake quickly reached Emperor Justin I (ruled 518-527) in Constantinople, the eastern capital of the Roman Empire. The emperor had served in Antioch during his military career and had fond memories of the city. He ordered the imperial court to wear mourning, and he suspended all public entertainments in Constantinople. On Pentecost, which is celebrated fifty days after Easter, Justin walked to the church of Saint Sophia in Constantinople in mourning. Rebuilding Antioch became his first priority. First, the emperor sent several government officials with large amounts of gold to seek out survivors and give them monetary relief. These officials were also ordered to assess the damage to Antioch and estimate how much money would be needed for restoration.

Once this was determined, the restoration began, although it was a slow process hindered by a second earthquake in November of 528. Residents of Antioch and nearby areas continued to emigrate from the region. Despite setbacks, Antioch was gifted by Emperor Justinian I (ruled 527-565) with several churches, a hospice, baths, and cisterns in celebration of his rise to emperor. After the second earthquake, he deemed the city free of taxation. Antioch had made little progress, however, when the Persians sacked the city in 540. In 542, remaining Antioch residents were hit by a devastating plague, thus destroying any hope of regaining the once-powerful city's grandeur.

Rose Secrest

FOR FURTHER INFORMATION:

Downey, Glanville. *A History of Antioch in Syria*. Princeton, N.J.: Princeton University Press, 1961.

"Killer Quake at Antioch: A Stroke of Nature's Fury Destroys a Brilliant Metropolis." In *Great Disasters: Dramatic True Stories of Nature's Awesome Powers*. Pleasantville, N.Y.: Readers Digest Association, 1989.

■ 1200: EGYPT

FAMINE

DATE: 1200-1202
PLACE: Across Egypt
RESULT: More than 100,000 dead

From the earliest beginnings of agriculture until the building of modern dams in the twentieth century, the people of Egypt depended on the annual flooding of the Nile for survival. In a typical year, the Nile began to rise in late June and reached its highest level in the middle of September. The water then receded, leaving behind a thick layer of silt that allowed crops to be grown. Without this flooding, the land surrounding the Nile would become a barren desert.

Two months before the flooding of the Nile began in the year 1200, the water in the river turned green and acquired an unpleasant taste and odor. Boiling the water did not improve it, and Egyptians began drinking well water instead. Abd al-Latif, an Arab scholar who left an eyewitness account of the famine, determined that the water was full of plant matter and correctly surmised that this was caused by a lack of rain at the source of the Nile. Although the water eventually returned to normal, the annual flooding failed to reach its usual level.

A level of about 28 feet (16 cubits) was considered necessary to produce sufficient crops. According to records kept for six hundred years, the Nile had risen to only 24.5 feet (14 cubits) twenty times and only 22.75 feet (13 cubits) six times. Previous failures of the Nile to reach adequate levels had led to famine. In 1064, a famine that lasted until 1072 resulted in between 25,000 and 40,000 deaths. On September 9, 1200, the Nile reached its highest point for the year, at a level below 22.75 feet (13 cubits).

Knowing that this extremely low flood level would lead to severe food shortages, thousands of Egyptians fled the country to seek refuge in other areas of North Africa and the Middle East. Huge numbers of farmers left their unproductive fields, leading to overcrowd-

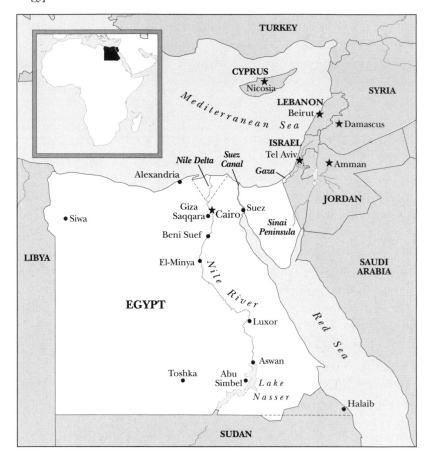

ing in the cities. By March of 1201, starvation in the cities reached the point where the poor were reduced to eating dogs, carrion, animal excrement, and corpses.

As the famine progressed, children, who were often left unprotected by the deaths of their parents, were killed and eaten. The government of Egypt sentenced all those who ate the flesh of children to be burned at the stake, but the murders continued. Latif records that he saw the parents of "a small roasted child in a basket" brought to the ruler of Egypt, who condemned them to death. Ironically, the burnt bodies of those executed for cannibalism were released to the starving populace for legal consumption.

The famine spread from the cities to all parts of Egypt. Adults as well as children were in danger of being murdered, even by the wealthy. Workers, brought into homes to perform their duties, and guests, invited to social events, were sometimes killed and eaten by their hosts. The corpses of those who died of starvation filled every town. In Cairo, between 100 and 500 bodies were carried away daily. Latif visited a pile of about 20,000 bodies in order to study human anatomy.

Meanwhile, in April of 1201, the water of the Nile again turned green, a sign that the annual flood would fail to reach the level needed to relieve the famine. In early September of 1201, the Nile's maximum level was about 28 feet (below 16 cubits), then immediately began to drop back. Although not as severe as the extremely low flood level of 1200, the rapid decline of the Nile ensured that starvation would continue.

The second year of the famine resulted in fewer deaths than the first year, mostly because the population of Egypt, particularly among the poor, had been greatly reduced. As an example of the reduced population, Latif records that the number of rush-mat makers in the city of Misr fell from 900 to 15. The population of the cities, so recently increased by refugees, fell so rapidly that rents decreased by as much as 85 percent. Even the price of wheat fell; although there was still a severe shortage of food, the number of buyers had been drastically reduced.

In early 1202, plague broke out in many parts of Egypt. The disease acted so rapidly that farmers fell dead while working their plows. In the city of Alexandria, funeral prayers were said for 700 people in one day. Between July of 1200 and April of 1202, the official number of deaths in Egypt was reported to be nearly 110,000. This number did not include many deaths that government officials failed to record.

In February of 1202, the Nile again turned green, leading to expectations that the annual flood would again fail to reach an adequate level. Many Egyptians began to suspect that the source of the Nile had been altered in some way, so that flood levels would never return to normal. On May 20, 1202, a series of violent earthquakes struck Egypt, adding to the number of deaths.

The Nile rose very slowly from the middle of June to the middle of July, discouraging those who hoped for relief from starvation. After the middle of July, however, the Nile rose more rapidly, reaching a level of about 5.25 feet (3 cubits) and remaining steady for two days. The Nile then swiftly increased to a maximum level of about 28 feet (16 cubits) on September 4, 1202. Unlike the flood of 1201, which had declined quickly, the Nile remained at this level for two days, allowing adequate silt to be deposited, then dropped slowly. The return of the Nile to its normal behavior brought two years of devastating famine to an end.

Rose Secrest

FOR FURTHER INFORMATION:

"Famine in Egypt: Failure of Nile Floods Brings Hunger to an Ancient Land." In *Great Disasters: Dramatic True Stories of Nature's Awesome Power.* Pleasantville, N.Y.: Reader's Digest Association, 1989.

Nash, Jay Robert. "Egypt: Famine, 1199-1202." In *Darkest Hours: A Narrative Encyclopedia of Worldwide Disasters from Ancient Times to the Present.* Chicago: Nelson-Hall, 1976.

Tannahill, Reay. "Ferocity and Famine." In *Flesh and Blood: A History of the Cannibal Complex.* Rev. ed. Boston: Little, Brown, 1996.

1320: THE BLACK DEATH

EPIDEMIC

ALSO KNOWN AS: The Plague, the Black Plague, the Pestilence, the Great Mortality
DATE: 1320-1352
PLACE: Europe, Asia, Middle East, and Africa
RESULT: 25 million estimated dead in Europe, perhaps more than double that amount worldwide

The Black Death was the worst pandemic in human history, one that annihilated at least one-third of all humanity during its thirty-year killing spree in the fourteenth century. No other disease has killed so many people so quickly as the Black Death. Some scholars call it the "greatest biological-environmental event" in history.

Despite many attempts to explain the reasons for the Plague, no one at the time understood what caused the disease or how it was spread. Today, however, medical experts know that the deadly disease was caused by the *Yersinia pestis* bacterium. Many researchers also believe the disease manifested itself in four distinct forms as it raged across most of the known world during the fourteenth century. The most common form was the bubonic plague. Victims of this malady suffered headaches, weakness, and feverish chills. A white coating on the tongue appeared along with slurred speech and a rapid pulse. Within days painful swellings the size of eggs, called buboes, erupted in the lymph nodes of the groin and armpits. Black purplish spots formed by subcutaneous hemorrhaging also appeared on the skin of most victims. This discoloration may have earned the disease the name the Black Death, though many historians believe this designation did not become commonplace until two centuries later, when Scandinavian writers used the term *swarta doden* (black death) to emphasize the dreadful aspects of the disease.

Most sufferers of the bubonic plague died within a week of contracting the disease. Though highly contagious, this form of the plague was not transmitted from one human to another as many fourteenth century observers believed. The real carrier of the disease was the *Xenopsylla cheopsis*, a flea that lived as a parasite on the European black rat and other rodents. In a complicated cycle of contagion, fleas were the first to become infected by the bacterium, eventually transmitting the disease to their rodent hosts. When rats died and became scarce, the infectious fleas searched for new warm-blooded hosts, such as human beings. Because so many people in the fourteenth century lived in cramped, squalid conditions, rats and fleas were ever-present in their daily lives. As result, plague-carrying fleas easily carried the disease from rats to people.

A pneumonic form of the plague that infected the lungs also developed during the colder periods of the pandemic. Death resulted from vomiting blood, coughing, and choking. Unlike the bubonic plague, the pneumonic form was transmitted by one human to another by sneezing and coughing contaminated mucous particles. Though less common than the bubonic form, the pneumonic plague was more lethal and killed up to 95 percent of its victims.

The deadliest of all the Plague's manifestations were two very rare forms of the Black Death. Septicemic plague attacked the bloodstream; death often came within hours. Almost no one survived. Equally lethal was enteric plague, which devastated digestive systems.

SPREAD OF THE DISEASE. Although historical records of the disease are imprecise, many historians believe the first major outbreak of the Black Death in human populations took place among the nomadic tribes of Mongolia in 1320. Alternating periods of drought, intense rain, and locust attacks throughout Asia may have produced severe ecological disturbances that upset the normal balance between plague fleas and rats in the wild. This disruption may have also caused rodents to come into closer proximity to humans. The result was an epidemic among humans unlike any ever seen before or since.

From the steppes of Mongolia, the Plague spread throughout China, India, and other Asian lands, killing tens of millions. Next, infected rats, fleas, and humans headed west by accompanying the numerous ships, barges, and caravans that traveled the trade routes connecting the East and West. By 1346 the Plague had spread into the lands along the Black Sea, but it had not yet reached medieval Western Europe. Europe's apparent immunity to the disease soon changed as a result of human conflict. According to Italian chronicler Gabriele de Mussis, a dispute broke out one day between local Turkish Muslims, or Tatars, and merchants from Genoa, Italy, who had established a trading post near the city of Kaffa (today called Feodosiya) on the Crimea. When fighting erupted, the Genoans retreated to their walled compound nearby and managed to keep their enemy at bay for months. The stalemate broke when the Black Death arrived and killed Tatars in great numbers. Distraught by their misfortune, the Muslims reportedly catapulted the corpses of their dead comrades into the Genoa compound to share the disease with their Christian enemies. Though modern scientists think it is unlikely that the Plague could be spread in this way, the volley of corpses prompted the Genoans to escape in their galley ships and head for friendlier ports in the West. They took with them the Black Death, presumably brought aboard by infected rats.

The returning Genoa ships, along with other seagoing vessels plying the trade routes, most likely introduced the disease to the various populated ports of the Aegean and the Mediterranean. Within a year, the disease swept through the Middle East, Arabia, Corsica, Sardinia, Sicily, and Africa. Muslim pilgrims making their way to Mecca may have helped spread the disease through the Islamic world. Genoese ships also arrived in the Sicilian port of Messina in October, 1347. On the ships were infected sailors. Though the terrified people of Messina drove the vessels away, the disease managed to infect the local human and rodent populations before departure. Soon, the residents of Catania, a nearby town, also began to die, and within weeks the disease raged across Sicily.

The Black Death next entered Italy through its many seaports and fishing villages. Millions of Italians, already weakened by famine, earthquakes, civil strife, and severe economic problems, quickly succumbed to the pestilence as it rushed across the peninsula. Venice lost 600 people a day during the worst of the disease; ultimately an estimated total of 100,000 Venetians died. As many as 80,000 may have perished in Siena. Matteo Villani, a plague survivor, estimated that 3 out of every 5 died in Florence.

The disease soon went beyond Italy. In 1357, it entered the port of Marseilles and swept through France, Europe's most populated country. In Narbonne, 30,000 died. The Plague destroyed half the population of Avignon, and in Paris 50,000 were killed. Within

An illustration of bubonic plague from a medieval Bible.

months the north and west of France also lay in the grip of the Plague. Mortality in many villages and towns often exceeded 40 percent. Next, the Low Countries (today Belgium, Luxembourg, and the Netherlands) became infected. By this time, Spain, Switzerland, Austria, Germany, and Hungary also suffered.

During the summer of 1348, while the Plague ravaged continental Europe and many other areas of the world, the English Channel seemed to offer a protective barrier to those living in the British Isles. Their security was breached in August, however, when plague-bearing ships finally arrived in England at the ports of Weymouth and Melcombe. Soon, Dorset, Devon, Somerset, and other settlements in the south of England were hit. Within months the disease had moved northward to London, where as many as 100,000 eventually died. By the summer of 1349 East Anglia and Yorkshire were also infected.

For a short while, many Scots welcomed the Plague as a divinely inspired punishment sent to strike down their enemy, the English. However, such wishful thinking soon vanished when the disease swept into Scotland. It also spread into Wales and made its way to Ireland. Before the year ended, infected ships reached Sweden and Norway, where the pneumonic form of the Plague may have destroyed 50 percent of the population. According to some accounts, the Black Death even reached Scandinavian settlements in Iceland and Greenland. The Plague also raced eastward and infected vast areas in Russia that had not yet been infected.

No place seemed safe from the Black Death. Outbreaks of the disease occurred in cities, towns, and villages throughout most of the known world. Though the rich were less likely than the destitute to contract the disease, all social classes suffered catastrophic losses. Everywhere, people died horrible deaths in their homes, on the streets, and in the fields. Animals died as well: Dead rats, dogs, cats, and livestock lay rotting alongside odiferous human cadavers. The living were horrified to see rats, vultures, crows, and wolves devouring the diseased bodies of beasts and humans alike.

By 1352, the worst of the Black Death was over, but the disease had not gone away forever. Instead it had become endemic to most countries it had struck. This new ecological situation meant that the plague recurred many times well into the eighteenth century. When it struck again in 1361 and killed a disproportionate number of the young, it became known as the "Pestilence of the Children." Wherever and whenever the plague took root, stunned survivors struggled to understand the calamity that had overwhelmed them.

THE SEARCH FOR ANSWERS. From every land came a host of explanations of why and how the Plague had come into being. Many religious leaders claimed God sent the disease as a punishment for the sins of humanity, such as avarice, usury, adultery, and blasphemy. Others blamed the devil or an antichrist. Even the most learned minds of Christendom and Islam believed in astrology during the fourteenth century, and many scholars cited astrological influences as causes of the disease. When asked by Pope Clement VI to explain the presence of the Black Death, an esteemed panel of doctors in Paris concluded that a conjunction of the planets Saturn, Mars, and Jupiter at 1 P.M. on March 20, 1345, caused the disease.

Phantoms were also accused of spreading the Black Death. Among them was an apparition called the Plague Maiden. Many panic-stricken Europeans claimed to have witnessed her ghostly form sailing into one home after another to spread her deadly contagion.

Some believed the Black Death materialized when frogs, toads, and reptiles rained down on earth. Priests in England insisted that immoral living and indecent clothing fashions were responsible. Comets were also blamed. The fourteenth century French surgeon Guy de Chauliac believed sick people spread the Plague merely by looking at another person.

Inordinate fear generated by the Black Death also produced theories based on hatred and hysteria, which resulted in massive scapegoating and persecution. Witches, Gypsies, Muslims, lepers, and other minorities were often accused of starting the Plague and were killed by crazed mobs. The worst abuses, however, were reserved for Europe's Jewish population, a religious minority that had long faced persecution in Europe. Despite condemnation from the papacy, mobs in Switzerland, Germany, France, Spain, Italy, and parts of Central Europe tortured, hanged, and burned alive tens of thousands of Jews in revenge for allegedly spreading the disease with secret poisonous potions. Though political leaders in a few countries such as Poland and Lithuania offered sanctuary to Jews, most civil authorities either did nothing to protect them or officially authorized the mass executions.

Others, meanwhile, sought more rational explanations for the presence of the pestilence. Basing their opinions on the ideas of ancient Greeks, many Christian and Muslim physicians of the fourteenth century suggested that bad air brought on contagion. This contamination was believed to have been caused by foul odors released by earthquakes, decaying corpses on battlefields, or stagnant swamps. Fogs and winds from the south were also suspected of producing plagues. Many medieval physicians also subscribed to another ancient Greek teaching, which claimed that illness resulted from an imbalance of the four humors—phlegm, blood, black bile, and yellow bile—believed to have made up the human body. At special risk, according to many physicians, were poor people whose "bodies were replete with humours."

MEDIEVAL PREVENTIVES AND CURES. Balancing the humors in the body through corrective dieting was one preventive measure undertaken by Europeans. Many people also burned pleasant-smelling woods, such as juniper and ash, to produce counterbodies in the air to ward off the Plague. Rosewater and vinegar solutions also were used to purify household air. Women often held bouquets of flowers to their noses to counteract bad air. Birds were allowed to fly free in some homes to keep the air stirred up and free of the Plague; bowls of milk and pieces of bread were also left out in various rooms with the hope of soaking up bad air.

Medieval physicians told their patients to shun more than bad air. They also recommended avoiding hot baths, sexual intercourse, physical exertion, daytime slumber, and excessive consumption of deserts. On the other hand, diets of bread, nuts, eggs, pepper, onions, and leeks were recommended to ward off disease. Antiplague pills were also available and consisted of dozens of substances, ranging from saffron to snake meat and various toxins. Europeans were also urged to keep their minds healthy and sound as the Plague approached. Physicians advised others to purge their minds of all ideas of death and to think only pleasant thoughts.

Another fourteenth century theory held the opposite view and contended that bad air should be counteracted with something foul. Accordingly, some Europeans bathed in urine or menstrual blood or deliberately inhaled the fumes of fecal matter to fumigate themselves of any plague-causing agents.

In addition to these preventive measures, medieval physicians relied on common medical procedures of their day to cure those stricken by the Black Death. Because medical knowledge was limited to mostly inaccurate theories from the ancient world rather than research and experimentation, their efforts invariably failed. Nonetheless, doctors practiced their craft the best they could. Many bled their patients to alter the balance of humors in a sick or dying person. Some punctured buboes to release evil vapors or applied dead toads or poultices directly to these swellings to absorb toxins. Muslim physicians treated the buboes with cold water. Above all, doctors urged their patients to pray for good health.

SPIRITUAL WEAPONS. The appeal to prayer found a receptive audience among most fourteenth century Christians and Muslims, who put more faith in their religious beliefs and institutions than anything their physicians had to offer. Both private and group prayer were rendered constantly to gain heavenly favor during the Black Death. In addition, religious pilgrimages, the construction of new shrines, and public processions of piety became commonplace attempts to gain spiritual strength in the fight against the Plague. Christians and Muslims also donned special religious charms to protect themselves. Not all clerics tried to stave off the Plague, however. Many stressed an acceptance of God's will. Muslim religious leaders, for example, often taught that fleeing the Plague was futile, if not contrary, to divine plan. Allah, they said, was responsible for all things, including pestilence.

Sometimes, the panic-stricken took spiritual matters into their own hands. Many Christians dug up graves of various Catholic saints to obtain relics of skull fragments or bones believed to have anti-plague powers. Others launched spiritual crusades against the disease. The biggest such campaign was the Flagellant Movement, which emerged in Germany and spread into France and the Low Countries. Detached from the Catholic Church, the movement urged atonement for personal sins and an end to the Plague through public acts of penitence and self-debasement. Members of the movement were called Flagellants because of the flagella or barbed whips they used to lash their naked backs in mass public demonstrations carried out in churchyards or town centers.

Sometimes numbering in the tens of thousands, the Flagellants marched on bare feet from one community to the next debasing themselves with whips, praying, singing, and seeking forgiveness before the eyes of thousands of onlookers. At times, their exhibitions also became fiercely anti-Semitic and resulted in mob violence against local Jews. Convinced the Flagellants were heretical and usurping Church authority, Pope Clement VI eventually ordered an end to their activities. Secular officials, including the kings of England and France, equally worried about civil disorder, provided enforcement of the papal order, and by 1350 the movement ceased to exist.

HUMAN RESPONSE. Wherever the Black Death raged, terrified humans responded in various ways. Displays of fear, rancor, suspicion, apathy, violence, and resignation, along with nobler responses of altruism, self-sacrifice, and heroism, all appeared wherever the Plague struck. Some people faithfully nursed those who lay sick and dying, while others shunned all Black Death victims and fled. Many, terrified of contagion, refused to tend to even their loved ones; many physicians and priests abandoned their duties and ran away. Fear even prompted many to avoid the possessions of the dead and dying. According to Italian author Giovanni Boccaccio in his collection of stories *Decameron: O, Prencipe Galetto* (1349-1351; *The Decameron*, 1620), many people of Florence isolated themselves from the sick and spent their time carousing and living lives of wild abandon until death came or the disease went away. Similar behavior was reported in other plague-stricken cities.

The Black Death caused panic and social breakdown wherever it struck. Merchants closed shops. Trade ceased. Construction projects halted. Crops and livestock were abandoned. Even some churches closed their gates to keep away terrified mobs. The English Parliament shut down twice during the worst days of the Plague. Though many civil authorities died or fled the disease, most governments did not entirely cease to function. Hard-pressed to maintain a semblance of law and order, those left in charge of civil matters often passed antiplague ordinances. Some of these decrees were designed to fight the Plague by improving public moral behavior to please God. Authorities in Tournai, France, for example, ordered men and women, who lived together outside of matrimony, to marry at once. They also banned swearing, playing dice, and working on Sundays. Medieval officials also imposed travel bans and quarantines on travelers to reduce contact with the infected. In many places, the sick were forced into buildings hastily designated as Plague hospitals, where they invariably died. Authorities in Milan took even more drastic measures by ordering laborers to seal up homes of Plague victims, entombing both the alive and the dead.

Disposal of the dead became a logistical nightmare for both church and civil authorities. Because most European Catholics believed Christian burials in consecrated graves were necessary for salvation, church graveyards quickly filled. As a result, grave diggers, if they could be hired, hastily dug new mass graves, into which corpses were unceremoniously dumped. In many communities, only the abject poor and released criminals were willing to nurse the dying or bury the dead. In Italy, for example, slaves from galley ships were freed and ordered to undertake these tasks. All too soon, however, the new class of grave diggers—called the Becchini—took advantage of their newfound freedom and robbed, raped, murdered, and extorted the living. Civil authorities, exhausted by death and desertion within their own ranks, were often too weak to control the Becchini and their counterparts in other cities and towns.

AFTERMATH. Humanity had never before witnessed such a massive death toll as that of the Black Death. According to a study commissioned by papal authorities, the Plague killed more than 24 million Europeans. Throughout Africa, the Middle East, and Asia, the Plague killed anywhere from 25 to 40 percent of local populations. Some scholars estimate that as many as 1 out of every 3 died throughout the Muslim Empire. Although exact figures will never be known, and many may have been exaggerated by shocked survivors of the disease, most modern historians agree the impact of untold millions of human deaths caused great trauma among the living. Some scholars, in fact, suggest that the widespread mental suffering caused by the Plague paralleled that of the world wars of the twentieth century.

Many people responded to the pestilence by becoming more pious, in an attempt to appease God and keep such a calamity from recurring. Religious faith for others, however, was shaken or destroyed by the horrors of the Black Death. Many disillusioned Christians failed to understand how a loving god they had worshiped had failed to protect them from the terrors of the Plague, nor could they readily forgive the priests who had fled and failed to administer last rites to dying Christians.

Some disenchanted Christians, including religious reformers such as England's John Wyclif and Bohemia's Jan Hus, openly questioned many Church doctrines and practices and may have paved the way for the Protestant Reformation two centuries later. Others rejected Christianity altogether and joined various new cults based on mysticism or even satanic beliefs. Though the Catholic Church remained a powerful institution in Europe, its authority was forever weakened.

The Black Death also brought about other major changes. According to many firsthand reports, outbreaks of immorality, crime, violence, and civil breakdown followed in the wake of the Black Death. In addition, a preoccupation with death and the macabre expressed itself in many areas. Young people, for example, in many plague-stricken areas began to socialize in graveyards, where they danced and played games, as if to flaunt their indifference to death. Various folk dances that emphasized death also appeared in parts of Europe. The death dance also became a popular subject for artists and writers who concentrated on the ghoulish and inescapable aspects of dying.

Although cities and towns were growing, a majority of Europeans lived as feudal peasants or poor urban laborers when the Black Death first struck. This situation began to change in the wake of the Plague, however. The massive loss of life caused by the disease produced a severe widespread labor shortage that ultimately benefited the working poor. For one thing, the dearth of workers caused a rise in wages and gave laborers more negotiating power with employers and greater mobility than they had ever had before. Farm workers, artisans, and workers of all types no longer felt obliged to adhere to fixed working conditions imposed by a ruling nobility. In response to the newfound economic strength of workers, the ruling classes imposed various sumptuary laws both to prevent chaos and to control inflation generated by rising wages. Some of these new laws set wages and fined any employer who violated the restrictions, but many others were established primarily to maintain distinctions among the social classes. Some of these rules, for example, attempted to control what kinds of clothes and food the poor could buy to prevent them from trying to imitate their social superiors. Though often effective, the sumptuary laws proved unpopular and hard to enforce.

Despite such attempts to maintain the old order, the shake-up caused by the Black Death helped to dismantle many of the centuries-old assumptions, traditions, and institutions of medieval Europe. The changes wrought by the Plague also lead to widespread questioning of the social and economic order that had existed in Europe for centuries. This assault on the old manner that had benefited a privileged class of nobles and the Church for centuries now opened the door for the coming of the Renaissance, the Enlightenment, and the modern age.

John M. Dunn

FOR FURTHER INFORMATION:

Benedictow, Ole J. *The Black Death, 1346-1353: The Complete History.* Rochester, N.Y.: Boydell Press, 2006.

Byrne, Joseph P. *The Black Death.* Westport, Conn.: Greenwood Press, 2004.

Cantor, Norman F. *In the Wake of the Plague: The Black Death and the World It Made.* New York: Perennial/HarperCollins, 2002.

Herlitly, David. *The Black Death and the Transformation of the West.* Cambridge, Mass.: Harvard University Press, 1997.

Horrox, Rosemary, trans. and ed. *The Black Death.* Manchester, England: Manchester University Press, 1994.

Karlen, Arno. *Man and Microbes: Disease and Plagues in History and Modern Times.* New York: Putnam, 1995.

Kelly, John. *The Great Mortality: An Intimate History of the Black Death, the Most Devastating Plague of All Time.* New York: HarperCollins, 2005.

Nohl, Johannes. *The Black Death: A Chronicle of the Plague Compiled from Contemporary Sources.* Translated by C. H. Clarke. London: Unwin Books, 1961.

Orent, Wendy. *Plague: The Mysterious Past and Terrifying Future of the World's Most Dangerous Disease.* New York: Free Press, 2004.

■ 1520: Aztec Empire smallpox epidemic

Epidemic

Date: 1520-1521
Place: Tenochtitlán, Aztec Empire
Result: 2 to 5 million dead

Spanish conquest and colonization of Mexico began in 1519 when Hernán Cortés was ordered by Diego Velázquez, governor of Cuba, to command an expedition to the mainland of Mesoamerica. The smallpox epidemic of 1520-1521 figured importantly in the unlikely conquest of an empire of millions by a much smaller force of Spaniards accompanied by their Native American allies. Landing on the Yucatán peninsula, Cortés marched inland, collecting allies en route to the capital of the Aztec Empire, Tenochtitlán, where he took the emperor, Moctezuma II, prisoner. In 1520, Cortés left Tenochtitlán, leaving some of his men behind to hold the city, in order to meet an expedition on the coast sent by Velázquez, who suspected the ambitious Cortés of exceeding his orders. Cortés convinced these forces to join him rather than arrest him, and he returned to Tenochtitlán. He found a capital where the Indians were in the throes of rebellion against the Spanish. In June of 1520 the Aztecs succeeded in repelling the Spanish. Few Spaniards survived *la noche triste* (the sad night). Cortés and the remainder of his troops retreated to Tlaxcala to rebuild his fighting forces.

Meanwhile, a smallpox epidemic was proceeding from Yucatán to Tenochtitlán. A soldier who had an active case of smallpox came with the expedition to arrest Cortés. According to some chroniclers his name was Francisco Eguia. He infected Indians with the viral disease, and it was quickly spread from person to person and from village to village, progressing rapidly from the coast to the interior. The disease was reported to have arrived in April or May of 1520; it spread inland from May to September, and it reached Tenochtitlán in September or October.

The effects of the outbreak in America were far greater than were experienced during an outbreak in Europe during the same period. The susceptibility of the American Indians compared to the Spanish can be accounted for by the fact that this disease was unknown to them. The Aztecs had no specific word in their language for smallpox and usually described it in their writings by its characteristic pustules. In Europe the disease had been extant for centuries, and when it re-appeared there were usually many persons who were immune because of previous exposure. In contrast, the Indian population was extremely vulnerable to the disease. There were no immune persons in the population, and the people were highly homogeneous genetically, which meant that the virus did not have to adapt to various genetic makeups to be successful in infecting the host. In addition, the first outbreak of a disease within a group is generally the most severe.

This disease wreaked disaster on the indigenous population. It is estimated that one-third to one-half of the population died during the epidemic. In contrast, only about 10 percent of a European population died in an outbreak in the sixteenth century. Because all segments of the population in America were vulnerable, there were few healthy caregivers to sustain the sick. In addition, many rulers were struck down. In Cortés's letters to the king, he reported that he was asked by many Indian groups who were allied with him against the Aztecs to choose a leader to replace someone who had died of smallpox.

Most important, the epidemic reached Tenochtitlán at a crucial moment in history. The Aztecs had forced Cortés to retreat, but during his time of rest and rebuilding he sent spies into Tenochtitlán to determine the strength of his opponents. He learned that the Aztecs had been struck down with smallpox and were greatly weakened. At times, the disease struck so many persons that no one in a family was able to give care to the others, and whole families died, not only of smallpox but also of thirst and starvation. Homes were destroyed with the corpses inside to diminish the fetid odor wafting through the once-great city. Bodies were thrown into the water, offering a wretched sight of bloated, bobbing flesh. Warriors who survived were weakened by the disease, and their chain of command was compromised. The emperor named to replace Moctezuma died of smallpox. The loss of continuity and experience in leadership greatly weakened the ability of the Aztecs to mount a defense against the Spaniards.

Having replenished his forces, Cortés struck Tenochtitlán again in May of 1521, and within months he had conquered the seat of the Aztec Empire. Debate continues over the role of the smallpox epidemic in this conquest. Cortés did not give it much weight in his chronicles, but Indian chronicles of the time emphasize its importance. The year 1520 is called the year of the pustules, according to Aztec chronicles. Though there is great disagreement among historians over the number of deaths and the importance of the smallpox epidemic in the conquest, there is no doubt that this epidemic was one of the most serious disasters in Mexico in the sixteenth century.

Bonnie L. Ford

FOR FURTHER INFORMATION:

Crosby, Alfred, Jr. *The Columbian Exchange: Biological and Cultural Consequences of 1492*. Westport, Conn.: Greenwood Press, 1972.

Diamond, Jared. *Guns, Germs, and Steel: The Fates of Human Societies.* New York: W. W. Norton, 1997.

Glynn, Ian, and Jenifer Glynn. *The Life and Death of Smallpox.* New York: Cambridge University Press, 2004.

McCaa, Robert. "Spanish and Nahuatl Views on Smallpox and Demographic Catastrophe in Mexico." *The Journal of Interdisciplinary History* 25 (Winter, 1995): 397-432.

Noble, David Cook. *Born to Die: Disease and New World Conquest, 1492-1650*. Cambridge, England: Cambridge University Press, 1998.

■ 1657: The Meireki Fire

Fire

ALSO KNOWN AS: The Furisode Fire, the Great Edo Fire
DATE: March, 1657
PLACE: Edo (now Tokyo), Japan
RESULT: More than 100,000 dead

The city of Edo, located where the eastern part of the central city of Tokyo stands today, became the most important city in Japan at the start of the seventeenth century. In the year 1600, Tokugawa Ieyasu defeated other daimyos (provincial military governors) at the Battle of Sekigahara. Tokugawa established himself as shogun (hereditary military dictator) of Japan, with his headquarters in Edo. Although the emperor of Japan remained in the ancient capital city of Kyoto as the symbolic ruler, the Tokugawa shogunate retained all political power until 1867.

Like all Japanese cities of the time, Edo was built of wood. Fire was always a potential hazard. The first official fire-defense system in Japan was established by the shogunate in 1629. At first, the shogunate employed a small number of resident daimyos to protect important sites within the castle and the family shrines of the shogun. By 1650, this system, known as the *daimyo hikeshi*, was expanded to include firefighters who watched over the residences, shrines, and temples of the daimyos who lived near the castle. This new system was known as the *jobikeshi*.

The Meireki Fire took place in March of 1657, the third year of the Meireki era. A year of drought had left the wooden buildings of Edo particularly vulnerable to fire. In addition, a wind blowing from the northwest at hurricane speed ensured that a fire would spread rapidly throughout the city. Because the fire was thought to have been caused by the burning of a *furisode* (young girl's kimono) during an exorcism ceremony, it was also known as the Furisode Fire.

The fire began in the Hommyoji Temple in the Hongo District of Edo. It quickly spread to the Kanda District, then south to the Kyobashi District and east to the Fukagawa District. Zacharias Waganaer,

a Dutch trader who left an eyewitness account of the fire, reported that the heat from the flames could be felt from a quarter of a mile away. He described the approaching wall of fire as a mile wide, with sparks falling from it "like a strong rain." The sun was completely blocked out by the huge amounts of black smoke.

The next day, the wind changed direction. The fire spread north to the Kojimachi District, destroying the houses of the servants of the daimyos. Soon the flames spread to the homes of the daimyos who lived near the castle, burning them to the ground. The castle itself

351

suffered extensive damage. Although the inner section was saved, much of the outer section was destroyed. The castle's central tower, about 200 feet tall, was lost and never rebuilt.

By the end of the third day, the wind and the flames decreased, but the smoke was so thick and the city so full of ruins that it was difficult to move from place to place for several days. Meanwhile, those who had lost their homes in the fire faced severe winter weather. More than 100,000 people lost their lives to the fire, either directly or as a result of exposure to the snowstorm that struck the city the day after the fire. When movement was possible again, the dead were loaded on boats and transported up the Sumida River to the suburb of Honjo. Here they were buried in large pits as funeral prayers were recited by monks of many different sects. A memorial temple, known as the Ekoin, was built on the site and remained until the twentieth century.

The shogunate responded to the disaster by setting up medical facilities and distributing food and money to those left homeless. The rebuilding of the city took two years and depleted the shogunate's treasury. The commercial sections of Edo were the first to be rebuilt, in an effort to restore the economy. The houses of the resident daimyos were not rebuilt; instead, the daimyos were sent back to their home provinces. The restoration of the castle was the last task to be completed. In an elaborate ceremony, the shogun entered the new castle in 1659.

The devastation caused by the fire led to reforms in fire prevention. During the rebuilding of Edo, the width of roads and the spacing of houses were standardized, in order to ease movement during an emergency. Special fire lanes were constructed at various intersections to allow for rapid motion. Laws were passed forbidding the common practice of stacking surplus goods along the banks of rivers, in an attempt to prevent fires from spreading by way of these large piles of flammable objects. The Ryogoku Bridge was built across the Sumida River in 1660, both to allow the city to expand and to ease movement across the river. Wide streets were placed on both sides of the bridge, in order to prevent fires from spreading to it. In 1718, volunteer firefighting units made up of commoners were organized in Edo. This system was known as the *machi hikeshi*. This system, which eventually included more than 10,000 volunteers, served as the main defense against fire in areas where the common people lived until the late nineteenth century. In 1868, when the emperor regained power from the shogunate, the *daimyo hikeshi* and the *jobikeshi* systems were disbanded, and the *machi hikeshi* system was reorganized into companies of firefighters known as the *shobogumi*. The *shobogumi* were placed under the control of the police in 1881, renamed the *keibodan* in 1939, and renamed the *shobodon* in 1947. In 1948, the first independent, professional fire departments in Japan were created.

Rose Secrest

FOR FURTHER INFORMATION:

Kornicki, Peter. "The Meireki Fire." In *The Cambridge Encyclopedia of Japan*, edited by Richard Bowring and Peter Kornicki. New York: Cambridge University Press, 1993.

McClain, James L., John M. Merriman, and Ugawa Kaoru, eds. *Edo and Paris: Urban Life and the State in the Early Modern Era*. Ithaca, N.Y.: Cornell University Press, 1994.

"Meireki Fire." In *Encyclopedia of Japan*. New York: Kodansha, 1983.

Naitō, Akira. "The Great Meiriki Fire." In *Edo, the City That Became Tokyo: An Illustrated History*. Translated by H. Mack Horton. Tokyo: Kodansha International, 2003.

Sansom, George. "The Great Fire of Meireki." In *A History of Japan, 1615-1867*. Stanford, Calif.: Stanford University Press, 1963.

■ 1665: The Great Plague of London

Epidemic

Date: May-December, 1665
Place: London, England
Result: Approximately 100,000 dead

Plague in England was a constant visitor for many centuries. The Black Death of the mid-fourteenth century had killed off between one-fourth and one-third of the country's population. In London, before the devastating Great Plague of 1665, there were serious epidemics in 1593 that killed 15,000; in 1603, 33,000; in 1625, 41,000; in 1636, 10,000; and in 1647, 3,600. In the interval between 1603 and 1665, there were only a few years in which London did not record any plague deaths.

Reasons for the Plague. In 1665, London was a city of fewer than 500,000 people. The core of this vast metropolis was the city itself, the historic area of about 1 square mile still enclosed by an impressive wall. Surrounding the city were growing suburbs, where most of the poor lived under wretched conditions. It is not known what brought the plague to London, but it is likely that it either came from abroad—perhaps from Holland, which experienced a terrible plague the previous year—or was already endemic to England and waiting for favorable conditions to break out. The Bills of Mortality, the official statistics that recorded deaths in London, reveal only 3 deaths from plague in the first four months of the year, but plague deaths jumped to double digits in May, and for the first time there was widespread concern about the plague. By the end of June, the weekly total had risen to 267; the plague was definitely spreading.

Unfortunately, neither the civic authorities nor the medical professionals had any knowledge of what the plague was or how it was transmitted. In fact, it was not until 1894 that the bacillus that caused the disease was isolated, discovered almost simultaneously by two scientists working independently of each other, Swiss bacteriologist

Alexandre Yersin and Japanese physician Shibasaburo Kitasato. It was given the name *Pasteurella pestis* (later *Yersinia pestis*), and eventually the method of transmission was also discovered. It was carried by the black rat, which in turn infected fleas. Unfortunately, the black rat was a sociable creature that lived comfortably with human beings, and this close proximity made it easier for fleas to transfer themselves from the rats, which became plague victims, to nearby human hosts.

The reason the plague was most ferocious in the summer months was likely due to the fact that rat fleas tended to flourish in hot weather. The type of plague that afflicted London was the bubonic variety, characterized chiefly by the telltale buboes that appeared on the body of victims, large swellings about the size of eggs that appeared in the joints, groin, armpits, and neck. The disease had an incubation period of usually two to five days, and the victim suffered from fever, chills, weakness, and headaches, eventually becoming lethargic or delirious. Bubonic plague had a death rate of 50 to 90 percent.

At the time of the plague, London was a filthy, unsanitary city, made up mostly of dilapidated, unventilated wooden dwellings, fronted by open sewers masquerading as streets and having no proper methods for disposal of garbage and human waste—in short, an ideal environment for rats. Conditions were most appalling in the suburbs, and the plague broke out in one of the worst slum areas, St. Giles-in-the-Fields, eventually spreading eastward, as well as to the south and west.

By the end of July the weekly plague figure had risen to over 1,800 victims, but the deadliest moments of the epidemic were in August and September, when the total plague deaths exceeded 46,000. In late October, the figures began to decline noticeably, and by the first week of December only 210 deaths were recorded. For the entire year, the official total was 68,596, of which the ravished suburbs accounted for 85 percent of the deaths. In general, this was a "poor man's plague" and a suburban phenomena. As alarming as these figures were, scholars believe the death toll was seriously undercounted, and a more likely total is about 100,000. Still, the plague lingered, and in the following year over 1,700 died. It was not until 1670 that London recorded no plague deaths for the entire year.

METHODS OF CONTAINMENT. A series of events conspired to make the death tolls even higher than they should have been, since the authorities often took measures that were counterproductive. For example, civic authorities mistakenly believed that dogs and cats may well have carried the disease, and officials ordered their extermination, resulting in the killing of tens of thousands of the creatures. Yet these were the very animals that could have possibly checked the rat population.

The most disastrous decision was to invoke a quarantine as the principal method of containing the plague. Authorities decreed that any house containing a case of plague was to be closed and locked, with all the residents sealed inside. Armed watchmen guarded the house to ensure that no one escaped from the infected dwelling. The door of the house was painted with a large red cross with the words "Lord Have Mercy upon Us" inscribed on it. This action simply guaranteed that the plague would likely spread to everyone trapped inside, and it was common for entire families to perish, one member after the other. In retrospect, a more successful policy would have been to separate the infected from the uninfected, perhaps by transferring all the infected to the local pesthouse or other such building, thus isolating the sick from the healthy.

Authorities believed that the contagion was carried in the air. Therefore, the city officials decreed in early September that fires should be burned throughout London, and for three days the city's air was fouled by a heavy pall of suffocating smoke and a terrible stench until rains mercifully doused these fires. Individuals had their own remedies for fighting the plague but all too frequently relied upon quack potions, amulets, charms, and mystical signs and numbers.

AFTEREFFECTS. London still managed to function during the plague, however imperfectly, despite the fact that the king, his court, and parliament fled the city for safety reasons. Among the few heroes to emerge from this period otherwise filled with much cowardice and stupidity were the Lord Mayor Sir John Lawrence and several of the city's aldermen. During the plague, they ensured a steady supply of food from the surrounding farmlands, kept prices from rising, prevented any riots, and raised money, mostly from private charities, to offer assistance to an increasingly destitute population.

A bureaucracy of sorts was established to cope with the demands of the plague. Watchmen were appointed to guard the infected houses. Nurses lived in the infected dwellings and administered to

A victim of the plague shows physicians the bubo under his arm. (Library of Congress)

the needs of the sick. However, this dangerous and depressing work was done only by the truly desperate, who quickly established a reputation for venality and callousness, frequently misusing their position to steal from their patients and even expedite their deaths.

Perhaps the most notorious workers were the "searchers," people who were to visit the houses of the deceased and establish the cause of death. This dangerous job was usually taken only by elderly impoverished women, who were often ignorant, illiterate, and corrupt. Frequently, they either misdiagnosed the cause of death or were bribed to attribute the cause of death to something other than the plague, so that family members could leave the house immediately and not be placed under further quarantine. Other unfortunates pushed their carts through the city during the night in order to collect those who died, shouting "Bring out your dead" to announce their arrival. Gravediggers, who were almost overwhelmed at times by the tide of thousands of people dying weekly, frequently had to dig mass pits into which bodies, nude or wrapped in sacks or cloths, were tossed, without the dignity of a coffin or proper burial service.

ECONOMIC RESULTS. London was economically devastated during the plague. Commercial activity almost vanished from the city. Shops were closed, the houses of the wealthy were shuttered, and many dwellings were kept under quarantine. Even the port of London, one of the most active in the world, saw deserted docks and little cargo, with foreign ships fearing to sail to this plague-infested destination and foreign customers reluctant to accept London goods that might be contaminated.

When the nobility and the professional classes fled the city by the tens of thousands, they often dismissed their workers or servants from employment. Newly impoverished, these unemployed sought cheap housing, which meant they were forced to live in the very suburbs that had the highest death tolls, thereby providing the human fodder that fed the deadly toll. There was a dramatic decline in human interaction. The authorities either forbade or discouraged large gatherings of people, whether in churches, alehouses, funerals, or inns. London, once one of the most noisy, bustling, and industrious of cities, became strangely silent and largely devoid of human activity.

THE LAST PLAGUE. This was the last major plague epidemic to afflict London. The question of why a plague never struck London again is one of the great historical mysteries. Although a precise answer has confounded both the historical and the medical professions, there are a number of possible explanations. First, it has been argued that the Great Fire of 1666, which burned almost the entire city within its ancient walls, destroyed the plague by burning the old unsanitary wooden city and killing off the rats in the process. However, this does not explain why the plague did not return to the unsanitary suburbs, which were untouched by the Great Fire.

Another popular explanation is that the brown or Norwegian rat supplanted the black rat as the chief urban rodent. Unlike its predecessor, the brown rat tended to avoid human contact, preferring sewers, garbage dumps, and other areas free of human beings. This may have eventually been an important component in containing the plague, but the brown rat did not supplant the black rat immediately after 1665. Rather, the displacement occurred over a period of several decades, thereby not accounting for the era before it became dominant. There are also medical theories concerning how human beings may have developed immunities to bubonic plague or that the plague's bacillus had mutated into a more benign form, but these ideas are considered suspect by medical authorities.

Perhaps the most persuasive explanation emphasizes measures undertaken by public authorities. Central governments around the globe developed sophisticated methods of isolating their nations from plagues by strict quarantines imposed upon ships and cargoes from infected regions of the world. Also, societies witnessed important developments in the areas of public health and standards of public sanitation. Over a period of decades and centuries, people have become healthier, water supplies purer, housing more sanitary, refuse collection more efficient, and disposal of human waste more effective. All these measures have made cities healthier and safer places to live. Undoubtedly, it was a combination of several of the above explanations that have helped modern society escape the horrors that London experienced in 1665.

David C. Lukowitz

FOR FURTHER INFORMATION:

Bell, Walter George. *The Great Plague in London*. Reprint. New York: Dodd, Mead, 1994.

Butler, Thomas. *Plague and Other "Yersinia" Infections*. London: Plenum Medical Books, 1983.

Cowie, Leonard W. *Plague and Fire: London, 1665-6*. New York: G. P. Putnam's Sons, 1970.

Moote, A. Lloyd, and Dorothy C. Moote. *The Great Plague: The Story of London's Most Deadly Year*. Baltimore: Johns Hopkins University Press, 2004.

Mullett, Charles F. "London's Last Dreadful Visitation" and "The Plague of 1965 in Literature." In *The Bubonic Plague and England*. Lexington: University of Kentucky Press, 1956.

Orent, Wendy. *Plague: The Mysterious Past and Terrifying Future of the World's Most Dangerous Disease*. New York: Free Press, 2004.

■ 1666: The Great Fire of London

Fire

DATE: September 2-6, 1666
PLACE: London, England
RESULT: 8 dead; 13,200 homes destroyed; 87 churches destroyed; 44 livery halls, 373 acres within the city walls, and 63 acres outside the city walls burned; more than 100,000 people left homeless; between 6 and 10 million British pounds in damage

The Great Fire of London, which raged from early Sunday morning, September 2, 1666, until early Thursday morning, September 6, 1666, was regarded by many contemporaries as the worst catastrophe in London's history. Coming shortly after the Great Plague of 1665 and during the Second Anglo-Dutch War (1665-1667), the fire caused substantial changes to be brought to London. Because much of older, medieval London was destroyed—an area 1.5 miles long by 0.5 mile wide—400 streets ceased to exist, and major landmarks such as St. Paul's Cathedral and the Royal Exchange burned, a major rebuilding project overseen by prominent architect Christopher Wren was undertaken. New regulations and strict building codes were implemented that aimed to prevent future conflagrations. Some have argued such massive destruction and the rebuilding of London was a factor in the prevention of additional outbreaks of the plague.

BACKGROUND. During the 1600's there were a number of substantial fires in London and throughout England. Fires in London in 1630 consumed 50 houses; in 1633 the houses on London Bridge plus 80 more burned; and a gunpowder fire in 1650 killed 27 people, destroyed 15 homes, and severely damaged 26 more. Provincial fires proved to be much more damaging: In 1644, 300 houses burned in Oxford; in 1653, 224 houses in Marlborough; in 1659, 238 houses in Southwold; and in 1665, 156 houses in Newport, Shropshire. The danger of fire was ever-present from household fires; clogged chimneys; and from the businesses of tradesmen, such as bakers, brewers, blacksmiths, and chandlers. No fire departments existed, and firefighting equipment was primitive by modern standards. Leather buckets for carrying water, fire hooks for pulling down buildings, ladders, axes, brooms, and "water engines" and "water guns"—devices for drawing water from wells, rivers, ponds, and aqueducts and spraying the fire—were of some use.

London, the largest city in the British Isles and the second largest in Europe, with a population of about 350,000 to 400,000, occupied 458 acres within the city walls and sprawled beyond the walls into the "out parishes" or suburbs. In April, 1665, King Charles II wrote to the lord mayor of London, Sir Thomas Bludworth, and the aldermen of the city, warning them of the danger of fire due to buildings overhanging the streets. He authorized them to imprison people who built overhanging dwellings and to tear the buildings down. Many superstitious people had feared that the year 1666 would bring disaster because of the number 666, which was viewed as a sign of the Antichrist mentioned in the biblical book of Revelation, and there were many predictions issued by self-proclaimed prophets about London's destruction as a result of God's judgment.

THE FIRE. The fire started in the house of the king's baker, Thomas Farriner (also spelled Farrinor or Farynor), between 1 and 2 A.M. Sunday morning on September 2, 1666, on Pudding Lane near London Bridge, in what is now EC3 in modern London. The streets in this part of London were congested and narrow, wide enough for only a wheelbarrow. Farriner's family escaped the fire by climbing out an upper-story window to the roof of the next-door building. A female servant's fear of heights prevented her from using this escape route, and she became the first fatality. Wood-frame buildings with pitch on their roofs and combustible materials, such as flax, rosin, oil, tallow, wines, brandy, and other alcoholic beverages, in warehouses on Thames Street fueled the fire, which was blown westward toward the center of the city by a strong wind. Samuel Pepys, the famous diarist, was awakened by Jane Birch, his female servant, at 3 A.M. to see the flames, but he was not concerned by the fire some distance from his residence.

Initially, the fire spread slowly, and most people were able to remove their belongings from their houses. Some ferried them down the Thames River and were charged exorbitant prices; others stored them in churches, only to have to move them again or lose them as

London during the Great Fire of 1666, from a print by Visscher. (Robert Chambers)

the fire spread more extensively than anyone could have imagined. Lord Mayor Bludworth was awakened and surveyed the scene around 3 A.M. and concluded that it was not serious. An inoperative "water engine" near the scene, low water levels, and the failure to pull down nearby buildings allowed the fire to continue to spread. Some contemporaries said that an alderman opposed pulling down the buildings because his home would have been one of the first to be destroyed. The occurrence of the fire on a Sunday caught officials off guard and added to the confusion.

Rumors spread quickly that the fire had been deliberately set by Catholics or foreigners, such as the Dutch or French, and London mobs began assaulting immigrants. A French Huguenot watchmaker, Robert Hubert, later "confessed" to having set the fire. Although his story was full of inconsistencies and changed repeatedly, he was convicted and hanged in October, 1666.

The fire spread throughout Sunday; the streets were clogged with people fleeing and with household goods. The Thames River became crowded with sightseers on boats and goods floating in the river. The sound of crackling flames, crashing buildings, occasional explosions, and peoples' cries filled the air. King Charles II and his brother, James, duke of York, alerted by Pepys, arrived on the scene and began to supervise and assist the firefighting efforts, as did William Lindsay, earl of Craven, who had stayed in London during the Great Plague the previous year.

People from the countryside came to London with carts and wagons to make money by helping to transport peoples' belongings. Some charged £30 for use of a cart, and thievery was commonplace. Some contemporary eyewitnesses were critical of citizens for being more concerned with saving their household belongings than with attempting to extinguish the fire. People rendered homeless by the fire began to congregate in large open spaces and fields in Moorfields, Finsbury and Islington, and Highgate in the north and St. Giles Fields and Soho in the west. Citizens of different social classes, along with whatever possessions they could transport, crowded into these areas. The fire's impact was unlike that of the plague the previous year; the plague killed the poor, while the rich had fled. The fire destroyed the property of both the rich and the poor.

Although the fire had advanced only 150 yards east of Pudding Lane to Billingsgate, damage caused by the northern and westward movement of the fire started to become substantial. Citizens had been reluctant to pull down buildings to create a firebreak because of ordinances requiring people to pay to rebuild any structures pulled down. Eventually, sailors and watermen from the Thames River began pulling down houses with ropes and using gunpowder to blow up buildings. Samuel Pepys was concerned enough by Sunday evening to move his money into his cellar and to have his gold and important papers ready to carry away if flames threatened his home. At about 4 A.M. Monday, September 3, Pepys moved his belongings in carts while riding in his nightgown. By Sunday's end, the fire had burned half a mile westward along the Thames.

The fire's spread on Monday, September 3, continued to cause astonishment, and it seemed as if the air itself had been ignited, with the sky resembling "the top of a burning oven," according to diarist and eyewitness John Evelyn. He also noted that the Thames was still choked with floating goods, boats, and barges loaded with all manner of items. Charles II, concerned about a possible breakdown in law and order and the lack of success in stemming the fire's spread, established eight "fire posts" throughout the city, with the duke of York in charge. These posts, under the command of a nobleman assisted by justices of the peace and constables and supported by soldiers, provided for the protection of property and were a symbol of authority in that chaotic time. Coleman Street in the east; Smithfield, Adlersgate, and Cripplegate to the north; and Temple Bar, Clifford's Inn Gardens, Fetter Lane, and Shoe Lane in the west were the locations of these posts. Militia from the counties surrounding London were called up to be ready to assist.

Hopes that the fire might be stopped along the Thames at Bayard's Castle, a large, tall stone structure, were dashed, as this building burned and the fire continued to move westward along the river. The portions of the city along the river that had been destroyed were the poorer ones, but as the conflagration remained unchecked it began to consume some of the wealthiest portions, including Lombard Street, where many merchants, bankers, and goldsmiths plied their trade. Most of these individuals moved their valuables, primarily money and bonds, to Gresham College much more easily than could the tradesmen who had bulky goods and materials stored in warehouses along the Thames. The most important structure lost to the flames on Monday was the Royal Exchange, the principal location in London for trading commodities, such as pepper and silk. The one bright spot on Monday was the halt of the fire at Leadenhall, a marketplace for grain and poultry products, in what would be EC2 in modern London, which marked the extent of the fire to the north and east. Although the financial center of London had been burned, its relocation along with the city government to Gresham College to the north was a positive development that provided for a semblance of financial and political stability.

The worst day of the fire was Tuesday, September 4. Contemporaries living in the countryside reported that the red glow of the fire could be seen 10 to 40 miles away at night, and residents of Oxford, 60 miles to the west, noted that the smoke obscured the daytime sunlight. A strong east wind blew embers, spreading the fire rapidly. The Guildhall in the north burned, and the fire jumped the city walls and moved into the out parishes. The Fleet River, which ran to the Thames to the west of the city walls, was regarded as a potential firebreak, but the flames leaped across it and continued westward.

St. Paul's Cathedral, the most prominent landmark in London, burned, along with 150,000 British pounds worth of books that booksellers had moved into its basement for safekeeping. Eyewitnesses reported that chunks of stone between 20 and 100 pounds fell from the cathedral, and lead from its roof melted into the streets. The Exchequer (national treasury) was moved to Nonesuch, Surrey, and the Queen Mother, Henrietta Maria, moved to Hampton Court, west of London.

The Tower of London was spared because the nearby buildings had been blown up, preventing the fire from reaching it. Had fire reached the stores of gunpowder in the Tower, a tremendous explosion would have resulted. Samuel Pepys and William Penn, father of the founder of Pennsylvania, dug holes in their gardens to bury their wine and cheese, believing that this would preserve them. Charles II and the duke of York helped to man water buckets and shovels and scattered gold coins among the workers as payment for their effort. Such actions helped elevate popular opinion of the monarchy.

Late Tuesday night the wind began to drop. Because of the abatement of the wind and demolition work, the fire began to be contained on Wednesday, September 5. The Temple, one of the Inns of Court (law school), was the last significant structure to burn. Rumors spread throughout London that the French and Dutch, 50,000 strong, had landed in England and were marching on London. Such notions were fueled by the fact that the postal service from London had been disrupted, and newsletters that were routinely sent to the provinces had stopped, causing puzzlement and suspicion. By Thursday, September 6, when dawn broke, the fire ended after it reached its furthest border at Fetter Lane in the west, where brick buildings halted the flames, Cock Lane in the north and west, and All Hallows Church, Barking, in the east.

Pepys noted that it was "the saddest sight of desolation" that he ever saw. Citizens who walked through the city noted that the ground was hot enough to burn the soles of their shoes; ash was inches deep, and debris was piled up in mounds. Fires smoldered in basements for weeks and even months, and acrid odors permeated the air.

AFTERMATH. On Wednesday, September 5, 1666, Charles II issued two royal proclamations to begin the process of recovery from the disaster. In order to feed the displaced and homeless, the king ordered local magistrates to bring bread to London. He also had markets set up throughout the city and let people store their goods in public places. The second proclamation urged the inhabitants of surrounding towns to accept refugees and allow them to practice their trades. On Thursday, September 6, the king went to Moorfields to address the thousands of refugees there and to explain that the fire was the judgment of God—not a conspiracy of Catholics, the French, or the Dutch. Charles II ordered 500 pounds of navy sea biscuits, or "hardtack," released for the refugees to eat, but the food was too dense for the people who were not used to it. Army tents were used to house the homeless, who also had built makeshift huts or had slept out in the open.

Another significant problem was sorting out the owners of the personal effects, household belongings, business papers, and wares that had been quickly deposited at several locations throughout the city. In the hope of recovering additional misplaced or stolen items, amnesty was declared for people who might have taken property illegally or by mistake. Scavenging among the ruins yielded items that were relatively undamaged or at least usable, especially precious and base metals that had melted. Although some merchants had no hope of such finds, the loss to booksellers was probably the most spectacular. Estimated at £150,000, it represented total ruin for a number of prominent merchants, and many scarce and rare titles were destroyed, leading to a substantial increase in the price of certain desirable volumes. Some contemporaries claimed that the price of paper doubled after the fire.

Another commodity that rapidly increased in price was coal, especially as cold weather would be coming in the following months; accusations of price gouging were common. Because of the massive destruction of housing and the large number of homeless people, competition for housing space was fierce, and rents quickly escalated, as they did for tradesmen seeking to relocate their businesses.

Because of the massive destruction, which left only a few recognizable landmarks standing, people had a completely clear view of the city from west to east, and the Thames River could be seen from Cheapside in the center of the city. The rebuilding of London was a daunting undertaking that started slowly. The London Common Council ordered inhabitants to clear the debris from the streets. Tradesmen and craftsmen were resettled, city offices were relocated, churchwardens were to report those who were in need of assistance, and donations came in from wealthy citizens who were either spared by the fire and from other cities. Because most charitable contributions for other previous disasters had come from London's citizens, the collection of donations was rather modest—£16,201 coming from collections in 1666 and 1668. Some provincial cities were concerned that the source of money to aid their plague victims would be reduced because that money had come from London, which was now in dire straits itself.

Rain on Sunday, September 9, helped dampen the embers, and contemporaries noted that the attendance at church was greatly increased. Ten days of heavy rain in mid-October brought additional misery to the homeless but helped extinguish remaining hot spots. On Monday, September 10, Charles II ordered Wenceslaus Hollar, the prominent landscape designer, and Francis Sandford, a historian and author, to make a survey of the city, and their report formed the basis for most of the statistical information about the extent of the damage caused by the fire. Their work was completed and published later in 1666 and showed a before-and-after perspective to visually indicate the extent of the destruction. The king issued another royal proclamation on Thursday, September 13, 1666, mandating rebuilding with brick and stone and allowing authorities to pull down houses built contrary to regulations. Streets were to be wide and a wharf, which was to be free from houses, was to run along the Thames River. October 10 was established as a day of fasting by royal proclamation. Also on that day, contractors or surveyors were appointed to prepare a list of all the properties destroyed and their owners or renters in preparation for delineating the path and layout of streets.

Within days of the end of the fire, several influential citizens, including John Evelyn and Christopher Wren, had submitted plans for rebuilding the burned area. Town planning was developed as a more serious undertaking in the seventeenth century, and the fire and such widespread physical damage in a major city offered an unprecedented opportunity to put it to the test. Wren was appointed Deputy Surveyor of His Majesty's Works, and he drew up a plan for rebuilding London, which improved access to London Bridge, developed a wharf from the Temple to the Tower along the Thames, set the Royal Exchange as the center of town, and redesigned St. Paul's Cathedral and 51 other churches.

Legislation established a special fire court, which first met on February 27, 1667, to settle disputes over land, rents, and rebuilding. The judges' verdicts were final, and they did not have to abide by ordinary court procedures. They could even order new leases and extend existing ones. The Rebuilding Act (1667) provided for the seizing of any land not built upon after three years and its sale to someone who would rebuild. Four types of houses were permitted: two-story houses built on lanes, three-story houses on streets, four-story houses on larger streets, and four-story "mansion houses" for wealthy citizens. For each style of home the thickness of walls and heights from floor to ceiling were specified. Guild regulations were set aside in order to facilitate rebuilding, and wages and prices of materials were fixed. The revenue for supporting this law was to be financed by a tax on coal of 1 shilling per ton, which was raised in 1670 to 3 shillings per ton. This was London's first major set of building codes.

Despite regulations and legislation, the actual rebuilding went slowly because of the increased cost resulting from the specifications set forth in the codes and the disputes that arose over the widening of streets, which caused a loss of property or a reduction in the size of property. Other factors that caused delay were the difficulties in obtaining building materials such as lead, timber, brick, tile, and stone. This did open up new trade opportunities in the Baltic Sea area, a major producer of timber. By 1667 the streets had been laid out, but only 150 houses had been rebuilt. Almost 7,000 had been completed by 1671, although as late as the 1690's there were fewer houses in London than before the fire. An important development in the rebuilding was Charles II's laying of the first stone for the reconstruction of the Royal Exchange on October 23, 1667, which was completed by September, 1669, when the merchants occupied it. Ironically, the Royal Exchange was destroyed by fire again in 1838.

Another major project was the straightening of the Fleet River and the building of quays on its banks, which became the location for numerous warehouses. The monument to the fire, a 202-foot high Doric column of Portland stone, was erected between 1671 and 1677 and stood 202 feet from where the fire started. An inscription that blamed the fire on Catholics was removed during the reign of Catholic king James II (ruled 1685-1688), the former duke of York. The rebuilding of St. Paul's Cathedral began in 1675 and was completed in 1710.

A number of positive developments resulted from the Great Fire. It destroyed a substantial portion of a very unsanitary city, fire insurance was developed, new fire equipment was purchased, and fires received quicker responses. The London Common Council developed a plan that divided the city into four fire districts, each of which was to provide buckets, ladders, axes, and water engines. In addition, the various merchants' companies were to store firefighting equipment. Such plans were copied by other English towns and cities, and London's redesign influenced the layout of Philadelphia, Pennsylvania, and Savannah, Georgia, in the United States.

Mark C. Herman

FOR FURTHER INFORMATION:

Evelyn, John. *The Diary of John Evelyn.* Edited by E. S. DeBeer. Oxford, England: Clarendon Press, 2000.

Hanson, Neil. *The Great Fire of London: In That Apocalyptic Year, 1666.* Hoboken, N.J.: John Wiley & Sons, 2002.

Pepys, Samuel. *The Diary of Samuel Pepys.* Edited by Robert Latham and William Matthews. Berkeley: University of California Press, 2000.

Picard, Liza. *Restoration London.* New York: St. Martin's Press, 1998.

Porter, Roy. *London: A Social History.* Cambridge, Mass.: Harvard University Press, 1995.

Porter, Stephen. *The Great Fire of London.* Phoenix Mill, Gloucestershire, England: Sutton, 2002.

Tinniswood, Adrian. *By Permission of Heaven: The Story of the Great Fire of London.* New York: Riverhead Books, 2004.

■ 1669: ETNA ERUPTION

VOLCANO

DATE: March 11, 1669
PLACE: Sicily, Italy
RESULT: More than 20,000 dead, 14 villages destroyed, 27,000 homeless

For three days in March of 1669, earthquakes shook Sicily's Mount Etna. Such seismic activity was not unusual. People who lived on the slopes of Sicily's highest mountain had experienced them frequently before, but they were aware that such tremors often preceded what they most feared: a devastating and catastrophic eruption of the smoldering volcano, whose frequent eruptions date to prehistoric times.

On March 11, 1669, the worst fears of the peasants who lived near the towering mountain became realities. Etna exploded in a series of eruptions stronger than anyone then alive could remember. The sky blackened as ash from the explosions rose toward the stratosphere. Debris fell over the eastern half of Sicily, even making its way well up into the southern Italian province of Calabria, across the Strait of Messina.

The eruptions were not confined to a single day. Two weeks after the first series, on March 25, the sky was still ominously dark and ash was falling everywhere. A wide river of molten lava was flowing relentlessly down Etna's south side, glowing orange in the subdued atmosphere. It hungrily devoured everything in its path, wiping out 14 villages in its course. Directly in the volcano's path lay the seaside town of Catania, whose population of about 20,000 people made it one of Sicily's largest cities. It lay just over 18 miles (29 kilometers) from Mount Etna's summit, and its sole protection against the oncoming lava flow were the city's defensive walls that dated back to the feudal era and surrounded the city.

These walls would prove useless against an adversary as enormous as the river of fire now lumbering toward the ill-fated town. By the time Etna returned to a quiescent state, it had reduced Catania's pop-

ulation from 20,000 to about 3,000. Another 3,000 people who lived in villages on Etna's slope died, mostly from suffocation, as the noxious fumes from the hot lava engulfed them.

A TOWERING GIANT. On a clear day, nearly everyone in eastern Sicily can see Mount Etna, rising almost 11,000 feet above sea level and towering over the plain below. The highest active volcano in Europe, it dominates the eastern half of Sicily, which is Italy's largest island. Sicily is situated to the east and slightly to the south of Italy's toe. A mere 2 miles across the Strait of Messina directly across from the town of Reggio in Calabria, Sicily was in prehistoric times a part of Italy's land mass. As the oceans rose, however, it came to be separated from what is now the lower part of the Italian mainland.

Mount Etna, named *Aitne* by the ancient Greeks and *Aetna* by the ancient Romans, is classified as a greenhouse type of volcano. Such volcanoes constantly belch gases out into the atmosphere, with Etna sending more than 25 million tons of carbon dioxide into the air above it every year. These emissions contribute significantly to the phenomenon of global warming. The typical products of the greenhouse type of volcano, besides carbon dioxide, are methane, ozone, nitrous oxides, chlorofluorocarbons, and water vapor.

The first recorded eruptions of Etna occurred in 475 B.C.E. They were noted and described in some detail by both the poet Pindar and the dramatist Aeschylus. Since then, over two hundred eruptions have been documented, but none so great or so devastating to human life as the one that occurred in 1669.

Mount Etna covers a substantial geographical area, a total of some 460 square miles. The Catania plain that lies below it is the largest lowland in Sicily. Around Etna's base runs a railway. Small villages and terraced fields in which vegetables are grown still dot its slopes. From the cone of the volcano, the area around which is usually covered with snow, rise thin ribbons of smoke. Travelers ascending the mountain first pass through cultivated areas, where produce grows well in the rich, volcanic soil available on the mountain's lower two-thirds. At higher levels, pine forests extend almost to the top of the mountain, where the landscape becomes more bleak and where strong winds usually blow and snow often falls.

THE LOOMING THREAT. Rumblings that occurred on Etna on March 8, 1669, alerted those who lived on its slopes to a possible eruption. Those who lived in villages below the volanco's summit had frequently experienced such rumblings in the past. They were concerned by them but generally were not unduly alarmed. They had survived such seismic activity before and had continued to grow their produce in the fertile soil that Etna's previous eruptions, dating to prehistoric times, provided for them.

It was three days before Etna finally erupted, with a force that had not been equaled by any of the previous recorded eruptions. Lava flows began to course down the mountain, hot rivers of molten lava that obliterated everything in their paths. Pine forests were quickly leveled. Small settlements disappeared, often with most of their inhabitants. Suddenly, the south side of the huge mountain turned into a cauldron of intensely hot molten rock that slid down its sides and seemingly could be stopped only by the Ionian Sea, which stretched out to the east of Catania. The flow continued for more than two weeks, resisting every effort to thwart it.

TRYING TO DIVERT THE LAVA FLOW. Desperate peasants whose dwellings were in villages that lay in the path of the great river of fire now advancing down the mountain had no defenses against the fiery onslaught. The air they breathed was poisoned by the fumes that rose from the volcano. Most fell helpless upon the ground, unable to breathe. They usually were dead before the molten lava reached their prostrate bodies.

The city of Catania, which from ancient times had endured Mount Etna's eruptions, was now threatened as it seldom had been before. Although some of the city's populace took the few possessions they could carry and tried to flee before the lava reached the city walls, a stalwart group of 50 men, led by Diego de Pappalardo, sought to divert the course of the flow. These men donned cowhides soaked in water to protect them from the incredible heat that the flow produced.

Carrying long iron rods, picks, and shovels, they ascended the mountain toward the slowly moving flow, which by now had created a well-defined central channel down the mountainside. High walls of cooling lava lined the channel through which the molten material was flowing. Working under extremely adverse conditions in air that was almost too polluted and fetid to sustain life, this stalwart band of brave men hacked an opening in one of the high lava walls, thereby diverting the flow of material down the central channel through which the molten lava was heading relentlessly toward Catania.

This heroic act of civil engineering appeared to be working. The flow in the central channel diminished considerably as a new channel formed outside the break in the lava wall. Keeping that break open, however, became a major problem. The Catanians were jubilant at the seeming success of their prodigious efforts, but their jubilation was short-lived.

Almost immediately, a group of 500 desperate citizens from the village of Paterno, noticing that the newly created flow was aimed directly at their village, assaulted the Catanians, forcing them away from the breaches in the lava walls that they had created with such great difficulty. Soon these breaches filled in, and the molten lava resumed its inexorable course down the central channel.

A consequence of the assault of the infuriated people from Paterno on the Catanians was the issuance of a royal decree stating that in the future no one was to interfere with the natural flow of molten lava from a volcano. Anyone doing so was to be held responsible for any damage that ensued from such efforts. This decree, in effect since 1669, was officially ratified in the nineteenth century by the Bourbon monarchy then in command. It was in force until 1983, when another eruption caused advanced engineering efforts to be employed in order to minimize the damage. The law was suspended so that these efforts could be carried out.

Actually, opening vents in the lava wall was not a viable long-term solution to controlling the lava flow during the 1669 eruption. At an elevation of about 2,600 feet, vents had been opened by the Catanians near the village of Nicolosi, but within less than twenty-four hours, the lava had flowed on and destroyed another village in its path about 2 miles farther downhill.

A century after the 1669 eruption, the devastating event was still prominently discussed by scientists. Sir William Hamilton, who published what is considered the first modern work on volcanology, *Campi Phlegraei*, in 1776, visited Mount Etna before he wrote his book, drawn there by what he had heard about the devastation in 1669.

THE DESTRUCTION OF CATANIA. Thirty-three days elapsed between the eruption of Etna on March 11, 1669, and the arrival of its lava flow at the feudal gates of Catania. Remarkably few of the city's citizens had fled as the oncoming lava approached the venerable walls, which accounts for the loss of some 17,000 Catanians in the disaster that followed.

Typically, as a lava flow proceeds on its downward journey, it builds up lava walls on both sides but also creates a lava roof, resulting in a tube through which the molten material passes. The result is that the lava stays blisteringly hot because it is not exposed to the outside air, which would reduce its temperature. This is what happened as the lava from the 1669 eruption flowed toward Catania and the sea.

This eruption was not the first to devastate Catania. In 1169, an estimated 15,000 Catanians were lost when an eruption of Mount Etna followed a huge tectonic earthquake that leveled most of the buildings in Catania and left many people dead in the rubble long before the lava flows reached the city. This disaster was on a scale comparable to that of the 1669 eruption.

R. Baird Shuman

FOR FURTHER INFORMATION:

Bonaccorso, Alessandro, et al., eds. *Mt. Etna: Volcano Laboratory.* Washington, D.C.: American Geophysical Union, 2004.

Chester, D. K., et al. *Mount Etna: The Anatomy of a Volcano.* Stanford, Calif.: Stanford University Press, 1985.

Rosi, Mauro, et al. *Volcanoes.* Buffalo, N.Y.: Firefly Books, 2003.

Scarth, Alwyn. *Volcanoes: An Introduction.* College Station: Texas A&M University Press, 1994.

_____. *Vulcan's Fury: Man Against the Volcano.* New ed. New Haven, Conn.: Yale University Press, 2001.

Sparks, R. S. J., et al. *Volcanic Plumes.* New York: John Wiley & Sons, 1997.

Sutherland, Lin. *The Volcanic Earth: Volcanoes and Plate Tectonics, Past, Present, and Future.* Sydney: University of New South Wales Press, 1995.

Wohletz, Kenneth, and Grant Heiken. *Volcanology and Geothermal Energy.* Berkeley: University of California Press, 1992.

■ 1692: THE PORT ROYAL EARTHQUAKE

EARTHQUAKE AND TSUNAMI

DATE: June 7, 1692
PLACE: Port Royal, Jamaica
MAGNITUDE: X on the Modified Mercalli scale (estimated)
RESULT: About 3,000 dead, more than 1,000 homes and other structures destroyed

In the late seventeenth century, the Jamaican city of Port Royal was a major trade center for the New World. Situated on a cay, or small low island, off the Palisadoes sands on Jamaica's southern coast, this Caribbean seaport owed its prosperity largely to smuggling and plundering. By the 1690's, Port Royal boasted at least 6,500 inhabitants and more than 2,000 densely packed buildings, some of which were constructed on pilings driven into the harbor.

Formerly a popular haunt for pirates, the city retained a reputation for hedonism and godlessness. Typical contemporaneous accounts called it "the most wicked and sinful city in the world" and "one of the lewdest [places] in the Christian World, a sink of all filthiness, and a mere Sodom." Those citizens who warned that Port Royal's widespread drunkenness, gambling, and debauchery were inviting divine retribution believed their fears were realized when, in the spring of 1692, a devastating earthquake destroyed most of the city.

Earthquakes were nothing new to Port Royal. Jamaica lies along the boundary between the Caribbean and North American tectonic plates and is seismically active. Since 1655, when England captured Jamaica from Spain and founded the port, settlers had reported earth tremors almost every year. However, most of these quakes caused little or no damage. One of the more severe quakes, which occurred in 1688, was large enough to destroy 3 houses and damage many other structures. The major earthquake that would follow it four years later was to prove far more destructive.

On Tuesday, June 7, 1692, between 11 A.M. and noon, a series of three strong earthquakes struck Port Royal within a period of a few minutes. After the third and most severe quake, a large tsunami pounded the seaport, snapping the anchor cables of ships moored in Kingston Harbor, smashing those ships nearest the wharves, and pouring into the city. In this case, not the crest but the trough of the tsunami struck land first, pulling out the harbor waters, then sending them back to finish off the town. The tsunami submerged half the town in up to 40 feet of water, pulling down what remained of the structures, causing hundreds more fatalities, and capsizing the vessels at anchor in the harbor.

One of Jamaica's two warships, the HMS *Swan*, had recently had its ballast removed during maintenance; the tsunami tossed this relatively light ship from the harbor into the middle of town and deposited it upright on top of some buildings. Such a ride through the city would have revealed streets littered with corpses, of those killed by both the quake and the tsunami, and those washed out of tombs by the waves. While the ship's masts and rigging were lost and its cannons dislodged, the *Swan* remained intact enough to serve as a refuge for more than 200 people who survived the devastation by clinging to the boat.

Multiple eyewitness accounts of the disaster describe the earth swallowing up whatever or whoever stood upon it, leading modern researchers to conclude that liquefaction played a major role in the devastation of Port Royal. In liquefaction, a process observed in loose, fine-grained, water-saturated sands subjected to shaking, the soil behaves like a dense fluid rather than a wet solid mass. This phenomenon is believed to be what caused "the sand in the streets [to]

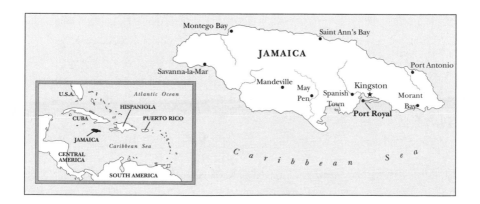

rise like the waves of the sea," as one witness reported, and many of Port Royal's buildings to topple, partially sink, or disappear entirely. Much of the city's population was also engulfed by the flowing sands.

The disaster killed roughly 2,000 people in Port Royal and left almost 60 percent of the city submerged below Kingston Harbor. Of those buildings left standing, most were uninhabitable. Two of the city's three forts, which had been heavily manned in anticipation of French attack, sank beneath the harbor. Several ships that had been moored in the harbor disappeared. Fill material that English settlers had dumped in the shallow marshy area between Port Royal and the Palisadoes to connect the cay to the sandspit was washed away. In Kingston Harbor, the bodies of the drowned floated with corpses the tsunami tore from the cemetery at the Palisadoes.

The devastation in Jamaica was not confined to Port Royal. In the settlement of Spanish Town, located 6 miles inland from Kingston Harbor, almost no buildings were left standing. On the island's north coast, roughly 1,000 acres of woodland slid into St. Ann's Bay, killing 53 Frenchmen. Plantations and sugar mills throughout Jamaica were damaged or destroyed. The island suffered about 1,000 fatalities in addition to those killed at Port Royal.

The evening of the disaster, with aftershocks still rattling Port Royal, pillaging and stealing began among the ruins of the city. Looters had free run of the seaport for almost two weeks. During this time, law-abiding citizens took refuge aboard ships in Kingston Harbor. With few doctors and limited medical supplies, many of the injured soon died. Still more survivors succumbed to illness spread by unhealthy conditions aboard the crowded rescue ships. Injury and sickness claimed about 2,000 more lives in the weeks immediately following the disaster.

Survivors hesitated to return to Port Royal and rebuild. What was left of the city appeared to be sinking gradually into Kingston Harbor, and there was concern that the entire island would slip beneath the water. Aftershocks large enough to feel persisted for at least two months after the June 7 disaster, contributing to the people's doubts concerning Port Royal's safety. Members of the Council of Jamaica (who were in Port Royal for a meeting on the day the quake struck) and Port Royal's remaining residents decided to establish a new town across the harbor, a settlement that later became Kingston.

While Port Royal was too important strategically for the English to abandon entirely, it never regained its importance as a commercial center. It became primarily a base for the British navy, and for the remainder of Jamaica's history as a British colony its civilian population remained small.

Karen N. Kähler and David M. Soule

FOR FURTHER INFORMATION:

Briggs, Peter. *Buccaneer Harbor: The Fabulous History of Port Royal, Jamaica.* New York: Simon & Schuster, 1970.

Marx, Robert F. *Pirate Port: The Story of the Sunken City of Port Royal.* Cleveland: World, 1967.

Pawson, Michael, and David Buisseret. *Port Royal, Jamaica.* Kingston, Jamaica: University of the West Indies Press, 2000.

Zeilinga de Boer, Jelle, and Donald Theodore Sanders. *Earthquakes in Human History: The Far-Reaching Effects of Seismic Disruptions.* Princeton, N.J.: Princeton University Press, 2005.

■ 1755: THE LISBON EARTHQUAKE

EARTHQUAKE

DATE: November 1, 1755
PLACE: Lisbon, Portugal
MAGNITUDE: In the 8.0 range on the Richter scale (estimated), X for the central city and IX for the outskirts on the Modified Mercalli scale (estimated)
RESULT: 5,000-50,000 or more dead

During the eighteenth century Portugal enjoyed one of its greatest periods of wealth and prosperity. Gold had been discovered in its colony of Brazil, which held the largest deposits then known of this precious metal. Moreover, extensive diamond fields were also found there. The greater part of this wealth flowed to the mother country and concentrated principally in the capital, Lisbon.

The population of Portugal was almost 3 million, with about 10 percent residing in Lisbon. This city, on the north bank of the Tagus River, was situated where the river, flowing from the northeast, bent gradually to the west and entered the Atlantic. The city was shaped like an amphitheater. It was flat in its central area, where the ports, together with the major commercial and royal government buildings, were located. In the low hills rising and arching around the center were houses, shops, churches, monasteries, and convents. A magnet of world trade, the city housed a cosmopolitan population. In addition, an exceptionally large proportion of its populace were members of the Catholic clergy and religious orders.

QUAKE, FIRE, FLOOD. The serenity and assurance of this city were irrevocably shaken on November 1, 1755, the holy day of All Saints. An earthquake of unprecedented strength and consequences struck the city, leaving it by dusk a broken ruin of its former self. For about ten minutes during midmorning the earth shook, rolled, and collapsed underneath the city three times. The shaking was so severe that the damage extended throughout southern Portugal and Spain and across the Strait of Gibraltar into Morocco.

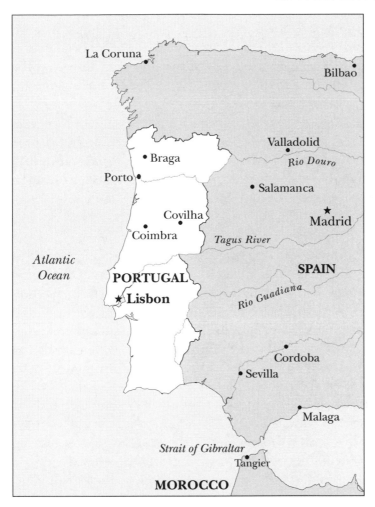

Near the port area, the quake leveled numerous major buildings and destroyed the royal palace. The king was not, however, in residence. Many of the city's over 100 religious buildings were damaged or leveled. Because it was a holy day and Lisbon was known for its religious fervor, most churches were filled with morning worshipers. They were crushed under the crashing walls and roofs. Aftershocks at almost hourly intervals caused further damage. Indeed, aftershocks of less frequent intervals but great violence would continue well into the next year.

Fires began to appear in the city, progressively becoming a general conflagration fed by a northeast wind. Lasting for almost a week, these fires charred part of the outskirts and the entire central part of the city. Their damage was the costliest because they destroyed the contents of opulent churches and palaces, consuming paintings, manuscripts, books, and tapestries.

In a final assault, three seismic waves from the sea struck the central harbor and coastal area just before midday. Some of these tsunamis towered at over 20 feet. What the quake had not shaken nor fires destroyed, water in crashing cascades now leveled. Thus, within a few morning hours, quake, fire, and flood had destroyed one of the major ports of Europe.

Deaths from this destruction were, in the days immediately following the events, estimated to be as high as 50,000 or more. A systematic, contemporary attempt through parish surveys to account for the dead was unsuccessful due to its uneven application. Modern estimates now go as low as 5,000 or 15,000 for the fatalities from this disaster.

However, not only death but also fear, hunger, and disease followed the destruction. To flee the conflagration and repeated tremors, thousands tried to escape the city for the countryside, struggling over blocked roads and passages. Prisoners escaped from jails and assaulted the living and the dead. Food could not be brought into the city. The thousands who had been injured but not killed languished without care, hospitals having been destroyed and caregivers having fled or been killed. Infectious diseases began to spread.

REBUILDING. The king's principal minister, Sebastião de Carvalho, later known as the Marquis of Pombal, energetically took control of recovery and rebuilding. Public health needed immediate attention. Bodies that had not burned in the fires were collected onto boats that were sunk in the Tagus. The army was called in to put out fires and clear streets and passages of debris. Anyone caught stealing was immediately executed. Prices for food and building materials were fixed. Field tents for shelter and feeding were erected.

The reconstructors of the city gave priority to replanning its layout. The new plan eliminated the old twisting, narrow streets. The flat central part of the city was redesigned to have straight streets that crossed at right angles in a grid pattern. These streets were 60 to 40 feet wide. Near the harbor area a spacious plaza was built, called Commerce Square.

To expedite construction, buildings were prefabricated. The sizes of doors, windows, and walls were standardized. To protect these buildings against future earthquakes, their inner frames were made of wood that could sway but not break under pressure. The style of building for these structures was a kind of simple or plain baroque and came to be known as "pombaline." These buildings were made according to the most advanced standards of hygiene so that there was adequate circulation of air and measures for sanitation. Because of the great wealth that Portugal commanded from its colonies, principally Brazil, Lisbon and other Portuguese cities recovered relatively quickly.

CONSEQUENCES. One consequence of the Lisbon earthquake was that as the result of the extensive rebuilding, the city's port and central area came to be among the best planned and constructed in eighteenth century Europe. Another consequence affected economic nationalism. Great Britain dominated Portuguese imports of manufactured goods. Indeed, much of the wealth that Portugal received from Brazil passed to English hands due to these purchases of British goods. To pay for the rebuilding, a tax was placed on the import of certain British products. This measure sought not only to raise reve-

A 1755 engraving titled The Ruins of Lisbon *shows a tent city outside the quake-ravaged port, criminal activity, and wrongdoers being hanged.*

383

nue for reconstruction but also to make British goods more expensive and thereby encourage the production of native Portuguese products at a relatively lower price.

The consequences of the earthquake were felt not only in terms of engineering and economics but also in theology and philosophy. In fact, it was in these areas that the quake had its most resonant social significance. No sooner had the quake struck than the clergy of Lisbon began preaching that the disaster represented the wrath of God striking against the city's sinful inhabitants. So strong was the fervor of these preachers that they aroused parts of the populace into paroxysms of hysterical fear. This hysteria made dealing with the crisis in an organized, rational manner difficult. The civil authorities begged the clergy not to preach such fear, but their admonitions were only somewhat successful.

Western Europe as a whole was in the midst of a period known as the Enlightenment, or Age of Reason. Pombal, with his rational, utilitarian views of government, was representative of this movement. Confronting the religious hysteria, reasonable men argued that the Lisbon earthquake needed to be studied not as a supernatural event but as a natural one. They demonstrated that thunder and lightning were known to be natural events, so an earthquake should also be considered as such. The Lisbon earthquake thus prompted a great debate between the emerging rational forces of the modern age and the declining religious emotions of the medieval.

A further philosophical debate also occurred among those who were followers of the Enlightenment. Many of them believed that in a reasoned, organized world everything happened for the best. Thus, they explained that while the earthquake in Lisbon was a horrible disaster, it nonetheless resulted in a rebuilt and modernized city.

Others argued that one could not be so sanguine and optimistic about the world. Among the leading voices of this point of view was the French philosopher and poet Voltaire. In a long poem written immediately after the earthquake and in a later, famous novel, *Candide* (1759; English translation, 1759), he argued that the Lisbon tragedy proved the existence of irrational, totally unbeneficial evil in the world.

Voltaire's hero, Candide, voyages the world, traveling throughout Europe, America, and Asia, encountering perils and dangers at every corner. He is in Lisbon during the earthquake. Numerous times he or his friends are tortured or almost killed. People around them lead miserable lives. He pursues a girl for a love that is ultimately futile. Accompanying Candide is a teacher, the philosopher Pangloss, who believes that everything that happens in the world happens for the best. Pangloss adheres to this belief to the end of the novel, despite all the horrors he witnesses. Ultimately, therefore, the reader of *Candide* learns that the superficiality and rigidity of the thought of Pangloss and people like him betray the inherent error of their position.

Voltaire maintained that it was naïve and self-serving to say that evil was always balanced by good. There were people everywhere who suffered for no reason and who would never be compensated for their suffering. He argued that those who believed that everything that happened was for the best were those who wanted to keep things as they were, who wanted acceptance of the status quo. Such an attitude ignored those who suffered under the conditions of the present and failed to respond effectively to alleviate their suffering. If ignored over a long period, such suffering could prove unbearable and violent. In relation to these arguments it should be noted that less than half a century after the Lisbon earthquake, the suffering and outrage of these masses burst forth against the Old Regime in the French Revolution.

The Lisbon earthquake resounded in Europe not only as a physical event but also as a cultural one. Its force shook not only the earth but also men's minds, in terms of old and new ideas.

Edward A. Riedinger

FOR FURTHER INFORMATION:

Braun, Theodore E. D., and John B. Radner, eds. *The Lisbon Earthquake of 1755: Representations and Reactions.* Oxford, England: Voltaire Foundation, 2005.

Brooks, Charles B. *Disaster at Lisbon: The Great Earthquake of 1755.* Long Beach, Calif.: Shangton Longley Press, 1994.

Davison, Charles. *Great Earthquakes, with 122 Illustrations.* London: Thomas Murby, 1936.

Dynes, Russell Rowe. *The Lisbon Earthquake in 1755: Contested Meanings of the First Modern Disaster.* Newark: Disaster Research Center, University of Delaware, 1997.

Kendrick, T. D. *The Lisbon Earthquake.* London: Methuen, 1956.

Laidlar, John, comp. *Lisbon.* Vol. 199 in *World Bibliographical Series.* Oxford: ABC-Clio Press, 1997.

Mullin, John K. "The Reconstruction of Lisbon Following the Earthquake of 1755: A Study in Despotic Planning." *Planning Perspectives* 7 (1992): 157-179.

■ 1783: Laki Eruption

Volcano

Date: June, 1783-February, 1784
Place: Southern Iceland
Result: Gaseous volcanic haze and its effects killed over two-thirds of the nation's livestock and caused a year of famine, resulting in 10,000 dead

Iceland is an island nation that sits astride the Mid-Atlantic Ridge in the north Atlantic Ocean. As the ridge and seafloor spread apart here at the rate of 0.8 inch (2 centimeters) per year—at the rift where the North American Plate is drifting westward and the Eurasian Plate is drifting eastward—Iceland is also on top of a hot spot of magma (molten rock) in the mantle below. It is thus one of the world's most volcanically active locations, on an island plateau formed primarily of basaltic lava rock. It is a land of volcanic fire and glacial ice, which is regularly reminded of the power and challenge of natural events—volcanoes, earthquakes, glacial flooding, and severe weather.

There are over 150 volcanoes in Iceland that have been active since the last ice age—ending about ten thousand years ago—and about 30 of them have erupted since settlement of the island, primarily by Vikings of northern Europe, eleven hundred years ago. Iceland has an eruption, on the average, every five years or so.

THE 1783 ERUPTION. It was here in 1783 that the largest lava eruption and flow of humankind's recorded history occurred. This geologic event devastated the agricultural environment, resulted in an ensuing famine in which over one-fifth of the nation's people died, and even altered the climate of the Northern Hemisphere for a couple of years. That latter consequence—the effect of volcanism on climate change—was speculated on for the first time in 1784 by Benjamin Franklin, then was seriously studied and explained after the 1980's, two hundred years later.

In early June of 1783, there were a number of small earthquakes in the region of the volcano Laki in southern Iceland. Its crater peak was undistinguished, rising only about 656 feet (200 meters) above its surroundings. Trending up to the northeast was a volcanic zone of fractured earth's crust where the plate-tectonic spreading of Iceland was inexorably occurring. About 30 miles (50 kilometers) to the northeast, now under the large Vatnajökull ("Vatna glacier"), was the occasionally active volcanic region called Grimsvotn.

On June 8, fissures from Laki and extending to the southwest began erupting lava, which flowed down the Skafta River Valley. There was little explosive venting of ash. In the area, fairly remote and sparsely settled, the event was termed the Skaftareldar ("Skafta fires"). Then fissuring and erupting lava appeared from Laki toward the northeast, with the lava flowing down the Hverfisfljot River Valley. Lava flowed southward as far away as 37 miles (60 kilometers) before cooling enough to congeal and then solidify to rock. The zone of fissures and the 110 to 115 erupting volcanic craters and vents extended 15 miles (25 kilometers) in total, with Mount Laki about in the middle.

By the time of the cessation of lava flows, eight months later in February, 1784, the Lakagigar ("Laki craters") eruption had produced a volume of basaltic lava of 434,368 cubic feet (12.3 cubic kilometers), mostly erupted in June and July, plus 10,594 cubic feet (0.3 cubic kilometers) of ashfall. The latter is solid-rock equivalent; the actual volume was about 30,017 cubic feet (0.85 cubic kilometers). That volume of lava is the largest of any eruption in recorded history. The volume of ashfall, while only a small part of this event, is itself about the same as the ashfall from the Mount St. Helens eruption in Washington State in 1980.

The lava flow covered 217 square miles (565 square kilometers), to an average depth of 72 feet (22 meters). That volume of lava would fill Yosemite Valley, California, to a depth of 984 feet (300 meters), or cover Washington, D.C. (61 square miles), to a depth of 256 feet (78 meters), or the state of Delaware (2,000 square miles) to a depth of 21 feet (6.3 meters). The Icelandic lava field from Lakagigar is now a jagged, jumbled plain of lava. It is mostly covered by a growth of lichens and moss, the only vegetation that can establish itself even after a couple of centuries because of the northern-latitude climate and slowness of rock weathering to soil there.

AFTEREFFECTS. The massive eruption itself caused no deaths and little damage. However, it did produce the most severe environmen-

tal effects, and threat to health and life, that Iceland has experienced in its one thousand years of documented human history.

The huge lava outpouring of the summer of 1783 was accompanied by some ashfall, which could be carried farther afield to affect crops and grasslands for grazing. More significant was the enormous amount of gas vented. The gases included carbon dioxide and water vapor, as well as unusually large quantities of the toxic gases sulphur dioxide, hydrogen sulfide, chlorine, and fluorine. It is estimated from chemical analysis of the volcanic products that 130 million to 490 million tons of sulphur dioxide and 5 million tons of fluorine were released into the atmosphere. Sulphur dioxide reacts with water vapor to produce sulphuric acid, a prime component of acid rain. Ejected high in the atmosphere, the result can be a sulphuric acid aerosol of tiny droplets.

As a result of the gas-rich eruption, a bluish haze or "dry fog" enveloped Iceland and drifted eastward over northern Europe for the winter months. In Iceland, the combination of volcanic ash and gases stunting grass and ruining pastures and fluorine contaminating the grass caused grazing livestock to be both starved and slowly poisoned. Half the nation's cattle and three-quarters of the horses (used for transportation) and sheep (used for wool and meat) perished. The loss of livestock, the damage to croplands, the short growing season in this northerly climate, and a severe winter combined to produce a devastating famine in the country. In the next couple of years, 10,000 people died—over one-fifth of the total population of 49,000—from starvation and disease, as well as the effects of the haze.

As a postscript to the great "haze famine" of 1783-1784, it might be noted that almost a century later, in 1875, Mount Askja—northeast of Laki in central Iceland—had an explosive eruption. Its 6.2-mile-diameter crater showered 70,629 cubic feet of ash over much of eastern Iceland. The resulting near-famine prompted many Icelanders to immigrate to the United States and Canada.

LONG-TERM AND GLOBAL EFFECTS. There was to be a more widespread, and unexpected, consequence of the massive 1783 eruption; it was a precursor to modern discussions of atmospheric conditions and global climate change. The sulfur-dioxide-produced acidic aerosol "dry fog" that reached Europe was more annoying than poisonous there, but it was present for much of the summer and fall of 1783. While it and some ash were carried over Europe by the prevailing winds—giving Scotland the "Year of the Ashie" and dropping ash dust in Italy, 2,000 miles (3,200 kilometers) from Iceland—haze was spread as far as central Russia.

Benjamin Franklin was American representative to France and the court of King Louis XVI from 1778 to 1785. A scientist, as well as an author, printer, statesman, diplomat, philosopher, and contributor to the cause of the recent American Revolution and its subsequent government, Franklin noted the prevalent blue haze and the abnormally cold and severe winter in Europe in 1783-1784. He speculated on a possible link between the "smoke" (fine ash and haze), perhaps being from the Iceland eruption the preceding year, and the cooling effect it might have on weather. He wrote a paper, "Meteorological Imaginations and Conjectures," which was subsequently delivered for him at a learned conference in Manchester, England, in December, 1784. It included the following:

> During several of the summer months of the year 1783, when the effect of the sun's rays to heat the Earth in these northern regions should have been greater, there existed a constant fog over all Europe, and a great part of North America. The fog was of a permanent

nature; it was dry . . . [The rays of the sun] were indeed rendered so faint in passing through it, that when collected in a burning glass [lens] they would scarce kindle brown paper. . . . The cause of this unusual fog is not yet ascertained . . . whether it was the vast quantity of smoke, long continuing to issue during the summer from Hecla in Iceland [Mount Hekla, a well-known volcano not erupting at the time, is just to the west of the Laki area], and that other volcano which arose out of the sea near that island [there had been a new volcano erupt and emerge from the sea off southwest Iceland in the spring of 1783], which smoke might be spread by various winds over the northern part of the world is yet uncertain.

The scenario now understood is that some major volcanic eruptions can eject enough sulphur dioxide to produce a sulphate (sulphuric acid) aerosol layer into the stratosphere, where it can reside for months or even a few years. This acts to absorb, or backscatter, the warming radiation from the sun, so there is less heating of the underlying troposphere—our zone of weather. This can result in global climate cooling in at least a belt of latitudes by a couple of degrees for many months, and thus in cooler local weather. Volcanic ash can also help to screen out incoming solar radiation, but except for an extraordinary explosion (such as dust from a large meteorite impact on Earth) it usually does not rise high enough or last in the stratosphere long enough to have a significant climate effect.

The Lakagigar eruption may be the most dramatic example in historical time of this connection between volcanically induced atmospheric change and the resulting climate cooling. In addition to the pronounced cooler winter in Iceland and much of Europe, the winter temperature during 1783-1784 in the eastern United States was 7 degrees Fahrenheit below the 225-year average there.

Similar detectable, but more modest, climate-cooling effects—by a degree or two for a couple of years, from ash and gas producing a high-altitude "mist"—were noticed for the eruptions of Krakatau in Indonesia in 1883, El Chichón in southern Mexico in 1982, and Mount Pinatubo in the Philippines in 1991.

It is believed that the magma for the Laki eruption had migrated and flowed laterally through crustal cracks opened by the ongoing tectonic rifting as Iceland spread apart astride the Mid-Atlantic Ridge.

The origin was probably the large active hot spot under the volcano Grimsvotn, under the Vatnajökull glacier. If the great 1783 Laki eruption had been localized under the glacier, the eruption would have been much more explosive—producing more ash as well as the gas—and would have created great ice melting and massive flooding.

In early October, 1996, there was a modest subglacial eruption near Grimsvotn, not far from the Laki eruption site. This one lasted for two weeks, caused subsidence of the overlying glacier over a fissure zone about 4.4 miles (7 kilometers) long, and produced a glacier burst of subglacial meltwater that flooded out and caused $15 million in damage to bridges, roads, and utility systems. A similar event had occurred there in 1938.

Robert S. Carmichael

FOR FURTHER INFORMATION:

Jacoby, Gordon, and Rosanne D'Arrigo. "The Laki Eruption and Observed Dendroclimatic Effects of Volcanism." In *Volcanism and the Earth's Atmosphere*, edited by Alan Robock and Clive Oppenheimer. Washington, D.C.: American Geophysical Union, 2003.

Decker, Robert, and Barbara Decker. *Volcanoes*. 4th ed. New York: W. H. Freeman, 2006.

Scarth, Alwyn. *Vulcan's Fury: Man Against the Volcano*. New ed. New Haven, Conn.: Yale University Press, 2001.

Sigurdsson, H. "Volcanic Pollution and Climate—the 1783 Laki Eruption." *EOS/Transactions of the American Geophysical Union*, August 10, 1982, 601-602.

Thorarinsson, S. "The Lakagigar Eruption of 1783." *Bulletin Volcanologique* 33 (1969): 910-927.

Witham, C. S., and C. Oppenheimer. "Mortality in England During the 1783-4 Laki Craters Eruption." *Bulletin of Volcanology* 67 (2005): 15-26.

Zeilinga de Boer, Jelle, and Donald Theodore Sanders. *Volcanoes in Human History: The Far-Reaching Effects of Major Eruptions*. Princeton, N.J.: Princeton University Press, 2002.

■ 1811: New Madrid earthquakes

Earthquakes

DATE: December 16, 1811-March 15, 1812
PLACE: Missouri; also Arkansas, Illinois, Kentucky, Indiana, and Tennessee
MAGNITUDE: Estimated 8.6 (December 16, 1811), 8.4 (January 23, 1812), 8.8 (February 7, 1812), with other quakes estimated up to 7.0
RESULT: 1,000 estimated dead, 5 settlements and 2 islands destroyed

In 1811, the New Madrid region encompassed the states of Kentucky and Tennessee, as well as the territories of Missouri, Mississippi, Indiana, and Illinois. Within this sparsely populated region, the town of New Madrid, Missouri, with a population of about 1,000, dominated boat traffic on the Mississippi River from the mouth of the Ohio to Natchez, Mississippi. Founded in 1789 by Colonel George Morgan, New Madrid was the third-largest city between St. Louis and New Orleans. It was situated at a point where high banks seemingly would protect it against even the highest flood and at a point where the current brought river traffic close to the western bank on which the town stood. Farmers, hunters, and fur trappers came to the town for supplies; riverboats stopped to buy and sell provisions.

New Madrid County stretched from the Mississippi River to within 30 miles of what would become the Missouri state western border. It included land 60 miles deep into what became Arkansas. Settlers in the entire county numbered only 3,200, but census figures did not include unknown numbers of slaves and Native Americans. These figures also would not have included isolated hunters and fur trappers.

THE EARTHQUAKES. In 1811, scientific knowledge could not have provided information about the New Madrid seismic zone, which includes northeastern Arkansas, southeastern Missouri, southern Illinois, western Tennessee, and western Kentucky. The towns of Cape Girardeau, Missouri; Carbondale, Illinois; Paducah, Kentucky; Memphis, Tennessee; and Little Rock, Arkansas, mark the boundaries of the zone; only Cape Girardeau existed in 1811. The unique events of

1811 and 1812 brought this zone, later, to national attention. The number of earthquakes and tremors, the length of time they continued, and the geographic area affected made the New Madrid earthquakes unique in U.S. history. The sparse population and the absence of multistory buildings were credited for the low death rate, about 1,000, during the quakes. In addition, many settlement residents had moved from log homes into tents after the initial quake. The death rate, however, may have been far higher than contemporary or later estimates. Deaths among Native Americans, slaves, and travelers on the Mississippi are not known.

The first tremors were felt about 2 A.M. on December 16, 1811. According to an anonymous New Madrid resident writing to a friend, the earth moved, houses shook, and chimneys fell, to the accompaniment of loud roaring noises and the screams and shouts of frightened people. At 7:15 A.M., a more serious shock occurred.

The shocks would continue. The Richter scale for measuring earthquake intensity had not been invented, but, in Louisville, Kentucky, engineer and surveyor Jared Brooks devised an instrument to measure severity, using pendulums and springs to detect horizontal and vertical motion. Working in Louisville, hundreds of miles from the probable epicenters, he recorded 1,874 separate shocks between December 16, 1811, and March 15, 1812. In New Madrid, according to eyewitness reports, quakes were an almost daily occurrence until 1814. The most violent shocks were felt on December 16, 1811; January 23, 1812; and February 7, 1812. Epicenters for the first two quakes were probably in northeastern Arkansas, about 60 miles south of New Madrid; the last was most likely in southern Missouri.

Eyewitnesses reported experiencing nausea and dizziness, sometimes severe, from the constant motion, saying that they could not maintain their balance during the worst of the quakes. Fissures, some as long as 600 to 700 feet, appeared in the earth. Various accounts told of eerie lights, dense smog, sulfurous smells, and darkness at the time of the quakes. Many pointed to unusual animal behavior before the quakes. Naturalist John Jacob Audubon, riding in Kentucky, was one of several people who found that horses refused to move for moments before the quakes. Bears, wolves, panthers, and foxes appeared in some of the settlements. After the quakes, panicked animals presented problems.

GENERAL GEOGRAPHIC EFFECTS. Settlements along the Mississippi River were obliterated by quakes and subsequent flooding or landslides. Other settlements were abandoned. Little Prairie, Missouri, was destroyed on December 16, 1811. As water rose, almost the entire population of the town fled, wading through waist-deep water, carrying children and belongings. They were surrounded by wild animals and snakes also struggling for their lives. Among humans and animals alike, the sick and injured had to be abandoned. The Little Prairie refugees finally reached New Madrid on Christmas Eve, only to find that town in ruins. New Prairie eventually was entirely flooded by the Mississippi River. Big Prairie, Arkansas, near the later town of Helena, was destroyed the same day, also by flood. Point Pleasant, Missouri, was destroyed by bank slides into the Mississippi on January 23, 1812, and in January and February, Fort Jefferson, Kentucky, was lost to landslides. New Madrid itself suffered serious damage from December through February and was finally obliterated by floods in April and May, 1812.

Decades later, New Madrid was reestablished north of the original site. Other settlements, such as Spanish Mill, Missouri, were abandoned when their economic base was destroyed. As the configurations of river channels changed, Spanish Mill was left without enough water to run its mill and without direct access to river traffic.

The land was also changed by the formation of many new lakes, some of them large, during the course of the quakes. These included Big Lake, on the Arkansas-Missouri border, 10 miles long and 4 miles wide, and Reelfoot Lake in Tennessee, 65 square miles when first formed. Native Americans reported that their villages were destroyed and that many persons drowned in the formation of the lakes. Elsewhere, large tracts of ground sank. Near Piney River, Tennessee, 18 or 20 acres sank until treetops were level with surrounding ground; the same thing happened to a smaller tract on the Illinois side of the River near Paducah, Kentucky.

Ultimately, the earthquakes were felt over an area of about 1 million square miles, including two-thirds of what were then the United States and its territories. Residents of St. Louis, approximately 200 miles from the epicenter, felt the first shocks around 2:15 A.M. on December 16, 1811. Windows and doors rattled, some chimneys were destroyed, and some stone buildings fell. At Natchez, Mississippi, 300 miles south, four shocks were felt on December 16. Tremors were felt from Washington, D.C., to Boston, Massachusetts; and from Charleston, South Carolina, and Savannah, Georgia, north to upper Canada and south to Mexico and Cuba. To the east, considerable damage was reported in Louisville, Kentucky. In Cincinnati, Ohio, the first quake tore down chimneys; the quake of February 7, 1812, destroyed brick walls. Almost 800 miles away, in Washington, D.C., residents woke on December 16, 1811, to the slamming of doors and the rattling of furniture and dishes. Dolley Madison, wife of U.S. president James Madison, was awakened by the shock, which also caused scaffolding around the U.S. Capitol to collapse. The quakes triggered landslides in North Carolina, where, at the statehouse in Raleigh, legislators adjourned, alarmed by the building's motion. In Charleston, South Carolina, clocks stopped, furniture moved, and church bells rang. During the severe quake of February 7, bells rang in Boston, more than 1,000 miles from New Madrid.

THE RIVER AND RIVER TRAFFIC. While damage to the Mississippi River and to river traffic was probably more severe than to the land itself, the extent is unknown. The number of boats, workers, and passengers and the amount of cargo on the river is impossible to gauge. Traffic probably was heavy, however, since the Mississippi was the only efficient means of transportation between the midwestern United States and the Gulf of Mexico.

Contemporary accounts point to dramatic effects of the earthquakes. One anonymous traveler saw violent movement of boats at the moment of the first quake. As the traveler watched, massive trees snapped in two. Another, hearing the crash of trees and the screaming of waterfowl, watched as riverbanks began their fall into the water. Eyewitnesses reported that the water changed from clear to rusty brown and became thick with debris tossed up from the bottom. Dead trees shot up from the riverbed into the air. Fissures, opening at the river's bottom, created whirlpools; water spouted. The quakes also created great waves, which overwhelmed many boats. The largest of the quakes caused the river to heave and boil.

The Mississippi was too dangerous to navigate after dark. River maps were unreliable; stumps and sandbars could shift. Thus, boats moored for the night. Those moored to river islands remained relatively safe, but many boats moored to the western shore were crushed by falling banks.

The most terrifying experience occurred on February 7, 1812, when the most violent of the quakes caused a huge series of waves in the river, in a phenomenon called a fluvial tsunami. This began about 3:15 A.M., when boats were still moored. Flooding New Madrid, the tsunami caused the Mississippi to run backward for a period that seemed, to observers, to last several hours. Lakes were created as the river poured into newly formed depressions, and thousands of acres of forest were dumped into the turbulent water.

The quake created temporary waterfalls, one about half a mile north of New Madrid and the other 8 miles downstream. A boatman, Captain Mathias Speed, had experienced the tsunami. Forced to cut his boat loose from the sinking bar to which it was moored, he found himself moving backward up the river. Safe on shore, he watched the disastrous effects of the waterfalls. River pilots had no way to anticipate the new hazards. Speed and his men counted 30 boats going over the falls. Twenty-eight capsized in the three days before the falls vanished as the river bottom settled. Those on shore could do nothing except listen to the screams for help. There were few survivors.

The first of the quakes, however, helped prove the value of steamboats. The *New Orleans*, commanded by Nicholas Roosevelt, was making its initial Mississippi River voyage in December of 1811. Provided with 116 feet of length, a 20-foot beam, and a 34-cylinder engine, as well as intelligent navigation, the boat arrived safely at New Orleans, despite the pilot's despair because all the normal navigation markers of the river had vanished. Since no one along the river had previously seen steam-driven craft, some blamed the subsequent disasters on the steamboat.

By the end of the quakes, the configuration of the river was altered. Many small islands vanished without a trace. Of the larger islands, some several miles in length, two were lost. Island No. 94, known as Stack or Crows Nest Island, inhabited by river pirates, disappeared on December 16, while island No. 32, off the Tennessee shore, disappeared on the night of December 21 while the *New Orleans* was moored there. Elsewhere, dry land became swamp, and wetlands were uplifted and dried. Smaller rivers that had flowed into the Mississippi were diverted, the shape of New Madrid Bend was changed, and three inlets to the Mississippi were destroyed.

Betty Richardson

FOR FURTHER INFORMATION:

Bagnell, Norma Hayes. *On Shaky Ground: The New Madrid Earthquakes of 1811-1812.* Columbia: University of Missouri Press, 1996.

Fuller, Myron L. *The New Madrid Earthquake: A Scientific Factual Field Account.* Washington, D.C.: Government Printing Office, 1912.

Logsdon, David, ed. *I Was There! In the New Madrid Earthquakes of 1811-1812 (Eyewitness Accounts by Survivors of the Worst Earthquake in American History).* Nashville: Kettle Mills Press, 1990.

Page, Jake, and Charles Officer. *The Big One: The Earthquake That Rocked Early America and Helped Create a Science.* Boston: Houghton Mifflin, 2004.

Penick, James, Jr. *The New Madrid Earthquakes of 1811-1812.* Rev. ed. Columbia: University of Missouri Press, 1981.

Stewart, David, and Ray Knox. *The Earthquake America Forgot: 2,000 Temblors in Five Months.* Marble Hill, Mo.: Guttenberg-Richter, 1995.

■ 1815: TAMBORA ERUPTION

VOLCANO

DATE: April 5-11, 1815
PLACE: Sumbawa, Indonesia
VOLCANIC EXPLOSIVITY INDEX: 7
RESULT: 92,000 dead

Tambora is located on Sumbawa Island near the eastern end of the Indonesian archipelago. For at least five thousand years prior to its great 1815 eruption, the volcano had exhibited only minor activity. This prolonged dormant period, however, set the stage for what is, to date, the world's largest known historic eruption and also its most deadly. Tambora, even today, is relatively remote and was much more so when the eruption took place. Nevertheless, a chronology of the events of that time have been pieced together by correlating the volcanic layers deposited during the eruption with eyewitness observations as reported by Sir Thomas Raffles, who in 1815 was the Dutch East Indies' temporary lieutenant governor.

Tambora began showing signs of life in the form of minor rumblings and earthquakes several years prior to the 1815 eruption, but the events that quickly led to the cataclysmic eruption began with an enormous explosion on the evening of April 5, 1815. The eruption produced a column of ash that raced upward 20.5 miles (33 kilometers) into the atmosphere. Although this was only a preliminary stage to the main eruption and it lasted just two hours, more ash was produced than during the entire Vesuvius eruption of 79 C.E., which buried Pompeii and Herculaneum.

Following this brief, violent outburst Tambora fell relatively silent until the evening of April 10, 1815, when, at about 7 P.M., an extremely violent explosion sent a plume of ash to an altitude of about 27 miles (44 kilometers). Observers reported columns of flame rising to a very great height from the crater and a rain of ash and pumice. As the violent eruption continued, the throat of the volcano became increasingly cleared of debris and grew wider, allowing it to

eject ever-increasing amounts of ash, pumice, and rock.

By about 10 P.M., three hours into the climactic event, the volcanic plume became so loaded that its density exceeded that of the surrounding atmosphere. At this point parts of the volcanic cloud began collapsing under their own weight to produce an incandescent cloud known as an ignimbrite flow. Survivors of the eruption reported this phase of the eruption as appearing like a flowing mass of liquid fire, and high winds attending the ignimbrite flows destroyed building and uprooted trees. The ignimbrite plunged down the volcanic slopes in all directions and out across the sea, where it interacted with water to produce steam explosions. These detonations hurled fine ash upward, dispersing it widely and plunging the region into two to three days of darkness. Ignimbrite flows entering the sea are also believed to be responsible for the mild tsunamis of from 3.3 to 13 feet (1 to 4 meters) in height that were recorded in the eastern Indonesian area during the eruption.

Tambora continued in violent eruption for about twenty-four hours with repeated explosions that were heard up to 1,616 miles (2,600 kilometers) away. About 1.8 million cubic feet (50 cubic kilometers) of magma was expelled from beneath Tambora and exploded into the atmosphere as some 5.3 million cubic feet (150 cubic kilometers) of porous ash and pumice. As a result, the unsupported central part of the volcano collapsed, reducing the volcano's height from an estimated 14,107 feet (4,300 meters) to 9,383 feet (2,860 meters), and forming a caldera 3.7 by 4.4 miles (6 by 7 kilometers) in diameter and more than 3,609 feet (1,100 meters) deep. Tambora's caldera is similar in size to Crater Lake, Oregon, but it contains only a small lake that comes and goes with the seasons and vents that still send vapors up along the caldera walls.

About 92,000 people, the greatest loss of any volcanic eruption to date, are estimated to have died on Sumbawa and the nearby island of Lombok. At least 10,000 people are believed to have perished directly from the volcanic blast and from the tsunamis it generated. Most of these fatalities occurred on the island of Sumbawa, where ignimbrite flows covered all but the western coast of the island. An estimated additional 38,000 people on Sumbawa and 44,000 on nearby Lombok died as a result of starvation and disease following the eruption. Moreover, the lingering effects of Tambora's fine ash and sulfur dioxide are believed to have had an affect on global weather patterns during the following year or two.

As with the caldera-forming eruption of Krakatau sixty-eight years later, spectacular sunsets and prolonged twilights were noted as far as England in the months following the Tambora eruption. The stars appeared less bright, and sunlight was dimmed to such an extent that sunspots were visible to the naked eye, even when the sun was well above the horizon. The geographic location of Tambora, only slightly south of the equator, allowed its eruption cloud to be dispersed in the stratosphere above both the Southern and Northern Hemispheres. Although an examination of temperature records and sunlight reduction suggests that the eruption of Tambora reduced global average temperatures in 1816 by less than 34 degrees Fahrenheit (1 degree Celsius), much colder weather was experienced in eastern Canada and New England. The summer of 1816, in fact, brought such misery to parts of North America and Europe that it became known as the Year Without a Summer.

Snow fell as far south as western Massachusetts in June of 1816, and northern New England experienced frost in July and again in August. Warm-weather birds were killed, and crops, particularly corn, were lost to the freezing weather. Cold, wet weather also affected Western Europe, where there were crop failures and famine. Ireland's famine led to a typhus outbreak, which by 1819 had become a European epidemic afflicting 1.5 million people and killing 65,000. The European wine harvest was unusually late, food was in short supply, and there was public violence related to food shortages. Those who could pursued indoor activities during the dank, dark, and stormy summer of 1816, but they too were affected. In Geneva, Switzerland, for example, Lord Byron produced a gloomy poem entitled "Darkness," while his acquaintance Mary Wollstonecraft Shelley worked on the famous gothic horror novel *Frankenstein* (1818).

Eric R. Swanson

FOR FURTHER INFORMATION:

Fagan, Brian. *The Little Ice Age: How Climate Made History, 1300-1850.* New York: Basic Books, 2000.

Francis, Peter, and Clive Oppenheimer. *Volcanoes.* 2d ed. New York: Oxford University Press, 2004.

Harington, C. R., ed. *The Year Without a Summer? World Climate in 1816.* Ottawa, Ont.: Canadian Museum of Nature, 1992.

Oppenheimer, Clive "Climatic, Environmental, and Human Consequences of the Largest Known Historic Eruption: Tambora Volcano (Indonesia) 1815." *Progress in Physical Geography* 27, no. 2 (2003): 230-259.

Stommel, Henry, and Elizabeth Stommel. *Volcano Weather: The Story of 1816, the Year Without a Summer.* Newport, R.I.: Seven Seas Press, 1983.

Stothers, Richard B. "The Great Tambora Eruption of 1815 and Its Aftermath." *Science* 224 (June, 1984): 1191-1198.

■ 1845: The Great Irish Famine

Famine

ALSO KNOWN AS: The Great Hunger, the Great Starvation
DATE: 1845-1849
PLACE: Ireland
RESULT: 700,000-1.1 million dead

The Great Irish Famine was the worst famine to occur in Europe in the nineteenth century and the most severe famine in the history of European agriculture. Indeed, some scholars argue that it was one of the greatest human ecological disasters in the history of the world. In addition to mass starvation, the Great Irish Famine changed the social and cultural structure of Ireland through eviction, mass emigration, and a heightened sense of Irish national awareness. It also hastened the end of the centuries-old agricultural practice of dividing family estates into paltry plots capable of sustaining life only through the potato crop.

This natural disaster, caused by a disease known as late blight (*Phytophthora infestans*) resulted in the country's potato-crop failure in successive years between 1845 and 1849. Ireland's population of almost 8.5 million people in 1844 plummeted to 6.5 million by 1850. Although historical sources differ (250,000-2 million dead), during the famine about 1 million people died from starvation, typhus, and other famine-related diseases. In addition, as many as 1.5 million of Ireland's people immigrated to English-speaking countries, such as the United States, Canada, Great Britain, New Zealand, and Australia, because of the famine.

HISTORICAL BACKGROUND. When the New World white potato (Irish potato), native to the Andes Mountains in South America, was introduced into Ireland in the seventeenth century, the new crop flourished in the damp Irish climate, quickly becoming the country's major food source. Before the introduction of the potato, beef, milk, butter, and buttermilk were the staples of the Irish diet. The potato grew in ever-increasing importance during the 1600's and 1700's, and the population exploded. The lower classes became more and

more reliant on the potato they called the "lumper." Before the famine, an average Irish man consumed daily between 7 and 15 pounds of potatoes. Children ate potatoes for their school lunch. Since many did not own knives, one thumbnail was grown long to peel the potato. After the potatoes were boiled, they were strained in a basket. The family would gather and sit around the basket in the middle of the floor. Potatoes, accompanied with buttermilk or skim milk, composed the entire meal, which peasant families ate at every mealtime gathering.

The historical record leading up to the Great Irish Famine, arguably Europe's worst natural disaster of the nineteenth century, must be examined so the impact of this tragedy can be understood. Since its colonization of Ireland in the twelfth century, Britain's primary economic goal was to extract the greatest amount of resources from its colony for the benefit of British and Anglo-Irish landowners. With the loss of its American colonies in 1775, and with the depression that resulted at the end of the Napoleonic Wars in 1815, Britain's attempts to increase agricultural profits in Ireland escalated. Seeking to force the Irish into greater submission, the British legislated penal laws that denied the Irish the freedom to speak their own language (Gaelic), to practice Catholicism, to attend school, to hold public office, or to own land. A tenant system was introduced into Ireland that gave British and Anglo-Irish landlords control of 95 percent of Ireland's land. Landowners who, for the most part, resided in England became known as absentee landlords and rented land to their Irish tenants, providing each tenant family with a cottage. Each cottage was surrounded by an acre and a half of land.

Some historians blame the ultimate depopulation of Ireland on the Malthusian notion of overpopulation, arguing that because the Irish population was too high, there was not enough food to feed everyone when the potato crops failed. After 1815, the expanding population increased the competition for land and forced peasant holdings to be divided and subdivided into ever-decreasing lots, eventually forcing many people to move to less fertile areas, where only potatoes would grow. The potato crop needed little labor to harvest, and a small acreage furnished a large crop yield. Some families had to survive on a quarter of an acre of land, and the potato was the only crop that would feed many mouths. Even before the famine, during the 1840's, it was common for laborers to hunger in the late summer before harvest. In addition, before the famine, housing and clothing were inadequate, and huts and rags were often the norm for the Irish peasants; a bed or a blanket was a luxury.

By the beginning of the 1840's, almost one-half of the Irish population, especially the poor agricultural communities, relied almost solely on the potato—which supplied vitamin C, amino acids, protein, thiamin, and nicotinic acid—for sustenance. In addition, the other half of the population consumed the starchy vegetable in massive amounts. Researchers explain that because of the nutritive value of the potato, Ireland's population had increased rapidly and reached 8 million by 1841. By then, two-thirds of the population depended on agriculture for sustenance. The Irish economy became completely dependent on the potato, and the failure of the potato crop in 1845 had disastrous results.

CAUSES OF THE FAMINE. The causes of famine are numerous and include drought, heavy rain and flooding, unseasonably cold weather, typhoons, and disease. In the late summer of 1845, the *Phytophthora* fungus, an airborne fungal pathogen that destroys both the leaves and roots (the actual potato) of the potato plant, and which originated in North America, established itself in Ireland, where it commenced to destroy the potato crop. The summer of 1845 also saw unusually cool, moist weather. Blight thrives in such climatic conditions and drastically affects even stored crops. In that season, the potato blight destroyed 40 percent of the Irish potatoes. After it struck in 1845, even more potatoes were planted because the pestilence was not expected to strike again. Unfortunately, the potato crop did fail again in 1846, and the results were even worse in 1847, when 100 percent of the crop was ruined. That year, 1847, when suffering reached its climax, is referred to as "Black '47."

In all, the potato harvest failed four years in a row, and the peasants had no food reserves. The famine situation continued unabated because of a deficiency of seed potatoes for new crops and the insufficient quantity planted for fear of continued blight. Unfortunately, the availability of only two genetic varieties of potato in Ireland at that time greatly increased the odds of crop decimation by famine. In hindsight, had other varieties of potato been available in Ireland the entire crop might not have failed.

Potato blight was not unknown in Ireland before 1845. A famine in 1740-1741 killed a quarter of a million people. The island nation struggled through crop failures and subsistence crises throughout the nineteenth century, including 14 partial and complete famines between 1816 and 1842. Because the Industrial Revolution never reached most of Ireland, there was little opportunity for employment other than agriculture.

EFFECTS OF THE FAMINE. Although at the beginning of the blight the potato plants appeared green, lush, and healthy, as they did most years, overnight the blight struck them down, leaving acre upon acre of Irish farmland covered with black rot. Leaves curled up and shriveled, black spots appeared on the potatoes, and an unbearable putrefying stench that could be smelled for miles lay over the land. When the fungus had run its course, Irish farmers saw that the crop they relied on for life was destroyed. Ireland was not the only country hit by hardship. Although infected crops were present the United States, southern Canada, and Western Europe in 1845-1846, the results were not nearly as severe or deadly as in Ireland. While other countries turned to alternative food sources, the Irish were dependent on the potato, so the results of the blight were disastrous. As harvests across Europe failed, the price of food soared.

The hardest hit were the landless laborers who rented the small plots of land to feed themselves and their families. When their crops failed, they had to buy food with money they did not have, and prices continued to rise. Although in 1845 only part of the entire Irish potato crop rotted in the fields, as the years went on the blight continued unabated. When much more devastating crop failures followed in 1846 and 1847, millions lost everything: their homes, their few belongings, their families, and eventually their lives. The hardest hit regions were the south and the west of Ireland. During this time, roughly 1 million people, previously well fed on a diet made up primarily of potatoes, died. Peasants forced to eat the rotten potatoes fell ill. People died of starvation in their houses, in the fields, and on the roads.

Disease became rampant and widespread, and most who suffered from long starvation finally surrendered to typhoid, cholera, dysentery, or scurvy. Entire villages fell victim to cholera and typhoid. Indeed, more people died of disease than of starvation. Money became so scarce that the dead were often buried without coffins. Some sources record that during the worst of the famine, peasants died in the night and their bodies would be found in the morning partially devoured by rats. As time went on, unmarked mass graves became the resting place for many Irish. At the worst in 1847, the dead were being buried in trenches. The famine together with the accompanying plagues became known as the Great Famine to the British, the Great Hunger to the Irish middle class, and the Great Starvation to the Irish peasantry.

RESULTS OF THE FAMINE. Before the famine struck, nearly half of all rural families lived in windowless, one-room cottages owned by landlords who were often ruthless. Also before the famine, some peasants were able to grow plots of oats or raise pigs to pay for the rent to their British landlords. After the famine, families who relied on the potato to keep themselves alive were left with nothing and had to choose between either selling their food to pay the rent or eating the food and facing eviction. If tenants failed to pay the landlord, the family was thrown out on the road and their homes were immediately burned to the ground so they could not return. During the Great Hunger, approximately 500,000 people were evicted, many of whom died of starvation or disease, while many others were relocated to poorhouses.

The British government legislated the Coercion Act in support of landlords who evicted those who failed to pay their rent. It also provided British soldiers and a police force to oversee the eviction of tenant farmers. Landlords evicted hundreds of thousands of starving peasants, who then flocked to disease-infested workhouses or perished on the roadside. Many times only grass made up their last meal. The streets swarmed with wretched, unsightly, half-naked beggars or, as they have been called, "the living skeletons" of the Irish. Villages were demolished; Cottages crumbled in ruins, abandoned by their tenants.

Britain provided financial assistance to Ireland in the form of loans amounting to 365,000 pounds sterling. In an effort to encourage an infrastructure to promote industrialization and modernize Ireland and avoid public revolt, the British government set up public works projects. However, these schemes proved useless because they were designed to not interfere with private enterprise. For instance, bridges were built over nonexistent rivers. Today, roads built by impoverished peasants—going from nowhere to nowhere—can still be viewed as part of the Irish landscape. For their efforts, the laborers received such low wages that they could hardly buy enough food to live on. In addition, this work was available to only a small percentage of the population. For example, in one Irish county, Kerry, in 1846, 400,000 people applied for 13,000 public works jobs. In March of 1847, the public works schemes were abandoned.

The responsibility to feed and house the poor fell to various charities. During the famine, 173 workhouses, built adjacent to dangerous fever hospitals, were constructed throughout Ireland. Some were so

In this 1880 Harper's Weekly *cover, a woman on the Irish shore beckons for help with her starving family at her feet and the specter of death looming over the country.* (Library of Congress)

overcrowded and inadequate that one workhouse in County Limerick, built to accommodate 800 occupants, housed over 3,000 destitute people. Workhouse residents were fed watery oatmeal soup and were forced to wear prisonlike uniforms. Families were split apart into male and female dormitories. Soup kitchens were set up throughout Ireland by religious groups such as the Quakers. However, many times the soup was so weak that it was of little nutritional value. Even this inferior food did not meet the demand as crowds waited for hours outside the distribution centers.

By August, 1847, as many as 3 million people accepted food at soup kitchens. Although soup was given free to the infirm, widows, orphans, and children, the Poor Law Amendment Act of 1847 maintained that no peasant with a holding of one-quarter of an acre or more was eligible for relief, which resulted in tens of thousands of farmers parting with their land. In its own efforts to alleviate Ireland's famine, the United States imported cornmeal, or Indian corn, which somewhat eased the food shortage, but the Irish found it unpalatable.

THE EMIGRATION OF THE IRISH. Emigration was the only alternative to eviction or the poorhouse. Although the practice predated the famine, emigration rose to over 2 million from 1845 to 1855. When landlords began to issue notices to their tenants to appear in court for nonpayment of rent, the fear of imprisonment caused families to flee their homes for English towns and cities, and if they had the money, to the United States, Canada, New Zealand, and Australia. Most who emigrated did so at their own expense and sent money back to their relatives to follow them. Although during the famine more than 1 million Irish fled their country, many of the Catholic peasantry remained in their native land. The Catholic Church in part discouraged emigration out of fear that the Irish would lose their faith if they lived in Protestant Britain and America.

The famine, however, continued to drive new waves of emigration, thus shaping the histories of the countries where Irish immigrants found new homes. The peak rate of emigration occurred in 1851, when 250,000 left Ireland, continuing through the 1850's and into the 1860's. Centuries after the famine, the far-reaching impact and results are evident in the number of Irish descendants scattered throughout the globe.

Even emigration proved no remedy for the plight of the starving Irish. According to British Poor Laws, landlords were responsible for 12 pounds a year support for peasants sent to the workhouses. Instead, some landlords sent their tenants to Canada at a cost of 6 pounds each. Many of those who survived later made their way across the Canadian border into the United States. Desperate Irish often crowded onto structurally unsafe, overcrowded, understocked, disease-ridden boats called "coffin ships." Thousands of fleeing Irish carried diseases aboard or developed fever on the voyage. Many never saw land again or died shortly after they reached their destination. In several cases, these vessels reached the end of their voyage after losing one-third to one-half of their passengers.

The survivors arrived in North America hardly able to walk, owing to sickness and starvation. The streets of Montreal, Canada, were filled with impoverished emigrants from Ireland, many with typhoid. The Grosse Île, Quebec, fever hospital was overrun with sick and dying infants. In August of 1989, during an address on Grosse Île, Dr. Edward J. Brennan, Ireland's ambassador to Canada, called the Great Famine Ireland's holocaust and the Irish people the first boat people of modern Europe.

IRISH ANGER RISES. The famine convinced Irish citizens and Irish Americans of the compelling necessity for intensified national awareness and political change. The poor did not readily accept their fate; food riots broke out, and secret political and militant societies increased their activity. Some greatly alarmed Irish believed that the potato would be permanently destroyed. Spiraling crime and disobedience were countered with repression and violence. The unemployed roamed the country, begging and sleeping in ditches. Fifty thousand British soldiers occupied the country, backed up in every town and village by an armed police force. Landlords were shot. During one of the worst famine years, landlord Major Denis Mahon was assassinated by his tenants following his attempt to mass-evict 8,000 of his destitute tenants from his 30,000-acre estate. Ireland was in ruins.

Although the British government spent an estimated £8 million on Irish relief, ineffective measures aimed at alleviating its neighboring island's distress resulted in deep and increased hostilities against British rule. Particularly disturbing was the increased exportation of Irish grain and meat to Britain during this time of famine because the starving Irish people could not afford to purchase these provisions themselves. Landowners continued to make profits through the export of Irish food as well as wool and flax. Historical records show that all through the famine, food—wheat, oats, barley, butter, eggs, beef, and pork—was exported from Ireland in large quantities. In fact, eight ships left Ireland daily carrying food that could have saved thousands of lives. About 4,000 shiploads of food sailed into Liverpool alone in the darkest famine year, 1847.

Despite famine conditions, taxes, rents, and food exports were collected in excess of £6 million and sent to British landlords. During the famine, an average of 2 million tons of wheat were annually shipped out of Ireland, an amount that could have fed the whole population. One scholar claimed that for every ship that came to Ireland with food, there were six ships sailing out. The British government's Coercion Act ensured that British soldiers and a police force were used to protect food for export from the starving.

RESPONSIBILITY FOR THE FAMINE. Many historians still place blame on Britain for allowing so many of Ireland's population to die. After all, Ireland was at this time part of the United Kingdom, the wealthiest empire in the world. Although the British government provided relief for Ireland's starving, it was severely criticized for its delayed response; their efforts to relieve the famine were insufficient. For instance, the first step the British took to relieve the catastrophic situation was to send a shipload of scientists to study the cause of the potato failure. The British were further condemned for centuries of political oppression of Ireland as the underlying cause of the famine. Starvation among the peasants was blamed on a colonial system that made Ireland financially and physically dependent on the potato in the first place. The Irish patriot labor leader James Connolly argued that the British administration of Ireland during the famine was an enormous crime against the human race.

No doubt insensitivity toward the Irish contributed to Britain's failure to take swift and comprehensive action in the force of Ireland's disaster. Charles Trevelyn, secretary of the British Treasury during the famine, claimed outright that the government's function was not to supply food, and Lord Clarendon, Viceroy of Ireland during the famine, referred to the evictions and emigrations that resulted from the famine as a blessing for the Irish economy. Additionally, although Prime Minister Sir Robert Peel attempted relief efforts in 1845 and early 1846 by repealing the Corn Laws (protective tariffs that enabled the Irish to import grain from North America), his successor, the liberal Lord John Russell, supported a policy of nonintervention, in keeping with the laissez-faire philosophy that dominated the era's British economic policy. Government officials maintained the belief that it was counterproductive to interfere in economics and placed the burden of relief for the starving peasantry unto the Irish landowners.

Historians today are attempting to shed light on the reasons behind the famine, stressing that although the potato crop failed, a state of famine per se did not exist in Ireland, because other food, such as grain, poultry, beef, lamb, and pork, was available. Basically, there was no shortage of food. Profits, some scholars stress, came before people's needs, and while the blight provided the catalyst for the famine, the disaster was essentially human-made—the Irish people were the victims of economics, politics, and ignorance. Well-known Irish short-story writer Frank O'Connor once observed that "famine" is a useful word used instead of "genocide" or "extermination." The author John Mitchell in 1861 declared that the Irish people died of hunger in the midst of food they themselves had created, and in 1904 Michael Davitt, the founder of the Irish Land League, called the Irish famine a holocaust.

LONG-TERM CONSEQUENCES OF THE FAMINE. The famine proved to be a watershed in the demographic history of Ireland. Ireland's population continued to decline in the decades following the famine, owing to emigration and lower birth rates, which ultimately allowed for increased landholdings. By 1900, 2.5 million more of Ireland's people had crossed the Atlantic. By the time Ireland achieved independence in 1921, its population was barely half of what it had been in the early 1840's. In their new homes, emigrant men were provided with manual labor jobs on construction sites, roads, and railways, while Irish women were hired as domestics. In time, Irish emigrants found opportunities for success never known in their homeland. For instance, automobile tycoon Henry Ford's grandfather was one such Irish famine emigrant, as was twenty-six-year-old Patrick Kennedy, the great-grandfather of President John F. Kennedy.

The famine was the most tragic and significant event in Irish history. Mary Robinson, the president of Ireland from 1990 to 1997, described the famine as the instrumental event in shaping the Irish as a people, defining their will to survive and their sense of human vulnerability. No one can fully voice the extent or the severity of the suffering endured by the Irish people from 1845 to 1850.

M. Casey Diana

FOR FURTHER INFORMATION:

Bartoletti, Susan Campbell. *Black Potatoes: The Story of the Great Irish Famine, 1845-1850.* Boston: Houghton Mifflin, 2001.

Donnelly, James S., Jr. *The Great Irish Potato Famine.* Phoenix Mill, Gloucestershire, England: Sutton, 2001.

Gray, Peter, and Sarah Burns. *The Irish Famine.* New York: Harry N. Abrams, 1995.

Kinealy, Christine. *The Great Calamity: The Irish Famine 1845-52.* New York: Roberts Rinehardt, 1995.

O'Cathaoir, Brendan. *Famine Diary.* Dublin: Irish Academic Press, 1998.

Tóibín, Colm, and Diarmaid Ferriter. *The Irish Famine: A Documentary.* New York: Thomas Dunne Books/St. Martin's Press, 2002.

Valone, David A., and Christine Kinealy, eds. *Ireland's Great Hunger: Silence, Memory, and Commemoration.* Lanham, Md.: University Press of America, 2002.

Woodham-Smith, Cecil, and Charles Woodham. *The Great Hunger: Ireland, 1846-1849.* New York: Penguin, 1995.

■ 1871: The Great Peshtigo Fire

Fire

Date: October 8, 1871
Place: Peshtigo, Wisconsin
Result: At least 1,200 dead, 2 billion trees burned

At 9 P.M. on October 8, 1871, a forest fire that had developed into a rapidly moving firestorm swept over the small lumber town of Peshtigo, Wisconsin. The fire began almost at the same minute as the Great Chicago Fire, which was raging some 240 miles to the south, and a similar forest conflagration burning to the east in Upper Michigan. Within half an hour Peshtigo was destroyed. The fire that engulfed and destroyed Peshtigo, Wisconsin, ranks as the deadliest fire in United States history to date. More than 1,200 people perished in the fire, and over 2 billion trees covering 1.25 million acres were destroyed. By the morning of October 9, 1871, the Peshtigo and Michigan fires combined to destroy 3.5 million acres of forest lands.

Peshtigo was a company town. The Peshtigo Company sawmill was owned by Chicago entrepreneur William B. Ogden and ran 97 saws, averaging a daily cut of 150,000 board feet of lumber. In addition, Ogden was principal owner of a three-story woodenware factory in Peshtigo. At the time it was the largest woodenware factory in the United States, producing thousands of wooden tubs, pails, shingles, clothespins, and broom handles daily. Lumber company officials, concerned for the safety of the factory and lumber mills located in the area, convened a management council to discuss the possible fire danger, but no decisive plan of action was agreed upon other than to clear a 30-foot-wide firebreak along the north side of the Peshtigo River and to fell trees in the immediate vicinity of the mills.

Conditions Leading to the Fire. During the late 1800's, the practice of clearing scrub brush and slash-and-burning in grassland regions of the eastern Dakotas, compounded by a year of regional drought and atypical meteorological conditions, established an environmental condition that started a chain reaction of unchecked prai-

rie fires that burned through the weeks of August and September, 1871. Driven by the prevailing westerly winds, the fires crossed the Minnesota and Mississippi Rivers into drought-inflicted areas of old-growth timberlands to the east and north. These forest fires spread rapidly by crowning, or traveling between treetops, then dropping to the ground and starting more intensive fires from the additional fuel on the forest floor. Strong thermal updrafts then carry sparks and firebrands to ignite more fires.

Communications in this region of the country were almost nonexistent. It was not uncommon for major fires to take a minimum of several days, and often several weeks, to be reported in metropolitan newspapers. The only warning of swift-moving fires was often issued by stagecoach and railroad passengers, or by those fleeing the fire's rapid advance. As a result, these great fires moved eastward unchecked and relatively unannounced. By September 1, 1871, a series of great interlinked prairie fires stretched from the Canadian border through Iowa and remained unreported to the communities far ahead.

By the end of the first week of September, 1871, the sky from the Straits of Mackinac in Michigan, throughout northern Wisconsin, and as far south as Chicago, Illinois, and South Bend, Indiana, were choking under a cloud of smoke. During the early days of September several small jump fires, caused by burning firebrands carried high into the sky by fire-generated convection currents and then blown downrange by prevailing winds, had occurred west of Peshtigo. The forests surrounding Peshtigo were thick-barked, old-growth timber, which were usually not harmed by ordinary forest fires. Fires were often considered a nuisance rather than a threat.

On September 23, 1871, a jump fire came within several miles of Peshtigo. A firebrand from this fire ignited the main sawdust pile of the Peshtigo Company, but the fire was extinguished by a bucket brigade of 60 men. After this episode the management of the Peshtigo Company, now mindful of the potential danger of the advancing range and forest fires and the unchecked spread of smaller slash fires caused by nearby railroad construction, ordered large barrels of water placed by the side of every business establishment, bunkhouse, and hotel. Flammable goods were packed in crates, moved from company-owned stores to the riverside, and covered with dampened earth. As a lumber town, Peshtigo was constructed almost entirely of timber-frame buildings, wood-shingle roofs, and wooden sidewalks. The roads were covered with sawdust and wood chips to control mud formation and dust. Workers at the local bank dug holes in the soil beside their buildings into which they could dump money and valuables if fire reached Peshtigo. Many families soaked woolen blankets and laid them over their cedar-shingled cabin roofs. However, by September 25, the winds abated, veered to the southeast, and the direct fire threat to Peshtigo was removed.

With the exception of a small fire the next week, ignited by careless railroad workers, mill operations and daily life returned to normal in Peshtigo. Autumn weather in the U.S. upper tier states is dominated by shifting winds as advancing cold fronts plunge southward

417

from the Arctic and meet moist tropical winds moving northward from the Gulf of Mexico. The clash of these air masses typically results in cold rains and churning winds, until winter snows begin. In 1871, however, the autumn rains did not arrive; drought conditions existed throughout the central United States. In the east, as far as New York City and Boston, the air was smoke-laden from the great fires burning unchecked to the west. Great Lakes shipping traffic was being negatively affected by the thick smoke because ships were unable to safely enter harbors due to poor visibility. Yet the fires continued to burn unchecked.

THE FIRE REACHES PESHTIGO. Just prior to 9 P.M. on the evening of October 8, 1871, a fine ash began to drift over Peshtigo. There was no wind, and the ash settled like a fine snow. Residents noted that as the ash fell wild birds and pet animals began to utter noises and act in frantic bursts of behavior. Then the sky to the southwest began to turn a dark red color, silhouetting the surrounding trees against the dark of night. Unknown to the residents of Peshtigo, over 300 families in the nearby Sugar Bush communities were being engulfed in a raging firestorm with flames estimated to have reached a height of over 200 feet. There is no record of what happened in Sugar Bush; nearly every resident of the communities perished in a matter of minutes as they tried to flee the advancing firestorm along the road to Peshtigo. There was no warning in Peshtigo.

The firestorm raced northeastward, spreading in all directions as it consumed old-growth trees and drought-ridden underlying ground cover. Winds accompanying the advancing fire, and driving it forward, are estimated to have been of hurricane velocity, swirling in gusts of over 100 miles an hour and even higher in the center of the firestorm.

Survivors of the fire reported that the previously still evening air suddenly developed a slight breeze, at which time the air instantly became very hot; survivors equated the rush of heat to that of a blast furnace. This was accompanied by a low moaning sound from the southwest, which grew louder, building to a deep rumbling roar like a train approaching from the distance. It was reported that as the roaring sound escalated, the sky to the west of Peshtigo flashed a brilliant red color almost blinding in its intensity, then faded to a glowing yellow as bright as the sun. Within seconds a violent wind struck the town, and the forest surrounding Peshtigo was engulfed in a wall of rolling and tumbling flames hundreds of feet high, moving at tremendous velocity. The rushing wind was so strong that trees were uprooted, roofs were lifted off of houses, and chimneys blew over.

THE EFFECTS OF THE FIRE. Many of the buildings in Peshtigo were reported to have simply exploded into flames; one second they were standing, the next they were blown apart into flaming pieces of debris. The tremendous heat of the oncoming firestorm ignited the wooden bridge and the wooden railroad trestle crossing the Peshtigo River while still nearly a mile away. It has been estimated that the forward edge of the firestorm may have been close to 2,000 degrees Fahrenheit. As Peshtigo erupted into flames the glow could be seen as far away as Menominee and across Green Bay to Door County.

The mill, wooden structures, sawdust-covered streets, and pine-plank sidewalks leapt into flames, cutting off the escape routes of many Peshtigo citizens. Many people tried to seek shelter within buildings. Though the Peshtigo River was being engulfed by walls of

A drawing of the Great Peshtigo Fire that appeared in an 1871 issue of Harper's Weekly. (Wisconsin Historical Society/#3728)

A deer carcass and charred tree trunks are all that remain of the town of Peshtigo, Wisconsin, following the fire. (Wisconsin Historical Society/#1859)

flame and jammed with toppled burning logs, it was the only location to offer any hope of safety. Humans, pets, draft and farm animals, and forest denizens all rushed to reach the river's waters. It was impossible to flee from the fire—it was moving too fast. Survivors reported seeing humans and animals running toward the river simply burst into flames. Other eyewitness accounts describe the thermal updrafts and convection currents of the fire as twisting like tornadoes. Others reported that the air seemed to be aflame as balls of fire would appear out of nowhere and suddenly disappear or as hot gases struck a supply of oxygen not yet consumed by the advancing firestorm.

The Peshtigo River was deep, and many of those who reached it drowned quickly. Others were injured by panicked animals, carried away by the current, or struck by logs and debris. Those citizens who reached the river slapped their hands on the water's surface and splashed each other in an attempt to cool their skin and hair. Many stripped off clothing and wrapped it around their heads to keep their hair from bursting into flames from the intense heat. Even with a continuous soaking of water, skin and cloth dried out almost immediately from the terrific heat. Flaming debris falling into the river burst into steam. When the woodenware factory exploded, it showered those in the river with flaming tubs, pails, shingles, and broom handles.

Within the town, anyone who sought shelter in a structure died. In one tavern, over 200 victims were trapped and incinerated. Only those who found refuge in the river and several more who struggled to a nearby marsh survived the inferno. Within twenty minutes, the town of Peshtigo had been obliterated, and at least 1,200 citizens had perished.

After nearly six hours, the few survivors climbed out of the water and waited until dawn for the ashes to cool so the search for possible survivors and noncremated bodies could begin. Three victims were found in a large water tank near the mill, but the water had become so hot that all of them died. Several people were found dead under similar circumstances at the bottom of a well. Many of the bodies were found huddled at the bases of trees.

Most of the bodies were burned beyond recognition. As a result, 350 victims of the fire were buried in a mass grave. Many victims who were not cremated died of suffocation as oxygen was sucked out of the air and into the firestorm. While the Peshtigo fire was the most deadly fire in American history, its destruction was overshadowed by the Great Chicago Fire that raged out of control the same night. For weeks after the disaster, the nation's press paid little attention to Peshtigo while devoting major coverage to the Chicago fire. The governor of Wisconsin was eventually forced to issue a special proclamation begging the nation to divert their charity and gifts from Chicago to Peshtigo.

Though much is known about the existing meteorological and environmental conditions at the time of the tragic Peshtigo fire, a new theory was offered in the late 1990's concerning the cause of the super outbreak of firestorms the night of October 8, 1871. Based on eyewitness accounts, regional observations, damage patterns, and the curious circumstance of several large conflagrations all igniting at approximately the same time over a wide, yet confined, geographic area, some investigators suggested the firestorms may have resulted from a Tunguska-like atmospheric meteor explosion.

Randall L. Milstein

FOR FURTHER INFORMATION:

Gess, Denise, and William Lutz. *Firestorm at Peshtigo: A Town, Its People, and the Deadliest Fire in American History.* New York: Henry Holt, 2002.

Lyons, Paul R. *Fire in America.* Boston: National Fire Protection Association, 1976.

McClement, Fred. *The Flaming Forests.* Toronto: McClelland and Stewart, 1969.

Pernin, Peter. *The Great Peshtigo Fire: An Eyewitness Account.* Madison: University of Wisconsin, 1999.

Soddens, Betty. *Michigan on Fire.* Thunder Bay, Ont.: Thunder Bay Press, 1998.

Wells, Robert W. *Fire at Peshtigo.* Englewood Cliffs, N.J.: Prentice-Hall, 1968.

■ 1871: THE GREAT CHICAGO FIRE

FIRE

DATE: October 8-10, 1871
PLACE: Chicago, Illinois
RESULT: 250 dead, more than 17,420 buildings destroyed, more than
100,000 left homeless, more than $200 million in damage

Undoubtedly one of the most crushing catastrophes ever to strike the city of Chicago, Illinois, was the Great Chicago Fire that raged for three days, from October 8 until October 10, 1871, twice jumping the Chicago River and igniting buildings on the other side. The city, tinder-dry after a virtually rainless summer and early autumn, had grown very rapidly as the United States experienced a great western expansion. Buildings erected quickly to house the heavy influx of new residents and to meet the requirements of the city's burgeoning industrial and commercial enterprises were often flimsy structures that served an immediate and pressing need but could not withstand the ravages of a raging fire propelled by strong winds.

When the final tally was in, 250 people lay dead, thousands were homeless, an estimated 17,420 buildings had been destroyed, and property damage was set at over $200 million, an inconceivably large sum at that time, representing about one-third of the city's total worth. The fire put the mettle of the city to an extreme test. Many thought this catastrophe would mark the death knell of Chicago as a major transportation crossroads and industrial hub. The city, however, soon emerged stronger than ever, fully meeting the challenge posed by its great loss.

THE CHICAGO OF 1871. In 1871, Chicago was unquestionably a boomtown. A decade earlier, it had been the site of the 1860 Republican National Convention, at which longtime Illinois resident Abraham Lincoln was nominated to run for the presidency of the United States. By 1870, its population of 334,000 exceeded that of St. Louis, Missouri, the only other contender in the Midwest for the title of metropolis. The city, intersected by the Chicago River, with Lake Michigan on its eastern border, enjoyed a virtual monopoly in transportation, with ships coming from the eastern United States by way of the Great Lakes and railroads from the East converging in Chicago with those serving the West. The city's industries produced meat, lumber, shoes, farm machinery, and scores of other items. Chicago was also among the country's largest distributors of farm products.

In the year of the fire, Chicago sprawled over some 23,000 acres, on which nearly 60,000 buildings had been erected. The overall property value of the city at that time was slightly more than $600 million. Prosperity was evident on every hand, and an ebullient optimism was in the air. People had flocked to Chicago because it offered them a better life than they could find almost anywhere else in the United States, certainly better than they could anticipate anywhere else in the Midwest. Immigrants from Eastern Europe, Scandinavia, Italy, and Greece poured into the city, which could offer them the immediate opportunity of employment.

BEGINNING AND SPREAD OF THE FIRE. Shortly after 9:00 on the evening of October 8, 1871, a fire broke out in a barn behind the cottage of Patrick and Catherine O'Leary at 137 De Koven Street in the southwestern part of the city, a working-class neighborhood whose humble structures were mostly wooden. Close to De Koven Street were planing mills, lumberyards, and furniture factories, all of which could add fuel to any flames that might rage near them.

When the alarm was sounded, the fire brigade rushed to the scene, realizing the danger that any such fire might pose when the town was so dangerously dry following a prolonged drought. A mere 2.5 inches of rain had fallen between July 3 and October 8, whereas normal rainfall for that period was between 8 and 9 inches. Only the night before, nervous spectators watched as 5 acres burned violently very close to the O'Leary barn, the site of the new fire.

Persistent legend has it that the fire in the O'Leary barn began when Mrs. O'Leary's cow kicked over a lantern that ignited some nearby hay. This bit of lore has never been substantiated, although it is altogether possible that this was the actual origin of the fire. What is known for sure is that when the fire bells sounded, the firefighters, exhausted from having fought a blaze that destroyed four blocks of the city the day before, arrived to find an inferno that was spreading rapidly. It was hoped that when the flames reached the four blocks

Chicago in Flames—The Rush for Lives over Randolph Street Bridge. (John R. Chapin)

that had been devastated the night before, the fire would be brought under control, but this was not the case, although this four-block barrier prevented the flames from spreading to the west, which was spared the worst of the damage during the conflagration.

By 10:30 on the evening of October 8, less than two hours after the first alarm was sounded, the fire on De Koven Street was declared out of control. Nearby residents were urged to evacuate their homes, but many, accustomed to hearing the fire warnings several times a week, paid little heed to the admonitions to flee, convinced that the danger was not great. The fire raged so strongly that by 11:30 a wall of flames had jumped the Chicago River and advanced into the business district.

What made the fire of October 8 an extraordinary one was that it was fed by gale-force winds out of the southwest that soon caused the great bursts of flames to become walls of fire. The air quickly became superheated; blinding ash and swirling dust were blown into people's faces by the fierce winds, blinding them and making breathing all but impossible; the force of the flames created a roar like that of a runaway locomotive. Soon those who had gone to their beds blandly assuming that this was just another fire found themselves facing a situation from which many could find no escape. The wind was so strong that no one could outrun it. Turmoil and confusion gripped all of those downwind from the fire as it proceeded in a northeasterly direction.

Before it was over on October 10, the fire, driven by the strong winds, had twice leaped across the Chicago River, proceeding as far as Fullerton Avenue, the city limits, and stopping only when it reached Lake Michigan to the east. It left a burned area 4 miles long and 0.66 mile wide. An estimated 1,687 acres had been burned by the fire, and nearly everything on those acres had been reduced to ash.

Frightened residents of Chicago flee the flames of the Great Fire, carrying what possessions they can. (Library of Congress)

GREAT PESHTIGO AND WESTERN MICHIGAN FIRES. It is a matter of mere coincidence that as the Great Chicago Fire was raging, another fire brought on by the dry conditions and high winds that plagued the Midwest on October 8, 1871, was raging north of Chicago in Peshtigo, Wisconsin, a small lumbering community north of Green Bay. This fire, once ignited, spread with such rapidity that there was no way to control it. The pine forests that surrounded the town provided ample fuel for the conflagration. As the flames hit the trees, they actually exploded, their sap igniting like gasoline.

As it turned out, the Peshtigo fire, although it is less well known than the Great Chicago Fire, was the most devastating in the history of the United States. It resulted in over 1,200 deaths. Everyone in its path perished. The Chicago fire received more publicity than the Peshtigo fire merely because Chicago was a commercial and transportation center through which many Americans had passed, thereby becoming familiar with it. The Peshtigo fire wiped out an entire small community; the Chicago fire almost destroyed a major metropolis.

On the evening of October 8, yet another fire erupted in western Michigan. This forest fire in a sparsely populated area claimed few lives, but it left nearly everyone in the area homeless, some 15,000 people losing their residences to the advancing flames. All sorts of rumors circulated about these three coincident fires. In each case, a parched landscape had somehow been ignited. Any parched landscape is vulnerable, sometimes being set ablaze by a lightning strike. Some thought that a comet had struck the earth or a meteor had exploded in the atmosphere.

EXTENT OF THE DAMAGE. Despite the vast destruction caused by the Great Chicago Fire, a few buildings in the city's central part remained in its wake, among them the Chicago Water Tower, which stands to this day as a city landmark. Ironically, the De Koven Street residence of Patrick and Catherine O'Leary was spared by the fire, although almost nothing was left standing around it. The famed Palmer House was completely destroyed, but the Michigan Avenue Hotel, whose panicked owner sold it for what he could get as the fire advanced, came through unscathed, much to the gratification and profit of its new owner, John B. Drake. It was saved because buildings adjacent to it were demolished before the fire arrived.

Only two of the exclusive residences on the elegant north side of

Chicago, home to such notable families as the Ogdens, the Ramseys, the McCormicks, and the Arnolds, remained standing after the fire. The courthouse, which had been built at a cost of $1 million and whose bell had announced such memorable and historic events as the assassination of President Abraham Lincoln in 1865, was destroyed, its bell crashing down from its dome at 2:30 A.M. on October 9. Crosby's Opera House, Hooley's Theater, and the Washington Street Theater also went up in flames. The celebrated Field and Leiter Department Store on State Street was soon consumed by the advancing fire, along with some $2 million worth of merchandise with which it was stocked.

One of the major problems posed by the fire was that the wind propelled it in such unpredictable directions that firefighters often found themselves caught by a raging inferno in front of them and another such inferno behind them. The speed with which the flames spread was phenomenal. The dry, wooden buildings that lay in its path virtually exploded when the fire reached them.

EARLY WARNINGS ABOUT FLIMSY CONSTRUCTION. Chicagoans had been warned well in advance about the dangers inherent in many of the buildings that had been built in great haste to accommodate the city's rapid expansion. The *Chicago Tribune*, whose own headquarters were completely destroyed by the fire, had warned its readers in a blistering editorial a month before the disaster that many of Chicago's brick buildings were only one brick thick. Their facades frequently crumbled and fell into the streets below. The cornices on many stone buildings had collapsed as the buildings weakened, sometimes crashing into the street and injuring pedestrians who happened to be in their paths.

Some of Chicago's most imposing buildings were impressive shells whose construction was so substandard that, had the fire not consumed them, they would surely have collapsed in the normal course of everyday use. The city's cast-iron buildings were not well secured on their foundations, so that even they were rapidly deteriorating and in some cases rusting away.

If the buildings in the business district were shoddy, residential construction throughout the city, particularly in the working-class neighborhoods such as De Koven Street, was even worse. Residential construction on the tonier north side of Chicago around Dearborn,

Rush, Ontario, Cass, and Huron Streets seemed elegant at first glance, but most of the mansions in these exclusive neighborhoods had been built more for show than for safety.

The houses on the north side of town were filled with valuable furniture, oriental rugs, paintings, statuaries, and tapestries, but these priceless treasures were displayed in buildings that would go up in flames instantly in the sort of dire situation that marked the Great Chicago Fire. It took just flames and a strong wind to turn Chicago's most illustrious neighborhood into a field of smoldering rubble.

FIREFIGHTING METHODS IN 1871. Certainly, given the firefighting equipment of that day, there was little chance of controlling a fire that advanced as quickly as the Great Chicago Fire. Much fire fighting at that time was done by bucket brigades, lines of people who passed buckets of water toward a fire. This meant that those fighting the fire, which generated a killing heat and which moved so rapidly as to threaten everything in its path, had to stand close enough to the conflagration to throw water upon it.

By 1871, Chicago was more advanced than many cities in its firefighting equipment. It had fire engines with steam-powered pumps to direct water onto fires that were burning out of control. However, these pumps were no match for the walls of flame that stretched nearly a mile wide in some places during the Great Chicago Fire.

By 3:00 on the morning of October 9, the pumps of Chicago's waterworks on Pine Street had failed, so the steam fire engines had little or no water to use in fighting the blaze. The only salvation now seemed to be Lake Michigan in the east, where the fire would necessarily stop. This natural barrier was some 4 miles from the fire's origin on De Koven Street.

LOOTING AND DRUNKENNESS IN THE FACE OF DISASTER. As the Great Chicago Fire advanced, chaos broke out in the city. Distraught citizens poured into the streets. The owners of saloons, fearing that the advancing crowds would ransack their establishments, rolled barrels of whiskey into the streets, where the assembled crowds drank freely from them. Soon the streets were filled with drunkards, many of whom thought that the end of the world was nigh.

Soon wholesale looting began as the less honest of the spectators broke into shops and residences, taking from them anything of value that they could carry away. Some of these miscreants, running away with their loot, misjudged the extent and speed of the fire and were burned in their tracks as they tried to escape.

It was not until October 11 that Lieutenant General Philip Sheridan led five companies of infantry, which had been rushed from Omaha and Fort Leavenworth, into the city where, declaring martial law, they were accorded all of the authority of the police department. The city's most respected citizens welcomed Sheridan and his troops after living for three days in a lawless and chaotic environment. These troops maintained order in the city for the next two weeks.

The imposition of martial law was deemed necessary because, although there was little left in the city to loot, many citizens feared that professional criminals and confidence men might flood into town trying to rifle buried safes and vaults and trying to exploit the homeless. Some thoughtful citizens, however, feared that it was dangerous to place a city under martial law in peacetime because soldiers had not been trained to deal with urban populations. They had been schooled to deal with enemies, and it was feared that they might now, under martial law, act as though innocent citizens were the enemies.

END OF THE FIRE. On the morning of October 10, the fire was beginning to burn itself out. At its northeastern extreme, it had been stopped by Lake Michigan. On the morning of the 10th, a steady rain fell upon the city, quenching most of the lingering flames.

As survivors straggled along the shores of Lake Michigan trying to find friends and family, they found that people, blackened by the smoke, were virtually unrecognizable. Many who had fled toward the lake as the flames moved in an easterly direction sought refuge on the beaches, but these beaches became so overheated that the only way for people to survive was to immerse themselves in the freezing waters of the lake, sometimes staying immersed for hours.

The morning was brisk and damp. Survivors of the fire huddled in shock in a cemetery near Lake Michigan that had recently been emptied of its corpses so that a park, eventually to become Lincoln Park, could be built. As they began to take stock, they realized not only that some 250 lives had been lost and many of the city's business establishments and residences destroyed but also that art museums, archives, public records, libraries, and other valuable and irreplaceable assets had been lost to the flames.

Much personal property entrusted to bank vaults for safekeeping

The corner of Dearborn and Monroe Streets after the Great Chicago Fire.

had been destroyed. The Federal Building at the northwest corner of Dearborn and Monroe Streets, which housed a major post office and a customs house, was no more. Inside it, over $1 million in currency had been incinerated. It is not surprising that some people thought Chicago could not rise from its ashes, but those who thought the matter through realized that its ideal location as an inland port would assure its endurance as a city of considerable note.

Aftermath. Remarkably, despite the massive havoc that the Great Chicago Fire wreaked, the city's infrastructure remained virtually intact. The water and sewer systems continued to operate, despite the temporary disabling of the Chicago Waterworks during the fire. Transportation facilities, both ports and railways, still connected Chicago with the rest of the country.

Had the sewer system been destroyed by the fire, epidemics might have broken out. Had the water system been severely compromised, the city would have been brought to its knees. As it turned out, however, Chicago was in an excellent position to rebuild. Before rebuilding, however, the legislature would pass ordinances that imposed stringent building codes upon those who were to reconstruct the city.

One of the outcomes of the fire was the election the next month of Joseph Medill as mayor of Chicago. Medill ran on a platform of stricter building codes and fire prevention and won handily, although one might question the validity of the vote—voting records had been lost in the fire so that allowing people to vote was a matter of faith. People who showed up at the polls and claimed to be registered voters were permitted to vote as long as they met two requirements: They had to be male and they had to be or appear to be of age.

The central business district of Chicago was laid waste by the fire. This main part of the city was built south and west of the Chicago River and extended as far as the railroad that ran along Lake Michigan to the east. Besides being the city's main shopping district, with its array of department stores and specialty shops, it was the home of a number of national corporations and of the renowned Chicago Board of Trade. This part of the city was now a shambles. A total of 3,650 buildings were destroyed in the central part of the city alone. Some 1,600 stores went up in flames, and 60 factories that employed thousands of people were totally destroyed. Temporary headquarters had to be set up for many businesses as plans were made to rebuild, this time with structures that passed the strict new fire codes that had been put into place as a result of the recent disaster. Six thousand temporary structures were quickly erected to house the thousands of homeless and to provide at least minimal shelter for the businesses whose buildings had been destroyed.

The elegant north side of Chicago accommodated almost 14,000 dwellings before the fire, ranging from the lakeside mansions of the rich to the humble cottages of those who served them. This section of town incurred the most substantial damage from the fire. When the flames had subsided, only 500 structures were left standing.

REBUILDING CHICAGO. Before long, a postfire building boom was under way. Such architects as Dankmar Adler, Daniel H. Burnham, and Louis H. Sullivan worked tirelessly to create a new Chicago that would be the architectural envy of the rest of the nation. The Home Insurance Company Building, opened in 1885, was the first of many steel-frame skyscrapers to be built. Within the next decade, 21 new steel-frame buildings ranging from twelve to sixteen stories in height graced the downtown area, which now has some of the highest buildings in the world, including the famed Sears Tower that rises more than a hundred stories above the street.

As an aftermath of the fire, Chicago's public transportation system also underwent a great revitalization. Trams—horse-drawn, cable-drawn, and electric—began to appear on city streets. The elevated train, which serves thousands of commuters every day, was erected to provide rapid transportation to the Loop.

Within three years of the fire, Chicago had rebuilt sufficiently to regain its stature as the preeminent city in the midwestern United States. Workers poured into the devastated city to help rebuild it. It was not unusual to see hundreds of new houses being built simultaneously in a given area. About 100,000 construction workers raced to build some 10,000 houses as quickly as they could.

R. Baird Shuman

FOR FURTHER INFORMATION:

Balcavage, Dynise. *The Great Chicago Fire.* Philadelphia: Chelsea House, 2002.

Bales, Richard F. *The Great Chicago Fire and the Myth of Mrs. O'Leary's Cow.* Jefferson, N.C.: McFarland, 2002.

Lewis, Lloyd, and Henry Justin Smith. *Chicago: The History of Its Reputation.* New York: Harcourt Brace Jovanovich, 1992.

Lowe, David, ed. *The Great Chicago Fire: In Eyewitness Accounts and Seventy Contemporary Photographs and Illustrations.* New York: Dover, 1979.

Murphy, Jim. *The Great Fire.* New York: Scholastic, 1995.

Pauly, John J. "The Great Chicago Fire as a National Event." *American Quarterly* 36 (Fall, 1985): 668-683.

Sawislak, Karen. *Smoldering City: Chicagoans and the Great Fire, 1871-1874.* Chicago: University of Chicago Press, 1995.

Waskin, Mel. *Mrs. O'Leary's Comet! Cosmic Explanations for the Great Chicago Fire.* Chicago: Academy Chicago, 1984.

■ 1872: The Great Boston Fire

Fire

Date: November 9-10, 1872
Place: Boston, Massachusetts
Result: 13 dead, 776 buildings destroyed, $75 million in damage

The Great Boston Fire originated in the basement of a warehouse on the corner of Kingston and Summer Streets near the bottom of an elevator shaft that extended to the attic. The warehouse was about 72 feet high, including a wooden mansard roof, and covered an area of 50 by 100 feet. As soon as the flames entered the shaft, they were carried upwards with tremendous convective force and burst through the roof shortly afterward.

The fire spread from the original building throughout the downtown area of the city by five major mechanisms. The primary mechanism of fire spread was from roof to roof by firebrands. A firebrand is a piece of burning material from a building that is carried by convective forces, such as wind, to a nearby building. The firebrands would land on the flammable wooden mansard roofs of adjacent buildings and spread the fire. The second method of fire spread was large tongues of flame that burst through window openings and spread the fire across narrow streets. Third, gas mains exploded in buildings and started new fires in adjacent buildings. It was not until hours into the fire that the gas mains were finally turned off. Fourth, heat was transferred by radiation from buildings on fire across the narrow streets. The fifth means of fire spread was explosions used by untrained personnel in an attempt to make firebreaks.

From Summer Street the fire raged north, consuming large areas of Franklin, Milk, Water, and State Streets before being stopped at the doors of historic Faneuil Hall. To the east it spread rapidly along High and Purchase Streets, destroying the waterfront area. The help of fire departments from 30 cities from as far away as New Haven, Connecticut, and Biddeford, Maine, was needed to bring the fire under control. This finally happened at 4 P.M. on Sunday, when it reached Washington, Broad, and State Streets because the engines

The Great Fire at Boston, November 9 & 10th 1872, *by Currier & Ives.* (Library of Congress)

could draw their water supply directly from the large water mains located there. A large number of water streams could finally be directed at the tops of the burning buildings with adequate pressure to reach the mansard roofs and penetrate through the windows into the interior of the buildings to extinguish the fire.

The factors that contributed to the conflagration can be placed into four major categories: urban planning and infrastructure, building and construction, natural factors, and fire service.

The streets were very narrow, with relatively tall buildings on all sides. Fire can spread across the narrow openings by convection and radiation once one building is fully involved in a fire. The height of the buildings limited the angle at which hose streams could be projected at them.

There was an insufficient water supply in the district where the fire occurred. The area had originally been a residential neighborhood, and the water mains and hydrants were drastically undersized for the amount of combustibles present in the warehouses. Water reservoirs were located under some of the streets, but their capacity was not adequate either. The hoses and hydrants had couplings of different sizes, which prevented the many fire departments assisting in the fire from coupling directly to the hydrants without using adapters. The pipes, which were only 6 inches in diameter to begin with, were restricted to 5 inches in diameter due to corrosion in the aging pipes. The hose streams projected at the buildings could not reach the upper stories or the roofs because of the limited pressure and the older-style hydrants. This was a major factor in the spread of the fire. Once an adequate quantity and pressure of water were available, the fire could be extinguished.

The mansard roofs were constructed of wood rather than the stone of the French buildings from which they were copied. The wood frame on the roof presented a large combustible surface to the fire, allowing it to spread rapidly above the heads of the firefighters. Wood trim around windows and doors, as well as timber floors, contributed combustible material to the fire. The granite veneers used on many buildings heated up and broke off or split apart, and the facades collapsed as the veneers separated from the main structure. The warehouse buildings were large, open-plan structures that were filled with great amounts of flammable contents. Compartmentation of the warehouses would have reduced the spread of the fire within the buildings.

Another problem was the warehouses' continuous vertical openings from the basement of the buildings to the roof. Once a fire begins in an open shaft, convective forces will naturally push the fire upwards. The fire will then spread onto intervening floors, moving horizontally as well as vertically, finally penetrating the roof.

Natural factors also existed. There was a 5- to 9-mile-per-hour wind the evening of the fire. Currents of air created by the fire gave the appearance of a firestorm or fierce wind. Large amounts of oxygen were drawn into the fire, creating local convective currents.

There was a critical delay in sounding the alarm for the fire because the policemen were between shifts. This allowed enough time for the fire to become fully developed in the building of origin before fire department personnel arrived on the scene. Many of the horses used to pull the fire engines were sick, and the engines and pumpers had to be pulled by firefighters from the stations to the fire. The firefighters became fatigued after fighting the fire for over twenty-five hours. The chief engineer could not command the entire fire front on foot.

As a result of the hearings held after the fire, the department was reorganized and placed under the Board of Fire Commissioners. All companies in high-value areas were staffed with full-time personnel. A number of new companies, including a fireboat company, were placed in service. Modern equipment was purchased, and additional hydrants were installed on larger pipes to improve water pressure. The fire-alarm system was transferred to the fire department, and district chief positions were made permanent. The board instituted a training program and a separate maintenance department.

In 1871 a bureau for the survey and inspection of buildings was established as the first agency to regulate building in Boston. Its authority was greatly expanded after the fire. Strict regulations were put into effect with regard to the thickness of walls and the materials to be used on the exposed portions of buildings. The fire service was reorganized. Boston thus entered the modern age of fire protection for its citizens after learning a valuable lesson in fire prevention from the disaster of 1872.

Gary W. Siebein

FOR FURTHER INFORMATION:

Bugbee, James M. "Fires and Fire Departments." *The American Review,* July, 1873, 112-141.

Coffin, Charles Carleton. *The Story of the Great Fire in Boston, November 9 to 10, 1872.* 1872, Reprint. Whitefish, Mont.: Kessinger, 2005.

Lyons, Paul R. *Fire in America!* Boston: National Fire Protection Association, 1976.

Sammarco, Anthony Mitchell. *The Great Boston Fire of 1872.* Dover, N.H.: Arcadia, 1997.

Schorow, Stephanie. *Boston on Fire: A History of Fires and Firefighting in Boston.* Beverly, Mass.: Commonwealth Editions, 2006.

1878: The Great Yellow Fever Epidemic

Epidemic

Date: August 13-October 29, 1878
Place: Memphis, Tennessee
Result: Over 100,000 cases of yellow fever, over 20,000 dead in the lower Mississippi Valley

The summer of 1878 was wet and hot in the lower Mississippi Valley. The climate provided the ideal breeding grounds for the *Aedes aegypti* mosquito, which dwelt up and down the Mississippi River. The female *Aedes aegypti* mosquito is the carrier, or vector, of the yellow-fever disease. When the female mosquito bites a person whose blood contains the yellow fever virus, subsequent bites infect susceptible individuals. However, in 1878, yellow fever, also known as Yellow Jack or the yellow plague, was still a mysterious disease of unknown cause. Yellow fever is endemic to West Africa, and it traveled to the Americas aboard trading ships importing slaves from Africa. With the open water casks on the ships, the mosquitoes easily survived the ocean crossings. Yellow fever then flourished wherever its vector could—where the temperature remained above 72 degrees Fahrenheit and where there was still water for the female mosquito to lay eggs.

The symptoms of yellow fever appear three to six days after the bite of an infected mosquito and range from mild, flulike symptoms to a severe, three-stage course of infection. Most Africans and their descendants exhibit mild to moderate symptoms of headache, fever, nausea, and vomiting. However, most victims recover within a few days. For Caucasians, Native Americans, and Asians, the first stage of the infection begins with a fever of 102 to 105 degrees Fahrenheit. The fever lasts three to four days and is accompanied by severe headache, backache, nausea, and vomiting. It is during this first stage that the patient is infectious and can pass the virus to a mosquito. In the second stage, which may last only a few hours, a remission of the fever

occurs, the headache disappears, and the patient feels better. Thereafter, in the third stage, the temperature rises rapidly again and the pulse rate drops. The first-stage symptoms recur but in a more severe form. Liver injury from the infection disrupts normal blood clotting, and some patients vomit blood, or a black vomit, and may also bleed from the nose, gums, and spots on the skin. Jaundice from liver and renal failure may yellow the skin, but the color is seldom as pronounced as the name "yellow fever" may suggest. Liver, heart, and renal failure often result in delirium. Most deaths occur on the sixth or seventh day after the reappearance of symptoms. Survivors remain ill for another seventeen to thirty days.

Reports of outbreaks of yellow fever in North American port cities began to appear in the late seventeenth century. The plagues in northern port cities, such as New York and Philadelphia, occurred only in the summer because the *Aedes aegypti* mosquito does not survive after a frost. It was in the tropical climates of the southern United States that the mosquito flourished and caused repeated epidemics. New Orleans' first reported epidemic occurred in 1796, and over the next century epidemics occurred regularly. Once people knew of the devastation of yellow fever, they lived in dread of its return. For people of the nineteenth century, the greatest fear of yellow fever came from a fear of the unknown—how it came about and how it was spread. What was known about yellow fever was that once it entered a city, it spread rapidly and easily among the people.

YELLOW FEVER STRIKES MEMPHIS. Before the Civil War, Memphis had a population of 22,000. By 1878, the population had risen to 48,000. At that time, Memphis was a major hub of cotton production in the United States. The city was located on the Mississippi River—a major trade route—and had three railroad lines. Yellow fever was no stranger to the citizens of Memphis. It had visited Memphis three times before, killing 75 people in 1855, 250 people in 1867, and 2,000 in 1873. As the city grew, the people realized that the attacks of yellow fever were growing worse. Although the disease was not spread from person to person by direct contact, it was understood that people fleeing from a city where yellow fever had struck could spread the disease to another community. Realizing that yellow fever patients must be isolated from other patients, staff members of a British hospital dressed the segregated patients in gowns with yellow patches to warn of their disease. The patients were nicknamed "Yellow Jackets" and the yellow flag flown over the quarantined area was known as the "Yellow Jack." Cities would also attempt to prevent escapees from other diseased communities from entry and prohibit their own inhabitants from entering affected areas.

When outbreaks of yellow fever in the West Indies, islands involved in trade with cities along the Mississippi River, were reported in the late spring of 1878, Memphis began to fear the possibility of another epidemic. Physicians and board of health members argued for quarantine measures. The city council rejected the quarantine so as not to interfere with Memphis's lucrative trade. In protest, the president of the Memphis board of health resigned his position. Outbreaks of yellow fever were reported in New Orleans by late July; however, a Memphis newspaper reassured the public that the sanitary conditions of the streets and private premises would prevent the arrival of the disease as long as the sanitary laws were enforced. When yellow fever was reported in Vicksburg, only 240 miles away from Memphis, on July 27, Memphis established quarantine stations for goods and people from cities south of Memphis on the Mississippi River.

On August 1, 1878, William Warren, a hand on a quarantined steamboat, slipped into Memphis and stopped at a restaurant located in Front Row along the Mississippi River. This small establishment was run by Kate Bionda and her husband, whose main trade was to cater food and drink to riverboat men. On August 2, William Warren became sick and was admitted to the city hospital. His illness was diagnosed as yellow fever, and he was moved to a quarantine hospital on President's Island, where he died on August 5.

Fear began to spread through Memphis as rumors of the riverboat hand's death multiplied, and on August 9, yellow fever was reported in the city of Grenada, Mississippi—only 90 miles south of Memphis. Again, newspapers tried to calm the public, cautioning them to avoid patent medicines and bad whiskey and to be cheerful and laugh as much as possible. By this time, Kate Bionda, age thirty-four, had become ill. On August 13, in her rooms above the snack shop, she died. A physician saw her, noted her symptoms and her jaundice and, after consulting with other physicians, diagnosed her as the first official case of yellow fever in Memphis in 1878.

On August 14, an additional 55 cases of yellow fever were announced. By August 15 and 16, the city of Memphis was in full panic. Thousands of people began to leave the city. There were processions of wagons piled high with possessions. Railroad companies attached extra cars, yet these were not enough for all of the people trying to flee the city. The city council members fled, and one-third of the police force deserted the city.

By August 17, four days after Kate Bionda's death, more than 25,000 people, over half the population of Memphis, had fled the city. However, news of the Memphis epidemic had spread just as swiftly. Other communities established quarantines against those coming from Memphis. Barricades were enforced with shotguns. Railroad trains from Memphis were refused by many cities, and refugees on riverboats were forced to stay on board for months as port after port denied them permission to land.

The refugees camped in forests and fled to small towns along the Mississippi River as well as to St. Louis, Louisville, Cincinnati, East Tennessee, and Virginia. Many did carry the yellow-fever virus, and over 100 Memphis citizens died outside the city. When the infected refugees entered areas where the *Aedes aegypti* mosquito lived, they continued the spread of the disease.

Of the 20,000 citizens who remained in Memphis, approximately 14,000 were African Americans and 6,000 were Caucasians. Through the first half of September of 1878, at least 200 people died per day. Survivors of the epidemic described some of the terrible conditions in the city. Carts would be loaded with 8 or 9 corpses in rough-hewn boxes, and the coffins were piled in tiers on the sidewalk in front of the undertaker's shop. Entire families were wiped out, and many victims died alone, covered with the black vomit characteristic of the disease.

Survivors recalled sights of piles of burned clothing and bedding outside houses—each a reminder that someone had died there. At first funeral bells tolled continuously, but the custom was suspended so as not to upset the sick and the dying. The stillness in the streets was occasionally broken by loud blasts of gunpowder, and at night burning tar barrels lit the streets—both futile attempts to clear the air of yellow fever. The weather remained unseasonably hot and humid for September and October, and ironically, one newspaper editor remarked that the mosquitoes were as vigorous and desperate as ever.

The African American population, which is usually resistant to the disease, also succumbed to the infection as never before. More than 11,000 African Americans in Memphis were infected, approximately 77 percent of their population. Of those infected, 946 died—a 10 percent mortality rate, considerably higher than in other epidemics. For Caucasians, the mortality rate was around 70 percent, with more than 4,000 deaths among the 6,000 that remained in the city. Other states quickly sent supplies and funds.

AID TO THE VICTIMS. Volunteer agencies arose to take care of the government and of the sick. The Citizen's Relief Committee was formed, composed mostly of prominent and wealthy citizens. Their first act was to establish a camp outside the city in an effort to remove any uninfected persons. About 1,000 persons occupied Camp Joe Williams, named for a Memphis physician who died of yellow fever in 1873, and only a few people died in the camp. The committee also assumed command of what remained of the police force. Under command of the African American janitor and cook, thirteen other African Americans were added to the police force. Fear of looting prompted them to call up the local militia, with both white and black companies guarding the city. Because business and commercial activity had ceased, people began to fear starvation. With donations of money and supplies from Memphis and elsewhere, the committee set up a welfare and rations program.

The difficult task of medical care was assumed by the Howard Association. Formed in Memphis in 1867, it was patterned after a similar group founded in New Orleans during the yellow fever epidemic of 1837. Its membership was composed mostly of businessmen, and its sole task was to serve in yellow fever epidemics. The members met on the day of Mrs. Bionda's death and assembled a corps of nearly 3,000 nurses and 111 physicians. Seventy-two of those physicians came from other states, because physicians in Memphis had enormous loads of patients. To treat yellow fever, many physicians relied on heavy medication, such as purges of calomel, rhubarb, or jalap (a plant root). Others used cold bath treatments, dousing the patients with cold water and then covering them with blankets to induce perspiration.

Most physicians, however, came to realize they could not cure yellow fever but could only alleviate its symptoms. Deeply frustrated, most Memphis physicians could only reduce fevers with sponge baths, alleviate warm chills with blankets, and give medicine to calm delirium. Few patients were admitted to hospitals as there were not enough beds for the thousands who were sick. Most of the sick were cared for in their homes by nurses. Both Caucasian and African American, male and female, most of the nurses were residents of Memphis. Nursing was not yet a recognized profession, and their function was mainly to sit with the patient. Much criticism was directed at the nurses. Although their motives ranged from a selfless devotion to the sick to a desire to make money, reports of theft, drinking, and misconduct by the nurses were common.

Despite physical and mental exhaustion, the physicians made attempts to understand the disease and performed about 300 autopsies. Yet afterward, they knew no more than they had before except that they probably had been confronted by a new and deadlier strain of the virus. More than 60 percent of these physicians gave their lives caring for the victims of the epidemic.

When the frosts of October 18 and 19 came, so did a decrease in the rate of yellow fever infection. On October 29, 1878, eleven weeks after the first reported case, the epidemic was declared over. Those who had fled the city returned home, and on November 28, Thanksgiving Day, the city held a mass meeting to praise the heroes of the epidemic, to thank the nation for its assistance, and to mourn their dead.

THE RESULTS OF THE EPIDEMIC. The yellow fever epidemic of 1878 had begun in New Orleans. It traveled up the Mississippi River to Vicksburg, then to Memphis, and to Cairo, Illinois, eventually reaching St. Louis. It was carried up the Tennessee River to Chattanooga, and up the Ohio River to Louisville and Cincinnati. Throughout the Mississippi Valley, over 100,000 had yellow fever, and more than 20,000 died. It was Memphis with its large population that felt the worst impact, however. Of the fewer than 20,000 who remained in the city, over 17,000 had yellow fever. Of the 14,000 African Americans, roughly 11,000 contracted the disease and 946 died. Of the 6,000 Caucasians, 4,204 died of yellow fever.

The future of Memphis was now in doubt, as it was considered an incurable pesthole. The value of lives lost was incalculable. Loss of trade was estimated as high as $100 million. Some outsiders suggested that the city be abandoned. However, under the direction of a new and more powerful board of health, Memphis began to clean itself up and accomplished remarkable improvements in public sanitation, with the creation of a waste-disposal system, approved water supply, street-paving program, and rigid health ordinances. Although still unaware of the cause of the disease, these cleanup measures did reduce the risk of yellow fever by eliminating the open sewers and outside privies where the mosquitoes bred.

The epidemic of 1878 also generated widespread interest in public health. The U.S. Congress instituted the National Board of Health, and a full-scale research program was also prompted by the epidemic. However, it would be another twenty-two years before members of the U.S. Army Yellow Fever Commission would discover that yellow fever was transmitted by the *Aedes aegypti* mosquito and that the agent of the disease was a virus.

The impact of the epidemic would be felt by Memphis for many years. The population had declined drastically, many businesses left the city, and others were dissuaded from moving to Memphis. Meanwhile, other cities such as Atlanta and Birmingham attracted new wealth and population in the South. Yet the city of Memphis would not forget the devastation of the 1878 epidemic nor the heroes who stayed to help its victims. Dr. John Erskine was the Memphis Health Officer in 1878. His fearlessness and tireless work to treat the plague victims were inspirational to his fellow physicians, yet he himself died of yellow fever. In 1974, the city of Memphis named one of its libraries in his memory and filled its shelves with accounts of the city's health disasters and triumphs. In 1990, St. Jude Children's Hospital in Memphis established an annual lectureship to honor his memory.

Mary Bosch Farone

FOR FURTHER INFORMATION:

Bloom, Khaled J. *The Mississippi Valley's Great Yellow Fever Epidemic of 1878.* Baton Rouge: Louisana State University Press, 1993.

Crosby, Molly Caldwell. *The American Plague: The Untold Story of Yellow Fever, the Epidemic That Shaped Our History.* New York: Berkley, 2006.

Gehlbach, Stephen H. *American Plagues: Lessons from Our Battles with Disease.* New York: McGraw-Hill Medical Publishing, 2005.

Hall, Randal L. "Southern Conservatism at Work: Women, Nurses, and the 1878 Yellow Fever Epidemic in Memphis." *Tennessee Historical Quarterly* 56, no. 4 (Winter, 1997).

Oldstone, Michael B. A. *Viruses, Plagues, and History.* New York: Oxford University Press, 1998.

Pierce, John R., and Jim Writer. *Yellow Jack: How Yellow Fever Ravaged America and Walter Reed Discovered Its Deadly Secrets.* Hoboken, N.J.: John Wiley & Sons, 2005.

1880: The Seaham Colliery Disaster

Explosion

Date: September 8, 1880
Place: Sunderland, England
Result: 164 dead

Under the rolling countryside of Durham County, located in the northeast corner of England, rested great coal fields. Evidence suggested that the early Romans who occupied England mined and burned coal in this region. The first recorded report of coal mining, however, came in the twelfth century. In 1183, Bolden Buke wrote of a coal miner providing coal for use at the ironworks of Coundon, a town located in Durham County. In the western part of the Durham coalfield, the coal seams were close to the surface of the earth and were relatively easy to mine. Most of the early mines were located along the bank of the Tyne River.

THE EXPLOSION. Coal mining in northeast England included a long history of disasters. One of the worst disasters occurred at Seaham Colliery on September 8, 1880. "Colliery" is the British term for "mine." Seaham Colliery, located near Durham and Sunderland, consisted of five seams of coal, one on top of another. These seams were between 38 and 600 yards below the surface. Three separate shafts connected the seams to the surface. The explosion occurred at 2:20 A.M., and it was loud enough to be heard by people on ships in the harbor and at a neighboring mine. Clouds of dust blowing skyward spewed from the shafts. The first people to arrive at the scene discovered that all three shafts of the mine were blocked. Cages used to raise and lower men from the mine were fastened in each shaft, blocking them.

A rope was tied around Mr. Stratton, a mine supervisor, and he was lowered a small distance down into the main seam. Although he was unable to proceed very far, he could hear men talking in the highest seam; they were believed to be safe and were later recovered alive. At

the time of the explosion, roughly 230 men and boys were working in the mine. In 1880, it was against the law for boys younger than twelve years of age to work in mines.

Initial rescue attempts were hampered by the debris in the shafts. Twelve hours went by before volunteers could be lowered into the shafts. A kibble, an iron bucket, was used because the cages were out of action. The main rescue work was conducted from what was called the High Pit shaft. From this shaft, 48 men were rescued alive and brought up in the kibble, while 19 survivors were brought up from the Low Pit shaft. Therefore, by midnight, twenty-one hours after the explosion, 67 men had been rescued alive. Tragically, 164 men and boys, some as young as fourteen, died in the explosion; 181 pit ponies, which were used to haul coal underground, were also killed.

Vast scenes of destruction met the rescue teams when they were finally able to reach the lower seams. Piles of stones were mixed with the mutilated bodies of miners and pit ponies. Several fires burning near the shafts needed to be put out before rescue attempts could continue. The potential for new explosions remained an ever-constant danger. As bodies were recovered, they were wrapped in flannel and canvas and numbered. Each miner's lamp was placed with his body, which was then transported to the surface by the kibble. Since the lamps were numbered, they aided in the process of identifying the bodies. Recovering the bodies was a slow and difficult procedure. By October 1, 1880, 136 bodies had been recovered. The final body was not retrieved until a full year after the explosion occurred.

INQUIRY AND OUTCOMES. In the seven months following the explosion, the Londonary Institute conducted an official inquiry. An official report was presented to Parliament in 1881. Two different theories were proposed regarding the cause of the explosion. The first theory stated that stones fell and released gases, which came into contact with a miner's safety lamp and triggered the explosion. The second theory focused on shots fired in the mine where holes were being enlarged. In the final report, the jury that studied the findings of the inquiry did not designate which theory was the actual cause. The report also stated that the issues of firing shots and clearing the dry coal dust, also considered a possible contributing factor to mine explosions, were best left to the mine managers.

The miners were unhappy that the report did not push for further study into the dangers of firing shots in mines and the presence of dry coal dust. Through their lawyer, Atherley Jones, the Miners Association—a union—requested that experimental chemists test the Seaham Colliery's coal dust. The miners' request was granted, and a series of experiments was initiated by Sir Frederick Abel at the Institute of Chemistry. Professor Abel amassed a document that included results of experiments conducted by him, as well as experiments from other countries. His work stressed the potential danger caused by large amounts of dry coal dust lying around. Despite this evidence, no new laws regarding mine safety were enacted until 1887.

Louise Magoon

FOR FURTHER INFORMATION:

McCutcheon, John. *Troubled Seams.* Reprint. Durham, England: County Durham Books, 1994.

Mitchell, William Cranmer. *A History of Sunderland.* Reprint. Manchester, England: E. J. Morten, 1972.

The New York Times, September 9-11, 1880.

Steinberg, S. H., and I. H. Evans, eds. *Steinberg's Dictionary of British History.* 2d ed. New York: St. Martin's Press, 1971.

Sunderland Daily Echo (England), September 8-10, 1880.

Wright, R. S. "Report on the Explosion Which Occurred at the Seaham Colliery on the 8th September 1880." *Durham Mining Museum.* http://www.dmm.org.uk/reports/2924-01.htm.

■ 1883: Krakatau Eruption

Volcano

Date: August 26-27, 1883
Place: Indonesia
Result: 36,417 dead, 165 villages and towns destroyed, 132 towns and villages damaged, two-thirds of island destroyed

In 1883, Krakatau (or Krakatoa) was a small, uninhabited island covered in lush vegetation. Lying in the Sunda Strait between Java and Sumatra, then part of the Dutch East Indies (now Indonesia), it was known to be volcanic but was thought to be extinct or at least insignificant. Native legends existed about an eruption there in 416 C.E., as well as a secondhand report from a Dutch official about another eruption in 1680, but the 1680 eruption was not widely reported and had been virtually forgotten by 1883.

Thus on May 20, 1883, when windows rattled and a noise like cannon fire was heard in the capital city of Batavia (now Jakarta) on Java, almost 100 miles away, no one's first thought was that the source was Krakatau. Some people thought they were experiencing an earthquake, but the noise was not coming from the ground. A volcanic eruption was then suspected, but still no one thought the source was Krakatau; when it was discovered that the volcano Karang, a much larger volcano than Krakatau in western Java, was not erupting, the thought was that perhaps one of the volcanoes across the strait in Sumatra was the source.

When some native fishermen reported to Dutch officials that they had been on Krakatau gathering wood and that while they were there an eruption had started beneath their feet, they were not believed at first. Reports soon came in to confirm their story: Krakatau was in eruption, producing clouds of steam, smoke, fire, and ash rising 6 or 7 miles high, along with lightning flashes, sulfurous fumes, and deposits of pumice on the surface of the sea.

The eruption cloud looked like "a giant cauliflower head," according to one eyewitness, the chaplain aboard the German warship *Elisabeth*, which was sailing through the Sunda Strait at the time. This wit-

ness also provided a striking account of the effect of ashfall; by May 21 it had turned a newly cleaned ship into something that looked "like a floating cement factory." All surfaces were covered with a gray, sticky dust more than 0.5 inch thick, which was aggravating to the eyes and lungs.

Ash continued to fall on the *Elisabeth* until it was more than 300 miles away. Ash also fell on other ships in the area and on the neighboring island of Verlaten (now Sertung), destroying the vegetation there. Vegetation on Krakatau itself was also destroyed. Ash fell as well on the two other islands in the Krakatau group, Lang (now Panjang) and Polish Hat, but did not destroy the vegetation there.

On May 22, the ship *Sunda* reported a heavy fall of ash when it was 7 miles from Krakatau; at a distance of 10 miles from the island it reported pieces of pumice floating in the sea, and at a distance of 30 miles the pumice was so thick that a bucket lowered into the sea came up filled almost entirely with pumice and hardly any water.

The May eruption caused no casualties and stimulated more interest than alarm. In fact, on May 27 a group of sightseers took a pleasure trip to the island and looked into the smoking crater of Perboewatan, one of Krakatau's three volcanic cones (the other two being Danan and Rakata). With steam billowing around them and explosions sounding periodically, some of the sightseers even clambered into the crater to pick up pieces of pumice and lava as souvenirs. One of them took photographs, the only ones that exist of Krakatau in eruption in 1883.

Volcanic activity decreased at the end of May but picked up again after mid-June. Explosions were heard on Java and Sumatra. One witness described a thick cloud of smoke and ash hanging over the volcano for five days in late June; when this cleared away, two dense columns of rising smoke could be seen. In mid-August, ships passing by Krakatau reported heavy ashfalls that turned the sky black, along with columns of smoke, rumbling noises, and flashes of lightning.

THE FIRST AUGUST ERUPTION. The eruption for which Krakatau is famous began early in the afternoon of Sunday, August 26, 1883. R. D. M. Verbeek, a Dutch geologist who later wrote the first full-length study of the eruption, reported that at 1:00 P.M. he heard a rumbling sound at his home in Buitenzorg (now Bogor), a town on Java about 100 miles from Krakatau. The director of the Batavia Observatory noted that the sound was first heard there at 1:06 P.M. At first it was mistaken for thunder and, as in May, even after residents realized that they were hearing a volcanic eruption, they assumed that some volcano other than Krakatau was producing the increasingly violent explosions.

Closer to Krakatau, there was no mistaking the sounds. The ship the *Charles Bal,* which passed within 10 miles of Krakatau, reported hearing explosions from the volcano that sounded like heavy artillery. The ship later reported "chains of fire" and white balls of fire at the volcano, along with continued explosive roars, choking sulfurous fumes, and a hail of pumice stone and ash which covered the decks to a thickness of 3 or 4 inches.

The captain of the *Medea,* 76 miles away, recorded two explosions from Krakatau at 2 P.M. that shook his ship, and he noted a black eruption cloud above the volcano, calculated to be 17 miles high. Later estimates put the height of the cloud at between 15 and 50 miles.

Reports from the Javanese port of Anjer, about 30 miles from the volcano across the Sunda Strait, noted that by 2 P.M. Krakatau was enveloped in smoke, and it had become so dark that people could not see their own hands. One witness said a column of steam rose above Krakatau, looking like thousands of large white balloons, and added that the sea looked agitated. Another witness said the eruption cloud kept shifting color between black and white; he, too, noticed the agitation of the sea, which he said was turning an inky black color. A third witness reported a fiery glare above the volcano and said that the explosions grew louder after nightfall. Houses shook, and panic set in. Residents of Anjer and other towns and villages gathered their belongings and prepared to flee.

There was panic even in Batavia. Even that far from Krakatau, the noise was so loud that the sound of the regular evening gun was almost inaudible. Doors and windows rattled, walls shook, and at 2 A.M. a powerful explosion knocked out the city's gas lighting system. Residents woke and rushed into the streets. However, there were very few casualties in Batavia. Most of the deaths occurred in coastal towns and villages closer to the volcano, and most were caused not directly by the eruption or the fall of ash and stone but from the massive tsunamis that ensued on Monday morning.

THE SECOND AUGUST ERUPTION. Overnight, ash continued to fall, and unusual electrical phenomena were reported on ships in the strait. The *Berbice*, about 50 miles to the west, reported hot ash falling, which burned holes in the sailors' clothes and the sails, and which was soon piled 3 feet deep on the deck. The ship was also struck by fireballs and flashes of lightning, and several members of the crew received electric shocks. On the *Gouverneur General Loudon*, 40 or 50 miles to the northwest, a mud rain fell, and lightning struck several times, creating phosphorescent effects (Saint Elmo's fire) on the masts and rigging. Saint Elmo's fire was also reported on the *Charles Bal*; its captain said "a peculiar pink flame came from fleecy clouds which seemed to touch the mast-heads and yard-arms." He also reported that the sky alternated between being pitch black one moment and ablaze with light the next.

It was not until after dawn on Monday, August 27 that the full force of Krakatau was felt. There had been numerous explosions before this, including a large one just after 5:00 P.M. on the 26th, but between dawn and 11:00 A.M. on the 27th there were four mammoth explosions (at 5:30, 6:44, 10:02, and 10:52) that dwarfed the earlier ones. The first three of these, especially the one at 10:02, were followed by tidal waves that caused most of the destruction associated with Krakatau.

Sometime between 6:00 and 6:30 A.M. a wave 33 feet high struck Anjer. The town was destroyed. All who did not flee died. The next day, a messenger sent to investigate returned from Anjer with the report that "there was no longer any such place." The houses and other buildings were gone, except for ruined remnants of the town fort;

the trees were all uprooted, except for a few leafless ones covered in ash; the Anjer lighthouse had vanished; and all the monuments in the town's cemetery had been washed away. The situation was summed up by one witness in a few brief words: "All gone," he wrote. "Plenty lives lost."

An even bigger wave struck at about 10:30 A.M. and destroyed the town of Merak, about 7 miles north of Anjer along the Java coast. All but 2 or 3 of the approximately 2,700 inhabitants died, even though many of them had taken shelter on a hill behind the town, where they had survived earlier waves. The 10:30 wave seems to have been higher at Merak than anywhere else, perhaps because of the funnel-shaped strait there formed by a tiny island just offshore. Estimates put the wave height at 135 feet; elsewhere the wave attained heights estimated at between 50 and 100 feet.

In Merak, as at Anjer, all the buildings vanished, except for the floor of the house of the resident engineer on top of the hill. The railroad line leading to the Merak quarry was torn up and twisted, and locomotives and railcars were battered and tossed aside. One locomotive was carried out to sea and lay 50 yards from the beach, a battered wreck with the waves breaking over it.

The area around Merak was similarly devastated. It was a "scene of desolation," according to one witness, who added: "For miles there was not a tree standing, and where formerly stood numerous campongs (native villages), surrounded by paddy fields and cocoanut

The island of Krakatau before the eruption of 1883. (Library of Congress)

groves, there was nothing but a wilderness, more resembling the bottom of the sea than anywhere else." He saw rocks of coral that the wave had deposited several miles inland, some of them weighing as much as 100 tons. Closer to Merak he noted remnants of bedding and furniture, along with shreds of clothing.

All together, in the Merak-Anjer area the death toll was set at 7,610. In the neighboring district of Tjiringin, another 12,022 perished, 1,880 of them in the town of Tjiringin, which was swept away by the 10:30 wave. Corpses lay on the ground in Tjiringin for days, and there was much looting.

SUMATRA. Parts of Sumatra, to the north of Krakatau, are closer to the volcano than Java and were directly in line with its blasts. In these areas, unlike the situation elsewhere, there were deaths from the volcano's hot ash and pumice in addition to deaths from the tidal waves. About 1,000 residents in the area north of Katimbang, on the southeast point of Sumatra 25 miles from Krakatau, died of burns; another 2,000 were burned but survived. The ash here struck not only from above but also, according to one witness, from below: spurting up like a fountain through cracks in the floor of the hut in which she had taken shelter on the slopes of Mount Radjah Bassa, north of Katimbang. Besides causing human casualties, the ash killed vegetation and, through its weight on roofs, destroyed many houses.

Even in Sumatra, however, most deaths were caused by the waves. Waves struck Katimbang as early as Sunday night, throwing small boats up on the shore. The whole town was washed away by the same wave that destroyed Anjer at 6:30 A.M. Monday.

Waves also struck farther west, at Teluk Betong on Lampong Bay, about 50 miles from Krakatau, beginning at 6:00 P.M. on Sunday, August 26. These early waves damaged a bridge and a pier and cast some boats on the shore. The real damage came the next day, primarily from the wave that struck at 10:30 A.M. Half an hour earlier the largest of Krakatau's eruptions had been heard in Teluk Betong; then ash and mud began to fall on the town, and it became dark as night, so dark that the effects of the wave that followed were not seen until the next day. Those who went to inspect then found only ruins, corpses, and iron government cash boxes. One witness described the scene by saying "there was no destruction. There was simply . . . nothing."

One of the most remarkable episodes in this area involved a

Dutch gunboat, the *Berouw*, which had been anchored in Teluk Betong harbor. Early Monday morning one of the big waves tore the *Berouw* from its moorings and carried it into the Chinese quarter of the town. The big wave at 10:30 A.M. lifted the *Berouw* again and deposited it almost 2 miles inland amid some palm trees. All 28 of its crew members died.

Altogether 2,260 people died in the Teluk Betong area, and it was difficult to send relief to the survivors because pumice in Lampong Bay made it impossible to reach the area by sea for weeks. However, amid all the devastation and suffering, one witness did note a positive result: All the mosquitoes in the area had been destroyed, by ash or mud.

SURVIVORS' TALES. In the midst of death and destruction, some people made miraculous escapes. The telegraph master at Anjer managed to outrun the tidal wave. "Never have I run so fast in my life," he said later, "for, in the most literal sense of the word, death was at my heels." An elderly Dutch pilot in Anjer told an even more remarkable tale. He was unable to outrun the wave but found himself swept by it into a palm tree. He stayed in the tree watching corpses float by him and later made his way to safety. One resident survived by riding on the back of an alligator. A Dutch auctioneer in a small village near Batavia survived by climbing on a dead cow that floated by, where he stayed until encountering a tree onto which he climbed. A Dutch official in Beneawang on Semangka Bay in Sumatra floated for hours, first on a shelf and then on a tree trunk, after his house collapsed around him.

AFTERMATH. In addition to the deaths and damage caused on Java and Sumatra, Krakatau caused much damage to itself. After the eruption, it was discovered that the northern two-thirds of the island had disappeared, apparently sunk beneath the sea. All that remained was a sheared-off part of one of the three volcanic cones, Rakata, and one tiny rock 10 yards square sometimes called by the name Bootsmanrots. The neighboring islet of Polish Hat also disappeared. On the other hand, the nearby island of Verlaten tripled in size due to rock landing on it from the volcano, and two new islands formed: Steers and Calmeyer. However, the latter two, being composed entirely of pumice, were washed away by the sea within months.

All plant and animal life on Krakatau seems to have perished in

A drawing of Krakatau in eruption. (National Oceanic and Atmospheric Administration)

the eruption, although some scientists have argued that seeds, insect larvae, and earthworms may have survived below ground. In any case, life did return to Krakatau fairly quickly: By 1889 plant life, bugs, and lizards were reported on the island.

Volcanic activity returned as well, in 1927, with the appearance of a new volcanic island where the northern two-thirds of the old island used to be. Anak Krakatau ("child of Krakatau"), occupying a small but growing portion of what used to be the northern part of Krakatau, has erupted periodically since its first appearance.

CAUSES OF THE WAVES. Besides the dispute over the survival of life after the eruption, there has been disagreement among scientists over the process that caused the massive tidal waves, or tsunamis, at Krakatau. Several theories have been put forward: that the pumice and other ejected materials landing on the water caused the waves, that some underwater explosion caused them, that they were caused by a "lateral blast" from the side of the volcano, that a pyroclastic flow of ash and heated volcanic gases was responsible, and that the collapse of two-thirds of the island into the sea produced the effect. The last view, which posits that by ejecting masses of material into the atmosphere Krakatau created a void beneath itself into which it eventually collapsed, seems to have the most support, but scientists remain divided because the evidence is inconclusive. One scientist, in discussing this issue, has remarked that Krakatau, though one of the best-known, is also one of the least-understood volcanic eruptions.

LONG-TERM AND LONG-RANGE EFFECTS. Even after the end of the eruptions, late at night on Monday, August 27, effects of Krakatau's blast continued to be felt. Darkness lingered for fifty-seven hours within 50 miles of the volcano and for twenty-two hours up to 125 miles away. Pumice choked the bays of Java and Sumatra until December and floated as far away as South Africa, nearly 5,000 miles distant, over the next two years. In the middle of the Indian Ocean, in December, 1883, the steamer *Bothwell Castle* encountered a vast field of pumice that stretched for 1,250 miles and was so thick upon the sea that the sailors were able climb onto it in some places and walk about.

The sounds of Krakatau also traveled to distant parts. In Singapore, over 500 miles from the volcano, vessels were sent out to investigate what sounded like the firing of a ship's guns. The explosion was also heard in Saigon (1,164 miles away), Borneo (1,235 miles away), Bangkok (1,413 miles away), Manila (1,800 miles away), and Ceylon (now Sri Lanka) and western Australia (up to 2,000 miles away). The most distant report came from Rodriguez Island in the Indian Ocean, 2,968 miles from the source of the blast. The waves produced by Krakatau also traveled long distances. High waves struck the coast of India on August 27, about 2,000 miles from the volcano. Tidal disturbances were also reported in New Zealand and even as far away as the English Channel.

The atmospheric effects of the eruption were among the most startling and long-lasting. Dust thrown up by Krakatau circled the globe and remained suspended in the atmosphere for two or three years. As a result, much of the globe was treated to spectacular, blood-red sunsets and a very odd-looking sun, which sometimes appeared blue or green. At times the sun also appeared with a pinkish halo around it; this halo, described at the time by the Reverend Sereno Bishop, has since been seen after other volcanic eruptions and is referred to as Bishop's ring.

Blue suns were reported in September in the Virgin Islands, Peru, and points in between. A green sun was reported in Hawaii, Panama, and Venezuela. In November the fire departments of Poughkeepsie, New York, and New Haven, Connecticut, were called out because a red glare in the sky convinced onlookers that a great fire was underway. There were so many fiery sunsets and brilliant after-sunset glows, especially in the winter of 1883-1884, that letters poured into the magazine *Nature*, which began a special department in its pages called "The Remarkable Sunsets."

Another probable consequence of the dust in the atmosphere was a cooling in the world's climate. There has been some scientific debate over this, but it is generally agreed that the volcanic dust reduced solar radiation reaching the earth by as much as 10 percent and that as a result world temperatures over the next three years dropped by 0.25 to 0.5 degrees Celsius. Cooler temperatures were especially noticeable in the Northern Hemisphere.

REPUTATION AND MISCONCEPTIONS. The 1883 eruption of Krakatau was one of the largest, loudest, and most devastating in recorded history. Perhaps as a result it captured the popular imagination, giving rise to numerous legends and erroneous reports. The very earliest newspaper stories contained wild statements about millions dying and sixteen volcanoes being in eruption. Years later, in 1969, Hollywood was equally inaccurate in producing a motion picture called *Krakatoa, East of Java* (Krakatau is west of Java).

It is also not true, at least according to the scientific consensus, that Krakatau blew off its top or decapitated itself and completely disappeared. Rather than blowing itself up into the air, Krakatau, as most scientists see it, collapsed into the sea. Moreover, not all of it disappeared; one-third of the original island survived.

The fact that Krakatau was uninhabited is also not widely known. It is true that Krakatau had been inhabited at earlier times in its history. Captain James Cook's ships landed at the island in the 1770's and discovered a village and cultivation; a village was also reported on the island in 1809, and there are reports of a penal settlement there. However, by the time of the eruption the island was completely deserted, except for local fishermen who occasionally visited it.

The popular view of volcanic destruction through ash and rock and fast-flowing lava also does not apply to Krakatau, which produced most of its deaths indirectly by tidal waves. On the other hand, the tidal waves resulted from volcanic processes; there was no simultaneous earthquake.

Finally, Krakatau was not located in some obscure, out-of-the-way region. On the contrary, it was right in the middle of a major shipping route, the Sunda Strait, not far from heavily populated coastal regions with access to the rest of the world by telegraph. It may be, in fact, that it is precisely because Krakatau was well connected to the rest of the world that its eruption has become world-famous.

Sheldon Goldfarb

FOR FURTHER INFORMATION:
Bullard, Fred M. *Volcanoes of the Earth.* 2d rev. ed. Austin: University of Texas Press, 1984.

Francis, Peter, and Clive Oppenheimer. *Volcanoes.* 2d ed. New York: Oxford University Press, 2004.

Francis, Peter, and Stephen Self. "The Eruption of Krakatoa." *Scientific American* 249, no. 5 (November, 1983): 172-187.

Scarth, Alwyn. *Vulcan's Fury: Man Against the Volcano.* New ed. New Haven, Conn.: Yale University Press, 2001.

Simkin, Tom, and Richard S. Fiske, eds. *Krakatau, 1883: The Volcanic Eruption and Its Effects.* Washington, D.C.: Smithsonian Institution Press, 1983.

Thornton, Ian. *Krakatau: The Destruction and Reassembly of an Island Ecosystem.* Cambridge, Mass.: Harvard University Press, 1996.

Winchester, Simon. *Krakatoa: The Day the World Exploded, August 27, 1883.* New York: HarperCollins, 2003.

Woolley, Alan, and Clive Bishop. "Krakatoa: The Decapitation of a Volcano." In *The Making of the Earth,* edited by Richard Fifield. New York: Basil Blackwell, 1985.

■ 1888: The Great Blizzard of 1888

Blizzard

Also known as: The Great White Embargo, the White Hurricane
Date: March 11-14, 1888
Place: Northeastern United States
Result: 400 dead, $7 million in property damage

The Great White Embargo, the Great Blizzard of 1888, the White Hurricane—whatever name the folklore legends give it, the March 11-14, 1888, snowstorm was one of the biggest to hit the northeastern United States. A roaring blizzard, sustained for four days by hurricane-force winds, extended from Maryland to Maine. It claimed 400 lives and caused $7 million in property damage. Two hundred boats off the coast and in harbors were swamped and sunk, taking the lives of about 100 seamen. Countless numbers of wild birds, animals, and livestock froze to death. New York was hardest hit, with 200 deaths reported there alone. The stock exchanges on Wall Street closed for three days.

The day before the blizzard, March 10, was unusually mild. At 9:30 P.M. the thermometer registered in the mid-50's. It had been the warmest day of the year, during one of the mildest winters in seventeen years. However, the following afternoon—Sunday, March 11—a drizzling rain turned to a downpour, and the temperature steadily fell.

If the meteorological equipment of the time had been more sophisticated, and communication between Washington, D.C., and New York more efficient than telegraph messages, perhaps the U.S. Signal Service's weather observatory in New York could have been warned about a severe storm brewing off the coast of Delaware. There, two massive weather systems were headed for collision. Frigid Arctic air, coming from northwestern Canada, was traveling south along the eastern coast of North America at 30 miles per hour. Warm, moisture-packed air from the Gulf of Mexico headed north, into the Arctic air. The two huge systems clashed, resulting in a winter hurricane saturated with moisture and fueled by violent winds. As the system turned to travel northwest, it picked up speed.

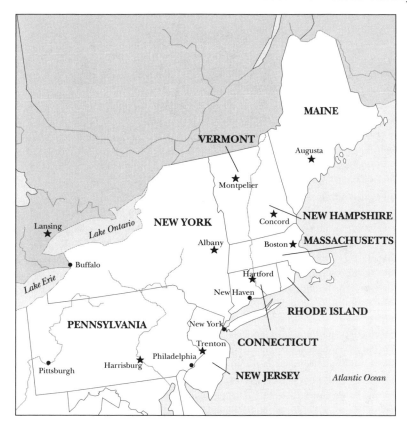

The first winds of the storm reached small craft and fishing boats on Chesapeake Bay late Sunday afternoon. The mercury plummeted, and the downpour quickly changed to a blinding wall of snow. Anchor cables on boats snapped, causing them to run aground or smash into each other. Vessels in the open waters were overtaken by the churning waters and sank. The storm, dubbed "The White Hurricane," moved from Chesapeake Bay north to Boston.

By midnight in New York, the rain had been replaced by snow, and the winds were gusting to 85 miles per hour. To qualify as a blizzard, the wind must blow at 35 miles per hour or more. During a hurricane, winds near the eye range from 74 miles per hour to as much as 150 miles per hour or more. The Great Blizzard of 1888 was virtually a hurricane with blizzard conditions. According to an eyewitness account from Arthur Bier, recorded in *Great Disasters* (Reader's Digest

Frank Leslie's Illustrated Newspaper *devotes an issue to the Great Blizzard of 1888 in New York City.* (Library of Congress)

Association, 1989), "The air looked as though some people were throwing buckets full of flour from all the roof tops," sometime after midnight on March 12, 1888.

DISASTER IN NEW YORK CITY. New Yorkers awaking Monday, March 12, found 10 inches of snowfall with drifts as high as 20 feet. In many areas one side of the street was blown free of snow, while the other side had snow piled to the second-story windows of buildings. Used to heavy snowfalls and trying to go about their business as usual, many New Yorkers bundled up against the weather and headed off to work. As the temperature continued to drop, and the snow showed no sign of letting up, the city slowly ground to a halt. Horse-drawn street cars struggled to remain on snow-covered tracks. The elevated trains ran very slowly, eventually coming to a standstill on frozen tracks. Commuters waited in vain, among the swirling snow and falling temperatures, on elevated-train platforms for trains that did not arrive. An estimated 15,000 passengers were stranded in the trains, elevated above the streets, across the city. With no way to get down they were at the mercy of enterprising "entrepreneurs" who carried ladders to the train cars but charged a steep fee of one dollar per passenger for the short climb down to the street. One train, stalled on the tracks between stations, was hit by another from behind. The collision killed an engineer and injured 20 passengers. Winds picked up to nearly 100 miles per hour. Abandoned streetcars were pushed over in these winds.

Fire stations were also immobilized. Many people tried lighting fires in their homes to keep warm. When the fires raged out of control, fire trucks could not reach the victims, and the raging winds spread the fire. Property damage from fire alone was estimated at several million dollars. Those left homeless or trying to survive with walls or roofs missing from wind or fire damage often succumbed to the elements and died of exposure.

The financial district on Wall Street actually shut down for three days, something unheard of even today, because only 30 of 1,100 members of the stock exchange showed up Monday morning. People braving the elements on foot were later found frozen to death in snowdrifts along the sidewalks. One such victim was George D. Barremore, a merchant from the financial district. Finding the elevated trains closed down, he decided to walk to work. He apparently collapsed in a snowdrift and froze only four blocks from his home.

Those who did make it to work found the buildings deserted and the return trip home too hazardous to make. Many people camped out in hotel or business lobbies. By Monday evening New York City was at a standstill. Thousands were stranded in a city with hotels so overcrowded that cots were set up in hallways and even bathrooms. Author Mark Twain was one such reluctant visitor. Having come in from Hartford, Connecticut, Twain is said to have sent word to his wife that he was "Crusoeing on a desert hotel." Some blizzard-tossed refugees found shelter on cots in the city's public buildings. One such location was the city's jails. At Grand Central Station an estimated 300 people slept on benches, since normal passenger traffic was immobilized. Business was brisk at pubs and places of entertainment, such as Madison Square Garden, where circus man P. T. Barnum performed to crowds of more than one hundred.

On Tuesday the East River was frozen. The ice bridge, connecting Manhattan and Queens, rarely formed because of the flowing waters of the river. Some adventurers bravely used the ice bridge as a shortcut between the two cities. When the tide changed, however, the ice bridge shattered, tossing some foolhardy travelers into the freezing waters of the river. Nearly 100 other adventurers were trapped on the ice floes and narrowly escaped with their lives.

On Tuesday afternoon the snow tapered off and the winds died down. By midday the thermometer began climbing from its 5-degree-Fahrenheit low. Wednesday, March 14, saw the snow yield to flurries. In the aftermath, a total of 20.9 inches had fallen, with drifts as high as 30 feet in Herald Square. This snowfall record would exist for at least the next sixty years.

OTHER LOCATIONS. New York saw light snowfall compared to other locations such as New Haven, Connecticut, which accumulated 45 inches. The driving winds there had also packed the snow into hardened drifts. Of the eastern cities, only Boston managed to avoid the worst of the storm. Alternating rain and sleet eventually led to an accumulated 12 inches of snow, but it did not bring the city to a standstill.

Traveling from Maryland to Maine, the Great Blizzard of 1888 affected one-quarter of the American population. High winds toppled telegraph poles from Washington, D.C., north to Philadelphia. Rail lines were blocked by the mangled cabling. In Philadelphia, freezing rain glazed the streets on March 12. When snow did fall, the ice-glazed streets were buried beneath 10 inches of drifts. Keene, New Hampshire, was blanketed in 3 feet of snow, and nearby Dublin received 42 inches. New York's state capital, Albany, received 47 inches, and Troy, New York, recorded 55 inches of snowfall—perhaps the largest amount of the Great Blizzard of 1888. City officials ordered paths plowed through the snow rather than having the snow completely removed. In New York City, men and boys eagerly worked at the drifts—using axes and picks on those of hard-packed snow—and earning between $2 and $10 for shoveling people out. An estimated 700 wagons and 1,000 workers cleared away the snow, dumping it along the piers of the Brooklyn Bridge. The public bill for the cleanup came to $25,000.

AFTERMATH. By Friday, New York City was that back to nearly normal. Bonfires lit to warm pedestrians, as well as the warming March sun, soon melted the mounds of snow piled alongside buildings and sidewalks. Cleaning up, restoring power, and counting the dead was a

A man stands next to a snow hut in Washington, D.C., following the Great Blizzard of 1888. (Library of Congress)

long task for the citizens. Melting snow revealed not only frozen bodies and dead animals but also heaps of debris discarded during the heavy snowfall. In areas outside New York hit by the blizzard, the melting snow revealed the bodies of thousands of dead birds, animals, and livestock.

The search for survivors was intense. In Brooklyn, at least 20 postal workers were pulled from the snow unconscious. New York's Republican Party leader, Roscoe Conkling, had collapsed in the snow from exhaustion. He became ill and died on April 18, making him the final victim of the White Hurricane.

Despite the devastation and loss of lives as a result of the Great Blizzard of 1888, it did have a positive impact on the largest cities shut down by the storm. To ensure that communications networks in the Northeast would never again be disrupted, the U.S. Congress decided that telegraph and telephone wires and public transit routes would be moved underground. Vulnerable gas lines and water mains, located above ground, were also redirected underground to safety. Within a quarter century, the subway systems for New York and Boston were proposed. New York's subway system was approved in 1894, with construction beginning in 1900.

Lisa A. Wroble

FOR FURTHER INFORMATION:

Allaby, Michael. *Dangerous Weather: Blizzards*. Rev. ed. New York: Facts On File, 2003.

Cable, Mary. *The Blizzard of '88*. New York: Atheneum, 1988.

Davis, Lee. *Natural Disasters: From the Black Plague to the Eruption of Mt. Pinatubo*. New York: Facts On File, 1992.

Erickson, Jon. *Violent Storms*. Blue Ridge Summit, Pa.: Tab Books, 1988.

Laskin, David. *The Children's Blizzard*. New York: HarperCollins, 2004.

Murphy, Jim. *Blizzard! The Storm That Changed America*. New York: Scholastic Press, 2000.

Ward, Kaari, ed. *Great Disasters*. Pleasantville, N.Y.: Reader's Digest Association, 1989.

Watson, Benjamin A. *Acts of God: "The Old Farmer's Almanac" Unpredictable Guide to Weather and Natural Disasters*. New York: Random House, 1993.

■ 1889: The Johnstown Flood

Flood

Date: May 31, 1889
Place: Johnstown, Pennsylvania
Result: About 2,209 dead, 1,600 homes lost, 280 businesses destroyed, $17 million in property damage

Strictly speaking, the Johnstown Flood of 1889 was not a natural disaster. Nature was only partly responsible; neglect and human error also contributed. Without the latter two, the disaster would not have occurred.

Flooding in the narrow valley of western Pennsylvania was a common occurrence, and while creating a certain amount of water damage in buildings, it also led to a casual attitude about these natural events. The great loss of life, however, was the result of a tremendous wave caused by the breaking of a dam 14 miles upstream from Johnstown.

JOHNSTOWN, PENNSYLVANIA. The first white settlers came to the valley around 1771, but the area was abandoned several times before it became a backwoods trading center. Population started growing when the canal system from Philadelphia to Pittsburgh was finished, and by 1889, ten thousand people lived in Johnstown, with a total of thirty thousand crowded in the narrow valley. Johnstown was built on a nearly level floodplain at the confluence of the Little Conemaugh and Stony Creek Rivers in Cambria County. In the early 1800's, Pennsylvania's canal system, when completed, had too little water in the summer to be usable; in 1836 the state legislature appropriated $30,000 for a reservoir dam on the South Fork River. The final cost was $240,000, and it was completed in 1852, six months before the Pennsylvania Railroad was built from Philadelphia to Pittsburgh, making the canal obsolete. The canal system was put up for sale in 1854 and in 1857 was bought by the Pennsylvania Railroad for $7.5 million.

In June, 1862, the dam broke after heavy rains. Little damage resulted downstream as the reservoir was only half-full, and a watchman had opened the valves and released much of the pressure before the break. The reservoir, then only about 10 feet deep, was abandoned until Congressman John Reilly bought it in 1875 for $2,500. Four years later he sold it to Benjamin F. Ruff, a onetime railroad tunnel contractor, coke salesman, and real-estate broker, for $2,000. Before selling it, Reilly removed the cast-iron discharge pipes and sold them for scrap.

The dam had been constructed according to the best engineering knowledge of the day. It was composed of layers of clay covered with an inner and outer coating of stones. A spillway, 72 feet wide, was cut at the eastern end of the rock of the mountain. The dam breast was more than 900 feet long and 20 feet wide, and the dam itself was 850 feet high with a 270-foot base, at the center of which were five cast-iron sluice pipes, each 2 feet in diameter and set into a stone culvert. These pipes were controlled from a nearby wooden tower. It was these sluice pipes which had been removed by Reilly, and the control tower burned in 1862.

In 1879, Ruff persuaded fifteen Pittsburgh men to buy shares in the venture, and on November 15 the South Fork Fishing and Hunting Club was chartered in Pittsburgh. Members, eventually numbering 61, included Andrew Carnegie; Henry Clay Frick, the coke king associated with him; several other Carnegie associates and officials; banker Andrew Mellon; Robert Pitcairn, the powerful head of the

Pittsburgh division of the Pennsylvania Railroad; and other industrial, commercial, and political leaders from Pittsburgh. Named president, Ruff boarded up one side of the stone culvert and dumped rock, mud, brush, hay, and anything else he found, including horse manure, into the hole left by the pipes; lowered the height of the dam several feet to provide a roadway wide enough for two carriages to be driven abreast on its top; installed a bridge over the spillway and under it a screen of iron rods to keep in the fish with which the lake was to be stocked; and built a clubhouse, boathouses, and stables. Sixteen members added private summer homes. Renamed Lake Conemaugh, 450 acres, 1 mile across and 2 miles long, it drained 60 square miles of mountainside, including many creeks, was 70 feet deep in the spring, and contained water weighing 20 million tons.

Watching this activity with some concern was Daniel J. Morrell, head of the Cambria Iron Works downstream, which had about $50 million invested in the valley. In November, 1880, Morrell sent John Fulton, an engineer and his designated successor, to look over the dam. Fulton's report, a copy of which Morrell sent to Ruff, noted that "repairs were not done in a careful and substantial manner, or with the care demanded in a large structure of this kind." He reported that the lake had no discharge pipe nor any other method to reduce or take the water out of the lake, and that it had been repaired badly, leaving a large leak at its center. In a brusque answer, Ruff maintained that there were no leaks, the weight of the water had been overestimated by Fulton, and the Iron Works was in no danger from the dam. He was later to declare that the "leaks" were springs at the base of the dam.

Still unsatisfied, Morrell, in a second letter, offered to cooperate in the work, helping financially to make the dam safe. The offer was declined, with renewed assurances of safety. Morrell died in 1885 and Ruff in 1887; two years later, Colonel Elias J. Unger, a retired Pittsburgh hotel owner, was named club president and manager and took up full-time residence at the lake.

In February, 1881, heavy rains had caused serious damage, and in June of the same year during a flash flood rumors flew that the dam was about to break. These rumors were renewed each year but for the next eight years proved groundless, leading to an attitude of complacency on the part of everyone in the area.

The first record of a flood in Johnstown is from 1808, when a small dam across Stony Creek, put in as a millrace for one of the first forges, was breached. As the years went by, floods became more serious because timber was being stripped off the mountainsides to provide lumber for building, and the river channels were narrowed to make room for buildings and bridges. Thus, there was less river to handle more runoff. From 1881 to 1888, seven floods were recorded, three of them serious.

THE YEAR OF THE JOHNSTOWN FLOOD. In April of 1889, 14 inches of heavy snow fell, then melted rapidly in the warm weather. In May rain fell for eleven days. On May 28 a storm that had originated out of Kansas and Nebraska caused hard rains over a wide area. On May 29 the U.S. Signal Corps warned the mid-Atlantic states that they were in for severe local storms, and parts of Pennsylvania had the worst downpour ever recorded; at the South Fork Club 7 inches fell.

On Thursday, May 30, a fine rain fell for most of the day, but by 4 P.M. the sky was lighter and the wind was up. People who lived in areas that had been flooded assumed the storm was over and the waters would recede. However, by 11 P.M. heavy rain and high winds had returned. During the night, families in the valley heard "rumbling and roaring" sounds as the heavy storm water tore big holes in the saturated ground. Crops washed away, roads became creeks, and little streams rampaged torrents.

By Friday morning the rain had eased off, but the sky was very dark and a thick mist hung in the valley. Rivers were rising faster than 1 foot an hour, and by 7 A.M., when men arrived for their shift at the Cambria mills, they were told to go home and take care of their families. By 8 A.M., much debris was observed in the lake, and it was rising rapidly. At 10 A.M. schools were let out. The Chicago and Pittsburgh trains arrived on time at Johnstown, but some areas of track were already in precarious condition, and at 11 A.M. a log boom burst up the Stony Creek, sending logs to jam against the massive Johnstown stone railroad bridge. By noon the water level in Johnstown was at a record high, and after the Stony Creek ripped out the Poplar Street and Cambria City bridges, George T. Swank, editor and proprietor of the *Johnstown Tribune*, started a running log of events.

Meanwhile, at the dam, young John G. Parke, Jr., new resident engineer for the South Fork Club, was busy that morning supervising twenty Italian laborers who were installing a new indoor plumbing system. Parke noted about 7 A.M. that the water level of the lake was only about 2 feet from the top of the dam, while the previous day it had been 4 to 6 feet below. He heard a sound from the head of the lake like "the terrible roaring as of a cataract." He went inside to have breakfast and then with a young workman took out a rowboat and surveyed the incoming creeks, finding the upper quarter of the lake filled with debris.

When Parke returned to shore, he was told he was needed at the dam immediately, and he saddled his horse to ride there. He found nearly fifty people observing the sewer diggers trying without much success to throw up a ridge of earth to heighten the dam. At the west end a dozen men were trying to cut a new spillway through the tough shale of the hillside but succeeded in providing a trench only knee-deep and about 2 feet wide. Local onlookers advised Colonel Unger, who was directing the work, to tear out the bridge and the iron-mesh spillway, but he did not want to lose the fish. At 11 A.M., the lake water was at the level of the dam, eating at the new ridge, and there were several large new leaks at the base.

Around 12:15, when Unger ordered the spillway cleared, it was too late: Debris had piled up to the extent that the bridge and mesh were jammed in, and the spillway was virtually blocked. At 12:30, Parke considered cutting a new spillway through one end of the dam, but he did not want to take the responsibility for ruining the dam. He reasoned that there would be no way later to prove the dam had been about to break. He went into the clubhouse for dinner. By 2 P.M. the water was running over the center of the dam, at its lowest point.

THE FLOOD ITSELF. The dam gave way at 3:10 P.M. John Parke insisted it did not break, it "just moved away." It took about forty minutes for the entire lake to empty. Civil engineers later calculated the velocity was akin to "turning Niagara Falls into the valley." They blamed the lack of outlet pipes, the lowered height of the dam in relation to the spillway (which was itself crammed with debris), and the fact that due to earlier damage the dam was weakest and lowest at its center.

The men stood and watched as huge trees were snapped off the ground and disappeared and the water scraped the hill down to bedrock to a height of 50 feet; the farmhouse and buildings belonging to

The aftermath of the Johnstown Flood. (Library of Congress)

George Fisher vanished in an instant, and Lamb's Bridge and the buildings of George Lamb climbed the 60-foot crest, then rolled and smashed against the hill. Then the valley turned sharply to the right and blocked their view. The Fisher and Lamb families had escaped minutes before, but at South Fork, Michael Mann, who lived in a shanty on the creek bank, was the first casualty. His body was found a week later, 1.5 miles downstream, stripped of all clothing and half buried in mud. South Fork Village, stacked on the hillside in a bend in the valley, suffered little damage: About 20 buildings, a planing mill, and the bridge were swept away and then deposited about 200 feet upstream by the water's backwash as it slammed into the mountain on the north side of the Little Conemaugh River. However, the 40-foot "mountain" of water, moving about 10 to 15 miles per hour, claimed another 3 lives.

For the first mile of its 14-mile journey to Johnstown, the river had only railroad tracks and equipment to swallow up. As the valley narrowed and twisted, the water height grew to over 60 feet. As it hit the tremendous stone viaduct built fifty years earlier and still used for the main line of the Pennsylvania Railroad, there was a booming crunch as debris piled up and momentarily formed another lake. Then the bridge collapsed all at once, and the water exploded with concentrated power down the valley, taking with it the entire small village of Mineral Point. Fortunately, most of the inhabitants had left earlier in the day as the water rose due to normal flooding, but the death toll reached 16 as those left went racing off downstream on their own rooftops or were caught in the maelstrom.

As the water advanced down the valley (average decline in elevation, 33 feet per mile), the debris caught in various places, damming up the water and then releasing it to flow more violently. The debris and the friction with the hillside also caused the top water to travel more rapidly, so that a "surf" effect developed, pounding debris and bodies deep into the mud and making later retrieval difficult. Now several hundred freight cars, a dozen or more locomotives, passenger cars, nearly a hundred more houses, and quite a few corpses were part of the wave that surged on down the valley. Past East Conemaugh, the flood was on a straightaway, and it began to gather speed. Woodvale with its woolen mill was wiped out, along with 314, or 1 of every 3, people in town. Miles of barbed wire from Gautier Works were added to the wreckage, which swept into Johnstown at 4:07 P.M.

In Johnstown, the floodwaters had actually begun to recede. Most people, perched in upper stories, never saw the water coming, but they heard it. It began as a deep, steady rumble and accelerated into a roar. Those who actually saw the wall of water, now an estimated 40 feet high, remembered "trees snapped off like pipestems" and "houses crushed like eggshells." Most impressive was the cloud of dark spray that hung over the front of the wave. Preceding the spray was a high wind.

The water hit Johnstown harder than anything it had encountered in its 14-mile course from the dam. It bounced off the mountain in its path and washed back up it 2 miles, carrying debris and people with it. The devastation took just ten minutes. However, the suffering and loss of life were more protracted.

The massive stone-arched Pennsylvania Railroad bridge on the downriver side of Johnstown had been protected by a curve in the river and held. Debris piled up 40 feet high against it, to an area of 40 acres, and as night came on it caught fire. Editor Swank, who had been watching everything from his *Johnstown Tribune* office window, wrote that the fire burned "with all the fury of the hell you read about—cremation alive in your own home, perhaps a mile from its foundation; dear ones slowly consumed before your eyes, and the same fate yours a moment later."

The finest and newest hotel in town, the Hulbert House, had been used as a place of refuge by many people seeking safety. It collapsed almost the instant it was hit by the flood. Of the 60 people inside the building, only 9 got out alive.

It was later wondered if so many lives were lost because no warning was given. Most of the blame for loss of life can be placed on the fact that flooding was common in the valley, and each year brought rumors that the dam was going to fail, but in the nine years since the lake had been filled no major upsets had occurred. Unger sent Parke to South Fork at 11:30 A.M. with a warning of danger, but two local men who had just gone to the dam said there was nothing to worry about. Sometime before 1 P.M., the East Conemaugh dispatcher's office received a message to warn the people of Johnstown that the dam was liable to break. He set it aside without reading it; his assistant read it and laughed. An hour later another message was sent to East Conemaugh, Johnstown, and Pittsburgh, and in thirty minutes another. Still, no one was unduly alarmed.

The only meaningful warning was received in East Conemaugh, when a railroad engineer whose crew was repairing tracks just upriver heard the water coming. He jumped into his engine, tied down the whistle and steamed down the tracks. Nearly everyone in East Conemaugh heard the whistle and understood almost instantly what it meant. Otherwise, as one telegraph operator noted of the messages, people paid no attention to the few warnings. As a matter of fact, the common attitude was that anyone taking any precautions was at best gullible and at worst a coward.

AFTERMATH AND CLEANUP. Dawn on Saturday, June 1, was dark and misty, and the river was still rising. A few random buildings stood amid the wreckage that was piled as high as the roofs of houses. Every bridge was gone except the stone bridge, and against it lay a good part of what had been Johnstown, in a blazing heap. Below the bridge

A house in Johnstown, Pennsylvania, lies on its side, pierced by a large tree trunk. (Library of Congress)

the Iron Works, though damaged, still stood, but at least two-thirds of the houses in Cambria City had been wiped out, and a tremendous pile of mud and rock had been dumped the entire length of the main street.

Amid the wreckage were strewn corpses and portions of corpses of horses and humans. Rescue parties had worked through the night to free people trapped alive in the burning pile, but an estimated 80 died. Now others helped bring the marooned down from rooftops and searched among the ruins for signs of life. Roads were impassable. The railroad had been destroyed. Every telegraph and telephone line to the outside was down. There was no drinkable water, little food, and no stores from which to obtain either.

Five Pittsburgh newspapers had sent journalists, and the first newspapermen arrived on foot at about 7 A.M. on June 1. The presence of reporters at the scene the following day and for several weeks to come, as well as later remembrances by people who lived through the event, provided records of individual experiences. Many of the contemporary newspaper accounts, however, were sensationalized and based on rumor as much as fact.

By noon rafts were built; people on the hillsides whose homes had escaped harm and farmers from miles out in the country began coming into town, bringing food, water, and clothing; unclaimed children were looked after. At 3 P.M., a meeting was called at the Adams Street schoolhouse. Arthur J. Moxham, a young, self-made, wealthy, and popular industrialist was put in charge of business. He immediately organized committees to establish morgues, remove dead bodies from the wreckage, establish temporary hospitals, organize a police force, and find supplies and funds. A fear of typhoid as well as concern for the survivors made retrieval, identification, and burial of the bodies imperative. Those who were not identified were numbered, their descriptions recorded, and they were buried. One out of every 3 bodies would never be identified. Hundreds of people who were lost would never be found; it is supposed that some simply walked away and never came back. Not for months would there be any realistic count of the dead, and there would never be an exact, final count. Two bodies were found as late as 1906. Ninety-nine whole families had been wiped out, 98 children had lost both parents, and hardly a family had not suffered a death. The flood had killed about 1 out of every 9 people.

On Sunday the weather eased off. Bodies were taken across the Little Conemaugh in skiffs and buried in shallow graves. A post office was set up, and all survivors were instructed to register. The first patients were cared for in a temporary hospital, and the first train came through. Supplies and volunteers, more newspapermen and police, doctors and work crews, a shipment of tents, an eleven-car train containing nothing but coffins with more to come, and a Pittsburgh fire department arrived, extinguishing the fire at the bridge by midnight. At the end of the day more than 1,000 people had arrived to help the 27,000 who needed aid. Thousands more were on their way.

On Tuesday, Moxham resigned, and James B. Scott, head of the Pittsburgh Committee, took over as civilian head of the area. From Washington, D.C., came nurse Clara Barton and her newly organized American Red Cross to set up tent hospitals and six hotels with hot and cold running water, kitchens, and laundries. In five months she distributed nearly half a million dollars worth of blankets, clothing, food, and cash. Upon her departure she was presented with a diamond locket by the people of Johnstown, and she was later feted in Washington at a dinner attended by President Benjamin Harrison.

By the end of the month a book on the disaster had been published, and within six months, a dozen would appear. Newspapers carried sensational stories for weeks and published extra editions, all of which sold out. Songs were written about the flood, several of which became best sellers. Sightseers with picnic baskets arrived and bought souvenirs. In all, cash contributions from around the world would total more than $3.7 million.

In spite of assiduous cleanup, including the sprinkling of four thousand barrels of lime over the area, typhoid broke out, affecting 461 people and killing 40. Everyone took it for granted that Johnstown would be rebuilt, and on its original site, and so it was. John Fulton made public the faults of the dam. In Pittsburgh, members of the South Fork Club met and officially decided that it would be best to say nothing about their role in the disaster. Suits were brought against them, but the club had nothing except the now-worthless site and widespread negative publicity; no one was awarded anything. Cyrus Elder, who had lost his wife and daughter and his home, and who was the only local member of the club, concluded, "If anybody be to blame I suppose we ourselves are among them, for we have indeed been very careless in this most important matter and most of us have paid the penalty of our neglect."

Erika E. Pilver

FOR FURTHER INFORMATION:

Degen, Paula, and Carl Degen. *The Johnstown Flood of 1889: The Tragedy of the Conemaugh.* Philadelphia: Eastern Acorn Press, 1984.

Evans, T. William. *Though the Mountains May Fall: The Story of the Great Johnstown Flood of 1889.* New York: Writers Club Press, 2002.

Johnson, Willis Fletcher. *History of the Johnstown Flood.* Reprint. Westminster, Md.: Heritage Books, 2001.

McCullough, David. *The Johnstown Flood.* Reprint. New York: Simon & Schuster, 1987.

———. "Run for Your Lives!" *American Heritage Magazine* 16, no. 4 (1966): 5-11, 66-75.

Walker, James Herbert. *The Johnstown Horror!!! Or, Valley of Death.* Philadelphia: H. J. Smith, 1889.

◼ 1892: CHOLERA PANDEMIC

EPIDEMIC

DATE: 1892-1894

PLACE: India, Russia, Asia, the United States, Great Britain, Europe, and Africa

RESULT: Millions dead, development of health departments and infectious disease surveillance

Cholera epidemics plagued humankind for most of the nineteenth century. The final worldwide cholera epidemic of that century occurred between 1892 and 1894. This epidemic was similar to the cholera epidemics that had preceded it in that it caused great devastation; millions of people died. The 1892 to 1894 epidemic was unique, however, in that it occurred just at the time when science was determining beyond a doubt that the cause of cholera was bacterial infection passed through contaminated water.

Cholera is caused by the organism *Vibrio cholerae*. It lives in various marine animals, which are consumed by humans, and it is present in contaminated water. Most humans become infected by eating raw fish or shellfish, or by drinking contaminated water. Not all people infected with cholera show symptoms, and they can spread the disease unknowingly. Cholera causes severe diarrhea and vomiting, which leads to a drastic loss of fluids within the body. Dehydration, collapse of the circulatory system, and death occur if the fluids are not replaced. Without treatment, cholera kills 20 to 50 percent of its victims and death occurs within hours. Today, prompt treatment can bring the death toll down to 1 percent.

Ancient Sanskrit writings from 2,500 years ago described a disease with symptoms that were similar to cholera. Although cholera existed before the 1800's, it remained primarily in the area of Bengal, with some brief occurrences in China. Originating in the Bengal basin at the delta of the Ganges and Brahmaputra Rivers, *V. cholerae* lived in the shellfish present in the waters. Hindu pilgrimages drew crowds of faithful to the Ganges River for ceremonies, where many were infected with cholera. Some died promptly; others carried the disease back to their villages, causing local infestations. These outbreaks of cholera remained local; thus, when cholera made its appearance throughout the world in the early 1800's, it was described as a new disease. In 1817, cholera spread from Bengal to other parts of the world. Over the next one hundred years the world would suffer six major outbreaks of cholera.

The spread of cholera was closely linked to the increase in international commerce, military actions, the increase in travel, and the increase in immigration of people. When cholera broke out in India in 1817, English ships and troops were stationed there. They carried cholera overland to Nepal and Afghanistan. Far more critically, their ships passed cholera along to Ceylon (now Sri Lanka), Indonesia, China, Japan, Arabia, and Africa. The Industrial Revolution and an increase in urban population and crowded living conditions also contributed to the spread of cholera.

The devastation caused by cholera was so great that port towns made attempts to control it by mandating quarantines. Ship were not allowed to disembark for weeks until they were determined to be free of disease. Scientists struggled to find the cause of the dreaded disease. Although Robert Koch, one of the great microbiologists of the nineteenth century, had found the bacillus that caused cholera back in 1883, his explanation was not accepted by other experts of the time.

In 1887, the federal government of the United States ordered a study of cholera to begin. Dr. Joseph Kinyoun directed the program, which later evolved into the National Institutes of Health. Dr. Kinyoun's research became more urgent in 1892, when an Asiatic cholera epidemic reached the United States.

When the cholera epidemic of 1892 struck the city of Hamburg, Germany, a unique situation within the area gave credence to Koch's theory that germ-contaminated water was responsible for spreading cholera. Hamburg obtained its water directly from the Elbe River, which was untreated. An adjacent town, Altona, had installed a water-filtration plant, so its citizens drank treated water. When the epidemic hit, the people in Hamburg succumbed, but the people of Altona were spared. The street that divided the towns experienced cholera on one side and none on the other side. Since the air was the same on both sides of the street and the ground was the same, it was apparently the water that made the difference.

The cholera epidemic of 1892-1894 appeared in India, Russia, Asia, the United States, Great Britain, Europe, and Africa. In Russia alone, over 1 million people died, including the great composer Peter Tchaikovsky. The exact circumstances surrounding his death were unclear. Some speculate that Tchaikovsky committed suicide by drinking water known to be contaminated; others believe that he took a poison that mimicked the symptoms of cholera. Tchaikovsky's doctor, however, pronounced him dead of cholera on November 6, 1893.

One result of the cholera epidemic of 1892 was the improvement in sanitation measures taken by the large cities. Water-treatment systems were instituted, and sanitation was greatly improved. Even in Asia, Africa, and Latin America, where resources were not available to provide sanitary water and sewage systems for all citizens, simple precautions like boiling drinking water made it possible to avoid exposure to waterborne infections.

Cholera epidemics prompted the formation of public health departments, which conducted surveillance and reporting of the disease. In the international classification of diseases, the code for cholera is 001 because it was the first disease for which public health surveillance was developed. Although cholera is still present in various parts of the world, improved sanitation, increased surveillance, and modern medical treatment have helped prevent the occurrence of new, widespread epidemics.

Louise Magoon

FOR FURTHER INFORMATION:

Bollet, Alfred J. *Plagues and Poxes: The Impact of Human History on Epidemic Disease.* New York: Demos, 2004.

Clemow, Frank G. *The Cholera Epidemic of 1892 in the Russian Empire.* London: Longmans, 1893.

Evans, Alfred S., and Philip S. Brachman. *Bacterial Infections of Humans: Epidemiology and Control.* 3d ed. New York: Plenum Medical Book Company, 1998.

Evans, Richard J. *Death in Hamburg: Society and Politics in the Cholera Years.* New York: Penguin Books, 2005.

Karlen, Arno. *Man and Microbes: Disease and Plagues in History and Modern Times.* New York: Putnam, 1995.

McNeill, William H. *Plagues and Peoples.* New York: Anchor Press/ Doubleday, 1998.

Markel, Howard. *Quarantine! East European Jewish Immigrants and the New York City Epidemics of 1892.* Baltimore: Johns Hopkins University Press, 1999.

■ 1896: The Great Cyclone of 1896

Tornado

Date: May 27, 1896
Place: St. Louis, Missouri
Classification: F4
Result: 306 dead, 2,500 injured, 311 buildings destroyed, 7,200 other buildings severely damaged, tremendous damage to river boats and railroad lines

Because the previous three weeks had witnessed violent weather across the United States, it must have come as a relief to St. Louis that the weather report for Wednesday, May 27, 1896, called for a partly cloudy day with only a chance of local thunderstorms. No one would have suspected that St. Louis could suffer the ravages of a tornado; it was considered common knowledge that tornadoes do not strike large cities. The tornado that nearly hit St. Louis on March 8, 1871, was believed to be as close as a tornado could come.

Until 3 P.M. on May 27, 1896, it was a hot, humid, and sunny day in St. Louis, just as the newspapers predicted. The city was a booming metropolis whose population already exceeded 500,000—it was the fourth-largest city in the United States. Union Station was in its second year of operation as the mid-America passenger hub of an increasingly mobile nation. Crowning its new status in industrialized America, preparations were well under way to house the Republican presidential nominating convention, scheduled for June. Across the mighty Mississippi River, East St. Louis had become a commercial railroad center with a rapidly growing population.

After 3 P.M. the sky slowly began to darken as the barometer and thermometer began to fall. By 4:30 P.M. large black and green cloud masses could be seen approaching the city. By 5 P.M. many parts of the city were enveloped in darkness, except for forked lightning illuminating the sky. Sizzling telegraph wires and burning telegraph poles cast an eerie bluish light pattern in the streets below. People scurried for the relative security of temporary shelter wherever they could find it, a fact substantiated by the location of bodies found after the storm. Shelter in cellars offered the best protection, providing that an individual was not crushed by the upper floors caving in.

At about 5:15 P.M. the tornado struck at the southwest edge of St. Louis. It widened into a 0.5-mile-wide complex of tornado and downburst wind, heading due east toward the central city area. Along its path it demolished 311 buildings and severely damaged 7,200 others. Stone and brick houses of the affluent were smashed almost as easily as the flimsy wooden houses of the poor. The tornado devastated 6 churches and damaged 15 others. Several city hospitals suffered varying degrees of destruction.

The storm cut a 10-mile path, leaving in many places a mile-wide swath of devastation. Witnesses described the tail of the storm as being like the lash of a whip, moving north to south, while the massive body of the storm slowly moved on its eastern path of destruction.

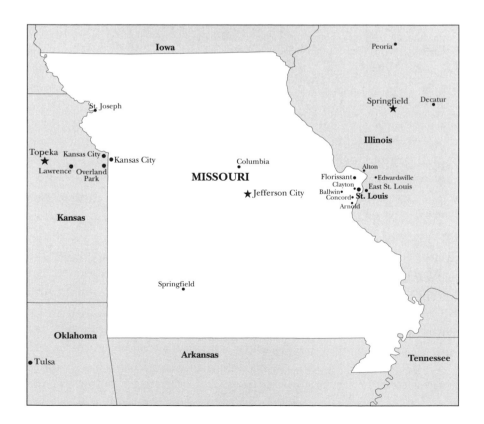

Entire neighborhoods, such as the Soulard area, were left in shambles. Nearly 500 workers were building a thirteen-building complex for Liggett and Myers Tobacco Company when the storm hit. Structures collapsed, and miraculously, only 13 workers died. However, at Seventh and Rutgers Street 17 people died when a three-story brick tenement collapsed. The new Ralston Purina Mill was also destroyed. However, a bank loan would allow the new headquarters to be rebuilt.

The storm reached maximum intensity when it came to the Mississippi River. Because of a slight turn in the storm, the tall buildings of downtown St. Louis were spared the test of whether or not they could survive tornadic winds. However, poverty-stricken families living in houseboats disappeared into the river. Sixteen boats moored in St. Louis harbor were wrecked. By the time they hit the Eads Bridge, tornadic winds were strong enough to drive a 2-by-10-inch wood plank through the $\frac{5}{16}$-inch thick wrought-iron plate of the bridge.

The great tornado then tore into East St. Louis, leveling half of the city. Thirty-five people died in the Vandalia railroad freight yard in East St. Louis. It took about twenty minutes for the worst single disaster in the history of the St. Louis metropolitan area to take its deadly and destructive toll. The storm system left 306 dead, over 2,500 injured, and 600 families homeless.

Drenching rains and lightning continued in St. Louis until about 9 P.M. Because the Edison Plant was destroyed, the city was without electricity. Rescue workers worked through the night by torchlight and through the sunshine of the next morning. Survivors were still being pulled from the rubble two days later. Meanwhile, long lines of friends, relatives, and the curious waited at the city morgue as the dead wagons unloaded their crushed and mutilated human cargo. Many bodies were blackened and unrecognizable. Others had been turned into human pin cushions as splintered wood and other debris had been hurled at tremendous speeds into their bodies.

As news of the disaster spread, the weekend brought tens of thousands of sightseers to St. Louis, anxious to see firsthand the destruction that was wrought. Among their number were hundreds of thieves, eager to uncover valuables from demolished homes and stores. On the Sunday following the "great tornado" over 140,000 people crammed through Union Station into the streets of St. Louis. Tours had already been organized to see the destruction. For weeks after the storm St. Louis newspapers were filled with stories of miraculous escapes, tearful tragedies, and tales of heroic citizens coming to the aid of other citizens. These accounts and others were pieced together by the Cyclone Publishing Company, a group of newsmen who copyrighted their work in Washington, D.C., only nine days after the storm. An eager American public read in awe and horror about the powers of nature and the human dimensions of natural disasters.

Irwin Halfond

FOR FURTHER INFORMATION:

Curzon, Julian, comp. and ed. *The Great Cyclone at St. Louis and East St. Louis, May 27, 1896: Being a Full History of the Most Terrifying and Destructive Tornado in the History of the World.* 1896. Reprint. Carbondale: Southern Illinois University Press, 1997.

Montesi, Albert, and Richard Deposki. "The Great Cyclone of 1896." In *Soulard, St. Louis.* Images of America. Chicago: Arcadia, 2000.

O'Neil, Tim. "The Great Cyclone of 1896." *St. Louis Post-Dispatch*, May 26, 1996.

"The Top Ten US Killer Tornadoes—#3: The St. Louis/East St. Louis Tornado of 1896." *The Tornado Project Online.* http://www.tornadoproject.com.

◼ 1900: The Galveston hurricane

Hurricane

Date: September 8, 1900
Place: Galveston, Texas
Classification: Force 12 on the Beaufort Scale; Category 4
Speed: At least 84 miles per hour, estimated 110-120 miles per hour
Result: 3,000-12,000 dead

The hurricane that swept in from the Gulf of Mexico and devastated Galveston, Texas, on Saturday, September 8, 1900, killed more people than any other natural disaster in the history of the United States at the time. It was a turning point in the lives of the people of the Upper Texas Gulf Coast.

Galveston Island was a low sand-barrier island, almost 28 miles long and from 1.5 to 3.5 miles wide. Its surface at that time rose to an average height of 4 to 5 feet above mean tide level. The average rise and fall of the tide at Galveston was 1.1 feet. The harbor at Galveston, on the bay side, served Texas and the Trans-Mississippi West Railroad. Rail connections, including those of the Southern Pacific and the Santa Fe along with smaller rail lines, focused upon Galveston.

The Formation of the Hurricane. In the first week of September, 1900, an air mass from the north cooled the island after a stifling period of heat. The weather front was known as a "norther." It was accompanied by a line of dark clouds from the northwest. At the same time a hurricane was reported first in the Caribbean Sea and then across Cuba in the Gulf of Mexico. It moved across Key West and then turned in a westerly direction, headed almost straight for Galveston. The cool front kept the slow-moving hurricane out over the Gulf of Mexico, where it gathered strength.

Until September 4, the storm had not developed a very destructive force. It did cause rough seas and heavy rains, however, dropping 12.5 inches of rain in twenty-four hours as it passed over Santiago, Cuba. On September 6, the center of the storm was reported a short distance northwest of Key West. In 1900, the Weather Bureau relied solely on information from its stations ashore. There were no reports radioed from ships at sea. Not until December 3, 1905, did a ship radio a weather observation to be received by the U.S. Weather Bureau. Not until August 26, 1908, was a hurricane report radioed from a ship, the SS *Cartago* off the coast of Yucatán.

The central office of the Weather Bureau ordered storm and hurricane warnings from Port Eads, Louisiana, on the Gulf to Cape Hatteras on the Atlantic. On Friday morning, September 7, the center of the hurricane was estimated to be southeast of the Louisiana coast. The hurricane flags were hoisted in Galveston that morning. Increasing swells were observed to the southeast, and cirrus clouds marked the blue sky.

THE EFFECTS OF THE STORM. By noon of Saturday, September 8, it was evident that the hurricane was bearing down on Galveston. The hurricane flags flew over the Levi Building, which held the Weather Bureau offices, and across the island. Families along the beachfront boarded up their residences and moved to higher ground in the city. The winds were rising constantly, and it rained in torrents. By 3 P.M. the waters of the Gulf and the bay met, covering the low areas across the island. By evening the entire city was submerged. Gigantic waves destroyed the houses nearest the beach first. Debris from these structures was then hurled into the next rows of houses. The wreckage from each street was then thrown by the pounding surf into the next. These buildings also fell and offered more wreckage for the storm to cast against the next block of buildings. The east and west portions of Galveston for three blocks inland were swept clean of residential and commercial structures.

Slate from the roofs flew through the air to endanger anyone out in the torrent. A disastrous fire in 1885 had destroyed a large section of the city, so slate roofs became a requirement in building construction. In the storm these were lethal weapons, but so were falling bricks and wood carried by 100-mile-per-hour winds. From 5 P.M. until midnight, the people were caught where they were, in homes and in buildings, until these collapsed around them under the pressure of the hurricane-force winds. The public buildings, courthouse, customs house, and hotels offered apparent safe refuge. They rapidly became overcrowded, however. Telephone, telegraph, and electric-light poles snapped, and the wires were strewn across the streets, which were becoming impassable. Corpses of people, horses, mules,

A house upended by the Galveston hurricane. (Library of Congress)

and pets began to float through the streets. The collapse of buildings and the cries for help could not be heard above the roar of the wind.

Nearly 1,000 people gathered in the large Ursuline Convent, two blocks from the beach. A 10-foot wall around the convent crumbled. People, animals, and debris were being washed against the walls of the building. Four expectant mothers gave birth during the storm in the nuns' cells. The babies were baptized immediately, for no one knew if they would make it through the night.

Shortly after 8:30 P.M., the wind blowing from the southeast shattered the east windows on the top floor of the city hall. The crowd that had gathered there nearly stampeded. The front part of the building collapsed shortly thereafter. Police Chief Edwin Ketchum was able to quiet the crowd at first, then lost control. Only music could quiet those who remained in the building. A few blocks away in the Telephone Building, the telephone operators were frantic until they began to sing. Strangely enough, one song was heard repeatedly—"My Bonnie Lies over the Ocean." The operators moved from room to room as the windows were smashed and the plaster began to give way.

Between 8 and 9 P.M., the water reached its maximum depth over Galveston Island. It was 15.6 feet deep above mean tide on the east side of the city at St. Mary's Infirmary. Downtown, the depth was 12.1 feet at the YMCA Building and 10.5 feet at the Union Passenger Station. Of the sick in St. Mary's Infirmary, together with the attendants, only 8 survived. St. Mary's Roman Catholic Orphans' Home on Fifty-seventh Street fell in portions—the east wing collapsed and then the roof and remaining part of the structure fell—during the height of the storm. All the children and the nuns, along with two workmen, perished. Many of the bodies were tied together with ropes, one nun to several children, in an apparent attempt to survive the storm. The numbers of dead children and refugees were never accurately ascertained.

Fort Crockett on the west side of the city near the beach was flooded. It held a heavy battery of 10-inch guns, a battery of eight 10-inch mortars, and a rapid-fire battery. Manning these guns were Battery O soldiers of the First Artillery. The men there rode out the first part of the storm in the barracks, but most soon left for higher ground and the safety of the Denver Resurvey School; three drowned on the way. The barracks building was destroyed, and the other men were lost. The shoreline at Fort Crockett had moved back about 600 feet. All fortifications except the rapid-fire battery at Battery O's Fort San Jacinto on Fort Point, on the eastern bay side of the island, were practically destroyed. At the fort every building except the quarantine station was swept away. Twenty-eight men of the Battery O were lost in the storm.

DAMAGE TO SHIPS. The 2-mile channel between Bolivar Peninsula and Galveston Island was the only passage for ocean-going ships into Galveston harbor. The channel was protected by two jetties extending from the peninsula and the island. Moored in the Bolivar Roads across from Fort San Jacinto and the quarantine station were three English steamships—the *Taunton*, the *Hilarious*, and the *Mexican*—in quarantine. The American *City of Everett* was also anchored in the Bolivar Roads. The federal government dredge boat *General C. B. Comstock* was tied up at the U.S. Army Corps of Engineers coal wharf, which was built out into the water from the south jetty near the quarantine station on Galveston Island.

Twelve other steamers were in port at Galveston, moored along the wharf on the bay side of the city. Among them was the English steamship *Kendal Castle* at Pier 31, on the west of the port facility. The American ship *Alamo* was docked at Pier 24, the Norwegian *Guyller* at Pier 21, the English ships *Benedict* and *Roma*, as well as the *Norna*, at Pier 15. The *Comino* was moored at Pier 14, and the *Red Cross* rested at Pier 12 on the east side of the wharf front. By midday, most of the ships were ordered to put out extra mooring lines. Later, the water on the rising tide began to submerge the wharves. The bay was rough, and a drenching rain soaked everything. Smaller craft—shrimpers, tugs, barges, and schooners—were dashed against the wharves.

Every ship in port battled for survival. The *Taunton* was driven by the wind 30 miles to Cedar Point on the mainland. The *Roma* broke its last moorings when the anchors parted from the chains. The ship was carried up the channel broadside to the current. The *Roma* careened into the *Kendal Castle*, then went broadside into the three railway bridges. It finally came to a stop between the last railroad bridge and the 2-mile-long wagon bridge that ran from Virginia Point to the island.

Galveston's rail traffic was cut off from the mainland for several days. The *Guyller* also plowed into the *Kendal Castle*, which began to drift when its lines broke. The ship was blown across Pelican Island, which was completely submerged, into the shallow water at the port of Texas City on the mainland. After the storm the *Kendal Castle* rested in 3 feet of water in the wreckage of the Inman Pier. The *Guyller* became stranded between Pelican Island and Virginia Point. The *Alamo* and the *Red Cross* broke loose and were driven across the channel to run aground on the eastern edge of Pelican Island. The *Comino* and the *Norna* stayed in their berths but were extensively damaged. For 10 miles inland from the shore on the mainland it was common to see small craft such as steam launches, schooners, and oyster sloops.

At the Bolivar Point Lighthouse, near the entrance to the harbor, people began to gather, because it was the best-built structure across the channel on the Bolivar Peninsula. About 125 people sought refuge from the storm there Saturday evening. The supply of fresh water was exhausted in a short time. An effort was made to collect rainwater in buckets tied to the top of the lighthouse. The lighthouse was 115 feet high, but the saltwater spray was blown over 100 feet in the air, mixing with the rainwater that fell into the buckets.

At 5:15 P.M., the U.S. Weather Bureau's anemometer blew away. The last recorded velocity was 84 miles per hour for the five-minute period the Weather Bureau accepted as official. The weathermen estimated winds later at a velocity of 110 or 120 miles per hour during the period from 6 P.M. to 10:45 P.M., after which they began to subside. Gusts were much higher.

At 7:30 P.M. the barometer fell to 28.05 inches. It then began to rise slowly. Galveston was awash in flood tide and debris; the water reached a depth of 8 feet on Strand Street, the heart of the financial district, by 10 P.M. The wind was in a southerly direction and diminishing. Then the water began to ebb and ran off very rapidly. By 5 A.M. of the next day, the center of the street was free of water. Slime an inch thick covered everything. People emerged, trying to find their loved ones. Others just wandered aimlessly through the streets.

RECOVERY EFFORTS. Death estimates ranged from 3,000 to 12,000 people. A partial list of the dead compiled by the Galveston *Daily News* after the storm comprised more than 4,200 names. Hundreds more were never identified. The best estimate is that more than 6,000 people lost their lives in Galveston and approximately 2,000 died on the coastal mainland. Morrison and Fourmey, publishers of the *Galveston City Directory*, also gave a figure of approximately 6,000 people dead.

Great piles of corpses, uprooted vegetation, household furniture, and fragments of buildings themselves were piled in confused heaps in the main streets of Galveston. Along the Strand close to the bayfront, where the big wholesale warehouses and stores were situated, great piles of debris lay in massive heaps where the tide had left them. The warehouses became tombs, holding human bodies and animal carcasses. The masses of debris were not confined to any one particular section of the city. There was hardly a family on the island whose household did not suffer loss or injury. In some instances entire families were washed away or killed. Hundreds who escaped from the waves did so only to be crushed by falling structures.

The days following the storm were ones of privation and sadness. There were enough provisions on hand to feed the remaining population in Galveston for a week, but the problem was in properly distributing the supplies. There was an immediate rush to obtain food and water, but this slacked off in time. After finding food and water, attention turned to the wounded and the dead. All pretense at holding inquests was abandoned. More than 2,000 bodies were carried by barge, weighted, and thrown into the Gulf. Hundreds were taken to the mainland and buried at Virginia Point. Ninety-six bodies were buried at Texas City, all but 8 of which had floated to the mainland from Galveston during the storm. Cases were known where people buried their dead in their yards. As soon as possible, the work of cremating bodies began. Vast funeral pyres were erected, and the fire department personnel supervised the incineration.

An estimated 4,000 houses were destroyed, as were many commercial, religious, and public buildings. The first three blocks closest to the water, running the entire length of the city, were completely destroyed on the Gulf side of the island. The water works' powerhouse was ruined, as was the electric plant, so that the city recovered from the storm without fresh water and in the dark. Every structure in the city suffered some storm damage, as the seawater completely covered the island to a depth as much as 15.2 feet above the mean tide. The highest elevation on the island at that time was about 8 to 10 feet above sea level.

After the railway bridges were repaired in a few days, Houston served as the center of relief distribution. It also served as the way out of Galveston for people seeking inland shelter over the next few weeks. Hundreds of refugees passed through every day. Free transportation was furnished to any point in Texas, provided people had relatives who would care for them. Clara Barton, head of the American Red Cross, came to Galveston to personally direct the Red Cross relief effort in cooperation with other agencies, such as the Salvation Army. She wrote during that first week:

> It would be difficult to exaggerate the awful scene that meets the visitors everywhere. . . . In those parts of the city where destruction was

the greatest there still must be hundreds of bodies under the debris. At the end of the island first struck by the storm, and which was swept clean of every vestige of the splendid residences that covered it, the ruin is inclosed by a towering wall of debris, under which many bodies are buried. The removal of this has scarcely even begun.

This description written by a lady who had witnessed many disasters provided a singular image of a city in desperate straits.

The 1900 hurricane that devastated the Gulf Coast caused a reduction in the volume of business in the South. Prices of staple commodities were higher during the weeks following the storm. There was a sharp rise in the price of cotton, which reached a ten-year high. There was little change in the price of manufactured products, however.

Mayor W. C. Jones took decisive measures in the days immediately following the storm. He organized the General Committee of Public Safety, which took charge of the early restoration of services in Galveston. The water-supply system was put back into order and was cleared of contamination. The mayor imposed price controls. Laborers were brought into the city to replace skilled mechanics in deposal of the bodies; they were then free to return to their regular jobs and repair of the industrial and residential structures and the infrastructure. The work of opening the streets and disinfecting them was pursued vigorously—the debris and garbage were removed by 250 vehicles of every description. They carried the waste out of the city, and it was burned. Eleven hundred tents were received by the Board of Health. All except 300, which were retained for hospital purposes, were distributed through the various ward subcommittees to shelter the homeless. As the rail bridges were repaired, Thomas Scurry, Adjutant General of the State of Texas, arrived with 200 volunteer guardsmen. The governor placed Galveston under martial law.

Galveston civic leaders had organized the Deepwater Committee in the late nineteenth century to promote the port facilities. In the first days after the storm, the Deepwater Committee was able to gain the attention of the Texas state legislature. Leaders such as I. H. Kempner proposed that Galveston be ruled by a commission system of government. The old mayor and ward system did not seem able to marshal the confidence and strength to start the reconstruction of Galveston. With the new system, each of four commissioners had control over one city department: finance and revenue, water and sewers, streets and public property, and fire and police departments. The Galveston model became one for the progressive movement in combating the "political machines" that ran many city governments at the time.

LOOKING TO THE FUTURE. The new city government hired General Henry M. Robert and two other engineers, Alfred Noble and H. C. Ripley, to devise some means of protecting Galveston from future storms. Robert had recently retired from the Army Corps of Engineers and had gained fame as the author of *Robert's Rules of Order* (1876). Their recommendation included a seawall and a grade raising of the city's elevation. Galvestonians approved a bond issue to raise the money to begin the work on the seawall. The state also agreed to rebate taxes for thirty-five years to help them finance the grade raising. The seawall was to extend from the east end of the island to Fort Crockett. The work began on October 27, 1902, and was

A man stands on a portion of the seawall constructed to protect Galveston, Texas, after the 1900 disaster. (Library of Congress)

finished on July 30, 1904. The seawall, 16 feet wide at the base and 17 feet high, was constructed of cement and stone around a network of steel pilings and reinforcement bars. Large blocks of granite from central Texas comprised a stone breakwater on the beach side of the wall.

The United States Army also planned to construct a protective seawall at Fort Crockett. Galveston County gave land to the federal government that expanded the fort by 25 acres. This allowed the Army seawall to connect with that on the Gulf side of the city. The Army agreed to fill in the gap and extend the seawall to Fifty-third Street. When completed, the seawall connected with the south jetty at the channel entrance to Galveston harbor at Eighth Street and Avenue A, angled to Sixth and Market, followed Sixth to Broadway, angled again from Broadway to the beach, then ran along the beachfront to Fifty-third Street.

The Goedhart and Bates engineering firm started work on raising grade level on the island around the time the first section of the seawall was completed. The contractors dredged a canal into the heart of the city, then built dikes around sections of the city. They filled the sections with silt their dredges had acquired from the bottom of the bay and the Gulf. Each existing structure was jacked up into place. The filled areas took weeks to dry. Residents had to walk to and from their houses on frame catwalks. The fill simply spread under the houses that had been raised above ground level.

Houses, churches, and commercial buildings all went through this process at the owners' expense. Some sizable masonry buildings were jacked up to new elevations. The grade raising took six years and was finished in July, 1910; all the streets had to be rebuilt. Utilities had to be relocated, and all the planting of trees and shrubs had to be done after the grade raising. The Galveston City Railway Company reestablished public transportation, completing the conversion to electricity from mule-drawn trolleys in 1905.

There was talk of restoring the wagon bridge after its destruction in 1900. Instead, the Texas Railroad Commission condemned the wooden railway trestle and ordered the construction of a causeway to carry rail traffic and automobiles, which were coming into widespread use. The causeway was modeled on a viaduct along the Florida Keys, utilizing twenty-eight concrete arches with 70-foot spans. In the center, a rolling lift gave a stretch of 100 feet for boat traffic to pass through. The bridge accommodated two railroad tracks, interurban rails, a highway for cars, and a 30-inch water main for Galveston from mainland wells. The causeway opened in 1912.

The population of Galveston increased again in the first decade of the twentieth century. The census of 1910 placed the total at 36,981, making Galveston the sixth largest city in the state. Its port facilities continued to be of importance to the U.S. Southwest. Galveston also grew as a popular tourist resort. All the rail lines serving Galveston ran excursions from Houston on Sunday mornings; there continued to be three sets of rail tracks. The railroads cut back on their excursion schedules when the Galveston-Houston Interurban service started in 1911. The Galvez Hostel opened in 1911 to provide visitors with beachfront accommodations on a grander scale than previously known in Galveston. Twenty-six passenger trains were going in and out of Galveston every day by 1912. Thus, in the twelve years after the great Galveston hurricane, the people of the city had completed a massive seawall, raised the level of the city, continued to compete as a deep-water port, and strengthened transportation links with the mainland.

A hurricane in 1915 proved to be of comparable strength to that of the 1900 storm. Tides were slightly higher, and the wind velocity was about the same. The storm came ashore on August 16, 1915, and the winds and tides continued to buffet the city through the next day. The hurricane washed away the earthen approaches to the causeway and broke the water main; every ship in the harbor suffered damage. At Galveston 8 people died, while elsewhere on the mainland the death toll was 267—compared to the 1900 storm, the loss of life was minimal. The protective devices built after the 1900 hurricane were successful in protecting the city in the 1915 storm. Flooding did take a toll, but this was almost entirely from the bay side. The seawall and the grade raising kept the storm losses at a bearable level. Other major hurricanes in 1943, 1961, and 1983 caused considerable damage but little loss of life. Technology had ensured that Galveston would continue to thrive as a city.

Howard Meredith

FOR FURTHER INFORMATION:

Bixel, Patricia Bellis, and Elizabeth Hayes Turner. *Galveston and the 1900 Storm: Castastrophe and Catalyst.* Austin: University of Texas Press, 2000.

Coulter, John, ed. *The Complete Story of the Galveston Horror.* New York: United Publishers of America, 1900.

Emanuel, Kerry. *Divine Wind: The History and Science of Hurricanes.* New York: Oxford University Press, 2005.

Green, Nathan C., ed. *Story of the 1900 Galveston Hurricane.* Gretna, La.: Pelican, 2000.

Greene, Casey Edward, and Shelly Henley Kelly, eds. *Through a Night of Horrors: Voices from the 1900 Galveston Storm.* College Station: Texas A&M University Press, 2000.

Halstead, Murat. *Galveston: The Horrors of a Stricken City.* New York: American Publishers' Association, 1900.

Larson, Erik. *Isaac's Storm: A Man, a Time, and the Deadliest Hurricane in History.* New York: Crown, 1999.

Lester, Paul. *The Great Galveston Disaster: Containing a Full and Thrilling Account of the Most Appalling Calamity of Modern Times.* Reprint. Gretna, La.: Pelican, 2000.

■ 1900: TYPHOID MARY

EPIDEMIC

DATE: 1900-1915

PLACE: New York State

RESULT: 3 dead, more than 50 ill from contact with "Typhoid Mary" Mallon

Mary Mallon, an Irish immigrant who served as a cook for various families and institutions, unwittingly spread typhoid fever to more than 50 people between the years of 1900 and 1915, and three deaths are linked directly to her.

Typhoid fever is a highly infectious disease caused by *Salmonella typhosa* bacteria and spread through contaminated food and water. Typhoid fever was a common epidemic until the early twentieth century, due to poor sewage and sanitation methods. The most common way of contraction was through contaminated drinking water. Symptoms include a high fever lasting a few weeks, pains, headache, cough, drowsiness, and chills. The bacteria lodge in the small intestine, where they proliferate and in severe cases may perforate the intestine or cause hemorrhaging. Typhoid ranges from mild, flulike symptoms to severe cases resulting in death within one or two weeks.

About 3 percent of individuals who have suffered from typhoid become carriers, which means that although they appear healthy and show no symptoms of the disease, their bodies contain the bacteria and they may spread it to others. Such is the case with Mallon, who either had typhoid before she could remember or had such a slight case in her early life that she thought it to be a minor influenza.

Mary Mallon was born in Ireland in 1869 and immigrated to the United States in 1883, where she began working as a domestic servant, cooking and cleaning in the homes of wealthy New Yorkers. In the summer of 1906, Mallon was working as a cook for a New York banker. When 6 of the 11 members of the household contracted typhoid fever, the house's owner hired George Soper, a sanitary engineer and specialist in typhoid fever outbreaks, to investigate the possible cause. Soper determined that Mallon had begun working for

DEVELOPMENT OF TYPHOID FEVER

Salmonella typhi bacteria enter digestive system after ingestion of contaminated water or food.

Phase 1 (2 weeks): Bacteria invade intestines' lymphoid tissue. Usually no symptoms.

Phase 2 (10 days): Bacteria invade bloodstream, often causing toxemia. Fever, immune system response.

Phase 3: Bacteria are localized in intestines' lymphoid tissue, mesenteric nodes, gallbladder, liver, spleen, occasionally bones. Lesions are caused by local tissue death (necrosis).

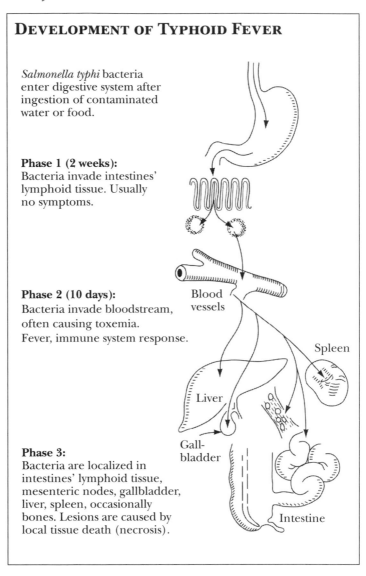

Blood vessels

Spleen

Liver

Gall-bladder

Intestine

the family shortly before the outbreak began. He traced Mallon's work history back through eight families she had worked for and discovered that seven of the families had been affected by the fever. All totaled, Soper found 22 cases of typhoid that he believed were linked to contact with food that Mallon had prepared.

The idea of a disease carrier was new to doctors and scientists, and the general public knew nothing about it. Soper believed Mallon to be a carrier but needed laboratory proof of his hypothesis. He approached Mallon, telling her she was spreading typhoid fever through the food she prepared, and that samples of her urine, blood, and feces were needed for testing. Mallon refused, and after further unsuccessful attempts the New York City Health Department called in the police to remove her. Laboratory tests showed high levels of typhoid bacilli in her feces, and Mallon was moved to an isolated cottage on North Brother Island, close to the Bronx in New York City and the site of Riverside Hospital.

Mallon was kept in isolation in the cottage for two years. In 1909 she sued the health department for release; the judge was sympathetic but sent Mallon back to the island. In 1910 a new city health commissioner allowed her to leave, on the promise that she would no longer work as a cook. Around 1914 the health department lost track of Mallon. She most likely had trouble making a living outside her expertise and returned to cooking. In 1915, after a typhoid fever breakout in Manhattan's Sloane Maternity Hospital, Mallon was found working in the kitchen, under the pseudonym "Mrs. Brown." She had infected 25 more people, 2 of whom died. She was apprehended and returned to the island, where she lived for the rest of her life.

Mallon came to be known as "Typhoid Mary," a term that began among the medical community as a descriptive term, perhaps to protect her identity, but came to signify anyone who is a public health threat. News reporters sensationalized "Typhoid Mary," turning her into a further outcast. Although the popular view in society declared that Mallon purposely infected others, there is no evidence to show this is true. Rather, her refusal to believe that she was a carrier was probably an extreme disbelief in new scientific thought. She denied the accusations until the end of her life, convinced that health officials were picking on her. Mallon resented her imprisonment and was extremely distrustful of the health personnel involved in her case. Her feces and urine were tested frequently, at times on several occasions per week, which added to her reportedly sullen and irritable nature with doctors.

Mallon was one of hundreds of healthy typhoid carriers tracked over a period of time in New York City, but she was the first to be monitored and the only one to be isolated for life. At the time of her first capture, the number of typhoid cases was greatly expanding. In New

York City alone, it was estimated that about 100 new carriers were added each year between 1907 and 1911, and this became the main cause of infection. New York State began following those who had recovered from typhoid but was able to find fewer than 20 of the estimated number of carriers.

The state had more success through epidemiological investigations into typhoid outbreaks, such as Soper's. Once a potential carrier was identified, their feces were tested for the presence of typhoid bacilli. If a person tested positively, the health department opened an individual record for the carrier, keeping close contact and checking to make sure carriers were not involved in food industries, teaching, or nursing. This was time and labor intensive and relied on much cooperation by the carriers themselves, most of whom were living under free conditions but had to submit to frequent testing. Some carriers became lost or refused to be tested, and some were traced to outbreaks and deaths as severe as those linked to Mallon. The problem of typhoid carriers continued on well into the 1920's.

Michelle C. K. McKowen

FOR FURTHER INFORMATION:

Bourdain, Anthony. *Typhoid Mary: An Urban Historical.* New York: Bloomsbury, 2001.

Gordon, Richard. *An Alarming History of Famous (and Difficult!) Patients: Amusing Medical Anecdotes from Typhoid Mary to FDR.* New York: St. Martin's Press, 1997.

Graf, Mercedes. *Quarantine: The Story of Typhoid Mary.* New York: Vantage Press, 1998.

Leavitt, Judith Walzer. *Typhoid Mary: Captive to the Public's Health.* Boston: Beacon Press, 1996.

■ 1902: PELÉE ERUPTION

VOLCANO

DATE: May 8, 1902
PLACE: Martinique
RESULT: Estimated 30,000 dead, city of St. Pierre destroyed

Pelée rises 4,583 feet above sea level. It is located at 14.8 degrees north latitude and 61.1 degrees west longitude. The name *pele*, meaning "bald," implies that the volcano was so named because its summit was, as it is now, an unvegetated dacitic lava dome. A lava dome was built during the eruption of the volcano in 1902, only to be destroyed by a subsequent eruption, then built up again. A stratovolcano composed mainly of pyroclastic rocks, Pelée is at the north end of the island of Martinique. It stands high over the coastal city of St. Pierre. The island is part of the Lesser Antilles volcanic arc formed by the subduction of the North American Plate under the Caribbean Plate.

Pelée is best known for the May 8, 1902, eruption, which destroyed Martinique's major city of St. Pierre, killing over 30,000 people. No other twentieth century eruption caused as large a number of casualties, resulting in the Pelée eruption being called the greatest killer volcano of the century. A nuée ardente, or "glowing cloud," type of pyroclastic flow and ash-cloud surge caused the destruction on the island. This nuée ardente detached from the lava dome and, pulled by gravity, flowed down the sides of the volcano. Pyroclastic flows, also known as volcanic hurricanes, are made up of hot incandescent solid particles; the term "pyroclastic" comes from *pyro* (fire) and *clastic* (broken).

Of six volcanic eruption styles identified by volcanologists, the most violent and extremely destructive type is Peléan volcanism. It is identified by glowing avalanches that spread down the mountain and over the ground, heavy with ash and pumice, at up to 62 miles (100 kilometers) an hour. Peléan volcanoes can flow over water as well as land. Sometimes described as a hot cloud traveling at tremendous speed, the volcanic hurricane can carry particles the size of boulders.

It may move silently and more swiftly than any atmospheric hurricane, reaching intensely hot temperatures. In fact, the heat is so intense that pyroclastic fragments can remain warm for over a year after the eruption.

This type of volcano was named for the 1902 Pelée eruption, which was the culmination of an eruption cycle that had been building for a few years. This cycle involved small eruptions that sent ash up from the volcano in a cloud to around 10,000 feet but that did not threaten to overflow the city. It can be assumed that the repeated activity had created an atmosphere of complacency that meant, in this case, that the population of 1902 assumed that the new volcanic activity was more of the same they had experienced over the past few years.

PELÉE ERUPTS. The first hint that there was activity in the volcano occurred on April 2, 1902, when new, steaming vent holes were seen in the upper part of a ravine called La Rivière Blanche. The ravine is on the south side of the mountain, facing St. Pierre, and leads from a secondary crater named L' tang Sec to the coast. Then, three weeks following the discovery of the holes, there were some tremors, ash clouds arose from the mountain's summit, and volcanic ash fell onto St. Pierre, the city at its base. The smell of sulfur filled the air as the volcano rumbled and shook.

Known as the Paris of the Caribbean, St. Pierre was a city of rows of well-built stone houses and downtown buildings, including an opera house, and served as the main port city for Martinique. The city rests on a large, open bay on the west coast of the island. St. Pierre was involved in an election campaign and ill prepared for the disaster about to befall it. Some people left as the ash began to fall, but most stayed so they could support the candidate of their choice in the election about to be held. Others came into the city from surrounding towns and villages to see the phenomenon of an active volcano.

By May the ash had thickened to the point that it blocked roads. Businesses were forced to close, and birds and small animals began to die from the ash and poisonous gases. On May 3 the newspaper *Les Colonies* wrote that the raining-down of ashes on the city "never stops." It reported that the ash was so thick that the wheels of moving carriages were silent as they passed through it, and the wind blew the ash from roofs and awnings into any open window.

The volcanologists of the time possessed only a primitive knowl-

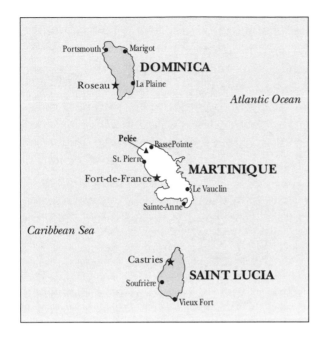

edge of the volcanic process and thus did not predict the disaster that was to occur. They were not aware of the existence of volcanic hurricanes and so did not urge people to leave the area. In fact, Gaston Landes, a professor at the St. Pierre high school, had said that the city could expect very little damage from the ash and the smell of sulfur. Even if there were lava flows, he told the city, they would be stopped by the ridges and valleys that lay between Pelée and the city. He assured them that even if the volcano should erupt, little damage would ensue. He was correct in that there was no lava in the flow that spewed out of Pelée. However, with the limited knowledge of volcanoes of that time, he was not aware of pyroclastic flows and of the heat they contained.

Early on May 8, ash clouds were still rising from Pelée. It seemed to the residents of St. Pierre to be just another day of ash falling on their roofs and streets. Suddenly, however, at 7:50 A.M. the volcano erupted with four blasts, sending a black cloud, which lit up with sharp lightning flashes, into the sky. The cloud of steaming hot gases reached temperatures of between 2,370 and 3,270 degrees Fahrenheit (1,300 and 1,800 degrees Celsius). Within five minutes a fifth blast sent an avalanche of boiling ash and gases down the mountainside. Glowing at 1,472 degrees Fahrenheit (800 degrees Celsius), the avalanche flowed so rapidly that in a few minutes the buildings and people of St. Pierre were buried and burned, covered by searing ash and gases.

Roughly 30,000 people were killed almost instantaneously, some perhaps surviving the initial avalanche until the fires claimed them. Others who survived the force of the flow died from inhaling the ash and gases that seared their respiratory systems. It is said that two people survived. One was a prisoner named Auguste Siparis, who was confined in an underground jail cell; the other was a shoemaker who managed to escape the fires. The story continues that the former prisoner became a performer in a circus sideshow as a survivor of the Pelée disaster.

In May, 1902, Pelée erupted in Martinique, causing 30,000 deaths—the most caused by a volcano in the twentieth century. (Library of Congress)

All that remained of the city was rubble and some partially standing walls. The heat had been enough to soften glass and windows, but copper remained unmelted. No clear volcanic deposit was found on the rubble because of the speed and violence of the flow and its makeup of ash and gases. On the volcano itself, the vegetation was stripped off, and any animals in the path of the flow were killed.

The hot ash had continued its flow to the sea, and 15 ships moored in the harbor capsized. The British steamer *Roddam* was torn free of its anchor and managed to flee to St. Lucia. It arrived with 12 dead crewmen and 10 suffering severe burns. One survivor from the *Roraima* stated that he watched red flames leap up from the top of the mountain, comparing it to the biggest oil refinery in the world burning on the mountaintop. It seemed to him that the mountain had blown apart without warning, its side ripped open, and he saw what seemed to be a solid wall of flame coming at those on the ships.

SUBSEQUENT ACTIVITY AND EFFECTS. Two months after the May 8 volcanic eruption, a second occurred. At that time two British scientists from the Royal Society were sailing past St. Pierre, studying the ruins of the city. They watched as a red glow surrounded the summit of Pelée, followed by an avalanche of heat and stones that poured down the mountain and across the ruins of St. Pierre. It took only a minute for the avalanche to reach the sea. They saw the black cloud, which seemed to consist of lighter particles of volcanic matter rising as heavier pieces fell to earth. The scientists described the cloud as globular, with a surface that bulged out. In fact, they said, it was covered with rounded bulging masses that swelled and multiplied, containing and moving with tremendous energy. It rushed forward toward them, over the waters, continually boiling up and changing its form. They saw it sweep over the sea, surging and moving while giving off brilliant flashes of lightning.

The scientists reported that the black cloud slowed its movement and faded, ash settling onto the surface of the sea. It then rose from the surface and passed over their heads, dropping stones and pellets of ash back down onto the sea. They smelled sulfuric acid and watched as the cloud moved out to sea, where it appeared to cover the sky—except for the horizon, which remained clear.

The major treatise on the eruption of Pelée, written by Alfred Lacroix of the French Academy of Sciences, named the phenomenon that destroyed St. Pierre a nuée ardente, or glowing cloud. Other terms are now used: glowing avalanche, ash flow, ignimbrite, fluidized flow, and base surge. Lacroix wrote that the pyroclastic eruption clouds move along the ground as hot, dense hurricanes, or "glowing clouds." It is suspected that a pyroclastic flow travels on a cushion of air, which allows it to rise from the surface of the land or water, and in some instances can even leave portions of the surface untouched by its destructive effects. This is why the scientists in a boat on the sea could escape unscathed by the avalanche that flowed over the water.

There had been two prior recorded eruptions of Pelée: one in 1792 and another in 1851. However, the 1902 eruption was unique in its destructiveness. The violence of the 1902 eruption drew attention to pyroclastic flows and opened a new area of research for volcanologists, in which they are still engaged. Recalling the serious effects of Pelée's eruption, in 1976 the French government evacuated the entire population of the island of Guadeloupe, fearing a similar eruption might occur from the volcanic mountain La Soufrière. It did not happen, but the memory of the destruction of St. Pierre in evidence on the island of Martinique, also French-owned, is strong in the French West Indies.

On Martinique, evidence of the killer volcanic eruption of 1902 still remains. Where volcanic ash was deposited, the land is a wasteland. The sand on that side of the island is black as a result of the black cloud of ash and gases that struck with such fury. The summit of Pelée was forever changed, with a large crater that formed from the explosion. It is now filled in by lava domes that, in an explosive volcanic eruption, form near the hole where the eruption occurred. The summit is a large garden of flowers and ferns surrounded by a heavy mist.

The city of St. Pierre never completely recovered from the explosion, and a small, quiet town exists where once there had been a bustling seaport. There is a volcanological museum with pictures and artifacts from the 1902 eruption of the volcano. The ruins of the opera house and other buildings are still visible.

Colleen M. Driscoll

FOR FURTHER INFORMATION:

Fisher, Richard V., Grant Heiken, and Jeffrey B. Hulen. *Volcanoes: Crucibles of Change*. Princeton, N.J.: Princeton University Press, 1997.

Morgan, Peter. *Fire Mountain: How One Man Survived the World's Worst Volcanic Disaster*. London: Bloomsbury, 2003.

Scarth, Alwyn. *La Catastrophe: The Eruption of Mount Pelee, the Worst Volcanic Eruption of the Twentieth Century*. New York: Oxford University Press, 2002.

_____. *Vulcan's Fury: Man Against the Volcano*. New ed. New Haven, Conn.: Yale University Press, 2001.

Zebrowski, Ernest. *The Last Days of St. Pierre: The Volcanic Disaster That Claimed 30,000 Lives*. New Brunswick, N.J.: Rutgers University Press, 2002.

■ 1906: THE GREAT SAN FRANCISCO EARTHQUAKE

EARTHQUAKE

DATE: April 18, 1906

PLACE: The northern coast of California, from King City to Humboldt Bay

MAGNITUDE: About 8.3

RESULT: Approximately 700 dead, 400 injured, 200,000 homeless, 28,188 buildings burned in San Francisco, and about $500 million in damage

In 1906, fifty-seven years after the 1849 gold rush, San Francisco was an active up-to-date city of 400,000. Although its central business district still included a handful of Spanish and Mexican adobe structures and comparatively few wooden buildings, the city comprised masonry and brick structures and newer multistory, steel-framed office blocks. Churches and public buildings of diverse construction were scattered throughout the city, while most residences, primarily wooden, were either closely spaced or shared common walls. In addition, most of the central business district, the waterfront, and the warehouse district was built on filled-in marshes, mudflats, and shallow water. Some newer commercial development and most of the residential district were perched on steep bedrock hills.

Before the 1906 earthquake, effective public utilities and fire and police departments served the bustling city. Numerous ferries crisscrossed the bay, steamers connected the city with Sacramento, and many railroad lines radiated from the busy city in all directions. The private Spring Valley Water Company pumped water through wrought iron or cast iron pipelines from the Crystal Springs, San Andreas, and Pilarcitos lakes, all impounded along the San Andreas fault, to University Mound, College Hill, and Lake Honda reservoirs inside the city. In turn, these reservoirs discharged water into the city's water mains. Additional water from Alameda Creek and Lake

Merrit entered the city via a pipeline beneath the South Bay. Several hundred firefighters manned 41 fire engines, 9 trucks, and 7 "chemical" engines as well as monitor and ladder trucks. Seven hundred police officers were assisted by sheriff's deputies, state militia, and the army's garrison at the Presidio.

REASONS FOR THE EARTHQUAKE. Most San Franciscans in 1906 did not expect a major earthquake. Prior to the 1906 earthquake, frequent small earth tremors caused trivial damage and occasional consternation. Spanish records from the second decade of the nineteenth century describe memorable earthquakes at the Presidio. A strong quake damaged City Hall and downtown buildings in October, 1865. In 1868, a severe earthquake across the bay at Hayward caused damage in downtown San Francisco and resulted in 5 deaths. Milder earthquakes occurred in 1890 and 1898. As a result, advanced construction codes had been adopted in San Francisco, and many buildings were designed to be fireproof. Thus, San Franciscans on the eve of the 1906 major earthquake judged the city well prepared to resist damage, but geologists and insurers were deeply concerned.

Earthquakes result from sudden, instantaneous lurches in a fault's movement, thought to be caused by temporary "freezing" of the fault that is followed by rupture. If the fault does not "freeze," movement is continuous and there are no major earthquakes. The San Andreas fault, responsible for the 1906 earthquake, is a right lateral transform fault separating the Pacific Ocean Plate from the North American Plate between Cape Mendocino and Baja California. This fault began shifting in the latest Cretaceous period, and by the present epoch cumulative movement has totaled about 370 miles. Thus, California as far north as Point Reyes and Santa Cruz was part of northern Baja California about seventy million years ago.

Today, movement on the San Andreas fault ranges up to 1.5 inches per year, requiring continual small repairs to structures spanning the fault trace. During the Great San Francisco Earthquake, apparently more than 240 miles of the San Andreas fault broke loose and shifted. Fissures with displacements mark the San Andreas fault from Point Arena, 100 miles northwest of San Francisco, to San Juan Bautista, 85 miles southeast. Severe damage at Priest Valley, 60 miles farther southeast, suggests an additional 60 miles of fault movement that failed to crack the surface. In addition, submarine observations in the later twentieth century traced fault-line topography to the San Andreas fault's juncture with the Mendocino Fracture Zone, a westward-trending fracture system passing far into the Pacific Plate.

Wherever displacement could be observed on the fissure, land southwest of the fault trace moved northward relative to the northeastern block. Just north of Tomales Bay this horizontal displacement was about 16 feet. Here the southwest block was lifted about 1 foot relative to the northeastern block. These displacements decrease to the north and south. Earthquakes along the San Andreas fault in historic time include 1812, Wrightwood (estimated magnitude, 7.0); 1838, San Francisco peninsula (7.0, estimated); 1857, Fort Tejon (8.0, estimated); 1906, San Francisco (8.3, estimated); and 1989, Loma Prieta (7.1, recorded).

THE EARTHQUAKE. The Great San Francisco Earthquake struck central California with a magnitude of about 8.3, on Wednesday, April 18, 1906, at 5:12 A.M. Fortunately, most people were still safely at home. In and around San Francisco, severe shaking lasted for about one minute. Before the main shocks, however, many observers noted two substantial preliminary shocks lasting several seconds. More than 1,000 aftershocks of intensity as great as V on the Modified Mercalli scale were recorded between April 18 and June 10 by a seismograph in Berkeley, California. Oscillatory ground movement during the main shock was principally horizontal and was estimated, in the city, at more than 2 inches on bedrock or firm ground. This was greatly amplified, however, on unconsolidated soil or sediment. Damage was substantial in a belt 20 to 40 miles wide paralleling the San Andreas fault from Eureka to Priest Valley. Thus, Santa Rosa, Salinas, San Mateo, Oakland, Berkeley, Vallejo, Petaluma, San Rafael, San Mateo, Palo Alto, and San Jose, in addition to San Francisco, suffered damage. Destruction was greatest adjacent to the fault trace, decreasing with distance from the trace. Indeed, the shock was felt as far away as Coos Bay, Oregon (390 miles); Los Angeles, California (350 miles); and Winnemucca, Nevada (340 miles). In addition, minor damage occurred 90 miles away on the east side of the San Joaquin Valley. As far away as Steamboat Springs, Nevada, wells and springs were affected by rising or falling water, interruption, stoppage and initiation of spring flow, and incursion of mineralized water.

Damage to buildings differed greatly according to construction

A house on Howard Street in San Francisco that was tipped by the 8.3-magnitude earthquake. (National Oceanic and Atmospheric Administration)

type and quality. Least damaged were buildings with solid foundations set on bedrock. Solidly built and well-braced one- or two-story wooden buildings suffered relatively little. The steel frames of structures as high as nineteen stories generally did not collapse, but masonry walls and cornices often shook loose. Most, however, were gutted by fire that caused poorly insulated beams to soften and crumple.

515

Heavy, well-constructed brick or stone buildings were also relatively resistant to damage, but poorly constructed masonry, or masonry with lime mortar, collapsed or disintegrated. Brick and stone clamped or braced by steel endured, as did massive concrete and brick fortifications. Finally, the single reinforced concrete building in the city of San Francisco, the Bekin Storage warehouse, survived with minor damage, as did the reinforced concrete portion of the Stanford University Museum.

Federal buildings, such as the mint and post offices, along with well-built churches, suffered least among masonry structures. However, shoddily constructed local governmental buildings, victims of low-bid and perhaps corrupt construction practices, such as the San Francisco and Santa Rosa city halls, the Agnews Insane Asylum, and the San Jose hall of records, were demolished. Private buildings differed greatly in their resistance. Many spires and towers collapsed.

The amount of damage was also greatly affected by the distance from the fault trace, topography, and the substratum, or soil foundation. For example, buildings straddling the fault trace were sheared. Although strong wood or steel-frame buildings generally did not break apart, they were twisted or rotated. Incredibly, a few stayed put, allowing the earth to shift beneath them, while larger structures either bent or were sliced apart but still stood. Concrete and earth-fill dams resisted damage. The earthen dams of the San Andreas and Pilarcitos reservoirs, built across the fault trace, survived the shearing. The massive concrete dam of the Crystal Springs Reservoir, immediately adjacent to the fault trace, also was undamaged. Buildings on weak or insecure foundations slid down slopes, while adjacent buildings with firm foundations attached to bedrock were relatively unharmed. Structures in the path of landslides and mudflows were severely damaged or destroyed.

Buildings not set on firm foundations reaching bedrock either collapsed or were severely damaged. For example, the Ferry Building, which rested on piles that reached bedrock, did not collapse; buildings on bedrock hills downtown and in the Western Addition were not very damaged. Approximately 20 percent of San Francisco, including the waterfront, the South of Market District, and most of the central business district, was built on filled-in mudflats and marshes. There, shaking was amplified by the soft, semiliquid substratum and generated actual wave movement; outright liquefaction also removed support for the buildings.

The earthquake reshaped the landscape in many ways. Fissures opened along the fault trace were, perhaps, most striking. Characteristically, these open rifts were generally about 5 feet wide and 10 feet deep. They sometimes occurred in zones as big as 50 feet wide. They were discontinuous, in many places consisting of a series of overlapping individual ladder breaks and somewhat inclined to the trace of the fault. In some places fissures did not open, and the fault trace was identifiable only by offset structures. Mudflows and landslides also occurred wherever blocks of surficial material shifted during the shock. These were concentrated along stream channels, where unstable land slumped into stream channels or on steep hillsides. In a landslide a coherent block of ground moves downhill in a more or less coherent mass, while in a mudflow, the dislodged material behaves as a liquid and flows.

In addition, liquefaction of water-soaked, unconsolidated subsoil was widespread. Parts of the mudflats in Tomales Bay simply flowed off into deep water. Here and at Bolinas, waves of compression, generated by shock along the fault trace, sent concentric giant ripples outward on the surface of the liquefied, unconsolidated material. After the shock passed, stability was restored in the liquified material and the ripples froze in place. Such frozen waves disrupted buildings, streets, and car tracks on the filled land in San Francisco. Compression at depth also spewed liquified sediment up to form mud volcanoes or craters on the surface.

THE FIRE. Although the event is referred to as the Great San Francisco Earthquake, the principal devastation was inflicted by the resultant fire. American cities of the time, including San Francisco, were largely built of wood. Consequently, nineteenth century American history records many great fires, such as the 1871 Great Chicago Fire. Actually, downtown San Francisco had been gutted by fire six times prior to 1906. As a consequence, most commercial builders favored brick, stone, and steel, but wood remained predominant in housebuilding. Immediately after the major earthquake shock, at least 10 large fires started among the closely spaced wooden buildings south of Market Street and in Chinatown, north of Market Street. Shattered chimneys, broken gas lines, and scattered fires readily ignited houses.

About 57 fires were reported before noon, despite the destruction of the city's modern alarm system. Also, Fire Chief Dennis Sullivan's fatal injury complicated the department's response. The capacity of the fire department to respond was far exceeded, and when an engine reached a fire, the firefighters found little or no water in the hydrants. The earthquake had broken the large mains bringing water into the city as well as the network of mains serving the hydrants from the subsidiary reservoirs. Thus, San Francisco's large, well-equipped fire department remained essentially unable to throw water on fires beyond reach of hose lines from the Bay Shore or one of the relatively undamaged reservoirs.

Mayor Eugene Schmitz and Fire Chief John Doughty implemented Chief Sullivan's emergency plan to pump water up Market Street through linked hoses, to establish a fire line along the city's broadest street. The already-blazing South of Market District was thus abandoned. Unfortunately, with Chinatown already ablaze and flames already jumping the street in a few places, the Market Street fire line soon failed. At the same time, a determined effort was made

The San Francisco earthquake of 1906 caused Union Street to buckle and become offset. (National Oceanic and Atmospheric Administration)

to check the westward advance of flames out of the South of Market District and into the Mission District. Frederick Funston, commanding the garrison at the Presidio in the temporary absence of his superior officer, General Adolphus Greeley, immediately ordered his troops into the city to fight fire and maintain order. Since he acted without official orders and without consulting his superior officers or civil authorities, his unconstitutional act was privately deplored by the War Department. The disciplined work of most of his men, however, as well as that of naval reinforcements, prevented looting and the breakdown of order. Thus, Funston, who eventually met with Mayor Schmitz and established cooperation with the police and fire departments, became a public hero and escaped discipline.

Strong measures were imperative to check the fire's spread. At 2 P.M., Mayor Schmitz obtained an opinion from a judge to clear the way for dynamiting buildings. Then, around 3 P.M., nine hours after the earthquake, he posted a proclamation announcing that gas and electricity had been cut off and warned people of the fire danger from damaged chimneys, gas pipes, and fixtures. Furthermore, he authorized summary execution of looters or persons defying the police or military. To enforce all of this, Schmitz also swore in 1,000 armed volunteer patrolmen. Although the proclamation of summary execution was illegal, Funston's men continued shooting looters and people ignoring orders. In this they were joined by police, the militia, and Schmitz's volunteers. Although the shootings effectively prevented civil disorder, there were many accusations of unwarranted, summary execution by rifle or bayonet. Most of this agitation was directed against relatively undisciplined militia and vigilantes, but controversy over the Army's role persisted.

In addition, Schmitz organized a committee of 50 prominent citizens to advise and assist him in fighting the fire. This committee first met at the Hall of Justice but relocated to Portsmouth Square when the building burned. By 8 P.M. on the first day, the fire front was a 3-mile-long crescent, and light from the flames was visible for at least 50 miles. Also by this time, Funston had met with the mayor and his committee at the Fairmount Hotel to outline plans to control the fire with a barrier of dynamited buildings. Thereafter, his troops set up a cordon along Van Ness Avenue, preventing entrance into the area to the east as troops forced all civilians out of the same area. Troops were also set to guard property west of Van Ness, and the dynamiting began on the east side of the avenue. Funston had made himself the de facto military governor of the city.

The fire continued spreading for a second day. On Thursday, April 19, the mansions on Nob Hill, the Fairmount Hotel, and the Barbary Coast below Telegraph Hill burned before 6 A.M. By 11 A.M., the U.S. Navy Pacific Squadron arrived, including the hospital ship the *Preble* and a water tender that immediately went to work bringing water to the city's fire engines. Sailors landed for demolition work, and Marines were deployed to protect waterfront property. In contrast to the Army, the militia, and the volunteers, they drew no criticism for misbehavior or wanton shooting. The Army, with the active participation of Funston's wife, Eda, set up a refugee camp on the grounds of the Presidio and in Letterman Hospital. Additional rations were ordered from Army stocks in Los Angeles and Seattle.

Ultimately, 20,000 people were estimated to be camping out in the Presidio. Other refugees, including the staff and patients from many of the city's hospitals, camped out in even larger numbers in Golden Gate Park. The inhabitants of St. Mary's hospital, however, escaped *en masse* on the steamer *Medoc*, which then stood offshore, eventually docking in Alameda. President Theodore Roosevelt requested that the Red Cross, insofar as possible, supervise relief operations at San Francisco. This first such effort established the Red Cross as the principal responder to mass disaster relief in America. By Thursday afternoon, thousands of people had gathered along the waterfront, where the fire department, aided by a Navy firefighting detachment and using more than 20 engines to pump water from the bay, had succeeded in saving almost all of the dock area. Every six minutes the Southern Pacific Railroad sent ferries loaded with refugees across the Bay without charge. In addition, a large number of Bay Boatmen also evacuated many, in some cases at exorbitant fees. Ultimately, the railroad transported 300,000 people across the Bay by ferry or onward by train to any point in North America. In time the wind changed, and by 4 P.M. the fire front was no longer wind-driven. Also, the water mains from Lake Honda had been repaired so that some water became available to the fire department. A small group of troops managed to organize a successful defense of part of the Russian Hill neighborhood. At 5 P.M., the Army, with the aid of a naval demolition squad, began blasting houses on the east side of Van Ness Avenue. This was soon supplemented by artillery fire.

The third day of the fire began with flames jumping the Van Ness Avenue fire line at midnight, but the fire department successfully checked this advance, and the firebreak was essentially maintained. At 5 A.M., Mayor Schmitz confronted Funston and ordered the cessation of dynamiting. One last blast, however, spread burning debris into an unburned area north of Green Street, and the fire, driven by the wind, expanded north and east. In the absence of troops to drive them away, Russian Hill residents successfully saved their neighborhood using water gathered in bathtubs, wet sheets, and even wine on the flames. At 5 P.M., Funston defied the mayor and ordered artillery bombardment along the Van Ness Avenue fire line. At 5:30 P.M. firefighters reported that the fire along Van Ness Avenue was out, and at 6 A.M. the following Friday morning, the Mission District was declared safe. At 7:15 A.M., the last flames were extinguished along the waterfront—seventy-two hours after the fire started.

Ultimately the fire was extinguished by a combination of factors. Fire lines established along Van Ness, Dolores, Howard, and Twentieth Street finally held when the wind either died down or shifted to oppose the fire's advance. Restoration of water service from the Honda Reservoir enabled firefighters to hold at Van Ness Avenue, and water pumped from the bay enabled firefightershters to save the waterfront. Ultimately, 4.7 square miles burned. Only a few isolated spots within the outer bounds of destruction survived: the south half of Russian Hill, a few downtown blocks, and part of Telegraph Hill. The strongly built mint, which contained a well in the basement, was successfully defended. The post office, thanks to thick walls and a determined crew of postal employees, managed to stave off the fire. The Palace Hotel also survived for six hours, until its cisterns were emptied and the roof sprays were cut off. Several additional buildings with solid walls and fire-resistant shutters or wired glass also stood unburned in the midst of the burned-out area.

AFTER THE FIRE. Because of the total confusion, actual enumeration of casualties was impossible, and many corpses were totally consumed by fire. Casualty estimates range from 450 to 1,000, with 700 the generally agreed estimate. While General Adolphus Greeley's official report listed 458 dead in San Francisco, only 315 dead were cited by city authorities. Four hundred injured were treated by medical authorities that kept records, and approximately 200,000 were left homeless. Subsequent to the fire, an outbreak of bubonic plague, caused by rats driven throughout the city, caused at least 160 recorded deaths.

Insurance companies were overwhelmed. The Fireman's Fund, for example, incurred liabilities of $11.5 million against total assets of $7 million. Companies reorganized under bankruptcy and paid claims, 55.6 percent cash and 50 percent in company stock. Only six major companies were able to pay claims without delay and in full. Fifty-nine companies spent months or even years fighting legal battles to avoid meeting their commitments.

Rebuilding San Francisco began immediately and, in the rush, plans that would have made the city more fire- and earthquake-resistant were essentially ignored. By December, 1906, plans were under way for the 1915 Panama Pacific International Exposition. By that year the city was rebuilt. Building codes were revised following publication of the California Earthquake Commission report. The codes curbed use of brickwork, outlawed heavy ornamental cornices, required improved bracing of steelwork, specified integration of walls and frames of buildings, and required installation of automatic sprinkler systems. In addition, a supplementary fire main system of saltwater, additional reservoirs within the city, refurbished cisterns, and acquisition of fireboats were recommended.

Earthquakes and other great disasters give rise to fanciful stories that persist in popular memory. The motion picture *San Francisco* (1936) dramatically shows a crevice suddenly opening in a crowded city street. Panicked people fall into it, to be engulfed when it promptly slams shut. This event never occurred. Also, a picture of dead cows in an open fissure at the south end of Tomales Bay has been published repeatedly as evidence of animals dying by falling into a fissure. In actuality, a rancher used the crevice to dispose of a dead cow, but the more dramatic story persists.

Folklore also has it that the San Francisco fire was stopped through heroic efforts by the Army to dynamite firebreaks, when in reality the dynamited wreckage of a building burns just as easily as the building, and even more readily if the building has stone or brick walls. Sober analysts of the California Earthquake Commission and of the Fire Underwriters heavily discount blowing up buildings as a way of stopping fires. A rumor that the U.S. mint was assaulted during the fire by an armed gang intending to rob it was repeated as historical fact in a San Francisco paper as late as 1956. Another incident wherein the carcass of a bull shot while charging and taken to Letterman Hospital to help feed refugees led to a rumor that dead horses from all over the city were being fed to unsuspecting victims.

Perhaps the most important result of the 1906 earthquake was that it made Californians actively conscious of the inevitability of periodic major earthquakes and the need for preparation. Thus, after every major quake, the California Uniform Building Code has been strengthened where found lacking. Also, continuing research on earthquake prediction provides growing understanding of what to expect and how to react. In spite of this, San Francisco again suffered severe damage in the 1989 Loma Prieta earthquake, escaping a major fire only because, fortuitously, winds were calm.

M. Casey Diana

FOR FURTHER INFORMATION:

Bolt, Bruce A. *Earthquakes.* 5th ed. New York: W. H. Freeman, 2006.

Collier, Michael. *A Land in Motion: California's San Andreas Fault.* Berkeley: University of California Press, 1999.

Colvard, Elizabeth M., and James Rogers. *Facing the Great Disaster: How the Men and Women of the U.S. Geological Survey Responded to the 1906 "San Francisco Earthquake."* Reston, Va.: U.S. Geological Survey, 2006.

Fradkin, Philip L. *The Great Earthquake and Firestorms of 1906: How San Francisco Nearly Destroyed Itself.* Berkeley: University of California Press, 2005.

Kurzman, Dan. *Disaster! The Great San Francisco Earthquake and Fire of 1906.* New York: William Morrow, 2001.

Smith, Dennis. *San Francisco Is Burning: The Untold Story of the 1906 Earthquake and Fires.* New York: Viking, 2005.

Winchester, Simon. *A Crack in the Edge of the World: America and the Great California Earthquake of 1906.* New York: HarperCollins, 2005.

■ 1908: The Tunguska Event

Meteorite or Comet

Date: June 30, 1908

Place: Tunguska, Siberia

Classification: 8 on the Torino Impact Hazard Scale; energy equivalent to at least 10 to 20 megatons of TNT released

Result: 2 dead, several nomad camps destroyed, more than 1,000 reindeer killed, 811 square miles (2,100 square kilometers) of forest flattened

Early on the morning of June 30, 1908, witnesses along a 621-mile (1,000-kilometer) path saw a fireball streak across the sky from the east-southeast. It was as bright as the Sun and cast its own set of shadows in the early morning light. The object exploded at 7:14 A.M., local time. Based upon seismic and barographic records, and upon the destruction caused, the explosion released energy equivalent to that of 10 to 20 megatons of TNT, making it the most devastating cosmic event on Earth during historical times. Depending upon the altitude of the explosion and the composition of the object, the energy released may have been as high as 50 megatons.

Had the explosion occurred over New York City, fatalities would have been in the millions. As it was, the object exploded over a sparsely inhabited forest in Siberia, roughly 43.5 miles (70 kilometers) north of Vanavara, a small village on the Stony Tunguska River. The region is one of primeval forests and bogs inhabited by nomads who tend large herds of reindeer. Near the epicenter (ground zero), trees burst into flame. Farther out, a great shock wave felled trees over an 811-square-mile (2,100-square-kilometer) area, pointing them radially outward, bottoms toward, and tops away from the epicenter. Right at the epicenter where the force of the blast wave was directly downward, a bizarre grove remained. Trees were left standing upright, but they were stripped of all their branches, like telephone poles.

An eyewitness in Vanavara said the sky was split apart by fire and that it was briefly hotter than he could endure. Because it was just after the summer solstice, the Sun remained above the horizon twenty-four hours a day north of the Arctic Circle. Dust, lofted high into the stratosphere, reflected so much sunlight back to the ground that even south of the Arctic Circle, in northern Europe and Asia, nights were not really dark for three days. People were amazed that they could read, or even take photographs, in the middle of the night. At least 1,000 reindeer were killed, and several nomad camps were blown away or incinerated. Some nomads were knocked unconscious, but remarkably, there are only 2 known human fatalities. An old man named Vasiliy was thrown 39 feet (12 meters) through the air into a tree. He soon died of his injuries. An elderly hunter named Lyuburman died of shock.

Scientists supposed that the seismic waves had been caused by an earthquake, but no scientists went immediately to investigate because of the remoteness of the site. It was not until 1927 that Leonid Kulik, the founder of meteorite science in Russia, reached the site after spending many days plunging through trackless bogs on horseback. Expecting to find a huge crater and a valuable nickel-iron mountain, Kulik and his assistant were amazed to find only a shattered forest stretching from horizon to horizon.

Careful research has since shown that the Tunguska object shattered about 5.3 miles (8.5 kilometers) above the ground. If it were a small comet, it must have been inactive, for there is no credible evidence of a tail. It must have been at least 328 feet (100 meters) in diameter and had an asteroidal core, because microscopic metallic particles were recovered that are more closely associated with asteroids than with comets. Russian scientists favor this hypothesis. The object's trajectory and timing are consistent with it being a fragment of Comet Encke. Western scientists favor the possibility that it was a small, dark, rocky asteroid, perhaps 197 feet (60 meters) in diameter.

When a solid object of this size plunges into the atmosphere, it piles up air in front of it until the air acts like a solid wall. The object shatters, its kinetic energy is converted to heat, and the object vaporizes explosively. Microscopic globules form as the vapor condenses. Such globules have been recovered from peat bogs and tree resin at the site, as well as from ice layers in remote Antarctica. The cosmic dust cloud truly spread worldwide. These globules have more of the elements nickel and iridium than normal Earth rocks do—clear signatures of their cosmic origins.

Charles W. Rogers

FOR FURTHER INFORMATION:

Chaikin, Andrew. "Target: Tunguska." *Sky and Telescope,* January, 1984, 18-21.

Fernie, J. Donald. "The Tunguska Event." *American Scientist,* September/October, 1993, 412-415.

Gallant, Roy A. "Journey to Tunguska." *Sky and Telescope,* June, 1994, 38-43.

Verma, Surendra. *The Tunguska Fireball: Solving One of the Great Mysteries of the 20th Century.* Cambridge, England: Icon Books, 2006.

Zanda, Brigitte, and Monica Rotaru, eds. *Meteorites: Their Impact on Science and History.* Translated by Roger Hewins. New York: Cambridge University Press, 2001.

■ 1908: The Messina earthquake

Earthquake

Date: December 28, 1908
Place: Strait of Messina, near Messina, Italy
Magnitude: 7.5
Result: 120,000 dead, numerous communities destroyed or severely damaged

In 1900 the Italian island of Sicily in the Mediterranean had a population of 3.8 million people. The island is separated from the province of Calabria on the Italian mainland by the 20-mile-long Strait of Messina. The strait is only 2 miles wide in the north, near the city of Messina, but expands to 10 miles in the south, near Reggio di Calabria. Even though much of the population of both Sicily and Calabria was employed in agriculture, one-fourth of it was concentrated in towns with populations of over 25,000, which proved disastrous during the earthquake in 1908. The Sicilian port city of Messina, which is located on the northern coast of the strait, claimed a population of 158,812 in 1905. It became Italy's fourth largest port, from which much of the citrus export was shipped to northern Europe. Ten miles southeast of Messina across the strait in Calabria is Reggio, another important Italian port city, with a population of 45,000 in 1908.

Sicily and the southern Italian region of Calabria are on the edge of the line that marks the collision between the European and the African continental plates. The mountain range that runs down the length of Italy and curves in southern Italy becomes the Calabrian Arc. The Messina Strait is on the southern point of the Calabrian Arc. The severe curvature of the Calabrian Arc causes lateral stretching of the earth's crust under the strait. Most of the earthquakes in Sicily and Calabria result from movement along the Messina fault, a fracture in the earth's crust that is 43 miles (70 kilometers) long and almost 19 miles (30 kilometers) wide. Between 1793 and 1908, twenty different earthquakes racked Messina and Reggio, although many were minor disturbances.

QUAKE. Earthquakes that reached at least magnitude 7 on the Richter scale have occurred repeatedly in Sicily and Calabria. An earthquake in 1783 resulted in 29,515 casualties, and another one in Calabria on September 8, 1905, produced property damage in excess of $10 million (1905 value). The most devastating earthquake to strike this region after 1783, however, occurred on December 28, 1908. The epicenter of this magnitude 7.5 earthquake was in the Messina Strait. The focus of the earthquake was 5 miles (8 kilometers) below the strait. Several weeks before December 28, shock waves were recorded in the region.

The day before the catastrophe was a mild day in Messina. That evening Giuseppe Verdi's opera *Aïda* was being performed at the local theater. People came from Reggio di Calabria, across the strait, to attend the performance, and the hotels in town were completely full. At 5:21 A.M., while it was still dark and most people were sound asleep, the ground moved for thirty-five seconds and destroyed or damaged an area from Terresa to Faro on the Sicilian coast and from Lazzaro to Scilla on the Calabrian coast. The shock, which some survivors compared to the noise of a fast train going through a tunnel, was most intense at the northern entrance to the strait, but it was felt in an area 100 miles in radius.

The earthquake's 30-mile path of destruction directly affected 40 communities north and south of Messina on both sides of the strait. The devastation was greatest in large towns, such as Messina and Reggio. Aftershocks were felt as late as early January, 1909. The initial shock was followed by a tsunami, or tidal wave, which reached heights of 8 feet in Messina and 15 feet in Reggio. The waves extended 219 yards (200 meters) inland and reached the island of Malta 115 minutes after the earthquake. In Messina the force of the water pushed a 2,000-ton Russian steamer from a dry dock into the bay. On the shore, embankments collapsed 6 feet under water, and cracks appeared on the ground 109 yards (100 meters) long and half a yard (0.6 meter) deep. In Reggio the wharf was wrecked, and freight railroad cars near a major ferry station overturned.

Few deaths resulted from either the tsunami or fires. Most of the 120,000 people who perished died because poorly constructed houses collapsed in the densely populated towns of Messina and Reggio. One-third of the population living in the 30-mile impact area

perished. In Messina the dead included soldiers of the local garrison, who died when their military barracks collapsed, and the U.S. Consul and his wife. The last survivors, a boy and two siblings, were rescued from the ruins eighteen days after the earthquake. Until order was restored by the Italian military, a number of criminals, who were freed when the prison in Messina collapsed, added to the carnage by pillaging. Witnesses claimed that former prisoners cut off fingers and ears of earthquake victims in order to collect wedding rings and other jewelry.

Gauged by the Modified Mercalli scale, the epicentral intensity of the destruction measured XI, which is only one level below the highest measurement possible on this scale. Both housing and infrastructure came down in clouds of dust and stones. The quake immediately destroyed the region's municipal electric, gas, and water facilities. Ports and banks were damaged or destroyed, and the telegraph cable was cut. The principal street in Messina, Corso Cavour, was demolished. In addition, 87 of Messina's 91 churches were destroyed, including the famous Norman cathedral. More than 1 million tons of debris had to be removed from Messina alone.

In addition to the destruction of the towns' infrastructure, in Messina and Reggio a majority of housing was completely destroyed. The most important reason for the extent of the destruction was the fact that most buildings were poorly built. In this poverty-stricken land, housing had to be constructed by local labor using available local material. Most walls were erected using rounded stones held together with weak mortar. Walls had weak girders and unsupported cross beams to support the weight of heavy roofs. These shortcomings of local construction had a long tradition. They were well known to French geologist Déodat de Gratet de Dolomieu, who described the poorly constructed housing in Messina in the aftermath of the earthquake of 1783. After that natural disaster, the Bourbon government of the kingdom of Sicily recommended construction of two-story timber-frame houses with the space between the timbers filled with stone embedded in mortar. This type of construction, called *baraccata*, was not enforced. Only the very rich could afford houses that were constructed adequately. A few of these *baraccata* buildings actually survived the earthquake of 1908 in Messina and in Castiglione. A doctor's house in Messina stood through the quake because its foundations were nearly 5 feet thick and the masonry was made of expensive lime and puzzolan mortar.

RESPONSE. Predictably, immediate reaction to the misery caused by the earthquake varied. The historian Gaetano Salvemini, a professor at the University of Messina who lost his whole family, lamented that he should have killed himself too. In one small Sicilian community that was not destroyed by the shock, people gathered in the church after the tremor. From there they followed their priest, who was carrying a statue of a saint to the center of the village in order to seek divine protection for the community. Journalists who visited destroyed communities reported that the population was apathetic, not religious, and gave the appearance of stupefaction and "mental paralysis." Outside Italy, the Russian poet Aleksandr Blok, reflecting on the achievements of modern civilization, asked whether fate was attempting to show how elemental forces could humiliate humankind, which in its hubris thought it could control and rule nature through technology.

Messina received foreign assistance two days before Reggio, where communications were interrupted longer. At first, help came from a variety of foreign ships, although one Italian warship in the region appeared soon after the catastrophe. The north German steamer *Theropia* left Naples on the afternoon of December 28 and reached the strait by daybreak the next day to offer assistance. By December 30, Russian and British warships were actively involved in rescue work. The injured were sent to Naples by ship and to Palermo and Catania by train.

Because of the initial lack of communication, the Italian government in Rome reacted slowly. Early reports suggested the loss of a few thousand people. Only after receiving a report from the prefect of Messina twenty-four hours after the disaster did the government appreciate the seriousness of the situation. King Victor Emmanuel III arrived in Messina by December 30. The pope offered financial assistance, but, because of health reasons, he could not make the journey to the stricken area. Systematic relief work did not come until a week later, when the Italian premier sent soldiers and imposed martial law. On January 9, 1909, the army secured Messina and helped in the rescue work. Looters were shot on sight. Military control lasted until February 14.

The world community reacted to the catastrophe with both an outpouring of sympathy and massive financial aid. By February 27, 1909, forty-three foreign countries, including even Peru, had provided assistance to this Italian region. The United States Congress voted for an assistance package of $800,000, and the Red Cross donated $1 million to the relief work by April, 1909. Additional funds were raised by a variety of papers and journals, ranging from the *Christian Herald* to *The New York Times*. The New York paper devoted front-page coverage to the earthquake from December 29, 1908, to

January 6, 1909. In addition, it published appeals for help from various American organizations, particularly the Italian American community.

In Italy a Committee to Aid was organized to assist the victims and to guide reconstruction. This committee included a number of politicians who wanted the aid to benefit primarily landowners and professionals rather than the masses. Peasants were urged to return to work on local citrus-fruit farms rather than rely on welfare in other parts of Italy. The duke of Aosta suggested that because of their poverty, the poor had lost little in the earthquake. The most extreme solution to the problem of recovery was suggested by the journalist Giuseppe Piazza, who thought that the Italian navy should bombard the ruins of Messina to the ground so that the city could be abandoned. Nonetheless, the population recovered and reached 177,000 by 1921. Also, by 1912, commerce in Messina reached 1909 levels and its port was again Italy's fourth-largest. Still, the earthquake left reminders. In 1958, 10,000 inhabitants of Messina still lived in "temporary" housing that had been built in 1909.

One long-term consequence of the earthquake was that it stimulated scientific studies on earthquake engineering. In early 1909 a committee was appointed, composed of nine engineers and five professors of engineering. Its task, as defined by the Ministry of Public Works, was to recommend earthquake-resistant buildings, which could be afforded by rural communities that had to rely on local raw material. The committee published its findings in Rome in 1909. Like many earlier studies after previous earthquakes, it summarized the weakness of housing construction in Messina and Reggio, ranging from poor mortar quality to unrestrained support beams. The committee recommended two-story wood-frame houses with walls filled with masonry. Based on these and subsequent findings, the Italian government between 1923 and 1930 passed more stringent construction laws, which in 1930 were more rigorous than those issued in earthquake-ridden Japan at that time. The task of meeting the challenge of earthquakes in this region is not finished. In 1970, the Italian government initiated studies on how to build a 2-mile (3-kilometer) single-span bridge across the Strait of Messina.

Johnpeter Horst Grill

FOR FURTHER INFORMATION:

Bosworth, R. J. B. "The Messina Earthquake of 28 December 1908." *European Studies Review* 11 (1981): 189-206.

Hobbs, William H. "The Latest Calabrian Disaster." *The Popular Science Monthly* 74 (February, 1909): 134-140.

Hood, Alexander Nelson. "Some Personal Experiences of the Great Earthquake." *The Living Age* 43 (May 8, 1909): 355-365.

Mulargia, F., and E. Boschi. "The 1908 Messina Earthquake and Related Seismicity." In *Earthquakes: Observation, Theory, and Interpretation*, edited by E. Boschi and H. Kanamori. Amsterdam: North-Holland, 1983.

Neri, G., et al. "Tectonic Stress and Seismogenic Faulting in the Area of the 1908 Messina Earthquake, South Italy." *Geophysical Research Letters* 31 (2004).

The New York Times. December 28, 1908-January 6, 1909.

Perret, Frank A. "The Messina Earthquake." *The Century: Illustrated Monthly Magazine* 55 (April, 1909): 921-928.

Wright, Charles W. "The World's Most Cruel Earthquake." *National Geographic* 10 (April, 1909): 373-396.

■ 1909: THE CHERRY MINE DISASTER

FIRE

DATE: November 13, 1909
PLACE: Cherry, Illinois
RESULT: 259 dead

The Cherry Mine is about 100 miles southwest of Chicago at Cherry, Illinois. Opened in 1904 by the St. Paul Mining Company, a subsidiary of the Chicago, Milwaukee and St. Paul Railroad, the mine existed solely to supply fuel for the railroad. Cherry, named for James Cherry, the railroad engineer in charge, was built to house miners. Almost all of the town's approximately 2,500 inhabitants consisted of miners and their families. On the morning of the disaster, 484 men went underground in the mine.

Up-to-date, well-managed, and prosperous, the Cherry Mine was a sought-after place to work. It was dry, gas-free, and, with the railroad as its owner, largely immune from seasonal layoffs. Also, the Cherry Mine was one of the first lit by electricity. Unfortunately, however, the electrical system shorted out three weeks prior to the disastrous fire, and oil torches were put temporarily into use. Such torches were, at the time, widespread in coal mines.

THE LAYOUT OF THE MINE. The Cherry Mine was entered through two shafts. The "second vein" (Illinois Springfield Number 5 Coal), a 5 foot, 2 inch seam mined at 316 feet, was the principal coal source when the mine burned. Beneath this, the lowermost of the three horizontal coal seams in the mine, the 3.5-foot "third vein" (Illinois Colchester Number 2 Coal) was mined at a depth of 486 feet. The "first vein" (Illinois Number 7, Streator Coal) at 271 feet was not mined in the Cherry Mine.

On both levels, miners were isolated far from the shafts. The main shaft hoist connected the second level to the tipple, or head frame, but did not run down the shaft to the third seam. A second hoist in the ventilation and escape shaft connected the second and third seams but did not reach the surface. Thus, men and cars from the lower level were lifted to the second level, proceeded 200 feet past

the mule stables to the main hoist and, at this point, were lifted to the tipple. There was no hoist in the air shaft above the second level, but an enclosed wooden stairway and ladders allowed miners to climb from the bottom to the top of the shaft. Two tunnels, mined through coal, passed around the stables to connect the shafts. These passages were propped with pine timbers and were partially lined with pine planks. About 75 mules were used to haul wooden mine cars between the working faces and the hoist landings. A "pillar" of unmined coal surrounded and supported the two shafts, stables, and entries.

The second level of the Cherry Mine was worked by the room-and-pillar method. Nearly a mile of "main entries," or tunnels, extended in an east-west direction from the shaft. Additional entries crossed the main entries at right angles to outline rectangular panels for mining. As coal was mined, "pillars," left in a rectangular arrangement, supported the "back," or roof.

The third seam was mined by the long-wall method because the seam was so thin that rock had to be excavated from the roof to permit men and mules to pass. Haulage entries radiated outwards from the shaft, and working tunnels branched out at acute angles. Here men had to crouch under a 3.5-foot "back." As the coal mining pro-

Smoke billows from the Cherry Mine after a fire there killed 259. (AP/Wide World Photos)

ceeded, the roof was allowed to collapse behind the miners, with only the tunnels remaining open. Miners on both levels were dependent on messengers for communication.

THE FIRE. At about 1:30 P.M. on November 13, 1909, a carload of hay was apparently ignited by kerosene dripping from the open torch at the second vein air-shaft landing. This small fire was ignored by miner Emil Gertz as he hurried to catch the 1:30 hoist. "Cagers," or hoist operators, Alex Rosenjack and Robert Dean continued hoisting coal for several minutes after they knew about the fire. Minutes later, Rosenjack and two others tried unsuccessfully to dump the burning car down the air shaft. Eventually, aided by a group of miners from the third vein, they pushed the car into the air shaft, where the fire died in the water-filled "sump" at the shaft bottom.

Meanwhile, however, timbers in the second level entries had ignited, and dense smoke already prevented miners from reaching the only water supply in the mine—a hose in the stables that supplied water for the mules. The fire raged out of control. At least forty-five minutes—too late for many to escape—passed before all men at the remote mining faces heard the warning. One cageload of men came up from the lower level before the cager fled, and a few additional men climbed the escape shaft stairs. Some second-vein men reached the hoist shaft from the side opposite the fire and escaped before smoke and flame blocked the shaft. Pit boss Alex Norberg then ordered the fan reversed to draw air down the main shaft, and mine manager John Bundy organized twelve volunteers to go down on the hoist to rescue trapped miners. After six successful trips, the seventh ended when the rescuers burned to death in the cage. Tragically, the hoist engineer, John Crowley, delayed lifting the men because signals from below were confused. At 8 P.M. the mine was sealed to smother the fire.

RECOVERY EFFORTS. Soon mine inspectors, firefighters, and rescue experts arrived to supervise further rescue and recovery. On November 14, R. Y. Williams and his assistant, from the University of Illinois, were lowered to the second level in the ventilation shaft wearing oxygen helmets and suits, but smoke and steam forced them out, and the shafts were again covered. The next day temperatures were fairly comfortable, but there was still too much smoke and steam underground. In an attempt to use the main shaft hoist, the fan was repaired to pull air down the main shaft. Ventilation, however, revived the fire, so both shafts were once again covered. On the fourth day, although the main shaft still retained excessive temperatures, a decision was made to enter the air shaft, and a temporary cage was constructed.

The next day, November 18, the "helmet men" retrieved a body from the air shaft. Also, a hose was lowered down to the second level late in the day, and fire fighting began. Chicago firefighters led the effort west of the main shaft all that night, and on November 19 they recovered four more bodies. Also, explorers got around cave-ins to reach the south entry and penetrated east almost to the air shaft. Repairs to timbering and removal of roof falls were done on these passages during the night. By the end of the first week, the fire was apparently under control in areas accessible from the main shaft landing.

Finally, on November 20, when the workings (tunnels and shafts) were stabilized and it appeared that no live men remained underground, the remaining mining inspectors left at 10:30 A.M. However, shortly after noon, 21 survivors, led by George Eddy and Walter Waite, were found on the second level. These men had sheltered behind barriers they erected to preserve breathable air, and all but one eventually recovered. After survivors were found, the mine inspectors hastily returned. Rooms east of the main south entry were explored that night and through Monday the 22nd, without finding additional living miners: About 100 bodies were removed. On November 23 and 24, the northwest entries were searched without recovering men or bodies. Northern workings east of the shaft, where many men had been employed, remained inaccessible. At this point, smoke began issuing from the main passageway connecting the west shaft with the air shaft. This passage was temporarily blocked by a roof fall and a temporary barrier. Exploration of the northwest section immediately ceased, the barrier was removed, and a hose was turned into the passage, dousing the fire.

Also on November 24, four men reentered the third vein for the first time since the fire began and found 3 to 4 feet of water in the workings. Groups of bodies were discovered in dry places. However, pumping preparations halted when fire began encroaching behind the shaft lining south and east of the main shaft. These fires could not be suppressed, so smoke spread west, practically driving out the rescuers. In addition, dense coal smoke from burning pillars aroused fear of noxious gases. Thus, after a unanimous decision that no survivors remained in the mine, both shafts were sealed with steel rails and concrete in order to smother the fire on November 25, 1909, two weeks after the fire began.

During the crisis, the Red Cross sent supplies and workers. The Catholic Church sent nuns to help the bereaved, and other churches organized relief committees. The *Chicago Tribune* gathered money and contributed food.

THE AFTERMATH. Restoration began February 1, 1910, after temperatures dropped to normal and the mine was ventilated. Finally, the fire was extinguished, and the lower level was drained. By March 5, 82 bodies had been recovered from the second level, and on April 12, 51 bodies were removed from the third level. Up to 6 men remained unaccounted for. Next, the second level was walled off, everything of value removed, and it was abandoned. By September 3, some third-level entries were cleared to the coal face, and the mine was expected to reopen October 10, 1910—one year and thirty-one days after the fire.

Results of the Cherry Mine disaster were many and varied. Public indignation made it necessary to bring in the militia to guard mine officials. Also, cagers Rosenjack and Dean fled the town, and hoist engineer Crowley was placed under protection. In all, 187 bodies were found on the second vein: 51 on the third vein and 12 victims burned to death during rescue efforts. Three of 256 dead listed in the state mining inspector's report were "American," 233 of diverse nationalities, and 20 of unreported nationality. The youngest miners were only fifteen and working in violation of the Factory Act, which prohibited those under sixteen from mining.

The Cherry Relief Commission collected a total of $256,215.72 from the state legislature and death benefits from the United Mine Workers, as well as money from the railroad, from churches, and from many individual donors. Also, an additional $400,000 settlement was negotiated with the mining company. These funds provided widows with lump-sum payments and, until they remarried, modest pensions, as well as child support for children too young to work. In 1910 and 1911 the Illinois state legislature passed several bills in response to the Cherry disaster. These required improved firefighting and prevention measures, telephones connecting the faces and cages with the surface, improved workers' compensation laws, and establishment of regional fire and rescue stations. The Cherry Disaster also was crucial in establishment of the Federal Bureau of Mines.

Cherry's annual memorial services and museum continue to draw large attendance. After the disaster, the St. Paul Mining Company continued with many of the original miners until 1927. By then unmechanized long-wall mines were obsolete, and the mine closed. In 1928, Mark Bartolo reopened the mine until its final closure during the Depression. Bartolo salvaged buildings and equipment and began to farm the site.

M. Casey Diana

FOR FURTHER INFORMATION:

Buck, F. P. *The Cherry Mine Disaster.* Chicago: M. H. Donohue, 1910.

Burns, Robert Taylor. "The Cherry Mine Disaster." *Outdoor Illinois* 8, no. 4 (1967): 36-40.

Curran, Daniel J. *Dead Laws for Dead Men.* Pittsburgh: University of Pittsburgh Press, 1993.

Hudson, Thomas. "The Cherry Mine Disaster." In *Twenty-ninth Annual Coal Report of the Illinois Bureau of Labor Statistics.* Springfield: Illinois State Journal, 1911.

Tintori, Karen. *Trapped: The 1909 Cherry Mine Disaster.* New York: Atria Books, 2002.

U.S. Department of Labor, Mine Safety, and Health Administration. National Mine Health and Safety Academy. *Historical Summary of Mine Disasters in the United States.* Beaver, W.Va.: Author, 1998.

Wyatt, Edith. "Heroes of the Cherry Mine." *McClure's Magazine* 34, no. 5 (March, 1910): 473-492.

■ 1914: The Eccles Mine Disaster

Explosion

Date: April 28, 1914
Place: Eccles (near Beckley), Raleigh County, West Virginia
Result: 181 dead

The Eccles Number 5 Mine was opened in 1905. It was owned by the Guggenheim family of New York City and managed by the New River Collieries Company until the Stoneage Coke and Coal Company took over operations in 1923. Stoneage operated the mine from 1923 until 1928. Eccles was a gaseous mine, as noted in the 1911 annual report of the Department of Mines of West Virginia. However, the ventilation required for gaseous mines was adequate and appeared to be up to standards. The Department of Mines was not expecting a major tragedy at Eccles.

At 2:10 P.M., an explosion in the Number 5 Mine killed every man among the 172 who were working there. While working the seam in the Number 6 mine, above the Number 5 Mine, 8 men were killed by the afterdamp from the Number 5 Mine explosion. Afterdamp is an asphyxiating gas left in a mine after an explosion of firedamp. Firedamp is a gas, largely methane, formed in coal mines and is explosive when mixed with air. Sixty-six men managed to escape from the Number 6 Mine.

The explosion that originated in the Number 5 Mine produced heat and violence so great that few of the 172 men in the mine workings could have lived any real amount of time after the explosion. About ten minutes after the first explosion in the Number 5 Mine, a second and less violent explosion occurred, which carried debris out of the Number 5 Mine's shaft. The first and more violent explosion, accompanied by flame, carried timber and quantities of mud up both mines' shafts and blew off the explosion doors of the fanhouse at the Number 5 Mine's shaft. The explosion did not, however, damage the fan. The explosion wave in the Number 5 Mine traveling toward the Number 6 Mine's shaft blew a large quantity of water from a depression up the Number 5 Mine's shaft. This quenched the flame and prevented it from entering the Number 6 Mine. Rescue workers entered through the Number 6 Mine's shaft.

REASONS FOR THE EXPLOSION. The official report filed by the mine inspectors gives the cause of the explosion as a barrier of coal being breached a short time before the explosion occurred. A contractor working on the south side of the coal barrier had been notified not to take out the barrier, as that would disrupt the ventilation in that portion of the mine. This barrier was intact on the morning of the explosion, as testified to by the night boss who examined it.

> After the explosion the body of [Seth] Combs [the contractor] was found on the north side of the barrier . . . while his work was on the south side, and it is assumed that some time during the day he had blasted out a hole in the barrier that he might have a shorter travel way to the north section of the entry. In doing so, practically one-third of the mine was left without ventilation and it seems that the explosion originated in the main south sections of the mine.

The mine was known to liberate explosive gas, and the coal in this section, varying in thickness from 8 to 10 feet, would allow the gas to accumulate next to the roof. Conditions suggested that this explosion was caused by the ignition of gas and its propagation throughout the various parts of the mine. This was aided, to some extent, by the presence of coal dust, as the force of the explosion traveled in all directions. It dropped the Eccles Number 5 Mine 500 feet down into the Beckley coal seam.

THE AFTERMATH. Of the 181 dead, 62 were positively identified. Of those, 15 percent were African American and 23 percent were of Italian descent. Some had Slavic surnames. Many of the dead miners were immigrants. About 39 percent were married. Those who could be identified were buried in family cemeteries if they were locals. Some of the Catholic immigrant miners were taken to Saint Sebastian cemetery in nearby Beckley. Those who were not identified were buried in the "Polish cemetery" above the tipple, where coal was emptied from the mine cars at the Eccles mines. In 1976, the bodies were moved to a new cemetery at the request of the Westmoreland Coal Company, which was then working the Eccles mines.

Dana P. McDermott

FOR FURTHER INFORMATION:

Dillon, Lacy A. *They Died in the Darkness.* Ravencliff, W.Va.: Coal Books, 1991.

Humphrey, Hiram B. *Historical Summary of Coal-Mine Explosions in the United States, 1910-1958.* Washington, D.C.: U.S. Government Printing Office, Bureau of Mines, 1959.

U.S. Department of Labor, Mine Safety, and Health Administration. National Mine Health and Safety Academy. *Historical Summary of Mine Disasters in the United States.* Beaver, W.Va.: Author, 1998.

Wood, James L. *Raleigh County, West Virginia.* Beckley, W.Va.: Raleigh County Historical Society, 1994.

■ 1914: *EMPRESS OF IRELAND* SINKING
FOG

DATE: May 29, 1914
PLACE: St. Lawrence River, Canada
RESULT: More than 1,000 dead in sinking of Canadian liner *Empress of Ireland* following collision with Norwegian freighter *Storstad* in heavy fog

The fame and historical significance of some disasters certainly overshadow other tragedies and accidents. Such is the case regarding the loss of the *Empress of Ireland*. The nationality, location, and date of the disaster all contributed to a general lack of knowledge about the ship's loss, despite the fact that more passengers lost their lives in the accident than in more famous incidents.

Empress of Ireland (completed in 1907) and its sister ship *Empress of Britain* were constructed by the Fairfield Shipbuilding and Engineering Company of Glasgow as flagships of the Canadian Pacific Line. At 14,200 tons, *Empress of Ireland* carried more than 1,000 passengers—310 first class, 350 second class, and 800 third class—on the Quebec-to-Liverpool route. For eight years the ship enjoyed a distinguished reputation for service and reliability and never once was involved in any sort of accident.

Empress of Ireland, with 1,057 passengers and 420 crewmen aboard, left Quebec on May 28, 1914. Many of its passengers were prominent leaders of the Canadian Salvation Army, on their way to Europe to attend the organization's worldwide convention. At approximately 1 A.M., Captain Henry Kendall, commanding the *Empress of Ireland* for the first time, paused to drop off pilot Adelhard Bernier at Rimouski, Quebec, at the point where the St. Lawrence River widens before the approach to the open sea. At about the same time, the Norwegian *Storstad*, a coal freighter, was approaching Rimouski to take on its pilot before entering the narrow portion of the river. The *Storstad*'s 7,000-ton displacement was further burdened by 11,000 tons of coal scheduled to be unloaded in Quebec the next day. On the *Storstad*'s

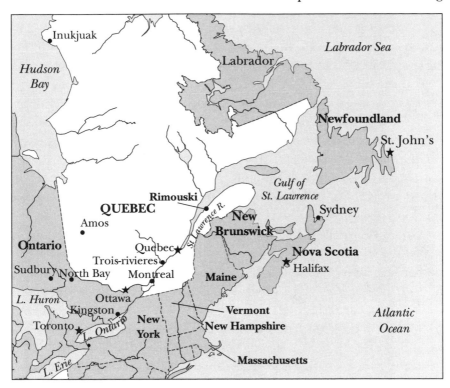

bridge First Mate Alfred Toftenes stood watch, peering into the darkness as intermittent fog began to develop over the river.

Not long after passing Rimouski, the two ships sighted each other. In the darkness without any visual references, both ships misjudged the bearing and speed of the other, with disastrous results. Before signals could be launched and positions verified, a blanket of fog obscured both vessels' view of the other, leaving the ships groping toward each other in the darkness. Both officers then took actions intended to prevent a collision, but which in retrospect proved the opposite. First Mate Toftenes, obeying the established maritime rules, proceeded on his original course and speed, presuming the other ship would do the same and pass cleanly to port.

Captain Kendell, however, did almost the opposite. He initially ordered all his engines to stop in order to allow the other vessel to pass ahead of him. The immense mass of the ship, however, carried the vessel forward anyway. To compensate, Kendall ordered the engines to full reverse to halt the *Empress of Ireland*'s forward momentum, announcing his intent to the unseen ship by three long blasts from his steam whistle. When First Mate Toftenes heard the whistle, he realized the danger of his situation. He immediately reduced forward speed and called the *Storstad*'s commanding officer, Captain Thomas Anderson, to the bridge. Anderson had just arrived on the bridge when the massive starboard side of the *Empress of Ireland* suddenly appeared out of the fog less than 100 yards dead ahead. Captain Anderson immediately reversed engines, while Captain Kendall went to full speed to avoid a collision, but their efforts were in vain. *Storstad* rammed the *Empress of Ireland* amidships, nearly cutting it in two.

Captain Kendall, realizing his ship was doomed, immediately ordered the helmsman to turn the ship toward shore and prepare the passengers for evacuation. Despite direct action, the *Empress of Ireland* and many of its passengers had no chance. The deep wound caused by the *Storstad* had flooded the boilers, and the *Empress of Ireland* came to a dead stop in the channel. Electrical power also failed, plunging the ship into darkness and disabling the public address system needed to alert sleeping passengers and crew. The gash in its side also admitted tons of water into the ship. Only ten minutes after the collision, the *Empress of Ireland* capsized, floated bottom up for several minutes, then sank in 150 feet of water.

Because of the loss of power and the quick demise of the ship, the death toll was staggering. Of 1,057 passengers, only 217 survived. More crewmen survived the tragedy because they were awake and working, but 172 of the 420 crewmen lost their lives. An additional 20 crewmen aboard the *Storstad* also died. Eager to place blame, a Canadian court of inquiry cleared Captain Kendall of all responsibility for the disaster. A Norwegian inquiry subsequently cleared the *Storstad* of any fault. In actuality both were to blame. Captain Kendall had acted indecisively and had not followed established maritime rules by failing to maintain his course. First Mate Toftenes also deserved blame for not summoning his commanding officer until the situation had deteriorated.

The loss of the *Empress of Ireland* has slipped into obscurity for several reasons. First, its loss was overshadowed by the sinking of the *Titanic* two years earlier. *Empress of Ireland* also sank in the St. Lawrence River instead of on the higher-profile passenger routes in the North

Atlantic. Finally, the growing war scare in Europe that would result in World War I only three months after the loss of *Empress of Ireland* dominated the news more than the loss of a passenger liner on a Canadian river.

Steven J. Ramold

FOR FURTHER INFORMATION:

Bonsall, Thomas E. *Great Shipwrecks of the Twentieth Century.* Baltimore: Bookman, 1988.

Croall, James. *Disaster at Sea: The Last Voyage of the "Empress of Ireland."* New York: Stein & Day, 1980.

McMurray, Kevin F. *Dark Descent: Diving and the Deadly Allure of the "Empress of Ireland."* Camden, Maine: International Marine, 2004.

Marshall, Logan. *The Tragic Story of the "Empress of Ireland."* 1914. Reprint. London: Patrick Stephens, 1972.

Wood, Herbert P. *Til We Meet Again: The Sinking of the "Empress of Ireland."* Toronto: Image, 1982.

Zeni, David. *Forgotten Empress: The "Empress of Ireland" Story.* Tiverton, N.Y.: Halsgrove, 1998.

■ 1916: The Great Polio Epidemic

Epidemic

Date: 1916
Place: 26 states, particularly New York
Result: At least 7,000 deaths, 27,000 reported cases

Nearly all Americans coming of age during the first half of the twentieth century have childhood memories that include the apprehension each summer brought, when polio epidemics could begin without warning, leaving many paralyzed or dead in their wake. Although poliomyelitis, or infantile paralysis, as it was also called, had existed for hundreds of years, the first large-scale epidemic of the disease hit the United States in 1916. An earlier outbreak had occurred in Stockholm in 1887, with 44 cases reported. There were also outbreaks in New York City in 1907, New York City and Cincinnati in 1911, and Buffalo, New York, in 1912, but none approached the horror and severity of the 1916 epidemic. Indeed, the 1916 polio epidemic set the pattern for polio epidemics through the middle of the twentieth century, both in the virulence of the disease and in the public's response.

Rate of Infection. Typically, in the early years of the twentieth century, the rate of polio infection in the United States was less than 7.9 cases per 100,000 people. In 1916, that figure rose dramatically, topping out at 28.5 cases per 100,000. People in 26 states were affected by the disease. All told, between roughly July of 1916 and October of 1916 some 27,000 cases were reported. Of these, about 7,000 people died. In New York City, the hardest hit area of the country, there were about 9,000 cases, and nearly all of these cases occurred in children younger than sixteen years of age. During the week of August 5, 1916, at the height of the epidemic, there were 1,151 cases reported in the city and 301 deaths. Many cases went unreported because the families of victims feared that they would be quarantined and unable to leave their homes.

Many victims of the disease suffered mild or no symptoms, often only complaining of a low-grade fever. However, others complained of stiff necks and backs and increasingly painful limbs. Sometimes, this muscular distress grew more severe, with the limbs becoming paralyzed. In the worst cases, the virus destroyed the nerves controlling the muscles responsible for breathing, leading inevitably to death. The swift onset of the disease, the often dire consequences, the mysterious nature of transmission, and its predilection for attacking adolescents and young adults in the prime of life made polio a terrifying word. During epidemics, horrified populations submitted to intrusive public health regulations that they never would have endured otherwise, all in the hope of quelling the infection's spread.

POLIO BECOMES EPIDEMIC. Ironically, some researchers believe that the improved sanitation in American cities in the twentieth century changed the way the population experienced the virus. The improved sanitation, while a boon in preventing many forms of illnesses, may have contributed to polio becoming a typically epidemic

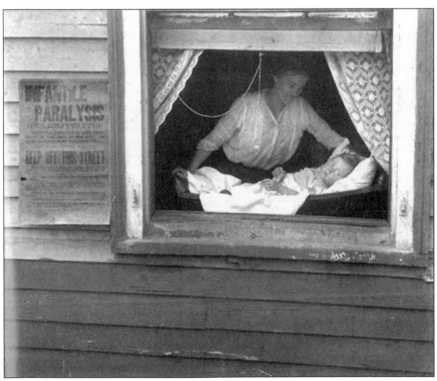

During the Great Polio Epidemic of 1916, quarantines were enforced in cities.

disease. In the years before the twentieth century, human feces containing large amounts of polio virus were the most common form of transmission. Water contaminated with feces led to many cases. Thus, before the twentieth century, polio infected almost all babies. These babies only suffered a mild reaction, generally no more than a low-grade fever or cold symptoms.

Sometimes babies who were infected did not exhibit symptoms at all. They were, nonetheless, immune to future infection by the virus. Further, polio had always been a far more serious disease in adults than in infants. Improved sanitation meant that fewer babies were exposed to the virus. As a result, more adults were susceptible to the disease. When the virus struck the largely unprotected population, it reached epidemic proportions as adolescents and adults passed the disease to other adolescents and adults, often with disastrous consequences. The illness this population suffered was of a far more serious nature, often leading to paralysis or death.

Although the cause of polio had been identified as a virus as early as 1909, no vaccine existed in 1916. Further, the medical community was uncertain how the disease was passed from person to person, and they did not know why the disease always peaked in the summer, only to ease in the winter. At the time of the 1916 outbreak, popular wisdom attributed polio to wildly different sources. Many believed that the disease was caused by poisonous caterpillars or moldy flour. Others thought that gooseberries or contaminated milk could cause polio. Still others thought that contact with human spit or sewage odors might be the culprit.

In spite of popular opinion, in 1916 medical researchers generally subscribed to the germ theory. That is, they believed that disease was passed from person to person via invisible germs. Much of the general public and some epidemiologists, however, still believed that most disease was caused by dirt. If there were such a thing as germs, they reasoned, then they must be spread by dirty people. Such reasoning led to the extreme measures to enforce quarantine and isolation that characterized the 1916 epidemic, particularly in New York City.

PUBLIC HEALTH RESPONSE. Public health officials undertook many measures to try to slow the spread of the disease in the summer of 1916. They placed quarantine signs on the doors of victims, in-

This card is furnished for the aid of interstate travelers. It should be retained and shown upon demand to proper authorities

U. S. Public Health Service,

Baltimore, Md.,.., 1916.

To whom it may concern:

This certifies that..

traveling {
from ....

to ....
}

with.................................children under 16 years of age has presented a satisfactory health certificate from the health authorities at point of departure that his premises are free from poliomyelitis (infantile paralysis). The children accompanying traveler have been inspected and show no evidence of that disease.

RUPERT BLUE,

Surgeon General, U. S. Public Health Service.

By...

In an effort to control spread of the disease, interstate travelers were required to carry a health certificate verifying the absence of polio.

structed that all bed clothing be disinfected, and required nurses to change their clothing immediately after visiting with patients. In the mistaken notion that dogs and cats could spread the disease, pets were not permitted to go into rooms with people suffering from polio. As the epidemic wore on, public health officials gathered up and destroyed many dogs and cats. On July 14, 1916, New York officials announced a new regulation forbidding travel in or out of parts of the city stricken with the epidemic. Further, New York City children had to carry identification cards certifying that neither they nor anyone in their families had polio before they were allowed to leave the city.

The public reaction in New York to the 1916 epidemic is particularly interesting because it reveals the deep resentment the upper and middle classes bore toward the poor and immigrant populations. When most public health and elected officials attributed the epidemic to dirty people, they did not have far to look in New York City, with its large, poverty-stricken immigrant population. As a group, the poor were generally ill educated and did not wield political clout.

Consequently, public officials took restrictive measures that were directly aimed at this population. For example, a New York City law required that any sick child living in a home without a private toilet and whose family could not provide a private nurse must be hospitalized. Thus, virtually any sick child who also had the misfortune to be poor was hospitalized. Since hospitals were often the sites of secondary infections, such hospitalization was not always in the best interest of the child. Even more extreme, poor children without symptoms were also quarantined, due to the public's belief that such children spread the illness to their middle-class and upper-class neighbors.

Residents attributed the large outbreak of polio in New Rochelle, New York, to its immigrant population. Indeed, the immigrant population was looked upon with growing suspicion as the epidemic dragged on through the summer. Immigrant children were banned from city functions and camps. In contrast, middle-class and wealthy children were sent out of the city for the summer, to places their parents deemed were "safe," often meaning to places that had low immigrant populations. More than 50,000 children were sent out of New York City over the course of the summer.

Several wealthy New York suburbs isolated themselves from the rest of New York, forbidding nonresidents from entering their towns. Hastings-on-Hudson, for example, refused to admit 150 families who wanted to summer there, and police intervention was needed to send them away. Some communities closed their beaches to nonresidents.

The polio epidemic of 1916, then, shows clearly how a public health issue can quickly become an issue of politics, race, economics, and class. In some places, such as Oyster Bay, a summer resort town, the interests of the less wealthy permanent residents were at odds with the wealthier summer guests. J. N. Hayes, in *The Burdens of Disease: Epidemics and Human Response in Western History* (1998), cites a study by Guenter Risse of the public reaction in Oyster Bay during the time of the epidemic. The permanent residents, many of whom made their living by supplying the summer residents with services, did not want a quarantine imposed that would destroy their livelihoods. At the same time, they did not want to pay through their taxes for health services for the rich guests. That many of the permanent residents were of Irish or Polish descent further convinced the summer guests that they were at risk in the resort.

As the epidemic continued, it became clear that the transmission model that most middle-class and upper-class members held was not accurate. Contact with poor and immigrant populations did not lead to the transmission of the disease; victims seemed randomly chosen. Some public health officials began to advocate for the eradication of the fly, on the grounds that flies spread filth and disease. Once again, the public backed these measures because it gave them a sense that there was something they could do. Nonetheless, killing flies did not stop the spread of polio.

CONCLUSIONS. While such reactions seem extreme, it is difficult to overestimate the panic the population felt with a serious epidemic underway, an epidemic that seemed impervious to modern medicine, and to all contemporary public health measures. During the 1916 epidemic, parents began keeping their children indoors and away from crowds, a pattern that repeated itself each summer until a vaccine was discovered.

During the polio epidemic of 1916, federal health officials kept many records and statistics in their efforts to better understand the cause and transmission of the disease. It took over two years to assemble and analyze the data and to release their report. The results of the report did nothing to allay public fear over future epidemics. The report said that the quarantine efforts had been a failure, and the federal health officials were unable to establish the way polio moved through communities. There was no indication that the disease was linked to family socioeconomic status or ethnic background. The report did raise hope that a cure or vaccine could be found if research efforts were focused on those people who had contracted the disease but had not become ill.

The polio epidemic of 1916 was only the first of a series of major polio epidemics that raced through the nation in the subsequent summers. This epidemic, along with the influenza epidemic of 1918, undermined public trust in modern medicine, which had held out such hope for the eradication of disease just a few years earlier. It would not be until nearly 1960 before children would once again populate beaches and pools in the heat of summer.

Diane Andrews Henningfeld

FOR FURTHER INFORMATION:

Daniel, Thomas M., and Frederick C. Robbins, eds. *Polio.* Rochester, N.Y.: University of Rochester Press, 1997.

Gehlbach, Stephen H. *American Plagues: Lessons from Our Battles with Disease.* New York: McGraw-Hill Medical, 2005.

Gould, Tony. *A Summer Plague: Polio and Its Survivors.* New Haven, Conn.: Yale University Press, 1995.

Hayes, J. N. *The Burdens of Disease: Epidemics and Human Response in Western History.* New Brunswick, N.J.: Rutgers University Press, 1998.

Kluger, Jeffrey. *Splendid Solution: Jonas Salk and the Conquest of Polio.* New York: G. P. Putnam's Sons, 2004.

Oshinsky, David M. *Polio: An American Story.* New York: Oxford University Press, 2005.

Rogers, Naomi. *Dirt and Disease: Polio Before FDR.* New Brunswick, N.J.: Rutgers University Press, 1992.

Smith, Jane S. *Patenting the Sun: Polio and the Salk Vaccine.* New York: William Morrow, 1990.

■ 1918: The Great Flu Pandemic

Epidemic

Also known as: The Spanish Flu Pandemic
Date: 1918-1920
Place: The United States, Europe, Africa, India, Japan, Russia, South America, and the South Seas
Result: 550,000 dead in the United States, more than 30 million dead worldwide

Influenza, an illness caused by a highly contagious, highly mutable virus, has been a part of human history for many years. It has been described as the kind of illness a doctor loves: everyone ill, but no one dying. Also known by a variety of names, including the grippe, catarrh, and knock-me-down fever, influenza generally kills only the very young and very old. However, in the spring of 1918, a new influenza virus began spreading throughout the world. Before the pandemic burned itself out sometime in late 1919 or early 1920, it had circled the globe and killed more people in less time than any other illness in recorded history. Even more frightening, it had targeted young, robust people in the prime of their lives.

Symptoms for most influenza viruses mimic a bad cold. The 1918 strain, however, devastated the human body, causing hemorrhages in the nose and in the lungs. People who were exposed to the disease came down with it in under three days and were often dead within three days of their first symptoms. Contemporary doctors at first doubted that they were dealing with influenza at all, thinking perhaps that the world was seeing a new plague of hemorrhagic fever.

Background. Influenza is caused not by one virus, but rather by several related viruses, which attack the respiratory system and are highly contagious. In general, influenza symptoms include sore throat, fever, sniffles, cough, and aches and pains. Sometimes it is difficult to differentiate influenza from the common cold; however, when large numbers of people in a given population begin to suffer the symptoms in a very short period of time, it is nearly always an influenza virus causing the problems.

One of the most troubling aspects of the flu virus is its ability to mutate quickly. Indeed, as it replicates itself, it makes small changes in its surface genetic material. Eventually, enough changes take place to render the virus impervious to the human immune system. That is, although the immune system produces enough antibodies to protect the person from further attacks by the same virus, once the virus mutates sufficiently, it is no longer the same strain that the person has become immune to. The immune system simply does not recognize the virus.

In 1889, the world saw the first influenza pandemic in history. Across the globe, many people suffered from the same strain of the virus. The pandemic reflected both the increased amount of travel and the increased speed of travel that the late nineteenth century technological revolution provided. As people moved around the globe, they carried their viruses with them.

OVERVIEW. It is likely that the 1918 influenza pandemic began in the midwestern United States. Many researchers believe that a widespread illness among the pig population of Iowa (a population that vastly outnumbered the human population of that state) presaged the human epidemic. Pig farmers fell ill, as did many sheep, bison, moose, and elk. Although the 1918 influenza is generally known as the Spanish Flu, all evidence points to an American origin.

Beginning in the United States in the spring of 1918, the pandemic spread to Europe and on to Africa, India, Japan, Russia, South America, and the South Seas, returning to the United States for a second, more deadly, round of illnesses. By very conservative estimates, some 30 million people died worldwide, with as many as 20 million dying in India alone.

Many have argued that World War I was the cause of the pandemic's devastating sweep of the world. While it is not possible to attribute the influenza epidemic to the war itself, certainly the war created conditions conducive to the spread and the virulence of the disease. Young, healthy men, a favorite target for this strain of influenza, were housed in close quarters as part of the armies of the combatants. In addition, they moved across the globe, pursuing their countries' political and military objectives. Consequently, they spread their viruses with them to each country they visited. Social upheaval and poor economic conditions also contributed to the high death rates in some nations.

SPRING AND SUMMER, 1918. In the spring of 1918, Europe was in the heat of combat. The United States had recently entered the war, and American troops were being rushed to the western front to fight a German offensive. Between March and April, over 200,000 troops left for Europe. These were the topics that grabbed the headlines in the spring of 1918; few noticed a flu epidemic that made its way across the United States. At that time, flu was not a reportable illness. As a result, although cases of influenza occurred in virtually every corner of the United States, the lack of a coordinated information-gathering system meant that health care workers could not assess the wave of flu for what it was: the first shot across the bow of what would become the worst pandemic in history. While there are few records from civilian sources, military and prison records suggest a pattern to the illness that was striking the country at large. First, many of the cases of influenza were followed by pneumonia. Second, the virus seemed to strike and kill not only children and the elderly but also young, healthy adults. While there was not a high death rate during March and April, the death rate for the latter group was considerably higher than one would expect.

Perhaps even more significant was the high rate of infection among men being prepared to fight the war in Europe. For example, an epidemic of influenza struck the Fifteenth U.S. Cavalry while en route to Europe. Consequently, the flu began to appear in and around the ports of disembarkation of American troops. By May, the virus was firmly entrenched in Europe. It had appeared in British and German troops in April. Not surprisingly, the German troops with the closest proximity to American and British troops were the earliest victims. It was widespread among French troops by May. From there, the virus spread to Italy and Spain. At this point, the influenza was named "Spanish influenza," not because it had originated in that country but because Spain did not censor the news from its borders, as did the countries actively involved in the war. Consequently, news of the European epidemic was largely limited to the cases reported by the Spanish, and people began to identify the influenza as a Spanish disease. Indeed, along with its many other nicknames, this flu was known as "the Spanish Lady."

Soon, the disease appeared in the civilian populations of Europe. Like the epidemic in the United States, the virus did not kill many of its victims at this time; however, a surprising number of the mortalities were among the young and healthy, a group that would be expected to survive an influenza epidemic. By June, the virus seemed to be dying out in the United States. However, it had appeared in Russia, North Africa, India, Japan, China, New Zealand, and the Philippines. In the following month, it appeared in Hawaii, the Panama Canal Zone, Cuba, and Puerto Rico.

The first cases were nearly always reported in port towns, where ships from nations already infected with the virus made landfall. Frequently, the sailors on the vessels were infected when their ships landed. From the port towns, the disease fanned rapidly outward among the indigenous populations. Roughly four months after its first appearance in the United States, the flu had circled the world. The disease, although widespread, was fairly mild. Nonetheless, estimates suggest that it had killed more than 10,000 people by the end of the summer.

AUGUST, 1918. By August, the death rates for respiratory illnesses began to inch upward in the United States, something that could not have been predicted by actuarial tables. Further, the virus had mutated as it traveled around the globe, sometimes manifesting itself in a milder form, sometimes in a horrifying, virulent form. During the third week of August, the flu exploded on three different continents, at three different ports. Alfred Crosby, one of the foremost historians of the pandemic, suggests that at this time, the milder form of the illness was homegrown. For example, English people who contracted the disease in England generally developed mild cases. On the other hand, when a British ship landed at Freetown, Sierra Leone, with 200 sailors ill with mild flu, the local workers who entered the ship became violently ill. On August 27, 500 out of 600 dock laborers in Freetown were unable to come to work due to illness.

The Sierra Leone workers then passed the virus back to the British on a different ship. This time, the British sailors were violently ill, and 59 died. Meanwhile, the civilian population of Sierra Leone became sicker and sicker. By the time this wave of influenza retreated, 70 percent of the population had flu and about 3 percent of the entire population had died.

A second port affected by the mixing of the flu virus through hosts of different nationalities was Brest, France, where most members of the American expeditionary force disembarked. Here, ill French soldiers and ill American soldiers passed the virus back and forth. Between August 22 and September 15, 370 had died and 1,350 had been hospitalized.

Boston, Massachusetts, was the first American city to experience the second wave of the flu virus. In the course of two weeks, the flu swept through 2,000 sailors before moving out into other military installations and to the civilian population.

SEPTEMBER, 1918. In 1918, the American army was as healthy as it had ever been. New sanitation methods and improved nutrition meant the army suffered far fewer illnesses. However, the ranks of the Army were swelling in 1918, as the United States sent an ever-growing number of young men to fight in World War I. Consequently, many Army bases were grossly overcrowded, in spite of relatively good conditions for the men.

In September of 1918, an illness began striking men in Camp Devens, Massachusetts, and then quickly spread to other camps. At first, the disease was not even recognized as influenza; it bore little resemblance to the flu that had become epidemic during the previous spring. The illness the Camp Devens soldiers contracted came on abruptly and devastated its victims. In addition, many of the men contracted pneumonia. Between September 7 and September 23, 12,604 soldiers out of a total population of 45,000 contracted influenza.

Even as the number of new cases of flu went down, the number of cases of pneumonia went up, and many were dying. The hospital at the base and the medical staff were completely overwhelmed, as was the morgue. When doctors performed autopsies on the dead, they discovered that the lungs of men who had been healthy and robust just days before were filled with bloody liquid. Some doctors speculated that this was some new form of hemorrhagic fever before they realized that it was a new, more deadly strain of influenza causing the illness. In any event, the doctors were horrified by the scope and the devastation of the disease.

THE EPIDEMIC IN THE UNITED STATES. The influenza spread rapidly throughout the United States. In general, while the U.S. Navy tended to spread the infection at the ports and at training centers, such as Great Lakes Naval Training Station, the Army moved across the interior of the United States by rail, infecting civilian populations

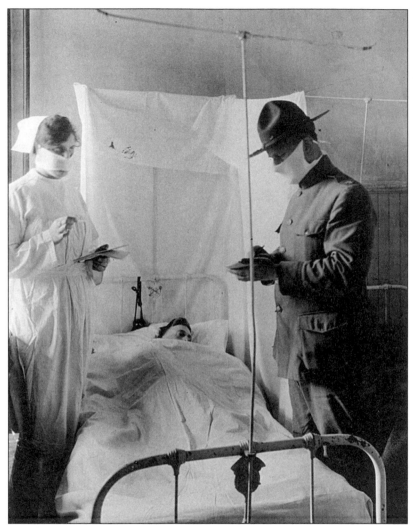

A soldier suffering from influenza in a New York Army hospital. (American Red Cross)

along the way. The overcrowded conditions on troop trains meant that a highly contagious, airborne infection would spread rapidly to all those on the train. In addition, the camps the new soldiers were moving to were overcrowded.

To make the situation even worse, the country was gripped by patriotic fervor. The United States, in need of more money to support the war effort, kicked off a Liberty Loan war-bond drive on October 4, 1918. Across the country, cities planned and carried out large-scale parades and systematic door-to-door solicitations in order to draw attention to the sale of bonds. While the sale of the bonds certainly raised money for the war effort, it also had the effect of spreading the influenza virus at a rapid rate.

The waves of influenza sweeping the country moved at different rates in different populations. The week ending September 28 marked the high point of the pandemic in the Navy, with 880 deaths due to influenza and pneumonia reported. In the Army, the peak occurred about two weeks later. In the week ending October 11, 1918, 6,170 soldiers died of influenza and pneumonia. In general, civilian populations became part of the pandemic a bit later than did the military.

Perhaps the hardest hit American city was Philadelphia. Alfred W. Crosby offers a horrifying look at the spread of the disease through that city in his book *America's Forgotten Pandemic: The Influenza of 1918* (2d ed., 2003). He attributes part of the problem to Philadelphia's proximity to Fort Dix and Fort Meade as well as the fact that the city had its own naval yard. In addition, Philadelphia had a huge Liberty Loan parade on September 28. Shortly after the parade, the virus ravaged the city. Schools, churches, and pool halls—any places that people gathered—were closed. By the time this happened, however, it was already too late, and there is little indication that the closing of public buildings did anything to prevent or ameliorate the spread of the flu.

Large cities such as Philadelphia and New York often had shortages of essential medical personnel. In 1918, the situation was worse than usual, however. During the pandemic, many doctors and nurses had gone to Europe to help care for the sick and the wounded on the western front. Thus, the medical and hospital facilities of large cities during the pandemic were totally inadequate to handle the numbers of sick and dying.

The infrastructure of large cities had trouble keeping up with the virus in other ways. Although by 1918 most cities had telephone services, there were too few operators healthy and on the job for the systems to work adequately. Garbage collectors stayed home sick, and garbage piled up in the streets.

The most grisly problem that large cities faced, and Philadelphia in particular, was what to do with the ever-increasing dead bodies. Crosby reports that the Philadelphia morgue was prepared to handle only 36 bodies. At the height of the epidemic, there were several hundred bodies stacked up in the corridors. Furthermore, there were not enough hearses to collect the dead bodies, and often corpses would stay in their homes or on the streets for days at a time. There were not enough coffins to bury the dead; cities that were not yet affected by the epidemic were warned by their not-so-fortunate sister cities to begin making coffins immediately in preparation for the inevitable arrival of the infection. Finally, there were not enough grave diggers to make enough graves for all the dead.

Between September 29 and November 2, 12,162 Philadelphians died of influenza and pneumonia. Although the very young and the very old died in the epidemic, the largest group affected consisted of people between the ages of twenty-five and thirty-four, just as they had been in the earlier, milder version of the influenza epidemic.

THE EPIDEMIC SPREADS. In September of 1918, a group of American soldiers were put on British troopships and sent, along with a troopship of Italians, to Archangel, Russia, an area under British control in the midst of the Russian Revolution. The soldiers brought influenza with them. Although there are no records of how many people in Russia ultimately died during the pandemic, it is estimated that about 10,000 in Archangel alone contracted the flu during October. As many as 30 people per day died during that month.

The effects of the pandemic were felt worldwide. As terrible as influenza was in the United States and Europe, it was many times worse in other parts of the world. In the United States, about 5 people per 1,000 died of the flu. Outside the United States, these figures were much higher. K. David Patterson and Gerald F. Pyle, in an important study, "The Geography and Mortality of the 1918 Influenza Epidemic" (1991), provide careful estimates of deaths worldwide. In Latin America, about 10 people per 1,000 died, while in Africa 15 per 1,000 died. In Asia, researchers estimate that as few as 20 and as many as 35 people per 1,000 died.

It appears that India was the most severely hit country in the world. In that country alone, researchers estimate that between 17 and 20 million people died. This works out to about 60 deaths per

1,000 people. In addition, although young men were the group most hard hit by the disease in the United States and in Europe, in India a disproportionate number of deaths occurred among women. Some scholars attribute the death toll among women to the stresses put on women by pregnancy. Others argue that the death toll was due to caregiving arrangements in India. Women almost exclusively provided care for the ill and dying. This rendered them most susceptible to becoming infected with the illness. In addition, when they fell ill in large numbers, there were few remaining women to provide care for them.

Colonial Africa was also hit extremely hard. The war in Europe certainly contributed to high death tolls among the indigenous people, for two reasons. In the first place, the African nations under European control had large numbers of European troops coming and going through their ports. European troops were stationed in Africa to protect these properties from other European troops. Thus, the Europeans brought their virus to Africa and exposed the civilian populations. Second, the demands of the war meant that there were few doctors or nurses available to help care for the colonial population. In addition, medical supplies, always in short supply in these areas, were diverted to the European front for use on soldiers there. As a result, the death figures were extraordinarily high. In Ghana, for example, there were about 100,000 deaths from influenza in just six months.

Research on the pandemic outside of Europe and the United States reveals that the poor tended to die in greater frequency than did the wealthy. The poor tend to have inferior nutrition, less accessibility to safe water supplies, and less adequate housing than do wealthier people, and these conditions render them susceptible to the bacterial infections that followed swiftly behind the viral influenza. Furthermore, there is some indication that deaths from other sources, such as kidney disease, heart disease, and diabetes, were much higher during the influenza epidemic. This may be partially due to the lack of health care in general or to the stress on the immune system that even a mild case of the flu caused.

Not only the heavily populated areas of the world and the large cities were affected, however. Often, small isolated areas fared worse than did larger countries. While the total death counts from these areas are not as high in total numbers as those from Philadelphia, for example, the death count per capita is often extraordinarily high. The South Pacific islands, often considered tropical paradises, became islands of death. In Tahiti, 10 percent of the entire population died in just three weeks. The influenza was brought to Tahiti by ship and immediately ravaged the civilian population. On Western Samoa, another island nation, 7,500 people died. This figure represents nearly 20 percent of Western Samoa's total population of 38,000.

In addition to these extraordinary figures, there were long-term, serious consequences for the nations involved. In most places, birth rates dropped dramatically. In India, the high death rate among women of childbearing age led to a much smaller number of women becoming pregnant.

CONCLUSIONS. The second and most deadly wave of influenza burned itself out by the spring of 1919. Although influenza made one more global sweep in 1920, it was less catastrophic, in all probability because so much of the surviving population was already immune. Scientists estimate that from 1918 through 1919, about 25 percent of the population of the United States suffered from influenza. The figures could be a good deal higher, however, for several reasons. First, flu was not a reportable illness in many places until the epidemic was well underway. Second, the shortage of doctors and nurses during the peak of the epidemic made it difficult for the remaining medical personnel to spend time compiling and reporting statistics. Finally, there were, in all probability, many people who had mild cases of the flu who never saw a doctor or reported their illness.

Another startling statistic to come out of the research is the number of deaths in the military due to influenza. More soldiers and sailors died of influenza than died of wounds during World War I. Crosby reminds readers that the total number of Americans killed by influenza in ten months, about 550,000, is higher than the total numbers of Americans killed in World War I, World War II, the Korean War, and the Vietnam War combined.

If it is difficult to ascertain how many Americans died in sum, it is nearly impossible to arrive at a worldwide figure. Some estimate that 30 million died; others suggest that the figures are far higher, at least 40 million or more. Even more elusive is the answer to the question of why this influenza virus turned so deadly. Researchers continue to investigate the causes and effects of the influenza pandemic. In the 1990's, frozen tissue from the lungs of influenza victims was scrutinized with technology unavailable in the early years of the century. Although preliminary reports suggested that the virus is a swine influenza, opinion would remain divided on the connection between the flu virus and the linked bacterial infections.

Another important question is why the virus attacked young people. Some researchers hypothesize that the immune system in young adults responded too strongly to the virus and caused the buildup of fluid in the lungs. Although there are no firm answers to all the questions surrounding the pandemic of 1918, there is little question that some strain of influenza virus will return every several years. Whether or not a pandemic of the scale of 1918 will ever happen again remains to be seen.

Diane Andrews Henningfeld

FOR FURTHER INFORMATION:

Barry, John M. *The Great Influenza: The Epic Story of the Deadliest Plague in History.* New York: Viking, 2004.

Bollet, Alfred J. "The Great Influenza Pandemic of 1918-1919." In *Plagues and Poxes: The Impact of Human History on Epidemic Disease.* New York: Demos, 2004.

Crosby, Alfred W. *America's Forgotten Pandemic: The Influenza of 1918.* 2d ed. New York: Cambridge University Press, 2003.

Hays, J. N. *The Burdens of Disease: Epidemics and Human Response in Western History.* New Brunswick, N.J.: Rutgers University Press, 1998.

Iezzoni, Lynette. *Influenza 1918: The Worst Epidemic in American History.* New York: TV Books, 1999.

Kolata, Gina. *Flu: The Story of the Great Influenza Pandemic of 1918 and the Search for the Virus That Caused It.* New York: Simon & Schuster, 2001.

Phillips, Howard, and David Killingray, eds. *The Spanish Influenza Pandemic of 1918-19: New Perspectives.* New York: Routledge, 2003.

■ 1923: THE GREAT KWANTO EARTHQUAKE

EARTHQUAKE

ALSO KNOWN AS: The Great Kanto Earthquake, the Great Tokyo Fire
DATE: September 1, 1923
PLACE: Kwanto area (including Tokyo and Yokohama), Japan, with the epicenter in Sagami Bay
MAGNITUDE: 8.3
RESULT: 143,000 dead

Over the past several centuries a major earthquake has struck the Kwanto District in Japan approximately every seventy years. Early in the twentieth century, seismologist Akitune Imamura, after lengthy studies, discovered that Tokyo was sitting on a seismic gap that would be corrected only when an earthquake of substantial size occurred. He predicted that there would soon be a very strong earthquake in the Kwanto District of Japan, an area that includes Tokyo and the seaport of Yokohama, 17 miles to the south. Imamura further predicted that the quake and consuming fires that would follow would result in over 100,000 casualties. This prediction was well publicized but was dismissed as irresponsible. It was, however, shortly fulfilled.

At one minute before noon on Saturday, September 1, 1923, the quake struck. Its epicenter was in Sagami Bay, 50 miles southeast of Tokyo near the island of Oshima. The initial shaking lasted for about five minutes and was followed shortly thereafter by a tsunami, or a tidal wave, that washed people and houses out to sea. In some of the smaller inlets the tsunami reached heights of up to 40 feet, resulting in many drownings. The tsunami had one advantage, however, in that it extinguished many fires that otherwise would have been uncontrollable.

Immense holes appeared in the streets, and buildings were tilted at strange angles. Tokyo's largest building, the twelve-story Asakusa Tower, split in two and collapsed. The earthquake knocked out the

seismograph at the central weather bureau in Tokyo. The seismograph at Tokyo Imperial University was still functioning, however; it recorded a series of 1,700 earthquakes and aftershocks that struck the Tokyo area over the following three days.

Fires followed the initial quake and in general did more damage than the quake itself. They were caused primarily by overturned charcoal braziers or hibachis that were being used to cook the noonday meal. Since the city was built largely of wood, the fires burned out of control. Gas mains ruptured by the quake and leaking oil from above-ground storage tanks added to the conflagration. A condition called a fire tornado was soon created, with a wind of such velocity that it would lift a person off the ground. These crisscrossed the city and either burned people alive or suffocated them with dense fumes of carbon monoxide. More than 30,000 people were reportedly killed at a single location, a park on the east bank of the Sumida River, when such a fire storm descended on refugees that had gathered there. Fire fighting was greatly hampered because much of the equipment was destroyed or could not be moved because of the rubble that blocked the roads. Water was not available to fight the fire because the water mains were ruptured by the quake. Safe havens were hard to find; bridges and narrow streets became deathtraps as fleeing people could neither go forward nor turn back. Hundreds of people who had attempted to cross one of the large bridges that spanned the Sumida River found themselves trapped and incinerated when walls of fire swept the bridge from both banks.

A party of 200 children on an excursion train trip were buried alive by a falling embankment. Hundreds of people tried to escape in small boats, only to be drowned by waves caused by aftershocks or to

This view of the Kwanto area of Japan shows almost complete destruction following the 1923 earthquake. (Library of Congress)

be burned to death in burning oil slicks. The liner *Empress of Australia* was able to save several thousand people by loading them aboard and heading out to sea to ride out the disaster.

The quake devastated a region of 45,000 square miles. In Yokohama, Japan's chief port, eyewitness accounts tell of the earthquake announcing itself as an underground roar, followed almost immediately by a frantic shaking. Communications were completely destroyed. The city authorities finally succeeded in getting messengers through to the capital begging for help, to little avail since that capital suffered the same plight. A great cultural loss was sustained with the destruction of the Imperial University Library, which contained one of the world's oldest and greatest collection of rare books, original documents, and priceless art objects.

The typical Japanese house of wood and paper construction was well suited by reason of its flexibility to withstand shaking, but the heavy tile roofs often collapsed, trapping the occupants. For the most part, steel-framed and reinforced concrete buildings remained standing with only moderate damage, but altogether 60 percent of the buildings in Tokyo and 80 percent in Yokohama were flattened by the quake or destroyed by the fires that followed.

The earthquake tested the design of the newly opened 250-room Imperial Hotel, a project of the famous American architect Frank Lloyd Wright. The hotel, financed by the royal family, was meant to be a showpiece. When the earthquake struck, many of Tokyo's notables were attending a party to mark its opening. Although he was not a seismic engineer, Wright incorporated into his design features that he thought would safeguard his structure from earthquake damage. He ruled out a deep foundation in the alluvial mud upon which the structure was built; he intended that the structure should float like a ship. He was mistaken in this theory, as experience gained in the quake demonstrated that soft earth amplifies the seismic shocks. The solidly constructed buildings in Tokyo with deep foundations withstood the quake better than the central section of the hotel, which sank 2 feet into the ground.

The hotel did survive, however, and Wright's other safeguards proved to be quite effective. They included reinforced and tapered walls and separation joints that isolated parts of the structure. The use of a light copper roof prevented collapse, which had entombed so many Japanese in their homes with heavy tile roofs. Rather than embedding utility pipes and conduit in concrete, as was the practice, Wright had them laid in a trench or hung in the open so that they would flex and rattle but not break in any seismic occurrence. Fortuitously, the hotel was designed with a large reflecting pool in front. This served as a firefighting reservoir that protected the hotel from the fires that raged following the quake when water was unavailable from the municipal system. The hotel stood until 1968, when the land upon which it rested became too valuable to accommodate it.

AFTERMATH. Aftershocks continued to shake the region following the quake. A soaking rain followed on the third day, which helped extinguish the fires that were still raging. Food shortages were rampant, and riots broke out, but there was no looting and little profiteering. Members of the Korean community were attacked as rumors accused them of setting fires and poisoning the wells. Several hundred were killed by vigilantes before the authorities could reestablish order.

A week after the quake 25,000 people were still living in the open. The prince regent, who later became Emperor Hirohito, tried by his presence to calm the terrorized citizens. He led relief operations and ordered the gates of the Imperial Palace opened to refugees. Many of the refugees returned to their homes looking for loved ones. Messages seeking missing family members were posted on public buildings, and collection centers for stray children were set up around the city. One of the biggest problems was disposing of dead bodies, many of which lay undiscovered in the rubble. Usually when located they would be piled up and cremated. The Sumida River was full of bloated and discolored corpses.

Within forty-eight hours of the earthquake, ships of the U.S. Pacific fleet arrived in Japanese ports, laden with water, food, and medicine. The American Red Cross set a goal of $5 million for relief supplies. Japan's low foreign debt and good credit rating made funds for rebuilding readily available. The most immediate effect on the economy was unemployment. An estimated 9,000 factories were destroyed. Massive reconstruction operations somewhat alleviated the unemployment problem, but the drain on the Japanese economy was ruinous. Foreign exchange dwindled, leading to a tight monetary policy that stifled growth.

A master plan for reconstruction was formulated under the leadership of the new home minister, Shimpei Goto. Narrow streets were to be replaced with broad avenues that would provide better access in and out of the area in a future quake and also act as firebreaks. Flammable wooden structures were to be banned in favor of fireproof structures limited in height. Before these plans could be implemented, however, those rendered homeless by the quake went to work rebuilding their houses in the old manner, resulting in the flammable and congested neighborhoods reappearing. Despite the threat of future earthquake damage, high-rise buildings, refineries, and chemical plants have been built on soft reclaimed land beside Tokyo Bay. Even a nuclear power station has been constructed at Shizuoka, about 100 miles from the center of Tokyo.

PLANS AND FORECASTS. Seismologists were of one mind that there would be a major earthquake in Tokyo or adjoining areas in the early twenty-first century. They cited as the most likely area the heavily industrialized Tokai region down the coast from Tokyo, which had not experienced a great quake since December 24, 1854. Studies indicate that tectonic forces have accumulated, and strains of these forces have deformed the adjacent land, indicating that the breaking points are inevitable. Following a historical pattern, this may be triggered by a sizable quake near Odawara, which is located a few miles south of Yokohama. The Japanese government designated this area for intensive civil defense measures. When a quake strikes, Tokyo will receive considerable damage but the industrial heartland in the Shizuoka prefecture will be devastated both by the quake and the tsunami that will follow.

Another place of concern is directly under Tokyo itself, where a *choka-gata* ("directly below") quake is likely to strike. A quake of this type struck in 1988, but because it was 55 miles under the surface, there was little damage.

Japan is the world leader in planning for earthquake survival. Disaster teams are trained and at the ready; stores of food, water, and blankets are on hand. Clearly marked evacuation routes have been laid out and reinforced against quake damage. An extensive public education campaign has instructed the population as to what to do in the event of a quake. Earthquake drills in schools and places of employment are a usual practice. Lines of apartment complexes are strung out to act as firebreaks in the event of a major conflagration among the crowded wooden houses behind them. The Tokyo fire department has detailed emergency plans to deal with a quake. Because a major quake will rupture water mains, it is likely that water will not be available from hydrants to fight the inevitable fires, so earthquake-resistant fire cisterns and underground water storage areas have been constructed. Measures have been taken to deliver water from the sea and streams for firefighting use.

On a national level, if unusual seismic activity is detected, six members of the Earthquake Assessment Committee are contacted immediately. They then analyze data and decide whether or not to advise the prime minister to warn the nation that a major earthquake is imminent.

Gilbert T. Cave

FOR FURTHER INFORMATION:

Davison, Charles. *The Japanese Earthquake of 1923.* London: T. Murby, 1931.

Hadfield, Peter. *Sixty Seconds That Will Change the World: The Coming Tokyo Earthquake.* Boston: Charles E. Tuttle, 1991.

Hammer, Joshua. *Yokohama Burning: The Deadly 1923 Earthquake and Fire That Helped Forge the Path to World War II.* New York: Free Press, 2006.

Poole, Otis Manchester. *The Death of Old Yokohama in the Great Japanese Earthquake of September 1, 1923.* London: Allen & Unwin, 1968.

■ 1925: THE GREAT TRI-STATE TORNADO

TORNADO

DATE: March 18, 1925
PLACE: Missouri, Illinois, and Indiana
CLASSIFICATION: F5
RESULT: 689 dead, more than 2,000 injured, $16-18 million in damage

The storm that spawned the Great Tri-State and several other tornadoes on March 18, 1925, was from a northeast Pacific storm. The depression was over western Montana on March 16. On the morning of the 18th, it was over northwestern Arkansas and was moving to the northeast at about 40 miles per hour. It was over southern Illinois during the early afternoon and southeastern Indiana by 8 P.M.

The U.S. Weather Bureau described 7 distinct tornadoes in Alabama, Tennessee, Kentucky, Indiana, Missouri, and Illinois generated by the storm. Thomas P. Grazulis, in *Significant Tornadoes: 1680-1991* (1993), describes the same 7 but adds an earlier one in Kansas and a later one in Kentucky on that date. All but the Kansas tornado were killers. Fortunately, the death toll was 4 or less for all but 2 of these tornadoes. One tornado started in Summer County, Tennessee, and traveled 60 miles to Metcalfe County, Kentucky, killing 39 and injuring 95. It was of F4 force and had a path width of about 400 yards. The Great Tri-State Tornado caused 689 deaths—741 deaths for the total storm, with the death toll for the other 6 tornadoes at 13, with 164 injuries.

The Tri-State Tornado was the most deadly and the most destructive. The Weather Bureau noted that it was different in another way. Most tornadoes occur in the southeast part of a storm system along a squall line or cold front. Seldom is a tornado formed in the center of a storm center, as the Great Tri-State Tornado was. It was especially devastating as it traveled on the ground along a ridge of mineral resources and parallel to a railroad. Thus, several mining and railroad towns were in its path.

MISSOURI. The tornado first touched down north of Ellington in southeast Missouri about 1 P.M. It traveled northeast to damage Leadanna, a mining town. It continued northeast to engulf Annapolis, 2 miles north of Leadanna. Annapolis was devastated, with 90 percent of the town destroyed and 2 dead. All but 7 of the 400 structures in Leadanna and Annapolis were badly damaged; the damage total was about $500,000 in the two towns. Fortunately, one schoolhouse that held 300 students was undamaged. The damage in and near Annapolis was 3 miles wide. Survivors remember that the sky became dark, and something like a smoky fog swept through the town. A funnel cloud was not seen.

The next damage occurred in and near the small towns of Lixville, Biehle, Frohna, and Altenburg. At least 32 children were injured in two county schools in Bollinger county. Deaths occurred in Biehle and Altenburg, 30 miles north of Cape Girardeau. In Biehle, there were 4 dead and 11 injured out of 100 villagers. For 3 miles near Biehle there were evidence and sightings of two parallel funnel clouds, which reunited later before passing into Illinois. A child was killed in a wooden schoolhouse 5 miles north of Altenburg. The toll in Missouri was 11 to 14 dead, 63 injured, and $564,000 in damage (in 1925 dollars).

ILLINOIS. The damage in Illinois was much worse. In Gorham, it had been dark and gloomy; the drizzle increased to pouring down a flood, then the air was filled with flying debris. The town of 500 was virtually wiped out. There were 34 deaths, and over half of the town's population was killed or injured. Seven of the deaths occurred at the school. Communications were cut off such that although the tornado struck at 2:35 P.M. no aid came until 8 P.M. There was not even a healthy doctor present until aid arrived. The doctor in town was giving an injection when the tornado hit; the patient was killed, and the doctor received a broken collarbone.

Murphysboro, population 11,000, was next to be decimated. The 234 deaths were the largest number in one city in U.S. history at the time. About 800 were injured and $10 million was incurred in damage. Three schools, built of brick or stone with little reinforcement, were caved in, crushing at least 25 people. The tornado affected 152 city blocks—72 percent of the residential section and 60 percent of the city. About 1,200 homes were damaged or destroyed, leaving

A school in Murphysboro, Illinois, where 17 children where killed by the tornado. (National Oceanic and Atmospheric Administration)

8,000 people, or two-thirds of the city, homeless. Fires ravaged the destroyed area and 70 more blocks in a residential district, demolishing homes still standing and burning victims caught under collapsed buildings. Fires could be seen as far as 60 miles away. The tornado had destroyed the water plant, as well as many of the hydrants. A "rigged" system restored water pressure to fight the fires. Other casualties of the tornado were the 2,000 jobs lost due to the destruction of the Mobile and Ohio Railroad shop, the Brown's Shoe Company, the Isco-Bautz silica plant, and other industries. Businesses sustained almost $1 million in damage but had only $122,000 in insurance.

The next town hit was DeSoto, a hamlet of 600, where 33 were killed at one school, setting the record for school deaths in a tornado. A total of 69 were killed in or around DeSoto. The town itself was obliterated. Only a dozen houses were left standing, none left undamaged. An outbreak of fires caused more damage to the ravaged town.

The hamlet of Bush was next in the storm's path; there, the tornado left 7 dead and 37 injured. It also left only one building standing in Hurst, a town of 200. The rural area between DeSoto and West Frankfort suffered 24 deaths. Even the Illinois Central railroad bridge on the Zeigler branch was shifted by 6 feet. One of the rescue jobs after the tornado was to clean the debris off of farmland so that planting could be done within the next few weeks.

Between West Frankfort and Orient was a small school attended by Mavis Flota. It was a warm day, but late in the afternoon it became so dark that the students could not read by lamplight. The clouds became streaked with lightning, and thunder boomed. A roar like the sound of a train told the teacher that there was a tornado coming. It tore off one room, spilling Flota onto the ground and into the golf-ball-size hail. When she stood, she was picked up by the storm and carried 2 miles, landing scratched and bruised but otherwise unhurt, except for the soles of her new shoes being pulled off.

The tornado cut across the northwest part of West Frankfort, the largest town in its path, with 20,000 people. This part of town was composed mostly of small residences, many of them miners' homes. Sixty-four blocks of houses were damaged in the 0.25-mile-wide path, and 13 blocks were wiped out. The 925 damaged or destroyed houses left 3,000 homeless and $500,000 in damage. There were 127 dead, 450 injured, and 117 hospitalized, with a total $800,000 in damage. Almost 800 miners were 500 feet below the earth's surface when they lost electrical power. They had to climb out a narrow escarpment and then face the damage and injuries caused by the tornado; many of the dead and wounded were women and children.

A small community, called Eighteen because it was near Number 18 Mine, was devastated. Nearby Parrish contained about 40 buildings, but only 3 were left after the tornado. Although the population was only 300, there were 46 deaths and 100 injured. There, the tornado was preceded by thunder and a violent succession of lightning flashes, and the funnel cloud was seen by Parrish inhabitants. It struck Parrish at 3:15 P.M. Hailstones the size of apples came after the tornado. Parrish never rebuilt, existing only as a few older homes.

In the forty-five minutes required for the tornado to travel through Gorham to Parrish, 541 people were killed. Leaving Parrish, the path of the tornado went through rural areas in Hamilton and White Counties before reaching Carmi, near the Indiana border. The destruction and death in the rural areas was unprecedented, as many farms were completely destroyed and 65 people were killed. At least three different White County schools claimed deaths from the tornado. It was estimated that 1,500 farms needed debris cleaned off of the land so that they could be planted.

INDIANA. The town of Carmi had 2 deaths and the border town of Crossville reported 1 before the tornado crossed into Indiana. In Illinois the tornado caused 606 deaths, about 1,600 injuries, and $13 million in damage.

Just beyond the Wabash River was the small town of Griffin. The tornado did not leave a habitable structure out of the 150 homes in Griffin. Two children on a bus were killed; the total death toll there was 34, with 200 injured out of 375 inhabitants. Identifying victims was difficult, as mud was embedded into their skin. Fires occurred in the ruins and added to the destruction and agony.

Leaving Griffin, the path of the tornado, 0.75-mile wide, veered north by 9 degrees. The new path would include Owensville and Princeton. At Owensville, 17 deaths occurred, including three generations of one family. In this rural area, 85 farms were totally destroyed.

Princeton, the county seat of Gibson County, was caught, like most other towns, unaware. A blackness moved over the south side of town, killing 45 and injuring 152 and causing $1.8 million in damage. One-fourth to one-half of the town was located in the devastated area, so after 200 homes were destroyed and 100 were damaged, 1,500 people were left homeless. The two largest industries, the $2 million Southern Railway shops and the H. T. Heinz factory, were demolished, as was the village of workers' homes nearby. Fortunately, only 3 people lost their lives at the industries (2 at Southern, 1 at Heinz). Luckily, the Princeton school had let out about twenty minutes earlier, and the children were out of the tornado's path; the school was caved in. An estimated 100,000 people visited Princeton to view the damage.

The deadly tornado finally lost its steam and lifted near Petersburg, 16 miles northeast of Princeton, about 4:30 P.M. East of Princeton, irregular-shaped chunks of ice as large as goose eggs were reported to fall. In Indiana, the tornado had appeared as three funnels for part of its path. Many people described it as a turbulent, boiling mass filled with debris. It often looked like a big black mass, similar to a thunderstorm. The tornado had killed 30 people in Indiana, injured 354, and caused $2,775,000 in damage.

CONCLUSIONS. The Great Tri-State Tornado is considered the single deadliest tornado in U.S. history to date. It maintained contact with the ground for the longest distance (219 miles) and for the longest time (3.5 hours). It was moving quickly for a tornado, at an average of 62 miles per hour—73 miles per hour in Indiana. The intensity did not vary as much with this tornado as with others; it simply destroyed everything in its way. Its path was wide, varying from 0.25 mile to 1 mile, with much of the path 0.75 mile in width. It traveled an exact heading of 69 degrees northeast for 183 of the 219 miles.

The killer moved so quickly that many were not able to seek shelter. Country residents indicated that only about five minutes passed after noticing the cloud before the tornado struck. However, shelter in the form of basements, which are usually places of safety, were deathtraps to several people. In some cases, the tornado caved the house into the basement, and the wood or coal stove then set the ruins on fire, burning the trapped survivors. Nine people were found around a stove in a Griffin restaurant.

C. Alton Hassell

FOR FURTHER INFORMATION:

Akin, Wallace E. *The Forgotten Storm: The Great Tri-State Tornado of 1925.* Guilford, Conn.: Lyons Press, 2004.

Cornell, James. *The Great International Disaster Book.* 3d ed. New York: Charles Scribner's Sons, 1982.

Felknor, Peter E. *The Tri-State Tornado.* Ames: Iowa State University Press, 1992.

Flora, Snowden D. *Tornadoes of the United States.* Norman: University of Oklahoma Press, 1953.

Grazulis, Thomas P. *Significant Tornadoes: 1680-1991.* St. Johnsburg, Vt.: Environmental Films, 1993.

_____. *The Tornado: Nature's Ultimate Windstorm.* Norman: University of Oklahoma Press, 2003.

■ 1926: THE GREAT MIAMI HURRICANE

HURRICANE

DATE: September 15-22, 1926
PLACE: Miami, Florida
CLASSIFICATION: Category 4
RESULT: 243 dead, about 2,000 injured

With winds approaching 138 miles per hour and a barometric pressure measured at a low 27.61 inches of mercury, the Great Miami Hurricane of 1926 is considered one of the most powerful storms to strike the U.S. mainland in the twentieth century. The hurricane began as a Cape Verde-type storm and initially was detected on September 11, 1926, as it moved nearly 1,000 miles east of the Leeward Islands. On September 16 it was located near the Turks Islands, where its winds were recorded at approximately 150 miles per hour. Passing north of Puerto Rico, the storm reached the Bahamas on the following day. Because no sophisticated tracking system was in existence at the time, residents of the Miami area were mostly unaware of the approaching storm. On the morning of September 17, the *Miami Herald* carried a small story on its front page noting the existence of the storm but indicating it was not expected to strike Florida. The U.S. Weather Bureau received its last report on the storm's location from Nassau in the Bahamas in the early afternoon of September 17, which prompted storm warnings to be issued for the Florida coast from Key West to Jupiter Inlet, 80 miles north of Miami. That same afternoon the *Miami Daily News* published a front-page story alerting residents to a "tropical storm." The paper also reported a warning issued by the Weather Bureau's chief meteorologist that late evening "destructive winds" could be expected in the area.

It was not until the late hours of September 17, as winds began to build, that citizens of Miami realized a major storm was about to pummel them. Until that point many of the area's residents, most of whom had recently settled in the region, either were unfamiliar with hurricanes or simply chose to ignore them. For the next eight hours,

hurricane-force winds battered the Miami region. The average wind velocity during this period was approximately 76 miles per hour. Never, in recorded weather history, had a hurricane sustained its winds for such a long duration. The persistent storm dumped nearly 10 inches of rain on the city and generated a storm surge that exceeded 13 feet.

The deluge inundated Miami Beach and swept ocean waters across Biscayne Bay into the city of Miami. All types of watercraft, from schooners to dredges, were blown onto shores, sunk, or capsized, including a steam yacht that was once owned by William II of Germany. Thousands of homes and office buildings were destroyed or damaged. A major contributing factor to the destruction was the fact that many of the buildings were constructed at substandard levels as a consequence of nonexistent or inferior code restrictions in effect during the real estate boom of the previous decade.

What was once considered the "playground" of America was left a scene of devastation as pleasure resorts were converted into temporary hospitals and morgues and office buildings into refugee centers. Water and debris were everywhere, transforming the appearance of an entire stretch of the Miami waterfront into something macabre. With roads washed out and causeways underwater, relief efforts were slowed considerably. Moreover, the persistent winds and absence of landing sites discouraged airplane pilots from attempting to enter the damaged areas. Instead, at least a dozen trains loaded with physicians, nurses, food, water, and other supplies descended on the city to help with the relief efforts.

Following its strike on the city, the storm moved on a northwesterly course toward the Lake Okeechobee area, where it proceeded to unleash its fury on the small community of Moore Haven, located on the southwestern side of the lake. In 1922 and 1924 heavy rains had raised the water level of the lake, which precipitated substantial flooding in the surrounding farm districts, though no lives were lost. As a result, the town's citizens decided to construct a muck dike to protect

Cars drive by boats washed ashore by the Great Miami Hurricane. (Courtesy, The Florida Memory Project)

the region from future flooding, but local and state officials greatly underestimated the impact a major hurricane would have on the lake.

In due course the relentless winds drove the waters over and through the dike, inundating the area to a depth of up to 15 feet and taking a heavy toll in death and property. A lone watchman assigned to patrol the dike in order to give warning in the event of potential danger was on patrol when the dike succumbed to the rising water. Washed away by the initial overflow, he managed to escape and immediately attempted to alert others. However, his warnings either went unheard or were disregarded in the midst of the chaos. The rush of water drowned scores of residents and left the town without food, water, or power. Nearly every structure in Moore Haven was destroyed, except for a row of brick buildings in the town's central commercial district. Several homes were swept almost 2 miles from their foundations. At one point, 34 bodies were lying in the town's old post office building, which served as an emergency morgue. Rescuers attempting to reach the stricken city were met by an exodus of people fleeing the area in small boats to points where they could continue on foot to safe ground. Entire families, forced to carry all of their remaining possessions in bundles, were seen straggling along open roads.

In the aftermath many residents of the district launched an organized protest against government officials, whom they blamed for keeping the lake's water above reasonable levels prior to the storm. They pointed out that if the state had permitted the locks to be opened during the storm season and allowed the water level to remain near the specified minimum depth of 15 feet instead of 19 feet above sea level, the damage caused by the floodwaters would have been considerably less.

After striking Moore Haven, the storm continued on its northwesterly course, eventually dumping large amounts of rain on Pensacola before moving further inland, over interior Alabama and sections of Mississippi and Louisiana, before dissipating. All together, the storm left 243 people dead and nearly 2,000 injured in its wake.

William Hoffman

FOR FURTHER INFORMATION:

Barnes, Jay. *Florida's Hurricane History.* Chapel Hill: University of North Carolina Press, 1998.

"Cities Built on Sand." *Weatherwise,* August/September, 1996, 20-27.

Kleinberg, Howard, and L. F. Reardon. *The Florida Hurricane and Disaster, 1926.* Miami: Centennial Press, 1992.

Williams, John M., and Iver W. Duedall. *Florida Hurricanes and Tropical Storms, 1871-2001.* Gainesville: University of Florida Press, 2002.

1928: St. Francis Dam collapse

Flood

DATE: March 12, 1928
PLACE: Near Saugus, California
RESULT: About 450 dead; 1,200 homes and other buildings severely damaged or destroyed; almost 8,000 acres of farmland stripped of livestock, orchards, crops, and topsoil; $15 million in damage

The St. Francis Dam, named after the San Francisquito (little Saint Francis) Canyon and Creek where it was located, was designed and built by William Mulholland, chief engineer for the Los Angeles Department of Water and Power (DWP) from 1886 to 1928. Its purpose was to create a 600-acre reservoir as a reserve water supply for the city of Los Angeles. Mulholland had devoted much of his life to making sure his beloved city had enough water to grow and prosper. Los Angeles had never had a reliable water supply until 1913, when Mulholland achieved world renown with the completion of the Owens Valley Aqueduct, at that time the longest aqueduct in existence. Its series of tunnels and concrete-lined channels transported 258 million gallons of water every day from the green Owens Valley south to the thirsty city of Los Angeles.

A boon to the growth of Los Angeles, the aqueduct brought death to the Owens Valley as the drought-plagued city sucked the Owens River dry. Owens Valley residents fought to prevent Los Angeles from taking all of their water. When peaceful means failed, a few desperate ranchers resorted to violence. The first dynamiting of the aqueduct occurred in May, 1924, and it continued sporadically throughout the remainder of the decade. Understandably, Mulholland began to worry about the fate of Los Angeles if the water supply were cut off for long periods of time. Because the aqueduct crossed the San Andreas fault, it was not just vulnerable to sabotage—potential earthquakes were another hazard. Mulholland's solution was the St. Francis Dam, with a reservoir big enough to hold an emergency supply of water capable of meeting the city's needs for at least one year. In fact, to ensure an adequate supply in drought years, the original 175-foot height of the dam was increased by 11 feet to allow for additional water storage eleven months after construction had begun. The base of the dam was not widened, however, a risky oversight in a gravity dam like St. Francis, which resists the enormous pressure of its pent-up waters through sheer weight alone.

The dam was completed in May, 1926. The St. Francis Dam was a massive curved concrete wedge about 200 feet high and 700 feet long. It was 156 feet thick at its base and 18 feet thick at its crest, and it contained over 134,000 cubic yards of concrete. Despite its imposing size, leaking cracks appeared in the dam during its initial filling in 1926-1927. Mulholland claimed they were caused by the curing of the concrete and had them sealed. In February, 1928, as the water level rose again with winter rains, fresh leaks appeared, which increased in intensity with the spring runoff.

THE DAM BREAKS. On March 7, 1928, the dam reached its maximum holding capacity of 38,168 acre feet (over 12 billion gallons), with water lapping within 3 feet of the parapet and wind-driven waves breaking over the spillways near the top. The previous year's leaks re-opened, keeping Mulholland's work crews busy. By Monday, March 12, the dam had been holding up its towering wall of water for five days. That morning, Tony Harnischfeger, the damkeeper, phoned Mulholland to report a new leak. Mulholland arrived at 10:30 A.M. with his assistant, inspected the dam for the next two hours, and left after assuring the damkeeper that the dam was safe. The damkeeper and his small son would be the first victims of the dam's collapse twelve hours later. Their bodies were never recovered.

The St. Francis Dam burst at 11:57 P.M., unleashing a 185-foot wave of destruction into the canyon below. About 50 miles to the south in Los Angeles, night owls who noticed their lights flicker momentarily had no idea they were witnessing the first signs of the deadliest disaster in Southern California history. Closer to the dam, at the Saugus substation of the Southern California Edison Company, the local electric power utility, one of the transmission lines shorted out, blowing up a switch and triggering an emergency alert. Edison personnel had no idea what had happened either.

At the electrical powerhouse directly below the dam, workman Ray Rising, a native of the Midwest's "Tornado Alley," awoke to the sound of what he thought was a tornado. Running to the door, he saw a 140-foot-high wave loom out of the darkness. He managed to resist being engulfed by climbing onto a rooftop that he rode like a raft through the twisting canyon, calling for his wife and children, until it dashed against the canyon wall, where he jumped to safety. Only 3 people survived out of 28 workmen and their families at the powerhouse. The powerhouse itself, a 65-foot concrete structure, was crushed like an eggshell by the wave 10 stories high.

Rolling over the Harry Carey Ranch near Saugus, the deadly tide, now 80 feet high, swept up miles of barbed wire ripped from the ranch's pastures. By 12:40 A.M. Tuesday, Edison employees at the Saugus substation knew the dam had failed and tried to phone a warning to an Edison work camp of 150 men 8 miles downstream from the dam on the banks of the Santa Clara River. The phone rang, but there was no answer, and then the line went dead. They knew what had happened this time. The flood arrived in Castaic Junction, a little town 40 miles from Los Angeles, at 12:50 A.M. and wiped it off the face of the earth. The lone survivor, George McIntyre, lived by grabbing the branches of a cottonwood tree. The bodies of his father and brothers were found near Santa Paula, 30 miles downstream.

At 1:30 A.M., highway patrol officer Thornton Edwards got an emergency call that would make him the Paul Revere of Santa Paula as he set out on his motorcycle with screaming sirens to warn the townspeople to evacuate. To his horrified amazement, he reached the Willard Bridge spanning the Santa Clara River only to see it crammed end to end with excited people waiting for the show to begin. He ordered the bridge cleared, posted a guard at either end, and drove on.

The flood reached the bridge by 3 A.M. As the flood surged over the top of the bridge, the latter snapped in half and disappeared. Meanwhile, Deputy Sheriff Eddie Hearne responded to his call by racing his squad car up the Santa Clara Valley toward the oncoming flood with both sirens wailing and lights flashing, first to Santa Paula and then to Fillmore. He got as far as crossing the Pole Creek bridge on the edge of Fillmore when he saw the road ahead inundated by a wide expanse of water, mud, trees, wreckage from buildings and vehicles, and other debris. He immediately raced back to Fillmore to phone a warning to evacuate the city of Oxnard and the adjacent plain.

Some of the debris remaining in San Francisquito Canyon after the St. Francis Dam collapsed in 1928, killing 450 people. (Courtesy, SCV Historical Society)

The entire Santa Clara Valley was awake by now and evacuating to higher ground. At Saticoy, a rancher woke 19 transients sleeping under a bridge to warn them. One refused to head for higher ground, saying there was not enough water in Southern California in which to take a bath, much less fill up the dry bed of the Santa Clara River. His body was found soon after daylight. By now, the speed of the water had decreased from 18 to around 5 miles per hour, but the flow had spread out to about 2 miles wide, consisting of about half water and half mud and trash. The flood narrowly missed Oxnard as it flowed to the sea. As dawn broke, hundreds gathered on the hills above Ventura to watch the final leg of the flood's journey. It left a dirty gray streak all the way out to the Channel Islands, over 20 miles from shore.

AFTER THE FLOOD. Within an hour of the St. Francis Dam's collapse, the entire reservoir had emptied, with a peak discharge rate of over 1 million cubic feet per second. The flood swept a path of devastation 55 miles through the Santa Clara Valley from the dam in San Francisquito Canyon to the Pacific Ocean between the towns of Ventura and Oxnard. The death toll from the flood—comparable to California's greatest natural disaster until that time, the 1906 San Francisco earthquake and fire—would have been much higher in a more populated area. However, the damage was still awesome.

The land lay in ruins. Bodies, both human and animal, were strewn everywhere. Forests had vanished, buried in silt. Orange, lemon, and walnut orchards were flattened. Towns were in shambles. Many valley residents staring at the wreckage the flood had left behind that Tuesday morning had never even heard of the dam that had wreaked such unbelievable carnage. Many wandered around aimlessly in shock. Fortunately, the Red Cross and other relief agencies had begun to arrive by 3:45 A.M. Doctors, nurses, and emergency equipment poured in from Los Angeles and San Francisco, but the doctors and nurses had little to do because there were very few people injured, aside from some suffering from exposure after being outside all night with little or no clothing. Fortunately or unfortunately, this unusual situation was due to the violent nature of the flood. Once caught in the floodwaters, most victims perished. The majority of survivors were either lucky or alert enough to escape before the deadly tide reached them and thus avoided injury. Many victims were never found, forever buried under tons of mud; the mounting number of mud-encrusted corpses was overwhelming to the survivors.

Bodies were transported from the lowlands in farm trucks, unloaded and stacked in piles near mortuaries, and washed down with garden hoses to make identification possible. One valley resident was so angry and disgusted that she stopped trying to shovel the mud from her home long enough to paint a sign she stuck in her front yard for all to see. The sign said, Kill Mulholland!

Did the state's greatest human-made disaster have to happen? Although William Mulholland accepted full responsibility for the tragedy that ruined his career, many DWP officials and others, including Mulholland himself, suspected that the dam might have been dynamited by Owens Valley terrorists. However, the overwhelming consensus is that the collapse was due to human error in the construction of the dam.

To avert further criticism, city officials decided to settle all claims for damages and loss of life as soon as possible without going through the courts. The city council passed an ordinance providing $1 million—an enormous amount of money in 1928—to start rebuilding and settling claims. About 2,000 workers with hundreds of tractors and other heavy equipment tackled the huge mess. It took ninety days working around the clock to finish the cleanup. All that remained were the broken pieces of the dam itself. Fourteen months after the disaster, an eighteen-year-old boy fell to his death while climbing on the ruins, and the city decided to demolish them. Mulholland's most infamous engineering project thus became an unremarkable pile of concrete rubble lying just upstream of where the dam once stood.

Despite the tragic proportions of the flood, the disaster had some positive outcomes. Among them were the formation of the world's first dam-safety agency, the adoption of uniform engineering specifications for testing of dam materials still in use around the world, a reassessment of all DWP dams and reservoirs, and an extensive retrofitting of the St. Francis Dam's twin, Mulholland Dam (renamed Hollywood Dam after the 1928 flood destroyed Mulholland's reputation). Perhaps most beneficial was the development of an efficient process for settling wrongful-death and damage suits that influenced disaster-relief legislation used extensively by victims of later floods, earthquakes, hurricanes, and other natural calamities.

Sue Tarjan

FOR FURTHER INFORMATION:

Davis, Margaret Leslie. *Rivers in the Desert: William Mulholland and the Inventing of Los Angeles.* Chicago: Olmstead Press, 2001.

Jackson, Donald C., and Norris Hundley, Jr. "Privilege and Responsibility: William Mulholland and the St. Francis Dam Disaster." *California History* 82, no. 3 (2004).

Nichols, John. *St. Francis Dam Disaster.* Chicago: Arcadia, 2002.

Nunis, Doyce B., Jr., ed. *The Saint Francis Dam Disaster Revisited.* Los Angeles: Historical Society of Southern California, 2002.

Outland, Charles F. *Man-Made Disaster: The Story of St. Francis Dam—Its Place in Southern California's Water System, Its Failure, and the Tragedy in the Santa Clara River Valley, March 12 and 13, 1928.* Rev. and enlarged ed. Los Angeles: Historical Society of Southern California, 2002.

Reisner, Marc. *Cadillac Desert: The American West and Its Disappearing Water.* New York: Penguin, 1993.

■ 1928: THE SAN FELIPE HURRICANE

HURRICANE

ALSO KNOWN AS: Lake Okeechobee hurricane
DATE: September 10-16, 1928
PLACE: Florida and the Caribbean
CLASSIFICATION: Category 4
RESULT: About 4,000 dead, 350,000 homeless

The San Felipe hurricane, also known as the Lake Okeechobee hurricane, was a ferocious Category 4 storm that claimed over 4,000 lives as it roared across the Caribbean islands of Guadeloupe, St. Kitts, and Montserrat; the Virgin Islands; and Puerto Rico before inflicting its full fury on Florida.

THE CARIBBEAN. The storm was spotted first by the crew of the ship SS *Cormack* in the Cape Verde Islands region in the eastern Atlantic in early September, 1928. By September 10, it had reached the mid-Atlantic, at which time it was classified as a Category 4 hurricane with winds of 135 miles per hour. The powerful storm crossed the islands of Guadeloupe, St. Kitts, and Montserrat on September 12. Its barometric pressure was recorded at 27.76 inches with winds between 160 and 170 miles per hour. The hurricane devastated the three islands. Buildings were destroyed, and roads were quickly inundated as 30-foot waves lashed against the shorelines. An estimated 520 people lost their lives, many of them in the flash floods spawned by the heavy rains accompanying the storm. The hurricane then proceeded south of St. Croix after dealing substantial damage to the Virgin Islands.

In the early morning hours of San Felipe Day on September 13, 1928 (the saint's commemoration day for which the storm received its name), the hurricane struck Puerto Rico near the port city of Arroyo, 32 miles southeast of San Juan, with the intensity of a Category 4 storm. Winds were registered at 135 miles per hour, with gusts up to 170 miles per hour, and blew steadily for four or five consecutive hours. In San Juan the wind reached its peak strength at about mid-afternoon. A short time earlier the Weather Bureau's anemometer registered 132 miles per hour, but the instrument was swept away by a gale.

The storm threw the city of San Juan into complete darkness and totally isolated it from the remainder of the island. All telegraph and telephone lines were destroyed, and all transportation was halted. Ships suffered extensive damage as a 19-foot storm surge swept ashore. The freight steamer *Helen* was ripped from its anchor during the peak of the storm, as were numerous smaller boats, and drifted onto rocks near the entrance of the harbor. The storm flattened the governor's palace and blew out its doors and windows, leaving it completely exposed to the torrential rains that soon flooded the building.

The hurricane wrought massive damage across the island. More than 19,000 buildings, representing 70 percent of the capital's homes and 40 percent of its businesses, were destroyed, leaving nearly 284,000 people without food or shelter. Trees by the thousands were uprooted, many of them smashing into homes or falling into streets.

Rainfall associated with the storm system was heavy and was a major contributing factor to the damage that occurred inland. Rain gauges recorded up to 30 inches of precipitation during the storm, which initiated mudslides and flash floods in the island's mountainous central regions. Whole villages were reported to have been destroyed by the onslaught. Altogether, over 1,400 people were killed in Puerto Rico during the storm that caused nearly $50 billion in damage to the island.

On September 15 the storm swept through the Bahamas, bringing heavy rains and 119-mile-per-hour winds to the eastern islands. Residents along Florida's east coast prepared to receive the full force of the approaching storm. On September 15 the Weather Bureau issued a warning that the hurricane was moving northwestward at a rate of 300 miles per day. Storm warnings were issued from Miami to Titusville, Florida.

Forecasters believed the storm could follow one of three paths: through the Florida Straits between Key West and Cuba and out into the Gulf of Mexico, to the north up along the East Coast, or straight ahead on a northwesterly direction that would take it to a point between Miami and Palm Beach.

FLORIDA. On September 16, the hurricane approached to within 200 miles of Miami. Storm warnings were posted from Miami to Jack-

A statue commemorates the San Felipe hurricane of 1928. (Courtesy, The Florida Memory Project)

sonville, an indication that forecasters believed the storm would move in a northeasterly direction across the state once it made land-fall. The Naval Radio Compass Station at Jupiter Inlet on the eastern coast, about 90 miles north of Miami, reported to the Navy Department that the storm was blowing with winds of more than 90 miles per hour and that the tide at Jupiter was more than 5 feet above normal. The compass station rode out the storm until early evening, when it reported that its radio tower had been blown down. It also sent a message informing the Navy Department that the barometric pressure had dropped to 28.79 inches and was still falling.

On the evening of September 16, the hurricane struck the coast near West Palm Beach, with winds estimated at over 100 miles per hour and a barometric pressure of 27.43 inches. An 11-foot storm surge, combined with over 10 inches of rain during the hurricane's passage, washed out numerous coastal roads. Many of the plush Palm Beach resorts and mansions perched along the shoreline received heavy damage. Close to 8,000 homes were either destroyed or damaged. Nearly 700 people were reported killed in Palm Beach County alone, many of them victims of the storm surge passing over the barrier island upon which the city is situated. The fashionable New Breakers Hotel was damaged severely when a tall chimney crashed through the roof, as was another elegant hotel, the Royal Poinciana, whose roof was torn.

From Boynton Beach to Lake Park, structures of all kinds were ripped from their foundations and carried for distances of hundreds of yards. Damage to the south in Miami was confined to broken windows and the scattered ruin of frail buildings, though some water destruction was also reported.

As predicted, the storm moved inland toward the Lake Okeechobee region. The storm that had brought devastation to the Palm Beach area was about to wield greater devastation.

Lake Okeechobee is the third largest freshwater lake within the United States. Located approximately 40 miles northwest of Palm Beach, it has a diameter of 40 miles and a maximum depth of 15 feet. Acting as a catch basin for the overflows produced by the rainy seasons, the lake served at the time as the chief water supply for central Florida. Dikes built around the lake were designed to restrain the overflows in order to protect the adjacent farming communities.

Almost totally unaware of the severity of the storm headed their way, residents of the tiny communities surrounding the lake, many of them migrant workers, carried on with their daily work routines. From the moment the storm struck, its exact path and the damage it was bringing were, for the most part, mysteries to inland inhabitants. There was no sophisticated communication system, so local residents had only rumors over the radio or unreliable wire communications to guide them.

As the storm moved across the lake's northern shore, driving all the water to one side of the lake, it caused the shallow waters to exceed the maximum height of 15 feet. In about thirty minutes the surge of water, combined with the heavy rainfall, overpowered the dikes protecting the lowlands at the lake's southern end. Hundreds of migrant workers were killed as a wall of water rushed through the region. Others clung to the tops of trees, houses, or any other objects they could grab hold of to ride out the surge. Several hundred women and children who sought safety on barges survived the storm when the two boats carrying them were washed ashore by the surge at South Bay. Some people had to walk as much as 6 miles through water higher than their waists before they were able to reach safety. It was nearly midnight before the storm began to lose some of its fury.

AFTEREFFECTS. Relief was slow in coming to the isolated region, since the attention of the country was focused on the damage done to the state's eastern shore. However, as relief workers battled their way into West Palm Beach over water-covered roads, they quickly spread the word of the enormity of the destruction that had occurred inland. The hurricane leveled every building in the nearly 50-mile stretch between Clewiston and Canal Point, except for a hotel which was converted into a shelter for fleeing refugees from the nearby towns of Belle Glade, Ritta, Bayport, Miami Locks, and other farming and fishing villages. A section of State Road 25 that connects Palm Beach and Fort Myers was left several feet under water. The Ritta Islands, located in the lake itself, were swept nearly clean by the winds. No survivors could be found on the islands following the storm.

The devastation from the storm was total. An expanse of land that stretched from the lake south into the Everglades was left in ruin. Eyewitnesses reported wreckage and debris scattered in every direction and numerous bodies floating in canals. The Red Cross placed the death toll in the region at 1,836, though there was no way to know the exact toll for certain. It was impossible for relief workers to gather the remains of the dead, and the original idea of sending individual coffins to dry areas such as Sebring and West Palm Beach had to be abandoned. Instead, funeral pyres were arranged to dispose of the bodies.

Domesticated animals and wildlife also suffered. Much of the lake's abundant fish supply was destroyed when washed over the dikes and left to die as the water receded. The surge also wiped out some farmers' entire stocks of cattle, pigs, horses, and chickens.

Following its strike on Lake Okeechobee, the hurricane curved north-northeast and skirted the city of Jacksonville. Trees in the city were uprooted by winds of 50 to 60 miles per hour, and several small shacks were toppled, though the major business and prominent residential sections escaped with minor damage. A roller coaster in Jacksonville Beach, 18 miles away, was toppled by the winds, and a portion of a dancing pier collapsed.

There were indications the hurricane was diminishing in intensity on its trail north, but it still carried enough strength to destroy communication wires between Tampa and Jacksonville. At one stage in the course of the storm, an entire portion of the state located below a diagonal line running from Palm Beach northward to the town of Brooksville was cut off from the outside world. As the storm curved back toward Jacksonville, another large section of the central part of the state as well as a portion of the East Coast became isolated. The storm eventually moved up the Georgia and South Carolina coast toward Hatteras, North Carolina, where it passed back into the sea.

Despite losing much of its strength, tremendous amounts of rainfall accompanied the remnants of the storm on its way north. Savannah, Georgia, reported 11.42 inches of rain and winds of 50 miles per hour, while Charleston, South Carolina, registering 7.18 inches of precipitation and winds of 48 miles per hour, reported its shoreline strewn with the wreckage of small boats and piers. Both cities were nearly isolated by broken communication lines.

The Lake Okeechobee hurricane is considered the most catastrophic storm to hit the state of Florida in terms of lives lost. The enormity of the disaster led federal and state officials to develop a plan to rebuild the dikes that failed on the lake's southern shores so that a similar disaster would not occur in the future. In the three decades that followed, the U.S. Army Corps of Engineers built a 150-mile dike constructed from mud, sand, rock, and concrete. It is named for President Herbert Hoover.

William Hoffman

FOR FURTHER INFORMATION:

Barnes, Jay. *Florida's Hurricane History.* Chapel Hill: University of North Carolina Press, 1998.

Kleinberg, Eliot. *Black Cloud: The Great Florida Hurricane of 1928.* New York: Carroll & Graf, 2003.

Longshore, David. *Encyclopedia of Hurricanes, Typhoons, and Cyclones.* New York: Facts On File, 1998.

Mykle, Robert. *Killer 'Cane: The Deadly Hurricane of 1928.* New York: Cooper Square Press, 2002.

Williams, John M., and Iver W. Duedall. *Florida Hurricanes and Tropical Storms, 1871-2001.* Gainesville: University of Florida Press, 2002.

■ 1932: THE DUST BOWL

DROUGHT AND DUST STORMS

DATE: 1932-1937
PLACE: Great Plains and the southwestern United States
RESULT: 500,000 homeless

Six years of severe drought combined with overuse and improper exposure of the soil in the semi-arid and arid prairie regions of the southeastern United States led to Dust Bowl conditions, wind erosion of the soil, and the displacement of 500,000 farmers and townsfolk in the region. Dust Bowl conditions include extensive and prolonged lack of rainfall extending over several years; depletion of soil moisture to the point where plant life cannot be sustained; increased heat in summer and increased cold in winter due to the effect of airborne dust particles on atmospheric heating and cooling; the transformation of soil into particles of dust, sand, and minerals; and an increase in the frequency and intensity of wind due to the combined effects of rapidly fluctuating daily air temperature, low humidity, and a decline in the vegetative barriers and ground covers.

HOMESTEADERS ARRIVE. Before settlement in the late nineteenth and early twentieth centuries, natural, deep-rooted prairie grasses held the soil in place. The grasses that established themselves on the prairie soil were able to survive severe and prolonged drought, hot summers, and cold winters. During most of the eighteenth and nineteenth centuries, the region of the Great Plains was known to most citizens as "The Great American Desert." In the post-Civil War period, railroads were given government land grants to encourage the western expansion of rail services. Promotional literature produced by the railroads and the national government encouraged settlement in the Great Plains, either along railroad lines or in homestead areas established in the western territories by the government. The older idea of the Great Plains as a desert was replaced by a new myth of an agricultural empire in the "Garden of the World" and a new marketing dictum that "rain follows the plow." This mistaken idea that settlement could change the climate encouraged farmers to continue plowing and planting their lands as the years of drought progressed, and discouraged the use of new agricultural techniques for semiarid soils even after these techniques were developed.

A period of western migration encouraged eastern, midwestern, and European immigrant farmers to relocate to the area. Government land-grant and homesteading programs, land marketing schemes by railroad companies, national policies encouraging increased agricultural production, and the invention of mechanized farming tools and tractors encouraged and supported this migration to the previously untilled land. The native grasses were plowed under, using the agricultural techniques of the day, exposing the newly turned soil to potential erosion. Most settlement and soil exposure occurred during periods of normal or increased rainfall, and the growing crops replaced the prairie grasses as protectors of the soil. Many farmers enjoyed bumper yields in the years preceding the drought.

The settlement of the American Great Plains was similar to the patterns experienced in semiarid areas of Australia, South Africa, and the Russian steppes. The settlers were primarily individuals with agricultural experience limited to the humid agricultural conditions of Western Europe or the eastern half of North America. The settlers began with an inaccurate perception of the possibilities and limitations of agricultural production in these arid and semiarid areas and lacked an adaptive technology to cope with extended drought. A severe drought in the Great Plains in the 1890's did not deter optimism concerning the agricultural potential of the region.

YEARS OF DROUGHT. The drought beginning in 1932 led to agricultural failure and to the repeated exposure of the land to wind erosion. Once tilled lands began to suffer wind erosion, the blowing dust together with the drought conditions caused the natural grasses on untilled land to wither and die, exposing more soil to erosion. Left unprotected, topsoil was lifted into the air, creating "black blizzards" of dust. The previously rich topsoil was blown away. On many farms, topsoil was eroded down to the clay base or to the bedrock. In many cases, even the clay began to fragment and become airborne in the wind. The loss of land fertility plus repeated crop failures led to the bankruptcy of thousands of farmers and the townspeople who provided services to the farmers. Many of these people became displaced migrants, with many traveling farther west to California or returning to the East in search of jobs and new land.

The harvest of 1931 produced a bumper crop of wheat, depressing the market price in the midst of the Great Depression, a national and worldwide decline in economic activity which began in the 1920's and which had already depressed prices for agricultural products. Farmers responded by increasing the acreage under cultivation hoping to restore lost income by increasing output, thus further reducing prices and exposing more land to potential erosion. The 1932 agricultural year began with a late freeze followed by violent rainstorms, a plague of insects, and a summer drought affecting 50 million acres in Kansas, Oklahoma, Texas, New Mexico, Colorado, and parts of Nebraska, South Dakota, and North Dakota. Drought conditions continued without relief until 1937 and gradually extended east, west, and north, involving most of North America in some form of drought. Lakes Michigan and Huron dropped to their lowest levels on record.

BLACK BLIZZARDS. The first great dust storm, or black blizzard, occurred in November, 1933. Vast quantities of dust particles were carried thousands of feet into the atmosphere by winter winds, block-

A collage of headlines about the Dust Bowl. (Library of Congress)

ing out the sun for several days at a time. Gritty dust and dirt blew into houses and other buildings under windowsills or through door jambs, covering and contaminating floors, food, bedclothes, furniture, and drinking water and damaging machinery and tools. Dust storms continued to occur regularly during the next few years. In parts of Texas and Oklahoma as many as 100 separate dust storms were recorded in a single year. In March of 1936, there were twenty-two days of dust storms over the Texas Panhandle. In April, 1935, twenty-eight days of dust storms occurred in Amarillo, Texas.

Storms in April, 1934, and February, 1935, were so severe that they darkened the skies over the entire eastern half of the United States, with dust from the Dust Bowl falling on Washington, D.C., New York City, and ships at sea. The finest dust particles were carried as far as Europe. An estimated 350 million tons of topsoil was blown away from what had been one of the world's richest agricultural areas.

Within the most severely affected areas of the Dust Bowl, crops sprouted only to wither and die. Drifts of dirt and sand smothered the remaining prairie grasslands, killed trees and shrubs, and blocked roads and railroad lines. Blowing dust scrubbed the paint off buildings and automobiles, caused human respiratory sickness, and created massive dry-weather electrical storms generating substantial wind gusts but no rainfall. Hundreds of people died of respiratory ailments. Cattle and wildlife starved or died of thirst. Birds found it impossible to nest successfully.

GOVERNMENT ACTION. In 1936-1937, Congress debated and eventually enacted a Soil Conservation Act, intended to relieve the economic impact of the Dust Bowl conditions and prevent future wind or water erosion of the soil. Dr. Hugh Hammond Bennett, working with the Roosevelt administration as the chief proponent of the bill, encouraged a congressional vote on the bill just as dust from a Dust Bowl black blizzard shrouded Washington, D.C., in a brown haze. The act allocated $500 million to subsidize farmers who converted from growing grain crops, such as corn and wheat, to soil-building crops, such as hay and legumes. These measures both helped stabilize the soil and helped reduce grain production, resulting in agricultural prices rising to pre-Depression levels. The Soil Conservation Act called for the establishment of agricultural and conservation education programs, the planting of trees around farms and along roads as windbreaks, and establishment of Soil Conservation Districts in each state. Later renamed Soil and Water Conservation Districts, these units of local government, encouraged by the national government and established in each state by acts of the state legislature, are an important force in encouraging farmers to add "best management practices" to their farming techniques, constructing vegetative barriers to reduce wind and water erosion of the soil, and protecting the soil and water resources of America.

Actions by the national government came too late for many farmers forced off the land due to mortgage foreclosures or the near-total loss of topsoil from their lands. Many migrated west to California or returned east to the industrial cities with only a few clothes and possessions and no money. Those with no skills other than farming worked as migrant farm laborers wherever they could find a harvest to work. These migrants put strains on the already overburdened government-welfare programs in these states and increased labor competition pressures. The migrants experienced anger and discrimination in the areas to which they migrated. Several states and many local governments enacted laws intended to prevent the migration and settlement of Dust Bowl migrants into their areas.

In 1937, the drought ended, and those who could return to agricultural production did, using new farming methods designed to protect the soil from both wind and water erosion. The 1937 crop yield nationwide was the largest on record. The good weather continued throughout the critical years of World War II, and the improved agricultural methods continued to protect the soil.

Gordon Neal Diem

FOR FURTHER INFORMATION:

Egan, Timothy. *The Worst Hard Time: The Untold Story of Those Who Survived the Great American Dust Bowl.* Boston: Houghton Mifflin, 2006.

Lookingbill, Brad D. *Dust Bowl, USA: Depression America and the Ecological Imagination, 1929-1941.* Athens: Ohio University Press, 2001.

Saarinen, Thomas F. *Perception of the Drought Hazard on the Great Plains.* Chicago: University of Chicago Press, 1966.

Stallings, Frank L. *Black Sunday: The Great Dust Storm of April 14, 1935.* Austin, Tex.: Eakin Press, 2001.

United States Great Plains Committee. *The Future of the Great Plains.* Washington, D.C.: U.S. Government Printing Office, 1936.

Worster, Donald. *Dust Bowl: The Southern Plains in the 1930's.* 25th anniversary ed. New York: Oxford University Press, 2004.

■ 1937: THE *HINDENBURG* DISASTER

EXPLOSION AND FIRE

DATE: May 6, 1937
PLACE: Lakehurst, New Jersey
RESULT: 36 dead (22 crew members, 13 passengers, and 1 person on the ground), travel by airship comes to an end

On May 3, 1937, the huge airship *Hindenburg* took off from Frankfurt, Germany, headed for Lakehurst, New Jersey. On board were 97 people—61 passengers and 36 crew members. The *Hindenburg* had already completed more than thirty ocean crossings in its first year of operation, having safely delivered more than 2,000 passengers and 375,000 pounds of mail and freight. The *Hindenburg* was a Nazi propaganda showpiece, with large black swastikas displayed prominently on its tail fins.

Over the years, German-built airships (lighter-than-air aircrafts), often called zeppelins, had acquired an excellent record for safety and dependability. An earlier airship, called the *Graf Zeppelin*, had logged more than 1 million miles without mishap on regular transatlantic flights from 1930 until it was retired in 1936.

THE CREATION OF AIRSHIPS. Ferdinand von Zeppelin (1838-1914) was born into a wealthy German family. As an army officer, he was sent to the United States in 1861 to observe military maneuvers during the Civil War. He had the opportunity to take a ride in a hot-air balloon, which can only drift with the air currents because it has no mechanism for steering or propulsion. That experience gave Zeppelin a lifelong motivation to design a lighter-than-air vehicle whose direction of flight could be controlled by a pilot on board. Other inventors had the same goal, but Zeppelin had the persistence and the financial resources to carry out his plan. By the time he died in 1914, Zeppelin had a fleet of thirty airships with a regular schedule of passenger flights between major cities in Europe.

The *Hindenburg* had the designation LZ-129, the one hundred twenty-ninth airship to be built by the Zeppelin factory since the first successful flight on the LZ-1 took place in the year 1900. The *Hinden-*

burg looked like an enormous sausage, 803 feet long and 135 feet in diameter. Most of its bulk consisted of a metal framework that held sixteen large gas bags filled with hydrogen. Hydrogen is much lighter than air, even lighter than the helium that is used in balloons. The total weight of the airship, including the framework, the gas bags, the passenger gondola, and the propulsion and steering apparatus must be less than the weight of air that it displaces in order for the airship to become buoyant. Like a submarine, which gets its buoyancy from the surrounding water, the airship literally floats in the air. Propulsion was provided by four 1,150-horsepower diesel engines that turned two relatively small propellers. Cruising at an average speed of 80 miles per hour, the transatlantic trip took only three days, less than half the time taken by the fastest ocean liners of the 1930's. The passenger gondola, about 60 feet long, was fastened to the bottom of the main balloon near its front end. It was designed for wealthy patrons who were accustomed to luxury. The sleeping cabins had comfortable beds and modern bathroom fixtures. The dining room had

The German airship Hindenburg *explodes into flame over Lakehurst, New Jersey.* (Courtesy, Navy Lakehurst Historical Society)

elegant furnishings, adjacent to a promenade deck with large observation windows. There was a dance floor with a stage for the band. The guest lounge was furnished with card tables and easy chairs. Because hydrogen gas is highly combustible, elaborate safety precautions were needed to prevent any open flame or sparks. Smoking was permitted only in a special smoking room, where the cigarette lighters were chained to the furniture. No cigarettes or matches were allowed anywhere else. The hallway walls had a rubberized coating to prevent buildup of static electricity. Riding in the gondola was very smooth compared to ocean liners because the great bulk of the balloon smoothed out any local air turbulence.

Because hydrogen gas is flammable, Germany had tried to buy helium gas from the United States. Helium is a lightweight, inert gas that provides almost the same amount of buoyancy as hydrogen. The U.S. government opposed exporting helium to Germany because Adolf Hitler's Nazi Party had come to power in 1933 and the threat of war was coming closer. During World War I, the German military had used zeppelins to drop bombs over London and other cities in Great Britain. In some fifty air raids, large buildings had been destroyed and over 500 people were killed. The terror caused by these air attacks left a lasting memory that firmly opposed selling helium to Germany as it was rearming itself.

THE *HINDENBURG* EXPLODES. On May 6, 1937, after a routine three-day flight across the Atlantic, the *Hindenburg* passed over New York City. Just after 7 P.M., the airship arrived at its landing field at Lakehurst, New Jersey. As it hovered above the mooring tower, ropes were dropped from the front of the ship to tie it down for unloading. A radio announcer and a newsreel photographer were on hand to report on the arrival because the passenger list frequently included international celebrities.

Without warning, the tail section of the *Hindenburg* suddenly burst into flames. The fire spread very quickly, and the airship sank down toward the ground because of the loss of hydrogen. Some of the panicked passengers jumped from the gondola and survived, but others were killed upon impact with the ground. Some waited too long to jump and died when their clothing and hair caught fire. The radio announcer spoke into his microphone, where his eyewitness words of shock were recorded: "It's burst into flames! Get out of the way! . . .

It's falling on the mooring mast and all the folks between us. . . . This is the worst thing I've ever witnessed!" Only thirty-four seconds after the initial explosion the *Hindenburg* lay on the ground with its metal skeleton twisted and wrecked. The fire did not last long because after the hydrogen had escaped, there was not much combustible material left to burn.

A circus performer named Joseph Spah was one of the miraculous survivors from the *Hindenburg* disaster. He was sitting in the dining room when the explosion happened. He smashed one of the window-panes and climbed out through the broken window, dangling from the ledge by his hands. He realized that he was too high to let go, so he waited for the burning airship to drop closer to the ground. The window ledge became very hot, searing his hands. When he thought he was about 40 feet from the ground, he let go, dropped to the ground, landed on his feet, and ran away from the fire. His only injury was a fractured heel.

There were some extraordinary acts of heroism during the disaster that helped to save lives. Some of the ground crew remained underneath the burning airship long enough to catch passengers who had jumped. Captain Max Pruss, who was in the control room, helped 7 crew members to escape through a window. He dragged an unconscious man to safety even after his own clothes had caught on fire. One of the casualties was Ernst Lehman, who had been in command of the *Hindenburg* on earlier flights. He was able to walk away from the blazing wreckage but died of burns later.

The *Hindenburg* disaster made headlines in all the major newspapers. Like the tragic sinking of the cruise ship *Titanic*, another technological marvel had come to a spectacular end, in spite of extensive safety precautions. In the 1930's, television was not yet available, but newsreel photography of major events was commonly shown at movie theaters before or after the feature film. Because a cameraman was all set up to film the landing of the *Hindenburg*, he was able to capture the whole disaster from beginning to end. Together with the voice of the radio announcer, it was shown to horrified audiences. It was the first major disaster with eyewitness photography. Pictures of burning victims trying to run away from the flaming wreck left an indelible image that travel by airship was too dangerous. The age of the airships came to an end with the *Hindenburg* disaster.

REASONS FOR THE EXPLOSION. What caused the *Hindenburg* to explode? As is customary after a major disaster, there was a formal inquiry, at which some of the survivors were able to tell their stories. Three possible scenarios emerged from the investigation. One was that an electric discharge from the atmosphere had initiated the explosion. Although no one had seen any lightning, there is frequently a buildup of static electricity between low-lying clouds and the ground. It had been raining earlier that day in Lakehurst, and newsreels did show a cloudy sky above the airship as it was landing. A second possibility was an electric discharge inside the balloon itself, perhaps produced by friction between gas bags rubbing against each other. It was almost impossible to prevent some leakage of hydrogen through the rubberized fabric of the bags, so a spark could have ignited the gas.

The third possibility, more of a speculation, was that it was an act of sabotage. Perhaps a member of the crew who was strongly opposed to Adolf Hitler's militarism and persecution of Jews had set a bomb that would bring a spectacular end to this airship that symbolized the dominance of German technology. However, no evidence of bomb material could be found in the wrecked remains of the *Hindenburg*.

Hans G. Graetzer

FOR FURTHER INFORMATION:

Archbold, Rick. *Hindenburg: An Illustrated History.* Secaucus, N.J.: Chartwell Books, 2005.

Botting, Douglas. *Dr. Eckener's Dream Machine: The Great Zeppelin and the Dawn of Air Travel.* New York: Henry Holt, 2001.

De Syon, Guillaume. *Zeppelin! Germany and the Airship, 1900-1939.* Baltimore: Johns Hopkins University Press, 2002.

Dick, Harold G. *The Golden Age of the Great Passenger Airships: "Graf Zeppelin" and" "Hindenburg."* Reprint. Washington, D.C.: Smithsonian Institution Press, 1992.

Mooney, Michael M. *The Hindenburg.* New York: Dodd, Mead, 1972.

Robinson, Douglas H. *Famous Aircraft: The LZ-129 "Hindenburg."* Dallas: Morgan, 1964.

Tanaka, Shirley. *The Disaster of the "Hindenburg": The Last Flight of the Greatest Airship Ever Built.* New York: Scholastic/Madison Press, 1993.

■ 1938: THE GREAT NEW ENGLAND HURRICANE OF 1938

HURRICANE

DATE: September 21, 1938
PLACE: Northeastern United States
CLASSIFICATION: Category 3
RESULT: About 680 dead, more than 1,700 injured, nearly 20,000 requests for aid, $400 million in damage

Some analysts call the Great New England Hurricane of 1938 a triple storm: hurricane, flood, and tidal surge. Unusually heavy rains beginning September 18, 1938, caused rivers and streams to rise and flood low-lying areas, and the rain that accompanied the up to 100-mile-per-hour winds during the brief course of the hurricane added to these conditions. In shoreline areas and cities on tidal rivers additional flood conditions were caused by the tidal surges common to hurricanes, when the high winds drive the tide upon itself. Several towns and cities also suffered from fires that were started when electrical wires were short-circuited by water or by ships that were driven by high winds and the tide into buildings along the coast.

THE FORMATION OF THE STORM. June of 1938 was the third-wettest June in New England weather records, followed by an abnormally wet and mild summer. It is suggested that a French meteorological observation at the Bilma Oasis in the Sahara Desert on September 4 noting a wind shift would, with modern radar tracking and satellite imagery not available then, have given the first hint of trouble. The shift resulted in an area of storminess off the west coast of Africa, entering the Atlantic in the Cape Verde region. On September 16 a storm of hurricane strength was reported northeast of Puerto Rico by a lightship and the Jacksonville office of the U.S. Weather Bureau. The bureau followed the storm's rapid progress westward, issuing a hurricane warning for southern Florida on September 19. The storm slowed and turned north, sparing Florida, and initially it was assumed to be heading out to sea.

This hurricane was abnormal in that it traveled northward at an average speed of 50 miles per hour rather than the more usual 20 to 30 miles per hour. In twelve hours it moved from a position off Cape Hatteras to southern Vermont and New Hampshire. More important from the standpoint of criticisms of inadequate warning by the Weather Bureau is the fact that less than six hours elapsed from its leaving the Florida area, traveling over water, until it hit Long Island, New York. Because of its rapid progress, the hurricane had destructive winds about 100 miles east of its center, while there was relatively little damage to property on the west side. Therefore, the worst of the destruction was concentrated on Long Island, Rhode Island, eastern Connecticut, central Massachusetts, and southern Vermont and New Hampshire. High winds lasted only about an hour and a half in any one area.

A storm surge causes giant waves to crash against a seawall during the Great New England Hurricane of 1938. (National Oceanic and Atmospheric Administration)

THE AFTEREFFECTS. In spite of its brief tenure, the hurricane had tremendous temporary and some important lasting economic impact. Whole seaside communities along the Connecticut and Rhode Island coasts were wiped out by wind and tides, which ranged from 12 to 25 feet higher than normal. New beaches were cut, islands were formed as the water ran through strips of shore, and navigational charts of the time became worthless. Roads and railroad tracks along the shore were undermined, buckled, and tossed. Railroad service was interrupted from seven to fourteen days while crews removed trees, houses, and several good-sized boats from the tracks.

Inland, bridges were wiped out, roads buckled where undermined by usually small streams, and trees fell on roads and buildings. Winds blew roofs, walls, and often top stories off brick and wooden buildings. Dams were breached by the high waters. Apples ready for harvest were blown off the trees, and whole groves of maples were snapped, affecting the maple-syrup industry for years to come. It was a rare church whose steeple escaped being torn down, and village greens were permanently altered by the toppling of stately mature elms and oaks that had lined the streets. Most important, some mills upon which a town's economy depended were never rebuilt after the damage. In New England, all old mills were originally powered by water, so they were located on dammed rivers.

Although not as hard hit, portions of northern Vermont and New Hampshire also suffered from fallen trees and flooding. Maine was the least affected, escaping flooding and damaged only by diminishing, although still high, winds. Boats were driven ashore from Portland south, and train schedules were disrupted and road traffic affected by downed trees.

EXAMINATION OF THE STORM. The major New England rivers were already at flood stage before the hurricane struck. The wet summer meant that the heavy rains in the three days preceding the high winds did not soak into the ground but ran off into streams, which in turn fed the rivers. Tributaries most affected were the Farmington, Chicopee, Millers, Deerfield, and Ashuelot Rivers of the Connecticut; the Quinebaug and Shetucket of the Thames; and the Contoocock and Piscataquog of the Merrimack.

New England is not often subjected to serious floods or hurricanes and is even less affected by tornadoes. Accounts of the 1938 hurricane are compared to the Great Colonial Hurricane of August 14 or 15, 1635 (as recorded by Increase Mather in his *Remarkable Providences* of 1684); the Great September Gale of September 23, 1815, recorded by Noah Webster and others; the ice storm of 1921; and floods of 1927 and 1936, the latter providing benchmarks for high water two years later.

The 1938 storm was termed "unique," "unusual," and "most interesting" by meteorologists, and a "freak," the "worst in the history of the northeast" by Dr. Charles C. Clark, acting chief of the U.S. Weather Bureau. It was not a tropical hurricane in the strict sense of the word because before it reached the northeastern states it was transformed into an extra-tropical storm, with a definite frontal structure and two distinct air masses—tropical maritime and polar continental, a peculiar temperature and wind distribution in the upper atmosphere. Although winds of 60 miles per hour were common at the hurricane's worst, geographic conditions contributed to winds up to 100 miles per hour in some areas. At slightly higher elevations, weather devices recorded much higher velocities: 186 miles per hour at the Harvard Meteorological Observatory at the top of Blue Hill in Milton, Massachusetts, and 120 miles per hour at the top of the Empire State Building in New York City.

THE EXTENT OF THE DESTRUCTION. Statistics, especially the count of dead and injured, vary considerably. An estimated 680 to 685 lost their lives. Estimates of those injured range from 700 to over 1,700. Nearly 20,000 applied for aid. There is no uncertainty, however, in the assessment that the $400 million in total damage was the highest for any storm to its date. One account lists 4,500 homes, summer cottages, and farm buildings destroyed; 2,605 boats lost and 3,369 damaged, with a total $2.6 million estimated in fishing boats, equipment, docks, and shore plants destroyed; 26,000 cars smashed; 275 million trees broken off or uprooted; nearly 20,000 miles of power and telephone lines down; and numerous farm animals killed. Some 10,000 railroad workers filled 1,000 washouts, replaced nearly 100 bridges, and removed buildings and 30 boats from the tracks. Bell System crews came from as far away as Virginia, Arkansas, and Nevada to help restore service. About half the estimated 5 million bushels of the apple crop was unharvested and destroyed.

On Fire Island, New York, the tide crossed from the ocean to the bay side over the land, sweeping everything from its path. In West-hampton, Long Island, only 26 of 179 beach houses remained, and most were uninhabitable. Every house in Watch Hill, Rhode Island's Napatree Point-Fort Road area was swept into Naragansett Bay, and only 15 of the 42 occupants in the 39 houses survived. Downtown Providence, Rhode Island, was flooded under 10 feet of water. New London, Connecticut, suffered $4 million in damage from water, 98-mile-per-hour winds, and the worst fire since General Benedict Arnold's troops burned the city in 1781. The fire was started by electrical wires short-circuited when a five-masted schooner was driven into a building. The town of Peterborough in southern New Hampshire also suffered from fire as well as wind and water damage when wires were short-circuited by floodwater. In one instance along the Connecticut shore, a railroad engineer nudged a cabin cruiser and a house off the tracks, loaded all his passengers into the dining and first Pullman cars, disconnected the remainder of the train, and brought his riders to safety. In several towns and cities, including Ware and North Adams, Massachusetts, and Brandon, Vermont, rivers changed their courses and took over main streets. While portions of Springfield, Massachusetts, and Hartford, Connecticut, were flooded, these cities were not damaged as much as might have been expected because of dikes built after the 1936 flood and sandbag walls added by volunteers in 1938.

On September 23, two days after the storm had passed, the Connecticut River crested at 35.42 feet. This was 2 feet below the 1936 record, but nothing else approaching this had been recorded since 1854. A total of 17 inches of rain had fallen in the Connecticut Valley in four days. However, the amount of rain varied greatly from one area to another, as did the velocity of the wind.

Electrical, telephone, and railroad services were interrupted for up to two weeks, and other services and activities were disrupted as well. Flooding and wind damage to buildings in town and city centers made food and provisions hard to find for days. Roads were blocked as well while crews removed the trees that had fallen across them, interrupting school activity and preventing many from reaching their homes. Business and public buildings as well as churches and homes had to be repaired or rebuilt. The disruption to lives cannot be adequately reflected in any of these statistics.

Erika E. Pilver

FOR FURTHER INFORMATION:

Allen, Everett S. *A Wind to Shake the World: The Story of the 1938 Hurricane.* Beverly, Mass.: Commonwealth Editions, 2006.

Burns, Cherie. *The Great Hurricane—1938.* New York: Atlantic Monthly Press, 2005.

Cummings, Mary. *Hurricane in the Hamptons, 1938.* New York: Arcadia, 2006.

Goudsouzian, Aram. *The Hurricane of 1938.* Beverly, Mass.: Commonwealth Editions, 2006.

Minsinger, William Elliott, comp. and ed. *The 1938 Hurricane: An Historical and Pictorial Summary.* East Milton, Mass.: Blue Hill Observatory, 1988.

Scotti, R. A. *Sudden Sea: The Great Hurricane of 1938.* Boston: Little, Brown, 2003.

Vallee, David R., and Richael P. Dion. *Southern New England Tropical Storms and Hurricanes: A Ninety-Eight-Year Summary (1909-1997).* Taunton, Mass.: National Weather Service, 1998.

■ 1946: THE ALEUTIAN TSUNAMI

TSUNAMI

ALSO KNOWN AS: The April Fools' Day Tsunami
DATE: April 1, 1946
PLACE: Primarily Hilo, Hawaii
RESULT: 159 dead in Hawaiian Islands (179 dead total), $25 million in damage on Hawaiian Islands

It was 7 A.M. on the morning of April 1, 1946, at Hilo, on the northeast coast of the big island of Hawaii, which is at the southeast end of the Hawaiian Island chain. Locally based ship pilot and U.S. Navy Captain W. Wickland was on the bridge of a ship moored in Hilo Bay. Sea level in the port began falling and rising and repeated this pattern twice more—much faster than would happen with any normal tidal variation. Then, as he would later report, "I looked out and saw what looked like a low, long swell at sea; way out, but coming in awfully fast. Seemed like three separate waves, each behind the other, came together in one monster wave. I was on the upper bridge, some 46 feet above the waterline. That wave was just about eye-level and probably two miles long."

THE ORIGINS OF THE TSUNAMI. A tsunami was rapidly but stealthily approaching Hilo and was about to wreak destruction. It had originated with an earthquake under the seafloor, which itself was at a depth of about 13,123 feet (4,000 meters) at the Aleutian trench. Its epicenter was about 81 miles (130 kilometers) southeast of Unimak Island, the latter being at the western end of the Alaskan peninsula. At the epicenter, with location 52 degrees 80 minutes north latitude and 162 degrees 50 minutes west longitude in the North Pacific, the seafloor disturbance had generated a sea wave that was now spreading outward in all directions.

The earthquake, having a magnitude of 7.4, occurred at 1:29 A.M. local time. Within several minutes, the long-length wave had grown in height as it rapidly approached the shallowing shore of Unimak Island, and a wave 98 feet (30 meters) high crashed onto the coast. It destroyed a lighthouse at Scotch Cap that was 32 feet (10 meters)

615

above sea level, killing the 5 inhabitants. The tsunami wave was also spreading southward. In the open, deep ocean, the distance between wave crests is typically greater than 62 miles (100 kilometers), the amplitude (wave height) about 3.3 feet (1 meter), and speed about 373 to 497 miles (600 to 800 kilometers) per hour; 497 miles (800 kilometers) per hour is about the speed of a jet airliner.

Four and a half hours after the earthquake, the waves were approaching the Hawaiian Islands, 2,400 miles (3,900 kilometers) to the southeast. As the seafloor shallows toward shore, the wave speed typically slows to perhaps 30 miles per hour and the amplitude of the wave crests builds dramatically.

HILO. It was now about 7 A.M. local time—Hawaii being in the adjacent time zone to the east of Unimak Island. The first wave of the sequence emptied the harbor of water at Hilo Bay, so that ships were now unexpectedly sitting on the newly exposed seafloor amid the coral reefs and some floundering fish. Then the large crest returned, uprooting and slamming the seaside buildings inland and against other buildings, taking out 7,500 feet of a 10,000-foot-long breakwater. With a great sucking sound it retreated out to sea, carrying with it much debris and several people. Twice more this process of retreat and destructive return was repeated. According to Captain Wickland, this tsunami had a crest that "broke, and tore up everything it touched. Some Coast Guard boats flew by, and a yacht was thrown up to the main highway. Every structure, building, and piece of equipment on shore seemed to take off."

THE AFTEREFFECTS. One-third of the town of Hilo vanished. The steel span of a railroad bridge across the Wailuku River was swept 328 feet (100 meters) inland. Heavy masses of coral were ripped up from the usually submerged reefs and strewn onto the beaches. The height of the tsunami waves had been from 23 to 32 feet (7 to 10 meters) at Hilo, as much as 59 feet (18 meters) locally elsewhere on the coast of the island of Hawaii, and up to 39 feet (12 meters) on the island of Oahu to the northwest. Hilo reported 96 dead, and another 63 were killed in other parts of the Hawaiian Islands—a total of 159. Twenty-six of the total died at the village of Laupahoehoe, about 25 miles (40 kilometers) up the coast northwest of Hilo, where the tsunami destroyed a schoolhouse and killed the 25 students and their teacher inside. Property damage in Hawaii was estimated to be $25 million.

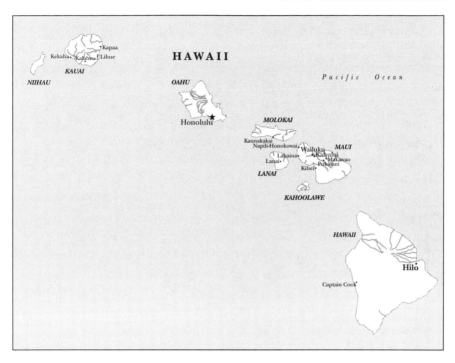

Twenty other persons died elsewhere from this tsunami; many of the deaths in Hawaii occurred when people—not aware that a tsunami was in progress—went down to the shore with curiosity after the first wave's water had withdrawn out to sea.

The following day in Hilo, bodies of a dozen people, recovered from the sea or from the wreckage on shore, were laid along the sidewalk under blankets. In the words of local resident Kapua Heuer, "You lifted the blanket to see if you could find those who you were looking for. The stark terror in their eyes—they died in terror."

The tsunami wave train continued spreading through the Pacific, at close to 497 miles (800 kilometers) per hour. It arrived at Valparaiso, halfway down the coastline of Chile, eighteen hours after the earthquake—and over 8,000 miles (13,000 kilometers) away from the epicenter—and resulted in a shore wave that was still 6 feet (2 meters) high. Tide gauges showed that the seismic sea waves were reflected back from Pacific coasts and hit the south side of Hawaii another eighteen hours later, then sloshed around the Pacific basin for the next couple of days.

OTHER HAWAIIAN TSUNAMIS. The Hawaiian Islands were hit by 7 tsunamis between 1924 and 2000, having waves at least 16 feet (5 meters) high. This includes the very early hours of May 23, 1960, when an earthquake the previous day off the coast of Chile generated a tsunami that resulted in waves at Hilo up to 23 feet (7 meters) high; 61 persons were killed, and 229 buildings were destroyed or severely damaged. On November 29, 1975, an earthquake of magnitude 7.2 on the island of Hawaii, 28 miles (45 kilometers) south of Hilo, created enough seafloor disturbance to produce waves up to 13 feet (4 meters) high at Hilo.

Tsunami-prone areas can reduce potential property damage by restricting building in low-lying coastal areas or at immediate portside. Hilo, after the destructive tsunamis of 1946 and 1960, limited commercial structures near the harbor. The area has been converted to a waterfront park that helps serve as a natural buffer for future high waves.

WARNING SYSTEMS. The best means of reducing danger and losses, particularly of life and injury, would be adequate warning of an oncoming seismic sea wave that could grow into a destructive tsunami. This shore-impacting growth into one or more walls of water depends in part on the local seafloor topography (bathymetry) and on the shoreline's shape and orientation with respect to the wave. Such a warning system is now in place for the Pacific region. In 1948, after the destructive Aleutian-generated tsunami that hit Hawaii in April, 1946, the U.S. government set up a Seismic Sea Wave Warning System. It is now known as the Pacific Tsunami Warning System and is administered by the National Oceanic and Atmospheric Administration (NOAA). With coordination and data processing at a Pacific Tsunami Warning Center in Honolulu, it quickly activates when any of its 30 participating seismic observatories, which are located around and on islands throughout the Pacific basin, detect an earthquake or other disturbance that could potentially generate a spreading tsunami. Another 78 stations have tide gauges for monitoring unusual changes in sea level, in order to detect a tsunami as it passes by. If such a wave is indeed spreading, an alert is issued, with prediction of arrival times, to Pacific nations, islands, and territories in the region.

The Warning System can typically issue a reliable Pacific-wide warning in about an hour after the occurrence of the source (such as an earthquake or volcanic eruption). This allows notice of an approaching tsunami for locations more than 466 miles (750 kilometers) from the source, because the wave train travels at about 750 miles per hour. This is adequate for trans-Pacific sites, as the tsunami travel time from, for example, Chile to Hawaii is about fifteen hours, and from the Aleutians to Northern California is about four hours.

The first use of the Warning System was on November 4, 1952, when an earthquake, detected as occurring off the Kamchatka Peninsula of eastern Russia, created a spreading sea wave. The Honolulu center predicted a time of arrival at the Hawaiian Islands about six hours from the time the earthquake occurred. People were evacuated inland, and ships or small boats were taken out to sea to ride out the subdued waves far offshore, and no lives were lost.

There are now regional systems of more localized monitoring stations and rapid data analysis, which give early cautionary warnings about ten minutes or so after an earthquake. This can be timely in reaching people and sites as close as 62 miles (100 kilometers) to a potential tsunami source. Such regional systems are in place in Hawaii, Alaska, Japan, the Kamchatka Peninsula, and French Polynesia. Before the Japanese regional system was established, there had been more than 6,000 people killed by tsunami waves in 14 events; after the system became operational, only 215 died from the next 20 tsunami events.

Robert S. Carmichael

FOR FURTHER INFORMATION:

Dudley, Walter C., and Scott C. S. Stone. *The Tsunami of 1946 and 1960 and the Devastation of Hilo Town.* Marceline, Mo.: Walsworth, 2000.

Dvorak, J., and T. Peek. "Swept Away: The Deadly Power of Tsunamis." *Earth 2,* no. 4. (July, 1993): 52-59.

Judson, Sheldon, and Marvin E. Kauffman. *Physical Geology.* 8th ed. Englewood Cliffs, N.J.: Prentice Hall, 1990.

Karwoski, Gail Langer. *Tsunami: The True Story of an April Fools' Day Disaster.* Plain City, Ohio: Darby Creek, 2006.

Satake, Kenji, ed. *Tsunamis: Case Studies and Recent Developments.* New York: Springer, 2005.

Shepard, F. P., G. A. Macdonald, and D. C. Cox. *The Tsunami of April 1, 1946.* Berkeley: University of California Press, 1950.

■ 1947: THE TEXAS CITY DISASTER

EXPLOSION

DATE: April 16, 1947
PLACE: Texas City, Texas
RESULT: 581 dead, 3,500 injured, 539 homes damaged or destroyed, $100 million in property damage in explosion of the freighter *Grandcamp*

Various cargoes, including sisal twine, peanuts, cotton, tobacco, small arms ammunition, and ammonium nitrate fertilizer were being loaded into the French Liberty ship *Grandcamp* as it lay alongside a pier at Texas City, Texas. Under certain conditions, ammonium nitrate can explode violently, but this fact was not widely known at the time. As a result, the longshoremen loading the ship failed to take proper precautions as they handled this dangerous cargo. Smoking was forbidden, according to signs posted on the dock and on the ship, but this rule was often violated. The longshoremen not only often smoked while working in the ship's hold but also sometimes laid lighted cigarettes down on the paper bags containing fertilizer. On April 14, two days before the disaster, a cigarette started a small fire among the bags. Luck was with the workers that day, and the fire was put out quickly.

EVENTS LEADING TO THE EXPLOSION. On the morning of April 16, 1947, longshoremen resumed loading ammonium nitrate into hold number 4 of the ill-fated ship. About 2,300 tons had already been loaded on previous days. Shortly after loading resumed at 8 A.M. someone saw smoke. It appeared to be coming from several layers deep in the hold. First the men poured a gallon jug of drinking water on the fire. Next, two of the ship's fire extinguishers were discharged. Unfortunately, neither of these measures did much good. A fire hose was lowered into the hold, but the captain refused to turn on the water because he knew the water would ruin the cargo. As a precaution the captain instructed the longshoremen to remove the small arms ammunition from hold number 5.

As the fire worsened the workers left the hold, and the hatch cov-

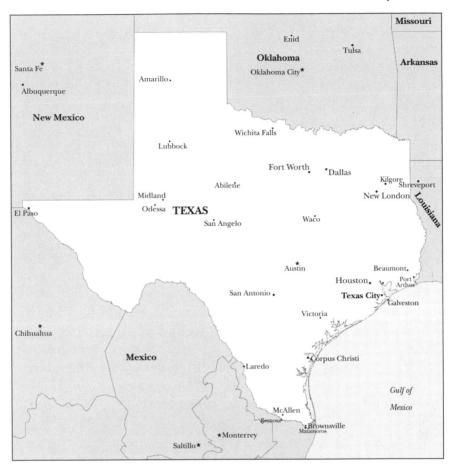

ers were reinstalled. This meant laying long wooden boards across the deck opening and covering them with tarpaulins. The ventilating system that circulated fresh air through the hold was turned off, and the steam-smothering system was turned on. Steam was admitted to the hold in the hope that it would displace all air and deprive the fire of the oxygen it needed. This did not work, because ammonium nitrate contains oxygen in its molecules. This oxygen is released as the fertilizer decomposes during a fire.

As steam pressure built up in the hold, it blew off the hatch covers at about 8:30 A.M. A photograph of the scene shows a fire hose spraying water onto the ship at about 8:45. Flames erupted from the open hatch around 9:00; at 9:12 there was a tremendous explosion that was heard as far as 150 miles away. Two small airplanes flying overhead were knocked out of the sky. A wall of water 15 feet high surged across the harbor and carried a large steel barge up onto dry land. Everyone still aboard the ship and in the immediate area on the dock was killed instantly. The ship's anchor, which weighed 1.5 tons, was later found about 2 miles from the site of the explosion.

RESULTS OF THE BLAST. Near the port area in Texas City were oil refineries, petroleum tank farms, and the Monsanto Chemical Company. Red-hot pieces of the exploding ship caused widespread damage at these facilities. Tanks of highly flammable chemicals exploded at various locations ashore. A residential area, inhabited mostly by poor African Americans and Hispanics, was just half a mile from the ship. Many homes in this area were damaged or destroyed, and many people were killed and injured.

The Monsanto plant was only about 350 feet from the explosion site; three-quarters of this facility was heavily damaged or destroyed. Monsanto's steam plant and powerhouse were destroyed. There were 574 people working at Monsanto that day. Of these, 234 were killed immediately or died of their injuries, and another 200 were injured.

Half of Texas City's firefighters, including its chief, and all of its firefighting equipment had been sent to fight the shipboard fire. These personnel and their equipment were wiped out by the explosion, seriously hampering efforts to extinguish the fires ashore.

Another Liberty ship, *High Flyer,* was tied up near *Grandcamp.* This ship was also loading ammonium nitrate fertilizer. When *Grandcamp* exploded, *High Flyer* was torn loose from its moorings and driven across the harbor, where it lodged against the *Wilson B. Keene.* The explosion killed one member of *High Flyer*'s crew. The others tied up their ship to the *Wilson B. Keene* and climbed over that ship to a dock. *High Flyer*'s hatch covers were blown off by the force of the explosion, which meant flying debris could fall into its holds and start fires.

Because the entire area was blanketed by heavy black smoke, officials were not aware that *High Flyer* was on fire. During the evening of April 16, a Coast Guard vessel discovered the burning ship, but the captain decided it was too dangerous to try to tow it out to sea. At about 1 A.M. on April 17, *High Flyer* exploded with a force at least as great as the earlier explosion of *Grandcamp.* It appears that 2 deaths and 24 injuries resulted from this second explosion. Casualties were relatively light because most people had left the port area.

RESCUE EFFORTS. Texas City's police chief, William Ladish, was in his office when the first explosion occurred. He was knocked to the floor by its force even though he was more than a mile from the ship. The police radio was knocked out by the blast, so Chief Ladish ran to the telephone exchange and called Captain Simpson of the Houston Police Department. Telephone-company officials called the National Guard and hospitals in Galveston and Goose Creek. Chief Ladish dispatched some of his men to set up roadblocks and some to assist the rescue efforts on the docks.

Mayor Curtis Trahan issued a disaster declaration and ordered the city's health officer, Dr. Clarence Quinn, to set up first-aid stations.

The explosion of the freighter Grandcamp *in Texas City, Texas.* (AP/Wide World Photos)

Fred Dowdy, the assistant fire chief, was out of town when the explosion occurred. When he returned, he took charge of what was left of the fire department. George Gill and a group of volunteers from the Carbide and Carbon Chemical Company, located at the edge of town, rushed to the scene with firefighting equipment from their plant. About two hours after the blast, officers and enlisted men from the Galveston office of the Army Corps of Engineers arrived on the scene with trucks and heavy equipment.

Texas City's three medical clinics were immediately overwhelmed with injured people in urgent need of medical care. The nearby city of Galveston activated the part of its hurricane relief plan having to do with emergency medical care. Galveston's three large hospitals and its Red Cross chapter were put on alert. Ambulances and city buses assembled at the hospitals; doctors and nurses carrying medical supplies boarded these vehicles and were transported to Texas City. An unused army hospital at Fort Crockett in Galveston was reopened and used to treat the wounded. More than 500 seriously injured people were transported from Texas City to Galveston by ambulance, bus, truck, taxi, and private car. About 250 were taken to hospitals in Houston.

It was impossible to keep accurate records of the names of the injured and where they were sent. As a result it was hours or days before families knew whether loved ones who had been in the port area were dead or alive. Both the Red Cross and Galveston radio station KGBC tried to collect this information, but they met with little early success.

A variety of law enforcement personnel converged on Texas City to help maintain order. The Texas Highway Patrol set up roadblocks. Texas Rangers kept order within the city, and a Houston police captain was responsible for order in the port area. Local police departments, sheriff's departments, and the state police also sent personnel.

Efforts to control the situation after the explosion were poorly coordinated because there was no emergency plan for the port. Port officials, city officials, U.S. Coast Guard, U.S. Army, Red Cross, and other organizations dispatched teams of people to help. Unfortunately, these groups were unable to communicate with each other. Telephones were knocked out by the explosions, and portable radio communications were not compatible between groups. Although the mayor of Texas City and the chief of police tried to establish a command center, they were unable to get a clear picture of the situation. Each individual group of rescuers did what seemed best at the time, and many heroic acts were performed, but no overall system of priorities was established.

CAUSE AND EFFECTS. Certainly the immediate cause of the disaster was careless handling of a very dangerous material, ammonium nitrate. During World War II this chemical was produced and transported under the supervision of the U.S. Army, and it was used as an explosive. The army insisted on very careful handling of the material. When the war ended factories continued to produce ammonium nitrate and sell it as fertilizer. Army supervision ended, and the people who handled the transportation of the fertilizer seem to have been unaware of its danger. The U.S. Coast Guard, which is responsible for the safety of ships, did not assume an active role. It appears that port officials and ship's officers did not know the potential for danger.

In the aftermath of the disaster some 273 lawsuits on behalf of 8,484 persons were filed against the United States government under the Federal Tort Claims Act. These suits were consolidated into a single case referred to as *Dalehite v. United States*. Early in 1950 Judge T. M. Kennerly of the U.S. District Court, Southern Division of Texas, found in favor of the people who sued. The judge's opinion stated,

> All of Said Fertilizer stored on the *Grandcamp* and *High Flyer* was manufactured or caused to be manufactured by Defendant [the U.S. government], shipped by Defendant to Texas City, and caused or permitted by Defendant to be loaded into such Steamships for shipment abroad. . . . All was done with full knowledge of Defendant that such fertilizer was an inherently dangerous explosive and fire hazard, and all without any warning to the public in Texas City or to persons handling same.

This decision was, however, overturned by the Fifth Circuit Court. In 1953 the Supreme Court voted four to three to uphold the action of the Fifth Circuit Court. Clark Thompson, U.S. Representative for Galveston, introduced a bill in Congress to compensate the victims. Enacted in 1955 this bill resulted in payments of almost $17 million to 1,394 individuals.

Perhaps some good came of this terrible event. It caused officials at many levels to reevaluate safety regulations and disaster plans. A hospital was finally built in Texas City in 1949. The National Red Cross, not satisfied with its ability to provide assistance to Texas City, revised its entire disaster relief program. Refineries and chemical plants upgraded their firefighting capabilities, and they entered into mutual assistance agreements. In 1950 the Coast Guard established a new port safety program, and in 1951 it reestablished the security provisions for handling dangerous cargoes, which had been in effect during World War II. These rules prohibited the handling of dangerous cargo near populated areas, required the stationing of trained guards, and restricted welding, smoking, and the movement of motor vehicles when such cargo was being handled.

Texas City recovered quickly from the disaster. Most of the people who fled were back in their homes within a few months. Retail businesses resumed normal operation, and many new homes were built. Refineries and chemical plants were rebuilt, and the city's population grew steadily. Port operations resumed, but cargo loading was limited to petroleum products. Ammonium nitrate was never shipped through Texas City again.

Edwin G. Wiggins

FOR FURTHER INFORMATION:

Barnaby, K. C. *Some Ship Disasters and Their Causes.* New York: A. S. Barnes, 1968.

Chiles, James R. *Inviting Disaster: Lessons from the Edge of Technology— an Inside Look at Catastrophes and Why They Happen.* New York: HarperBusiness, 2001.

Cross, Farrell, and Wilbur Cross. "When the World Blew up at Texas City." *Texas Parade,* September, 1972, 70-74.

Mabry, Meriworth, et al., eds. *We Were There: A Collection of the Personal Stories of Survivors of the 1947 Ship Explosions in Texas City, Commonly Referred to as the Texas City Disaster.* Texas City, Tex.: Mainland Museum of Texas City, 1997.

Minutaglio, Bill. *City on Fire: The Forgotten Disaster That Devastated a Town and Ignited a Landmark Legal Battle.* New York: HarperCollins, 2003.

Stephens, Hugh W. *The Texas City Disaster, 1947.* Austin: University of Texas Press, 1997.

■ 1952: THE GREAT LONDON SMOG

SMOG

DATE: December 5-9, 1952
PLACE: London, England
RESULT: More than 4,000 dead

The city of London is situated along the valley created by the Thames River. On the afternoon of Thursday, December 4, 1952, a high-pressure air mass encompassed the Thames Valley in which the city is located. Cold air moving westward from the European continent displaced a warm air mass that had settled over much of London, creating an inversion in the atmosphere and trapping the gases created both by industry and by coal-burning heaters in homes.

That evening the chill resulted in many Londoners piling extra soft coal in their furnaces. The result was an increased buildup of smoke, soot, and sulfur dioxide in the air. By the morning of the 5th, a dense pall had settled over most of the city. As the day progressed, the smog became so thick that public transportation was suspended, even in the suburbs. Traffic backed up, and motorists began to abandon their cars. All river traffic came to a halt.

Because of the cold temperatures, most people continued to burn coal fires in their homes, creating even more smoke and pollutants in the now completely still air. By Sunday the 7th, the cover had become so dense that sunlight could not even penetrate most areas. The smog was situated over an area covering hundreds of square miles; all traffic remained at a halt as visibility was reported to be less than 5 yards on most roads. In addition to the difficulties in breathing for many individuals, the heavy smog contributed to numerous accidents. A commuter train ran over a gang of workmen, killing 2. On Monday, December 8, two commuter trains collided near London Bridge.

The first evidence for the deadliness of the smog came on Friday, December 5. At the London livestock exhibition, it became necessary to slaughter a prize heifer that began to suffocate from the soot-laden air. Other cattle were saved only when their owners placed over their faces improvised gas masks made from whiskey-soaked grain sacks. By that evening, physicians began to observe a sharp rise in patients suffering respiratory distress, usually presenting as an irritating cough, but sometimes including vomiting and black phlegm expelled while coughing.

Hospital admissions rose to four times the normal level by the third day of the smog. Coroners began to report a significant increase in the number of deaths they were called to investigate; an unusual number involved persons who were either sleeping or sitting quietly while reading or sewing. On both Sunday and Monday, the reported number of deaths in the city was triple the normal average.

By Tuesday the 9th, the smog began to lift as fresher air entered the city. Nevertheless, delayed effects from the smog continued to result in an increase in the number of deaths. A conservative estimate as to the total number of deaths directly attributable to the smog was approximately 4,000. However, excess deaths continued for some twelve weeks after the Great London Smog, and the total number of dead may have reached as high as 8,000.

In response to the tragedy, London began to set in place a smog-control program. The Clean Air Act, passed in 1956, allowed local governments to take emergency measures to quickly deal with potential disasters. Coal as a source of heat was gradually replaced. Although heavy buildup of smog would continue to occur at intervals, the number of deaths that occurred in the 1952 disaster was never approached again.

Richard Adler

FOR FURTHER INFORMATION:

Davis, Devra L., Michelle L. Bell, and Tony Fletcher. "A Look Back at the London Smog of 1952 and the Half Century Since." *Environmental Health Perspectives* 110, no. 12 (December, 2002).

Dooley, Erin E. "Fifty Years Later: Clearing the Air over the London Smog." *Environmental Health Perspectives* 110, no. 12 (December, 2002).

Lewis, Howard. *With Every Breath You Take: The Poisons of Air Pollution, How They Are Injuring Our Health, and What We Must Do About Them.* New York: Crown, 1965.

Nagourney, Eric. "Why the Great Smog of London Was Anything but Great." *The New York Times*, August 12, 2003.

Wise, William. *Killer Smog: The World's Worst Air Pollution Disaster.* New York: Ballantine, 1970.

■ 1953: The North Sea Flood

Flood

Date: February 1, 1953
Place: The Netherlands, Great Britain, and Belgium
Result: 1,853 dead

Although the greater portion of the devastation wrought by the North Sea storms and flooding of late January to early February of 1953 occurred in the southwestern provinces of the Netherlands, considerable damage and loss of life also took place in the low-lying coastal regions of eastern Great Britain and coastal Belgium.

The people of the Netherlands, though seasoned through a centuries-old history of progress and setback in their struggle with the North Sea and prepared for ordinary emergency situations, were confronted in February, 1953, with an unprecedented set of circumstances that unleashed overwhelming natural forces on their coastal defenses.

The Flood in Great Britain. By the early hours of January 30, 1953, an exceptionally severe atmospheric depression had developed in the North Atlantic Ocean roughly 250 miles northwest of the Isle of Lewis in Scotland's Outer Hebrides. It gave rise to formidable gale winds, which had moved into the North Sea by the morning of January 31 and had assumed a south-southeasterly course.

After having caused gale-force winds and high tides in Scotland and along the Irish coast, the storm shifted to the northern sector of the North Sea, pushing large masses of water southward. Such depressions, with severe storms, are not an unusual occurrence in the North Sea region. The difference in this instance was that, whereas most depressions pass across the North Sea itself quite rapidly, the 1953 depression moved very slowly. This allowed the buildup of an exceptionally massive amount of water that, driven southward by the gale winds and coinciding with the high, seasonal spring tides, led to an unforeseen calamity.

Along the coast of east England, gales were recorded at the highest velocity up to that date for Great Britain—113 miles per hour. The evening of January 31 and the morning of February 1, 1953, is when most of the destruction and resultant deaths occurred.

In Great Britain the areas most devastated were the coastal regions and the lowlands of the main river estuaries, stretching roughly from the Humber in Yorkshire to the Thames, a distance of approximately 180 to 200 miles. Particularly vulnerable low-lying areas were totally submerged, including the tourist resort towns of Mablethorpe and Sutton-on-Sea, and nearly the entire Lincolnshire coast. Sea walls were breached at Heacham, Snettisham, and Hunstanton, while those at Salthouse, Cley, Great Yarmouth, and Sea Palling were heavily damaged.

Massive evacuation was undertaken, with at least 32,000 individuals being removed, including virtually the entire population (13,000) of Canvey Island in the Thames estuary and all the inhabitants of Mablethorpe and Sutton-on-Sea along the coast. In Norfolk, east England, the Ouse River overflowed its banks, covering the historic town of King's Lynn with over 7 feet of water. Farther south, where the Orwell River overflowed, Felixstowe was also inundated. In Suffolk, property damage was most extensive at the ferry port of Harwich, as well as at Tilbury, Great Wackering, and Jaywick Sands. Foulness Island in Essex was completely submerged.

In the Thames region, severe pollution problems occurred when the three major oil refineries at Coryton, Isle of Grain, and Shellhaven suffered substantial damage. Spreading south down the Kentish coast, the gales and tides submerged parts of Gravesend, Herne Bay, Dartford, Margate (where the harbor lighthouse was destroyed), and Birchington. Sheerness's naval dockyard and facilities were also rendered useless.

AFTEREFFECTS. On February 2, 1953, Prime Minister Winston Churchill declared the storm to have created a state of "national responsibility." Attempts at collecting relief funds and supplies for the afflicted coastal and river areas were spearheaded by the London Lord Mayor's appeal fund, which raised some £5 million.

The death toll in Britain reached 307, 156,000 acres were flooded (one-third of the total acreage went under salt water), and the total for lost livestock—mainly cattle and sheep—was estimated in the hundreds of thousands. About 500 residences were completely demolished and another 25,000 damaged. Monetary loss through damage was estimated at between £40 and 50 million.

On March 5, 1953, a special committee under the chairmanship of Lord Waverly was appointed to investigate the causes for the catastrophe and issue recommendations. The Waverly Committee released its findings and recommendations in August of 1953. The decision was made to implement an early gale warning system along the east coast to be in effect from September 15 to April 30 each year.

The tragedy led to the passage of the Coastal Flooding (Emergency Provisions) Act on May 20, 1953. Special river boards throughout the east coast were appointed and then granted extraordinary powers in case of emergency. The minister of agriculture was further granted the authority to compensate and otherwise provide relief to farmers and farm families whose property had sustained damage as the result of flooding.

THE FLOOD IN BELGIUM. In Belgium between January 30 and 31, 1953, the same tidal storm caused 22 deaths and wreaked devastation in the low coastal plain between the ferry port of Ostend and the Dutch border. The Schelde River overflowed its banks, breaking the dike at Antwerp and flooding a part of the metropolitan area. Massive damage was inflicted upon the town and harbor of Ostend as well as Zeebrugge, where the lock of the sea canal was battered. Although the dikes at Malines were breached, damage to the town itself was not as extensive as elsewhere. The greater proportion of the domiciles in the towns of Knokke, Blankenberge, and La Zoute were heavily damaged.

The disaster in Belgium had serious political repercussions as King Baudouin had made a trip to the French Riviera in order to recuperate from a bout with influenza. His absence during a time of national emergency was much resented and vehemently criticized in the Belgian press. The royal family, and the monarchy itself, were in considerable jeopardy in the wake of the 1951 abdication crisis centering around former king Leopold III. The political atmosphere was so charged that King Baudouin felt compelled to return for a three-day tour of the devastated area before going back to the Riviera on February 12.

THE NETHERLANDS. By far the most massive blows dealt by this catastrophe fell on the Netherlands, which had been waging a continual, centuries-old battle to reclaim its low-lying agricultural land (polders) from the North Sea and was particularly vulnerable to the inroads of storm tides because of the large amount of land lying below sea level. Of these, the spring tides had usually been the highest and the most dangerous. Storm tide depredation had been a recurring peril along the lower islands of Zeeland Province and the estuaries of the Meuse, Rhine, Schelde, and Ijssel Rivers. The most destructive of these storm tides had occurred in 1421-1424, 1570, 1682, 1715-1717, 1808, 1825, 1863, and 1916. The 1953 storm tide would surpass all others since 1570 in the sheer scope and dimensions of its devastation.

The potential for future danger had been acknowledged in the 1930's, when plans were formulated for the construction of a more modernized series of protective dikes, dams, and bridges along the estuaries of both the Schelde and the Meuse. These plans had been interrupted by the Nazi invasion of the Netherlands in June, 1940, and the subsequent German occupation from 1940 to 1945. By 1953, the construction schemes were virtually forgotten.

The combination of the delayed, northeasterly gale winds causing the North Sea to rise to unprecedented levels and the spring tides led to most of the inundation. Estimates of the dead and missing vary slightly, but the figure of 1,524 is conventionally accepted (for a total of 1,853 when tallied with the tolls for Britain and Belgium). An estimated 988,400 acres of land were saturated, some 50,000 buildings were destroyed or damaged, 89,000 to 100,000 individuals were evacuated, and 300,000 were left homeless. In monetary terms the damage was estimated to have totaled 1.5 billion guilders. Nearly 6 percent of the farmland in the Netherlands, mainly in the provinces of Zeeland, Brabant, and South Holland, was left under water. The loss of enormous numbers of cattle, chickens, and sheep brought forth major concerns over the danger of epidemics caused by rotting carcasses and wastes.

Almost entirely inundated were the islands Schouwen and Duiveland, Overflakkee, Walcheren, Tholen, North Beveland, and South Beveland. Flushing Town suffered flooding of up to 9 feet in its center, after the sea wall had fractured in five separate places. The largest urban centers effected were Rotterdam and Dordrecht, which had extensive flooding in the outlying districts, though not in the center.

At Rotterdam, the Hook of Holland Canal was destroyed, as was the Moerdijk Bridge.

North Holland Province sustained far less damage and loss of life but nevertheless experienced substantial coastal flooding in resort areas. The Netherlands' largest and most popular seashore resort, Scheveningen, was flooded, and much of its beach was temporarily washed away.

As a general rule most of the fatalities occurred in situations where either there was no warning or the reports of danger were taken too lightly. Many remembered wartime flooding in 1944-1945, which was not as severe as had been feared, and therefore downplayed the magnitude of the 1953 storm and underestimated the perilous nature of their situation. The village of Goedereede (population 2,000) proved to be a model of vigilance and cooperation. The majority of the villagers fled to the upper rooms of their houses, reacted calmly, and assisted one another in the survival and evacuation processes. Goedereede sustained no casualties as a result of the tragedy.

RELIEF EFFORTS IN THE NETHERLANDS. Relief efforts were directed from the Zeeland center of Middelburg, which had escaped the flooding, by the Dutch Red Cross through communications with the local burgomasters (mayors) and other available authorities. The speed and effectiveness of the assistance varied according to the degree of damage and isolation of a given village or community. Helicopter units of the British Royal Air Force, the U.S. Air Force, and the Swiss air force were sent in to assist the Dutch military in its rescue efforts. Some 2,000 stranded individuals, many trapped on the roofs of their houses, were rescued.

Ironically, the Dutch government, only days prior to the flooding disaster—on January 27, 1953—had informed the United States government that the Netherlands had sufficiently recovered from the ravages of World War II and had no further need for U.S. financial assistance, thus terminating the Marshall Plan in that country. On February 6, 1953, the Dutch requested a temporary resumption of U.S. aid under the Marshall Plan to recoup from the storm-tide catastrophe. February 8 was proclaimed by Queen Juliana a day of official mourning, and on February 16 the state of emergency was lifted.

In the wake of the disaster the schemes of the 1930's were revived in the form of the Delta Plan. The Delta Commission, appointed to recommend and accelerate improvements, rendered its report on July 10, 1953. By the end of the year, setbacks in April and November due to high tides notwithstanding, there had been remarkable progress made in the region's recovery. The last of the breaches in the dikes were closed in September, the Schouwensee Dike had been raised 16 feet, and a mobile storm defense was set up at the mouth of the Ijssel estuary, just east of Rotterdam. Reclamation of polderland, augmented by the efforts of a motley collection of international student volunteers and the use of concrete caissons of World War II vintage, was completed by early December.

Raymond Pierre Hylton

FOR FURTHER INFORMATION:

Lamb, Hubert. *Historic Storms of the North Sea, British Isles, and Northwest Europe.* New York: Cambridge University Press, 1991.

McRobie, A., T. Spencer, and H. Gerritsen, eds. "The Big Flood: North Sea Storm Surge." *Philosophical Transactions of the Royal Society of London* A363 (2005): 1261-1491.

Pollard, Michael. *North Sea Surge: The Story of the East Coast Floods of 1953.* Suffolk, England: Terence Dalton, 1978.

"SEMP Biot #317: The Catastrophic 1953 North Sea Flood of the Netherlands, January 11, 2006." *SEMP (Suburban Emergency Management Project).* http://www.semp.us/biots/biot_317.html.

Studies in Holland Flood Disaster 1953. 4 vols. Washington, D.C.: National Research Council, 1955.

■ 1957: HURRICANE AUDREY

HURRICANE

DATE: June 27-30, 1957
PLACE: Louisiana and Texas
CLASSIFICATION: Category 4
SPEED: Maximum wind unofficially 144 miles per hour, officially 105 miles per hour
RESULT: More than 500 dead, about $150 million in damage

On June 17, 1957, the U.S. Weather Bureau predicted the hurricane season that year would begin early. Only a week later, on Monday, June 24, the prediction came true, as a tropical depression developed west of the Yucatán Peninsula in the southernmost part of the Gulf of Mexico. At 10:30 that night, the Weather Bureau issued its first advisory about the storm; at noon on Tuesday, June 25, the wind having already reached hurricane speed, the Weather Bureau declared a hurricane watch for the coasts of Louisiana and Texas. By 4 P.M., Hurricane Audrey was moving north, its rotating wind increasing in speed.

On Wednesday, June 26, at 10 A.M., the Weather Bureau issued a hurricane warning, which said in part: "Tides are rising and will reach 5 to 8 feet along the Louisiana coast and over Mississippi Sound by late Thursday. All persons in low exposed places should move to higher ground." Although a revised warning, issued twelve hours later, mentioned tides of 9 feet, many people of Cameron Parish, in the marsh country of the southwest corner of Louisiana, thought they could safely spend Wednesday night in their homes. Furthermore, adults from Acadia and other families that had long lived in that part of Louisiana tended to think that their houses, built on sandy ridges called *chênières*, stood on the "higher ground" to which the Weather Bureau referred, because previous storms had not flooded the houses; newcomers to the parish, however, generally evacuated. When the families that had remained in or near the towns of Cameron, Creole, and Grand Chenier tried to leave at dawn on Thursday, June 27, rapidly rising water, combined with unexpectedly early hurricane wind and rain, made driving away virtually impossible, and the disaster began for them before 8 A.M., the hour when the eye of the hurricane reached the coast about halfway between the town of Cameron and the Texas state line.

HEIGHT OF WATER. Before Audrey arrived in Cameron Parish, its wind and the resultant waves of 45 or 50 feet in the Gulf of Mexico had already sunk a fishing boat and capsized an oil rig. On shore, or on what ordinarily would have been shore, it was not the wind directly, not even the several tornadoes generated by the hurricane, but the storm surge—the high tide with huge waves—that caused the most harm. For a shoreline at which normal tidal variation is small, the tides produced by Audrey were enormous, reaching 10.6 feet above mean sea level in Cameron itself, 12.1 feet on the beach due south of that town, 12.2 feet at Grand Chenier, 12.9 feet near Creole, and 13.9 feet midway between Creole and Grand Chenier. The onshore waves rose at times from 10 to 15 feet above the high-tide mark and smashed almost every building in their path.

Although no other area suffered as much as Cameron Parish did during Audrey, the hurricane brought flooding in Louisiana from the Texas border in the west to the Delta of the Mississippi River in the east. In western Louisiana, floodwaters reached as far north as Lake Charles. Even in east Texas, located west of where Audrey's eye met land and generally less damaged by Audrey than southwest Louisiana, significant water damage occurred.

PROPERTY DAMAGE. In Port Arthur, Texas, storm rain accumulating on the roof of a nine-story building led to massive structural collapse. In Louisiana, a huge supply barge rammed into a storage tank on land. The fishing schooner *Three Brothers* washed ashore, as did many other vessels, including the shrimp boat *Audry*. At Grand Chenier, the hurricane totally destroyed about one-tenth of the houses; at Creole, it left only one building on its foundation; and in Cameron, where about 3,000 people had lived before June 27, only two buildings remained mostly intact—the parish courthouse, which served as a shelter during the storm, and an icehouse, which served briefly as a morgue in the storm's aftermath.

DEATH, SURVIVAL, AND HEROISM. Because Cameron Parish was rural, property damage was small in proportion to what it would have been had Audrey struck a low-lying urban area like metropolitan New

Orleans. What made Audrey especially horrible was the toll in human lives. Not since the hurricane that destroyed Galveston, Texas, in 1900, had so many people in the western half of the U.S. Gulf Coast died because of a tropical storm. Some people apparently died alone, like thirty-five-year-old Harry Melancon of Broussard, Louisiana, who happened to be driving an oil tanker truck in Cameron Parish when Audrey arrived and whose body was not found for five months. Others died after having taken what shelter they could with members of their family; eight-year-old Thelma Jo Gibbs, whose body was found in 1958, was one of those.

Some families lost only one member; others lost many. Eighteen members of one family died after they had taken shelter in the home of Robert Moore on the Front Ridge, southeast of Cameron. Ironically, some members of the family would have lived had they remained in the house of Susan Rose Moore, Robert Moore's mother, because it remained intact. Robert Moore's house, though newer, was swept off its foundation and broken apart by the storm surge.

Among the men in Robert Moore's house was Albert January, whose story suggests the struggle and terror common as hurricane victims fought for their own lives and those of their loved ones. When the house broke apart, January, his wife, their three children (ages eight, seven, and two years), and many other people held onto the roof while it floated away. Three times waves shoved Mrs. January and the children off, and three times Mr. January rescued them. A fourth wave, however, proved deadly for Lucy LaSalle January and her children, Arthur Lee, Annie Lee, and John Randall, when Mr. January's rescue effort failed.

The story of Dr. Cecil Clark presents a similar sorrow but another kind of heroism. Thirty-three years old, Clark was the only physician in Cameron, where he had charge of the Cameron Medical Center. He and his wife, Sybil Baccigalopi Clark, a nurse-anesthetist, had five children: John (eight years), Joe (seven years), Elizabeth Dianne (three years), Celia Marie (eighteen months), and Jack Benjamin (three months). John and Joe had spent Wednesday night at the home of Dr. Clark's mother in Creole; they survived Audrey the next day by being tied to tree tops.

Meanwhile, early Thursday morning, to try to evacuate patients from the twelve-bed hospital at the medical center, Dr. and Mrs. Clark had left their three younger children at their presumably safe home in the care of Zulmae Dubois, their housekeeper. Their trip thwarted by rising water on the road, they returned, but Dr. Clark tried to go back again, this time without his wife but with a neighbor. Still unable to get through, Dr. Clark eventually had to ride out the storm in the concrete-block house of Mr. and Mrs. Philbert Richard, from which, after the storm had abated, he waded amid debris to the courthouse and began long hours of treating hundreds of sick or injured persons, among whom were the patients from the little hospital, whom nurses and deputy sheriffs with boats had evacuated in Dr. Clark's absence.

A common grave in Lake Charles, Louisiana, for unidentified dead from Hurricane Audrey. (Library of Congress)

Not until Friday evening did Dr. Clark learn that his wife and their two older children had lived through the disaster. Although knocked unconscious momentarily, Mrs. Clark had swum and then drifted on wreckage until people in a little boat had rescued her from driftwood miles from where her house had stood. Late that night, during a short respite at a friend's home in Lake Charles, Dr. Clark learned of the deaths of his three younger children and Mrs. Dubois, who had all drowned when the waves destroyed the Clarks' house. Despite his own grief, he soon returned to Cameron to treat survivors. By late 1957, Dr. and Mrs. Clark had had the Cameron Medical Center rebuilt, and in December the American Medical Association awarded Dr. Clark a gold medal as "General Practitioner of the Year."

Not all of Audrey's more than 500 fatalities drowned. Some probably died of heart attacks under the stress of the storm, although the exact number of heart-attack deaths will never be known because the great number of dead bodies made performing routine autopsies virtually impossible. Similarly, some people probably died from snakebites, although only one such case was confirmed. Seven-year-old Steve Broussard, Jr., of Pecan Island in Vermilion Parish, immediately east of Cameron Parish, survived the floodwaters that took the lives of his sisters Larissa, Veronica, and Estelle when their house floated into White Lake and then broke apart. In the dark of the morning of Friday, June 28, however, while he was floating on a part of the roof of his family's home, one of the thousands of water moccasins dislodged and infuriated by the hurricane crawled onto the wreckage and bit him on the ear. Hours later, after his father had braved hundreds of other snakes and fought off a maddened cow in an attempt to get help, the child died on his way to a hospital in Abbeville.

AFTERMATH. Lessening in intensity as it moved inland, Audrey nevertheless brought strong wind and much rain from the Gulf Coast all the way up through the Ohio Valley states, New York, and New England and Canada. The storm damaged more property and caused more deaths, including four in Canada, before it ended.

In the United States, President Dwight D. Eisenhower declared the severely affected communities disaster areas. In southwest Louisiana, where the death toll was the worst, thousands of people joined in an effort to rescue and comfort survivors; to find, identify, and bury the dead; to retrieve sealed concrete tombs washed out of low-lying cemeteries; to clear away the big, innumerable piles of debris; to round up hungry and often hostile cattle and return them to their owners; to restore telephone service, electricity, gas, and safe drinking water; to rebuild homes and businesses; and to help victims resume something resembling ordinary life.

Amid heat, mosquitoes, and water moccasins, rescuers searched on foot and by boat for the living and the dead. Helicopters crisscrossed the sky. Military personnel, including members of the Coast Guard and the National Guard, were among the relief workers, as were men and women from the American Red Cross and the Salvation Army. Responding to reports that Audrey had impoverished some survivors, Governor Earl Long pressured insurance companies into paying great claims to Louisiana citizens for wind damage, despite the companies' contention that the insured had no flood coverage and that it was water that had caused most of the damage to homes and businesses.

Of the approximately 40,000 persons whom Audrey drove from their homes, about 22,000 went to Lake Charles, where many stayed at McNeese State College. In Lake Charles was the big, makeshift morgue that replaced the original one at the icehouse in Cameron and another one at a Lake Charles hospital. In shed 5 at the dockyard, hundreds of survivors walked calmly past the dead bodies cooled with blocks of ice and tried to identify those whom they had lost. The unidentified dead were eventually buried in special plots in several cemeteries.

Only slowly did some grieving people accept their loss. For a time after Audrey, one Cameron Parish resident reported, mothers would go to the border of the marsh, listen to the calls of the nutria (semiaquatic rodents), and hear in those mammalian sounds the cries of their missing babies, victims of the storm.

Victor Lindsey

FOR FURTHER INFORMATION:

"Disasters: Audrey's Day of Horror." *Time,* July 8, 1957, 12.

Harris, D. Lee. *Hurricane Audrey Storm Tide.* Washington, D.C: U.S. Department of Commerce, Weather Bureau, 1958.

"In the Wake of Disaster." *Newsweek,* July 8, 1957, 22-24.

Menard, Donald. *Hurricanes of the Past: The Untold Story of Hurricane Audrey.* 2d ed Rayne, La.: Author, 1999.

Post, Cathy C. *Hurricane Audrey: The Deadly Storm of 1957*. Gretna, La.: Pelican, 2007.

Ross, Nola Mae Wittler, and Susan McFillen Goodson. *Hurricane Audrey*. Sulphur, La.: Wise, 1997.

"Story of Hurricane Audrey—and the Warnings That Many Ignored." *U.S. News & World Report,* July 12, 1957, 62-63.

U.S. Army Corps of Engineers. "Descriptions of Hurricanes." In *History of Hurricane Occurrences Along Coastal Louisiana*. Rev. ed. New Orleans: U.S. Army Engineer District, 1972.

■ 1959: THE GREAT LEAP FORWARD

FAMINE

FAMINE

DATE: 1959-1962
PLACE: The People's Republic of China
RESULT: Casualties so vast they can only be estimated at between 15 million and 50 million dead

The greatest famine—and perhaps the greatest natural disaster—in the twentieth century occurred virtually unnoticed in the outside world. So tight was the control of information coming out of the People's Republic of China in the late 1950's that the Great Leap Forward famine was unpublicized. The starving millions in China knew that something was wrong in their area, but the national press was reporting on the spectacular success of the government's programs and acknowledging only food shortages due to bad weather in some localities.

It is hard to say how much knowledge even the Chinese leaders had of this tragedy. Surely the government knew that many of its citizens were hungry, but the lack of a free press meant each leader had to rely on limited personal experience or on government reports from village to county to province to the capital that were inflated every step of the way. In many cases, these reported on bountiful harvests, when the villagers had in fact already eaten the seed needed to plant the next year's crop before the onset of the harsh unproductive winter season. One year the government reported total grain production of 375 million tons when only about 200 million tons had been produced.

In the Great Leap Forward famine, the losses were so great not even the numbers of victims—let alone their names—are known. So far is the world from knowing the exact number of casualties that they can be estimated only by a demographic analysis of the number of "excess deaths." Scholarly estimates of the number of deaths range from a low of 15 million to a high of 50 million, a measure so imprecise as to give a range of deaths that could be off by a factor of 3 or as

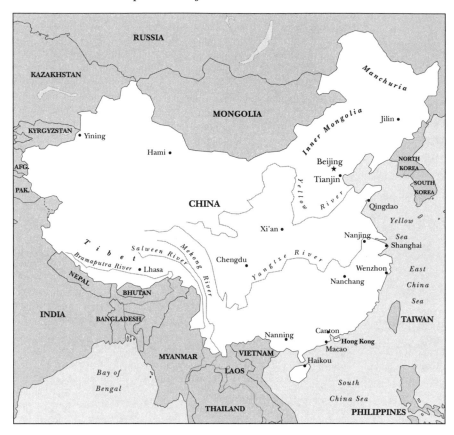

much as 300 percent. Thirty-five million people could have died without any record of it.

Geography—both physical and human—contributed to this catastrophe. Since ancient times, China has been home to the world's largest population and today has well over 1.3 billion people, or about a quarter of the world's total population. China also has the world's third-largest land area—trailing only Russia and Canada. This might seem to be adequate, but well over two-thirds of Chinese land is virtually uninhabitable desert and mountains, so China must feed 25 percent of the world's people with only about 7 percent of the world's arable (farmable) land.

Even in good times, avoiding hunger in China is difficult. With so large a land area, China has too much water (flooding) in some regions and not enough water (drought) in others in any given year.

The key to a good national harvest is to have relatively fewer floods and droughts than normal. In 1959-1961, the odds turned against the Chinese in that a higher number than usual of both floods and droughts occurred. The 1960 weather conditions are considered the worst in twentieth century China.

Yet weather is only part of this story, and perhaps not even the most important part. Some scholars attribute only 30 percent of the catastrophe to the weather, reserving the brunt of the blame for failed government policies. To the outside world, the late 1950's anti-Western Chinese Communist system seemed monolithic, and China

Food for starving Chinese is unloaded from a ship during the Great Leap Forward famine. (National Archives)

was thought to have only minor differences with its ally the Soviet Union. In truth, there was a massive split between the two countries, with corresponding differences among the Chinese leaders. They were torn between a highly bureaucratized central planning system recommended by the Russians and a chaotic, voluntaristic path recommended by China's Communist Party leader, Mao Zedong.

While Mao's plan seemed to prevail, conflicts marred its execution in many areas. Mao's Great Leap Forward plan was supposed to stimulate Chinese production so dramatically that China would overtake the British in fifteen years by fostering an ongoing revolutionary fervor among the Chinese. Many Chinese did respond enthusiastically, even accepting Mao's idea that steel production could be stimulated by having villages build backyard iron furnaces. This idea led many to melt down perfectly good iron skillets and dismantle high-quality steel train rails, throw them into backyard furnaces, and turn out third-rate pig iron. While peasants were busy with this unproductive activity, they often failed to plant crops or to harvest ripe yields at the right time, further compounding the catastrophe.

In reality, neither of the paths was suitable for the crisis China faced. While industrial production slipped, grain production plunged disastrously, to about 75 percent of the level before the Great Leap Forward. Worse, much of this grain was siphoned off to pay for "aid" the Chinese were receiving from the Soviets. This meant that the grain available to feed the Chinese people became even less, exposing those most at risk—the sick, elderly, and children—to the horrors of this massive famine. The government's policies clearly aggravated this unprecedented natural disaster.

Richard L. Wilson

FOR FURTHER INFORMATION:

Becker, Jasper. *Hungry Ghosts: Mao's Secret Famine.* New York: Henry Holt, 1998.

Blecher, Marc. *China Against the Tides.* London: Pinter, 1997.

Christiansen, Fleming, and Shirin Rai. *Chinese Politics and Society: An Introduction.* London: Prentice Hall/Harvester Wheatsheaf, 1996.

MacFarquhar, Roderick. *The Coming of the Cataclysm, 1961-1966.* Vol. 3 in *The Origins of the Cultural Revolution.* New York: Columbia University Press, 1997.

_____. *The Great Leap Forward, 1958-1960.* Vol. 2 in *The Origins of the Cultural Revolution.* New York: Columbia University Press, 1983.

Yang, Dali L. *Calamity and Reform in China: State, Rural Society, and Institutional Change Since the Great Leap Famine.* Stanford, Calif.: Stanford University Press, 1996.

Zhao, Kate Xiao. *How the Farmers Changed China: Power of the People.* Boulder, Colo.: Westview Press, 1996.

■ 1963: THE VAIONT DAM DISASTER

LANDSLIDE

DATE: October 9, 1963
PLACE: Belluno, Italy
RESULT: Almost 3,000 dead

During the early 1960's a magnificent concrete dam (*Diga del Vajont*) was constructed about 10 miles (16.2 kilometers) northeast of Belluno, an Italian town along the Piave River. The dam spans the Vaiont gorge, an old glacial trough in the heart of the spectacular Italian Alps. The area is within the southern part of the majestic Dolomites of the northern Italian region. This region is characterized by near-vertical cliffs composed mostly of massive carbonate rocks. The dam, which cost approximately $100 million to build, is 11 feet (3.4 meters) wide at the top and 74 feet (22.7 meters) wide at the base and stands 875 feet (265 meters) high at the highest point. It was designed to create a large lake for the generation of hydroelectric power. The dam impounded a reservoir of 316,000 cubic feet (8,943 cubic meters) of water. The curved, thin-arch dam still stands as an engineering marvel and a testament to humanity's ingenuity.

Downstream from the dam, the gorge intersects the Piave River Valley near the mountain villages of Pirago and Longarone. Casso, a small highland village, is along the northern edge of the valley on Mount Pul. This farming community overlooks the Vaiont dam and reservoir. Upstream from the dam, the village of Erto is situated along the highland area of the Vaiont Valley.

LOCAL GEOLOGY. The stratigraphic sequence in the area consists mostly of Mesozoic rocks. The Jurassic Dogger epoch formation creates steep cliffs along the valley. These rugged rock walls consist mostly of dolostone, a rock composed of the mineral dolomite, calcium magnesium carbonate. The Dogger stratus is underlain by Triassic rocks; the subjacent Cretaceous and Tertiary strata are composed mostly of limestone but contain some argillaceous units. These clay-bearing layers represent potential zones of weakness in the rock

648

column. Limestone near the dam site has been weakened by solution features, such as joint fissures, sinkholes, and underground caverns.

Structurally, the dam is situated along an east-west-trending asymmetrical syncline designated the "Erto Syncline." This fold plunges to the east, or upstream. The limbs of the syncline dip from 25 degrees to 45 degrees toward the Vaiont Valley. The steep dips and fractured strata, as well as the weak layers within the stratal packet, render the area landslide-prone. There is evidence of earlier slope failure at some places, and in 1960 a large slide block composed of 916,000 cubic yards (700,000 cubic meters) of debris moved downslope from Mount Toc into the reservoir. Although the slide did no significant damage because of the low water level, it did alert local citizens and scientists associated with the project to a potential problem. Geologists investigated the slide area and determined that it was part of a much larger landslide block. The slide block was about 1.1 miles (1.8 kilometers) long and 1 mile (1.6 kilometers) wide. The total volume of the block was estimated to be more than 787 million cubic feet (240 million cubic meters), much larger than originally suspected by engineers.

A landslide results from the movement of a mass of rock and soil downslope in response to gravity. This movement can be either slow or rapid. If infinitesimally slow, the movement may not be evident to the casual observer but can be recorded by sensitive instruments placed within the unstable mass. During 1960 and 1961 monitoring stations within the slide at times recorded 10 to 12 inches (up to 25 to 30 centimeters) of creep per week; the rate of creep slowed to 0.5 inch (about 1 centimeter) per week during 1962 and 1963. This reduced level of creep led most scientists to the conclusion that the imminent danger of mass movement was probably over.

However, heavy rains occurred at times during the late summer and early fall of 1963. This precipitation soaked into the slide area, adding weight to the mass and hydrating some of the clay layers. Data recorded at Erto indicated that more than 90 inches of rain fell in the area from February to early October in 1962 and 1963. This excessive rainfall was probably the trigger that led to the major disaster in the area.

THE VAIONT DISASTER. On October 9, 1963, instruments within the slide mass recorded as much as 32 inches (80 centimeters) of movement per day. The creep rate had become dangerously high, and people in local villages were warned of possible flooding. Animals grazing south of the reservoir probably sensed the movement and abandoned the area a few days before the disaster. Late on the evening of October 9, at 10:41 P.M., disaster struck. During a heavy downpour, about 350 million cubic yards (270 million cubic meters) of rock and soil slid off the flank of Mount Toc and moved at a rate of 68 miles per hour (30 meters per second) into the reservoir.

Initially, there was a loud noise and rush of air that caused damage to some homes in Casso; water from the reservoir was lifted 792 feet (240 meters) up the north slope of the gorge and more than 325 feet (100 meters) vertically above the top of the dam. The displaced water rushed down the valley and entered the Piave River, where it moved both upstream and downstream. The wave that flowed upstream engulfed most of the town of Longarone. A photograph taken after the flood shows almost total destruction of the southeast part of the village. The strip along the river was swept clean of buildings and trees. In less than five minutes the raging waters destroyed most of the village and left more than 2,000 people dead. Some water was diverted downstream along the Piave more than 1.4 miles (2 kilometers). In the uppermost part of the reservoir the wave bypassed the town of Erto but hit with full force the village of San Martino at the northeast end. In all, nearly 3,000 lives were lost, including engineers, technicians, and workers living in barracks along the crest of the dam.

AFTERMATH. According to author Patrick L. Abbott, the event has been called the world's worst dam disaster. The final tragedy was played out when the chief engineer of the dam project, Mario Pancini, packed his bags for a trip to court at L'Aquila in southern Italy and "taped the cracks around the doors of his Venetian room and turned on the jets of his gas range." The dam stands today not only as a stark monument to humankind's engineering expertise but also as a grim reminder of its ineptness in selecting a geologically safe site for construction.

Donald F. Reaser

FOR FURTHER INFORMATION:
Abbott, Patrick L. *Natural Hazards.* Dubuque, Iowa: Wm. C. Brown, 1996.
Coch, Nickolas K. *Geohazards.* New York: Prentice Hall, 1995.
Kiersch, G. A. "The Vaiont Reservoir Disaster." In *Civil Engineering,* Vol. 34. New York: American Society of Civil Engineers, 1964.
McCully, Patrick. "When Things Fall Apart: The Technical Failures of Large Dams." In *Silenced Rivers: The Ecology and Politics of Large Dams.* New York: Zed Books, 2001.
Montgomery, Carla W. *Environmental Geology.* Dubuque, Iowa: Wm. C. Brown, 1989.

■ 1964: The Great Alaska Earthquake

Earthquake

ALSO KNOWN AS: The Good Friday Earthquake, Black Friday
DATE: March 27, 1964
PLACE: Alaska
MAGNITUDE: 8.3-8.6, possibly as high as 9.2
RESULT: 131 dead, $500 million in damage

The 1964 Great Alaska Earthquake was one of the highest in magnitude ever recorded, between 8.3 and 8.6 on the Richter scale. This magnitude has since been revised to 9.2, making it the strongest earthquake ever recorded in North America. It released as much as eighty times the energy of the 1906 earthquake of San Francisco. The quake took place 125 miles below the earth's surface but near the shore, so that most of the damage was caused by waves heaving up onto the land and sweeping away whatever was in their path.

REASONS FOR THE EARTHQUAKE. Normally the Pacific Plate moves in a northwesterly direction at a rate of about 5 to 7 centimeters per year. The continents, the ocean basins, and everything else on the surface of the earth move along on these plates that float on the underlying convecting material. However, where the plates come together, as is the case in southern Alaska, the movement causes the earth's crust to be compressed and warped, with some areas being depressed and others uplifted.

As far as scientists can understand, in 1964 the Pacific Plate subducted, or slid under, the North American Plate at the head of Prince William Sound, 56 miles (90 kilometers) west of Valdez and 75 miles (120 kilometers) east of Anchorage. It caused the earth under the water in the harbor to split open and crack. A tsunami, or harbor wave, resulted. Water rushed in at great force to fill the open areas and was pushed up by the section of the seafloor that was uplifted. In the Alaska earthquake, 100,000 square miles of earth uplifted or

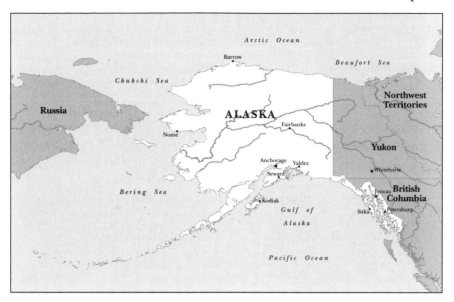

dropped. Areas north and northwest of the epicenter subsided as much as 7.5 feet. Areas south and southeast rose, over wide areas, as much as 6 feet. Locally, the uplift was much greater: 38 feet on Montague Island and more than 50 feet on the seafloor southwest of the island. The Homer Spit and all the coastline of the Kenai Peninsula sank 8 feet. Cook Inlet and Kachemak Bay protected Seward, but the Seward area dropped 3.5 feet. Tsunamis devastated every town and village along the outer coast and the Aleutian Islands. Also, horizontal movements of tens of feet took place in which the landmass moved southeastward relative to the ocean floor, moving more earth farther than any other earthquake ever recorded, both horizontally and vertically. The area of crustal deformation stretched from Cordova to Kodiak Island. Beginning in Prince William Sound, it moved toward Kodiak at 10,000 feet or about 2 miles per second. The shock was felt over a range of 50,000 miles.

The strong ground motion caused many snowslides, rockfalls, and landslides both on land and on the ocean floor. It smashed port and harbor facilities, covered plants and salmon beds with silt, disturbed and killed salmon fry, leveled forests, and caused ocean saltwater to invade many coastal freshwater lakes. In areas where the land sank, spawning beds, trees, and other vegetation were destroyed. In areas where the seafloor rose, marine animals and plants that need water for survival were forced above ground.

It is thought that the duration of the quake was three to four minutes; however, no seismic instruments capable of recording strong ground motion were in Alaska at the time. The quake served as a test of manufactured structures under extreme conditions and as a guide to improvements in location and design.

An earthquake sends out waves known as aftershocks. There were 52 large aftershocks in Alaska, which continued for a year after the quake. The first 11 of these occurred on the day of the quake, and 9 more happened in the next three weeks. The aftershock zone spanned a width of 155 miles (250 kilometers), from 9 miles (15 kilometers) north of Valdez, for 497 miles (800 kilometers) to the southwest end of Kodiak Island, to about 34 miles (55 kilometers) south of the Trinity Islands.

GEOGRAPHY. South central Alaska and the Aleutian Islands compose one of the most active seismic regions in the world. One thousand earthquakes are detected every year in Alaska, thirty-seven of which measure 7.25 or more on the Richter scale. Anchorage itself rests on a shelf of clay, sometimes called "Bootlegger Clay," named

A boat beached by the tsunami that followed the Great Alaska Earthquake. (National Oceanic and Atmospheric Administration)

for Bootlegger Cove, once a rendezvous for rumrunners. This clay assumes the consistency of jelly when soaked with water. In 1959 the U.S. Geological Survey cited a number of places along the bluffs of Anchorage where the clay had absorbed water. However, people did not attend to the report, and the geologists were referred to as "catastrophists" because they predicted a catastrophe where seemingly there was none. When the quake hit, many homes and businesses, especially on the west side of city, sank out of sight.

Thanks to the Good Friday holiday, there were very few fishing boats on the water at the time of the quake. However, one boat, the *Selief*, had been sailing toward the harbor with $3,000 worth of Alaskan king crab in its hold. The captain of the ship heard warnings on the radio, but, unable to avoid the tsunami, he found himself uplifted by the waters and deposited about six blocks inland from the shore. Another boat, a freighter, was docked in the harbor and unloading its cargo in Valdez. When the quake hit, 31 men, women, and children, who were standing by and watching, were swept away and killed by the wave. The boat rose about 30 feet and then dropped, rose again, and dropped. The third time it was able to get free from its mooring and move out to sea. Two men died of falling cargo, and another died of a heart attack.

EFFECTS OF THE EARTHQUAKE. The Alaska earthquake has been called the best-documented and most thoroughly investigated earthquake in history. Within a month, President Lyndon B. Johnson appointed a Federal Reconstruction and Development Commission for Alaska, a commission that thoroughly researched every aspect of the disaster. The committee divided itself into panels, each representing the major disciplines involved in the data gathering: engineering, geography (human ecology), geology, hydrology, oceanography, biology, and seismology. Each of these panels gathered scientific and technical information.

Other prevention measures for the future included the establishment of the Alaska Tsunami Warning Center (ATWC) in 1967, located in Palmer. Strong-motion seismographs and accelerographs were installed in Anchorage shortly after the quake. Risk maps for Anchorage, Homer, Seward, and Valdez, based on extensive geological studies, were prepared by the Scientific and Engineering Task Force of the Reconstruction Commission and were used as a basis for

The Great Alaska Earthquake caused this bridge over the Cooper River to fall. (National Oceanic and Atmospheric Administration)

federal aid to reconstruction and as guides to future builders.

The earthquake provided seismologists with a rich field of study, but it also turned the nation's attention again, and sharply, to the problems of improving the elements of a national natural-disaster policy: zoning and construction codes, prediction and warning systems, rescue and relief organizations, disaster data collection and analysis, and disaster insurance and reconstruction aids.

There were 131 lives lost in the earthquake, a very small number for so great a catastrophe. There are several reasons for this. First, the earthquake happened on a holiday, when the schools were empty and most offices were deserted. Second, it was an off-season for fishing, so there were very few boats in the harbors. Third, there were no fires in residential or business areas, and fourth, there was a low tide at the time, which left some room for water to flow. Most people who died were swept away by tsunamis, 16 of whom were in Oregon and California. The extensive military establishment provided resources that reduced the loss of life, eased some of the immediate suffering, and restored needed services promptly.

The office of Emergency Planning, under the provisions of the Federal Disaster Act, provided additional aid. This included transitional grants to maintain essential public services, an increase in the federal share of highway reconstruction costs, a decrease in the local share of urban renewal projects, debt adjustments on existing federal loans, federal purchase of state bonds, and grants for a state mortgage-forgiveness program. In all, the earthquake generated $330 million of government and private funds for rescue, relief, and reconstruction.

Because Anchorage is the most populated and most developed area in Alaska, most of the financial losses occurred there. A J. C. Penney building was destroyed, and a Four Seasons apartment building, which was under construction and not yet occupied, totally collapsed. Many other buildings were damaged beyond repair. The Denali Theater on Fourth Avenue in Anchorage was showing a late afternoon matinee when the entire building sank 15 feet. All the children in attendance were able to crawl out, once the building stopped shaking. Almost all the schools in Anchorage were demolished.

Railroads twisted, and a diesel locomotive was thrown 100 yards from the track. Oil storage tanks at Valdez, Seward, and Wittier ruptured and burned. Many bridges, ports, and harbor facilities were destroyed. An incredible 75 percent of Alaska's commerce was ruined—$750 million worth. A landslide at Turnagain Heights destroyed about 130 acres of residential property, including 75 houses. Another landslide at Government Hill caused severe destruction.

A wide area outside the state of Alaska also felt the effects of the quake. Buildings in Seattle, 1,000 miles away, swayed. The tsunami hit Vancouver Island, California, Hawaii, and even Japan. Water levels jumped abruptly as far away as South Africa; shock-induced waves were generated in the Gulf of Mexico. An atmospheric pressure wave was recorded in La Jolla, California. The day became referred to as Black Friday, because of the death and destruction.

Winifred Whelan

FOR FURTHER INFORMATION:

Cohen, Stan. *8.6: The Great Alaska Earthquake March 27, 1964.* Missoula, Mont.: Pictorial Histories, 1995.

Herb, Angela M. *Alaska A to Z: The Most Comprehensive Book of Facts and Figures Ever Compiled About Alaska.* Bellevue, Wash.: Vernon, 1993.

Hulley, Clarence C. *Alaska: Past and Present.* Portland, Oreg.: Binsfords & Mort, 1970.

Lane, Frank. *The Violent Earth.* Topsfield, Mass.: Salem House, 1986.

Murck, Barbara W., Brian Skinner, and Stephen C. Porter. *Dangerous Earth: An Introduction to Geologic Hazards.* New York: John Wiley & Sons, 1997.

National Research Council Committee on the Alaska Earthquake. *The Great Alaska Earthquake of 1964.* Vols. 1 and 2. Washington, D.C.: National Academy of Sciences, 1969-1970.

Paananen, Eloise. *Earthquake! The Story of Alaska's Good Friday Disaster.* New York: John Day, 1966.

Ward, Kaari, ed. *Great Disasters: Dramatic True Stories of Nature's Awesome Powers.* Pleasantville, N.Y.: Reader's Digest Association, 1989.

■ 1965: THE PALM SUNDAY OUTBREAK

TORNADOES

DATE: April 11, 1965

PLACE: Parts of Indiana, Illinois, Iowa, Michigan, Ohio, and Wisconsin across a path 350 miles long and 150 miles wide

CLASSIFICATION: 2 tornadoes—in Elkhart, Indiana, and Strongsville, Ohio—estimated as definitely F5; 17 of the other 49 tornadoes estimated as F4 or F5

RESULT: 271 dead, 3,148 injured, more than $200 million in damage

The Palm Sunday tornado outbreak of April 11, 1965, was the most devastating, until that time, in the United States. As of 2006, it was second in size and destruction to the 1974 Jumbo Outbreak. The Palm Sunday disaster resulted when a mass of cold dry air rapidly moving down from western Canada collided with a mass of warm moist air moving up from the Gulf of Mexico. The colliding air masses produced large storms in Texas and Oklahoma, which grew in intensity as they rapidly moved northeast. These storms followed an unusually intense jet stream that took them to the upper Midwest.

A PLEASANT SUNDAY. In the six states that were struck in the Midwest, it was a warm and balmy Palm Sunday. It seemed like a good day for puttering in the garden or preparing for Easter celebrations. However, it was obvious to some weather experts that conditions were also ideal for the formation of tornadoes, a fact that troubled the U.S. Weather Bureau early that morning. Consequently, tornado warnings were issued throughout the morning. Yet many radio and television stations were closed for Palm Sunday or had a skeletal staff. The forecasts were not widely or adequately communicated.

Investigations after the tornado revealed that most areas had between thirty-five minutes and five hours of warning time, a situation that revealed an additional problem. The public was slow to react and dulled by the numerous tornado watches in "Tornado Alley." Also, many were outside enjoying the warm spring temperatures on a balmy Palm Sunday and were away from their radios. Lack of adequate communication and lack of response was underscored by government investigators as a major cause of the high fatality rate.

DEVASTATION. The first small tornado struck at 1:20 P.M. south of Dubuque, Iowa. An hour later six other tornadoes were reported in Iowa, Wisconsin, and Illinois. By 3:15 weather forecasters in Chicago were able to see a 100-mile-long line of thunderstorms stretching from De Kalb, Illinois, to Madison, Wisconsin, with tornadoes, and even colonies of tornadoes, spewing forth. One tornado near Crystal Lake, Illinois, leveled the Crystal Lake Shopping Center and Colby Estates housing subdivision, wreaking havoc on a path 1 mile wide and 10 miles long.

The scene was repeated throughout the day. Fifty-one tornadoes over a twelve-hour period occurred along a path 300 miles long and 150 miles wide, leaving 266 dead. More than half of the dead were in Indiana. In Russiaville, Indiana (population 1,200), every building was damaged, while in Goshen over 100 trailers were crushed into masses of torn metal. Lower Michigan also was hit hard. Two powerful tornadoes tore through Branch, Hilsdale, Lenawee, and Monroe Counties, killing 44 and causing more than $32 million in damage. Half an hour apart, the tornadoes followed a similar course. Ohio was the third state to bear the brunt of the tornadoes. Devastation was particularly severe south of Cleveland in Strongsville, Ohio. Near Toledo, 370 homes were destroyed along a 10-mile path. Every home in Toledo's Creekside neighborhood was destroyed.

Most tornadoes result in stories of miraculous escapes and pitiful tragedies. In the Palm Sunday tornado there were a number of fortuitous escapes. In Crystal Lake, insurance man Charles Swanson was sucked out of his shower and into the street as his house crashed in around him. Seventeen-year-old Dan Avins was asleep at home near Cleveland when the tornado hit; he awoke to find himself still in bed, 35 feet from his house. James Petro, Jr., an eight-month-old baby living in Strongsville, was hurled 175 feet from his demolished house, suffering only a black eye. Unfortunately another baby in Strongsville was ripped from his mother's hands, along with her wedding ring, and sucked out of the house. Only the mother survived.

THE AFTERMATH. In the aftermath of the destruction, President Lyndon B. Johnson toured the devastation and walked among the twisted steel and rubble of Dunlap, Indiana, which had been torn apart by twin tornadoes. Federal disaster relief was issued rapidly, and insurance agents swarmed into the wreckage. In general, insurance companies received praise for the rapidity at which claims were paid. Among the productive activities was the work of one weather expert who traveled 7,500 miles in four days to make an aerial survey of the tornadoes' destruction. Professor Theodore Fujita of the University of Chicago noticed from the air that tornado tracks paralleled each other and seemed to move in clusters. Where one tornado destruction path would end, another would begin nearby. He also noticed cycloidal marks in open fields, providing indications of a parent tornado with rotating funnels attached to and revolving about the child tornado. These observations helped piece together the Fujita scale of tornado intensity, which has been in use since 1971 as a standard means of classifying tornadoes.

The failure of the public to respond to what seemed to be ample tornado warning was an issue seriously studied by National Weather Service investigators. In succeeding years, recommendations for improved telecommunications and siren warning systems were enacted in many localities vulnerable to one of nature's great cataclysms.

Irwin Halfond

FOR FURTHER INFORMATION:

Bluestein, Howard. *Tornado Alley: Monster Storms of the Great Plains.* New York: Oxford University Press, 1999.

"Disasters: Up the Alley." *Time*, April 23, 1965, 29.

"First the Wind, then the Waters." *Newsweek*, April 26, 1965, 25-26.

Grazulis, Thomas P. *The Tornado: Nature's Ultimate Windstorm.* Norman: University of Oklahoma Press, 2003.

Rosenfeld, Jeffrey. *Eye of the Storm: Inside the World's Deadliest Hurricanes, Tornadoes, and Blizzards.* New York: Basic Books, 2003.

"When 35 Tornadoes Hit 6 States 'Like Bombs.'" *U.S. News & World Report*, April 26, 1965, 50-52.

■ 1966: The Aberfan Disaster

Landslide

Date: October 21, 1966
Place: Aberfan, Wales, United Kingdom
Result: 147 dead (116 children, 31 adults), 32 injured, a school and
8 houses destroyed

The tightly knit mining village of Aberfan lies in the valley of the Taff River, one of many steep-sided valleys that cut through the mountains of Wales. The area had been the site of coal mining for two hundred years. During that time, huge tips (dumps or stockpiles) of mining waste, debris, and ashes piled up on the mountain slopes. The coal mine that was served by the miners of Aberfan had produced such tips, one of which was 700 feet high by 1966, after thirty years of continuous use, and which was being added to by some 36 tons each day.

The coal mine in question, the Merthyr Vale Colliery, had been in private hands until 1947, when, with the nationalization of the British coal industry, it passed into the hands of the National Coal Board, which then assumed responsibility for its working safety. The miners came largely from the village of Aberfan and surrounding villages. The younger children of the village attended Pant Glas Primary (Elementary) school, which was sited on Moy Road and lay directly under the 700-foot tip. On the other side of Moy Road were houses. Between the foot of the tip and the back of the school lay a small farm and the schoolyard.

Heavy rain had fallen in October of 1966, with almost continuous rain on October 19 and 20. Tip workers had noticed some cracks at the top of the tip, caused, it was believed, by the crane or derrick that upended the waste trucks as they were hauled up from the colliery on the valley floor. The crane was ordered moved back, which it was.

The Slide. The morning of Friday, October 21, was a dark, foggy, damp morning. It was the last day for Pant Glas school before the usual midterm break. The 7:30 A.M. shift at the colliery began as normal, with the tip workers setting out for the top. By the time they had

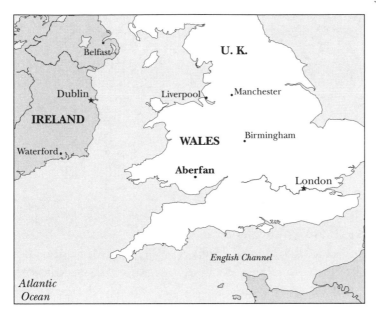

reached it, around 9 A.M., and peered through the fog, they saw only a crater in front of them. The whole side of the tip had slipped down onto the school, the farm, and the houses opposite on Moy Road.

In fact, a solid wall of mud and sludge, made up of water, ash, and coal waste, had crashed down on the school and other buildings and, like an avalanche, engulfed and filled them, as well as demolished parts of their structures. The resulting deaths were therefore as likely to have been caused by suffocation as by the impact of falling debris and collapsing buildings. At the same time, a black dust engulfed the village.

The school itself was a solid Victorian brick edifice, two classrooms in depth, consisting of an assembly hall, some six juniors' classrooms, and two infants' classrooms. The landslide hit those juniors' classrooms facing toward the tip, largely demolishing them. Those facing Moy Road were less severely affected. The two infants' classrooms, being at one end of the school, were largely undamaged. Opposite the school, several houses had also been demolished. At one point, it was estimated that the sludge lay 45 feet deep in the schoolyard.

THE CHILDREN'S EXPERIENCE. For the children attending the school, at 9:15 A.M. assembly had just finished and classes had just begun. One of the surviving children in one of the worst-affected class-rooms described her experiences: They first heard a tremendous rumbling sound; the whole school seemed to go dead, and everyone was terrified. The sound grew louder and louder until they could see the blackness descending outside the window. After that she was knocked unconscious, waking to find her leg trapped and broken under a huge radiator that had been ripped from the wall but which had saved her from suffocation. Most of her classmates were not so fortunate.

Another student described the landslide like water pouring down the hillside. She saw two boys run right into it and be sucked away. It hit the school like a huge wave, splattering everywhere, crushing the buildings. Another child, the last one to be brought out alive, had been completely buried but had managed to stick her fingers through a gap and to call out.

Some surviving children suffered horrific injuries. One boy lost three fingers and suffered a fractured pelvis and an injured leg. He would have bled to death because of his internal injuries, but the mud caked around him. As it was, his ear was ripped off and had to be sewn back on. A few children were more fortunate. One fourteen-year-old boy was late for school. He arrived just as the head teacher was letting all the unscathed children go home.

The first rescuers, who included many of the mothers, climbed through the windows and began to pass children back out. Hearing so many cries, they worked frantically, deep in mud, which was up to 5 feet deep in some classrooms, trying to find those buried. Some of the children managed to escape on their own. The rescuers did not dare move anything, however, in case there was further collapse. Some of the rescuers were themselves injured and needed hospital treatment.

As soon as the colliery was informed, the shift was halted and the miners rushed to the scene, to be joined by other miners from a nearby colliery. The slide was still moving, the fog on the valley floor still persisted, and the road was narrow and a dead-end, so rescue conditions were very difficult, though, in a community used to mining disasters, never chaotic. The dead and injured had to be evacuated, and the sludge had to be dug through and cleared to allow access and to find bodies. Some 25 houses were evacuated by the police.

Engineers with heavy bulldozers were brought in to try to halt the flow of the slag, a move made more urgent by the fear of further rain. However, by the time they arrived the chances of finding anyone else alive were slim. In fact, the last person to be found alive was rescued at 11 A.M., less than two hours after the initial impact. Nevertheless, it took a further six days to recover all the bodies. Many of the truck drivers worked up to six hours at a time clearing the debris; some miners worked for ten hours at a time. The police also joined in the initial digging.

Of 254 children on the school roll, 74 had been declared dead by the end of the first day. Another 2 children had been killed in the farm, together with their grandmother. Eight other adults had been identified as dead, including 3 teachers. About 36 people were in the hospital, and some 80 people were still missing. The deputy head teacher, Mr. D. Beynon, was found clutching 5 children in his arms, dying as he tried to protect them. All of the 38 children in his class appeared to have died. As badly affected was the senior class, those studying for the examinations to gain entrance into high school, where Mrs. M. Bates and 37 children had been killed. In the other senior class, the teacher had been brought out safely, but some 27 children were unaccounted for.

IMMEDIATE AFTERMATH. The engineers had been unable to halt the flow of sludge on the first day. On the next day, Saturday, military rescue units arrived. By the end of the day, the torrential flow of water finally ceased its ferocity. At its height, the tip had been discharging 100,000 gallons of water per hour.

By the end of the day 137 bodies had been recovered—106 children and 16 adults being identified, and a further 15 still unidentified. At least 32 people were still in the hospital. Most of the school had been cleared, but it was feared that up to 60 people could be buried in the surrounding rubble. In fact, there were 8 bodies recovered the next day, Sunday, and 1 body a week later, bringing the final toll to 147, plus 1 of the injured, who died in hospital. Twenty-six rescuers were injured. Almost the entire age range of nine- to eleven-year-old children of the village had been wiped out.

The whole nation was deeply shocked by the disaster. The same day as the accident, the British prime minister, Harold Wilson, promised a high-level independent inquiry, and he himself traveled to Merthyr Tydfil, the nearest town, to meet with local officials. The next day, Saturday, the duke of Edinburgh, the queen's husband, visited the disaster. An appeal fund was immediately set up that day, which grew later to tremendous proportions. Princess Margaret, the queen's sister, appealed for toys for the injured and bereaved children. Also on that day, the public inquiry, which was to become one of the biggest ever held in the United Kingdom, was set up under the Tribunals of Enquiry Act of 1921, to be conducted by Lord Justice Edmund Davies, a respected lord justice of appeal, who had been born only 2 miles from Aberfan and who had known the area all of his life. The speed of such moves was unparalleled. The necessary legislation for the tribunal was put before Parliament and cleared by October 25.

One unfortunate repercussion of this was that all comment on the tragedy was banned by the attorney general, as the affair was now in the hands of the law. Many felt uneasy about this, believing that fair comment was being censored. However, legal aid was granted to all who had been affected, so that they could be legally represented at the inquiry.

An inquest was opened on Monday, October 24, in a small chapel vestry. Over 60 relatives crowded in, and feelings ran high. "Our children have been murdered," was a common cry. The coroner gave the causes of death as asphyxia and multiple injuries but had to explain that it was not his job to apportion blame; that was for the tribunal of inquiry.

The first funerals were held on Thursday, October 27. At the Baptist Church, the minister performing the service had lost his own son. A mass burial was arranged for the Friday, to which an estimated 10,000 people came. Two 8-foot trenches were dug for the coffins, and a 100-foot-tall cross was made from the wreaths sent. It was said that there was little weeping. Some years later, the appeal fund constructed a memorial garden and cemetery for the victims on the site of the demolished school. On Saturday, October 29, the queen and the duke of Edinburgh visited the village, and flags were flown at half-staff throughout the nation.

LONG-TERM AFTERMATH. The psychological scars on the surviving children and their parents remained for a generation; many needed medical and psychological rehabilitation. The survivors had to be moved to other schools; finally, a new school was built nearby.

The village remained in deep shock for many years but never lost its cohesiveness. The nation as a whole was also deeply affected for months, even years. For some, it became a crisis of faith.

The inquiry lasted five months and took statements from 136 witnesses. The National Coal Board was held legally liable for not maintaining their property, the disaster being the result of waste materials being allowed to block an original watercourse. The water, instead of escaping out at the bottom of the tip, as was normal, soaked into the tip and built up enormous pressure within it. The rains of the preceding few days finally rendered the whole tip unstable, and it had therefore collapsed with considerable force.

As a result of the tribunal report, the Mines and Quarries Act of 1989 was passed by the British Parliament, giving the government wide-ranging powers to supervise the safety of mines, quarries, and tips. An earlier act, the Industrial Development Act of 1966, which was designed to help reclaim derelict land but whose implementation had been hampered by lack of funds, was reenergized, especially in Wales. By 1967, the secretary of state for Wales had published a policy document that in future years led to large-scale reclamation of mining sites in South Wales.

In July, 1968, it was decided to remove all the tips of the Merthyr Vale Colliery, though the colliery itself did not cease working until 1989, as part of the overall decline of the Welsh coal-mining industry. The forestry commission replanted much of the wasteland, and the area became a recreation site, which attracts visitors from around the world. The appeal fund was used not only to relieve the suffering of the families affected but also to build new facilities for the village, as well as fund educational research.

David Barratt

FOR FURTHER INFORMATION:

Austin, Tony. *Aberfan: The Story of a Disaster.* London: Hutchinson, 1967.

McLean, Iain, and Martin Johnes. *Aberfan: Government and Disasters.* Cardiff, Wales: Welsh Academic Press, 2000.

Madgwick, Gaynor. *Aberfan: Struggling out of the Darkness—A Survivor's Story.* Blaengarw, Wales: Valleys and Vales Autobiography Project, 1996.

Miller, Joan. *Aberfan: A Disaster and Its Aftermath.* London: Constable, 1974.

Morgan, Louise, and Jane Scourfield, et al. "The Aberfan Disaster: 33-Year Follow-up of Survivors." *The British Journal of Psychiatry* 182 (2003): 532-536.

Rapoport, I. C. *Aberfan: The Days After—a Journey in Pictures.* Cardigan, Wales: Parthian, 2005.

■ 1969: HURRICANE CAMILLE

HURRICANE

DATE: August 15-18, 1969
PLACE: Mississippi, Louisiana, Alabama, Virginia, and West Virginia
CLASSIFICATION: Category 5
RESULT: 258 dead, $1.5 billion in damage

Packing winds of nearly 200 miles per hour and a barometric pressure of 26.84 inches, Hurricane Camille was a storm of immense intensity and at the time only the second on record to strike the U.S. mainland with Category 5 force. From the time it was first designated a hurricane on August 15, 1969, as it moved from south of Cuba to its point of dissipation over the North Atlantic, Camille left a staggering amount of devastation, including 258 storm-related deaths and an estimated $1.5 billion in damage, much of it concentrated in the Gulf Coast regions of Louisiana and Mississippi.

THE BEGINNINGS. For several days in its early stages, Camille moved at a leisurely pace across the Atlantic as a relatively disorganized tropical system. The storm was spawned on August 5 by a tropical wave moving off the coast of Africa. By August 9 it had reached tropical disturbance level, approaching the northern Leeward Islands, before passing through them on the following day. The same day a satellite photograph indicated it was no more than a weak cloud mass. On August 11 satellite imagery revealed the system had become an isolated block of clouds located between Puerto Rico and the Lesser Antilles and that it had broken into two circular air masses.

For a brief time officials at the U.S. Weather Service believed the tropical disturbance was unlikely to reach the status of a major storm. A hurricane hunter who flew into the tropical wave reported little organization in the cloud formation. However, after reaching the warm waters of the Caribbean, the disturbance rapidly intensified and was designated a tropical storm as it moved within 350 miles of Cuba. Camille's central pressure had dropped dramatically to 29.50 inches, and its sustained winds topped 65 miles per hour.

Coursing through the Caribbean, the storm continued its rapid intensification, with winds climbing to over 80 miles per hour and its barometric pressure falling to 28.67 inches. On August 15, the storm was upgraded to hurricane status, as it moved through the Yucatán Straits on its way northwest. Maximum winds were recorded at 115 miles per hour, with gales extending out 125 to 150 miles to the north of the storm's center and 50 miles to its south. Its forward movement was measured at 7 miles per hour.

Camille swept over the western tip of Cuba with 115-mile-per-hour winds, driving hundreds of residents to higher ground with its torrential rains. The weather station at Guane, center of a rich tobacco area, reported winds of 92 miles per hour. As the storm meandered toward the eastern Gulf of Mexico, it dumped nearly 10 inches of precipitation on the Isle of Pines, immediately south of the Cuban mainland. At the time, the U.S. Weather Bureau placed the storm's center about 250 miles south-southwest of Key West.

The region of Cuba struck by the storm is an area highly vulnerable to flooding owing to the runoff of rain that rushes down the mountainsides to the sea. The sugar crop and tobacco crop, both mainstays of the Cuban economy, suffered extensive damage during the storm's passage. In the central town of Puerto Cortes, 50 houses were destroyed. In many communities along the coast, power and telephone communications were cut off and large ranches and farms were isolated by the flash floods.

CAMILLE CONTINUES TO INTENSIFY. Camille continued on a track that took it through the Yucatán Channel, and on August 16 its eye moved into the Gulf of Mexico. The storm's forward movement was measured at 12 miles per hour. It was located 400 miles south of the Florida panhandle and moving in a north-northwest direction. Camille's winds covered 80-mile-wide circles and buffeted across 200 miles of Gulf waters. Its barometric pressure tumbled to 27.13 inches.

Hurricane Camille not only continued to intensify but also surprised storm watchers by changing its course to a more northwesterly direction toward the Louisiana-Mississippi-Alabama coastlines. On August 16 a hurricane watch was put into effect, stretching from Biloxi, Mississippi, to St. Marks, Florida. As the storm moved to within 250 miles of Mobile, Alabama, Camille's winds were estimated at 160 miles per hour and its speed at 12 miles per hour. The storm continued its on its track toward the mouth of the Mississippi River, prompting officials to extend the hurricane warning as far west as New Orleans.

Late in the evening on August 16, Camille's eye crossed into the Pass Christian, Mississippi, area with winds up to 200 miles per hour, accompanied by a monster tide 24 feet above normal. The hurricane skirted the mouth of the Mississippi River some 90 miles southeast of New Orleans in an area lined with small islands, bays, and harbors. On August 17, a final Air Force reconnaissance flight recorded a barometric pressure of 26.61 inches with maximum surface winds at more than 200 miles per hour. The barometric reading was second only to the 26.35 reading for the Labor Day Hurricane of 1935, the lowest ever recorded at the time. Later in the day, at 9 P.M., the National Hurricane Center issued a warning that Camille was "extremely dangerous" and was bringing 15- to 20-foot tides with it along the Mississippi-Alabama coast. Areas along the coast were advised to evacuate immediately.

EVACUATION AND LANDFALL. The main damage inflicted by the storm throughout the low coastal region was from the floods produced by the high tides and heavy rainfall. In Gulfport, Mississippi, all evacuation centers had run short of food and water even before Camille's arrival. The storm's track along the coastline was marked by a series of local communication and power failures. In a clear sign of the severity of the storm, the Mississippi River Bridge at New Orleans was closed to traffic, and the world's longest bridge, the causeway that crosses Lake Pontchartrain, was shut down. Camille's winds lashed the causeway at more than 60 miles per hour and churned the lake's water into a caldron of violent waves.

Evacuations were ordered all the way from Grand Isle, Louisiana, to the Florida Panhandle. Over 100,000 people spent the night of August 17 in Red Cross shelters, in the area extending from New Orleans to Pensacola. Residents of the fishing villages of Louisiana's marshlands evacuated by the thousands. Nearly 90 percent of the population left their homes to take refuge. The Red Cross announced it had set up 394 evacuation centers in the Mississippi Delta area, with over 40,000 people reported in shelters as far away as Alexandria, Louisiana, 200 miles to the north, and Lafayette, located in the southwestern corner of the state. U.S. Coast Guard helicopters had to risk the storm's winds to rescue 30 men stranded on an oil rig in the Gulf of Mexico. Waves of 12 to 14 feet were reported at a rig located offshore from Timbalier Island, which is situated about 40 miles west of the mouth of the Mississippi River.

Following its swipe at southern Louisiana, Camille washed ashore near Gulfport just before midnight on August 17. Its barometric pressure stood at 26.84 inches, and its winds continued to whirl at 180 miles per hour. When ranked by size, Camille was a relatively small hurricane, with an eye less than 5 miles in diameter. Its hurricane-force winds reached out 45 miles in all directions, with gales extending out 150 miles. Mobile, located nearly 95 miles east of the storm's center, registered 44-mile-per-hour winds, while New Orleans, situated nearly 45 miles closer to the storm's core, received sustained winds of 52 miles per hour.

THE DAMAGE. Camille's lethal combination of high winds and high tides brought almost total destruction to the coastal areas from southeastern Louisiana to Biloxi. Because of the many shapes and sizes of the bays and inlets, surge heights varied at different locations. In several places in Louisiana, from the Empire Canal south to Buras, Boothville, and Venice, the surge poured over the levees on both the east and west banks of the Mississippi River, only to be trapped by the back levees, leaving the built-up areas between the embankments flooded with up to 16 feet of water. The east-bank levees were nearly destroyed as the wave action of the water severely eroded the landside slope before reaching the back levees. The regions within the levees were almost totally destroyed. Few structures survived intact, and those that did ended up floating about until dumped between or on the levees.

The waves nearly wiped the small community of Buras off the map when the town was inundated with 15 feet of water in a matter of minutes. In one bizarre incident, a 200-foot barge loaded with combustible solvents was dumped by the waters in the middle of a highway running through the center of the town. As the storm surge swept over the river's east-bank levee, a swift influx of tidal waters disrupted the normal flow of the river, elevating its water level for a considerable distance upstream. Close to 66 percent of the total land area in Plaquemines Parish, representing about 414,000 acres of land, was flooded.

Along the coast, fires raged out of control, as firefighters were unable to reach them in the wake of the inundating tides. Buildings in Bay St. Louis, Mississippi, a scenic coastal town located 15 miles west of Gulfport near the Mississippi line, burned furiously. Its business district, comprising mainly a lumber mill and seafood packing center, was concentrated on a single street, half of which caved into the bay. An estimated 95 percent of the homes in the city were damaged.

Thousands of people in Louisiana, Mississippi, and Alabama were left homeless as the storm made its way across the coastline. The destruction wrought by Camille stretched along 50 miles of beach from Waveland, Mississippi, to Pascagoula, near the Alabama state line, and three or four blocks inland. The storm raised the Gulf of Mexico nearly 3 feet higher than normal as far as 125 miles east of Pass Christian, Mississippi, and 31 miles to the west. The U.S. Army Corps of Engineers later estimated that 100,000 tons of debris had to be cleared away in order to make passable nearly 530 miles of road. U.S. Highway 90, the main coastal road, was covered with sand in many sec-

Hurricane Camille was one of few storms to achieve Category 5 status at landfall. (National Oceanic and Atmospheric Administration)

tions; piled high with lumber, furniture, refrigerators, mattresses, and other debris in some stretches; and completely washed away in others. Nearly one-third of the Bay St. Louis Bridge and one-half of the Biloxi-Ocean Springs Bridge were damaged when the high tides shoved the spans off their supports. An estimated 50 percent of the resort properties in the Biloxi area were damaged and the other half destroyed. Fourteen counties in Mississippi suffered electrical power failures, some lasting for several days. Telephone service also was affected, as nearly 15 percent of telephones were put out of service, with the number jumping to 67 percent along the Gulf Coast. Pascagoula faced a problem of another kind when it was invaded by hundreds of poisonous cottonmouth snakes seeking higher ground. One woman reported hundreds of black water moccasins and cottonmouths in her mother's backyard.

Homes and buildings that had withstood previous hurricane-level storms proved no match for Camille. Water stood 10-feet deep in the lobby of the plush Broadwater Beach Hotel. A wave of 22 feet inundated Pass Christian Isles, including the Richelieu apartment complex, where a decision by a group of people to ignore the warnings and ride out the storm with a "hurricane party" ended in tragedy when 23 of them died in the onslaught. Along with the storm surge, heavy precipitation, between 5 and 10 inches, moved inland with Camille. Rainfalls from 2 to 6 inches extended to portions of southeast Louisiana, central and northern Mississippi, and northwest Florida.

Stately oak trees that had also survived previous hurricane-force winds fell victim to Camille. Pine trees were blown down in forests nearly 70 miles inland. Roofs were torn from barracks at Camp Shelby, an Army base located more than 65 miles from the coastline.

WIND SPEEDS AND TIDES. Based on wind speeds measured at reconnaissance flight levels and measured surface pressure, maximum surface winds reached 201.5 miles per hour near the center of Camille on August 17. As the storm moved inland, many of the recording instruments were damaged or destroyed. The highest actual wind reading was taken on a drilling rig recorder, located about 15 miles from the storm's center, which registered a gust of 172 miles per hour. An Air National Guard Weather Flight unit located at Gulfport Municipal Airport estimated sustained winds at over 100 miles per hour with gusts ranging between 150 to 200 miles per hour.

Keesler Air Force Base in Biloxi measured winds at 81 miles per hour with gusts up to 129 miles per hour.

In Pascagoula, sustained winds of 81 miles per hour were recorded at a shipyard, while a local radio station reported winds at 104 miles per hour before it was knocked off the air. Wind speeds west of Camille's center were lower than those extending east. Although Lakefront Airport reported sustained winds of 87 miles per hour with gusts of 109 miles per hour, winds at New Orleans generally ranged from 40 to 60 miles per hour with gusts up to 85 miles per hour. On the other hand, eastern portions of St. Tammany and Washington Parishes were raked by winds estimated at well over 100 miles per hour. As Camille moved ashore, sustained hurricane-force winds were generally confined to the storm's center, extending east of New Orleans to Pascagoula, with gusts reaching from New Orleans to Mobile Bay.

Enormous tidal surges marked Camille's arrival. The small towns of Pass Christian, Bay St. Louis, and Waveland were all but destroyed by a giant wave generated by the storm's backlash. Record-breaking tide levels were recorded from Waveland to Biloxi. Tides in some areas were measured up to 24 feet. Generally, they ran from about 15 to 22 feet above normal. The storm generated tides as high as 3 to 5 feet above normal as far away as Apalachicola, Florida. West of the storm's center, tides ranged from about 10 to 15 feet above normal but then dropped off substantially, running only 3 to 4 feet above normal west of the Mississippi. Grand Isle, located only 60 miles west of the hurricane, reported a tide of 3.6 feet.

THE DEATH TOLL AND AFTEREFFECTS. Many of those who perished in the surge were found lashed together, usually family members or husbands and wives who were attempting to survive the rising waters. Every home in Pass Christian, a town of 4,000 people, was damaged. Nearly 100 bodies were discovered in the debris, including all 13 members of one family. At a local high school where residents had gathered, rescuers found a cluster of parents holding their children overhead to protect them from the raging floodwaters below. Generally, buildings located on hills of about 20 feet survived the high winds and storm surge, while structures situated around the 10-foot level were overwhelmed. As the winds diminished, National Guard troops in amphibious vehicles rushed in to rescue survivors clinging to trees and remnants of houses.

All together, 143 people were killed along the coast from Louisiana to Alabama. The storm also took a toll on fish and wildlife, especially in the estuary region lying east of the Mississippi River. Many deer and muskrats were killed. Only 40 to 50 of a deer herd of 500 roaming the area were believed to have survived. Millions of fish were killed, as were some shrimp, and oyster seedbeds located in the bays and inlets received considerable damage from debris deposited on them during the storm.

The storm caused little intrusion of saltwater into the lower reaches of the Mississippi River. Samples taken at the water supply intakes at New Orleans and Port Sulphur did not reveal any significant increases in salinity, though some locations along the eastern Louisiana coast did experience brief periods of additional salinity during Camille's passage.

Camille dealt a severe blow to the region's commercial shipping industry. A surveyor noted that 24 vessels, ranging from tugs to freighters, were found aground. Among the boats was the container ship *Mormacsun*, which only recently had been launched and was being outfitted at a shipyard when its mooring lines snapped, driving it aground. The storm caused the collision of two vessels set adrift in the waters, the 4,459-ton Greek freighter *Lion of Chaeronea* and the 10,648-ton U.S.-flagged *Windsor Victory*. Both ships suffered only minor damage. Three cargo ships in Gulfport harbor, the *Alamo Victory*, the *Hulda*, and the *Silver Hawk*, were severely damaged and washed ashore. A tug, the *Charleston*, in the process of towing the barge *City of Pensacola*, was in danger of sinking and had to be beached. Another victim, the 10,250-ton U.S.-flagged freighter *Venetia V*, docked in Mobile, was ripped from its moorings and set adrift.

The storm also inflicted severe damage on the area's petroleum industry, particularly in the offshore areas east of the Louisiana delta. Installations at South Pass, Main Pass, and Breton Sound were battered by the storm, as were facilities situated in the marshes and shallow bays, including Quarantine Bay, Cox Bay, and Black Bay. Two large oil slicks formed south of New Orleans, one a result of a leaking offshore well in Breton Sound, the other from a ruptured storage tank near the town of Venice in Plaquemines Parish. Because Venice was still under water from the high tides, the oil riding the top of the water lapped at the inundated houses and other buildings.

Facilities located west of the Mississippi River fared better, receiving only light damage. At least 4,000 oil wells, stretching from the Mississippi Delta to the St. Bernard Parish line, representing close to 10 percent of Louisiana's wells, were shut down and 3,000 employees evacuated prior to the storm's arrival. As a result of the precautionary measures, there were no reported injuries to petroleum industry personnel, despite direct hits on the facilities. All together, Camille destroyed 4 platforms, 3 drilling rigs, and 7 wells. In addition, 2 platforms, 7 drilling rigs, and a well suffered heavy damage.

An aerial survey by the U.S. Forest Service of 14 counties in southern Mississippi indicated that nearly 1.9 million acres of commercial forestland sustained damage. The storm completely defoliated some of the area's hardwood forests, with the pine forests suffering somewhat less damage. Agricultural and timber losses in Louisiana included 8,000 cattle and 150,000 orange trees in Plaquemines Parish, oyster beds in Plaquemines and St. Bernard Parishes, and over $40 million in damages to tung oil trees and timber in St. Tammany and Washington Parishes.

CAMILLE MOVES INLAND. As Camille moved inland across Mississippi, its strength diminished, and on August 18 it was downgraded to a tropical storm. By the time it reached the northern Mississippi border, it had been downgraded to a depression, though its rainy core remained surprisingly intact and its eye clearly visible on satellite photographs after more than a day over land. Its remnants finally merged with a moisture-filled air mass to produce record amounts of rainfall, in some cases more than 25 inches, throughout Tennessee, Kentucky, and Virginia. As it moved through West Virginia, the storm deposited nearly 5 inches of rain in the southern portions of the state.

The combination of weather factors produced rainfall amounts that rank with other record rainfalls throughout the world. Some amounts exceeded 25 inches, and totals in excess of 4 inches fell in an eight-hour period over a region 30 to 40 miles wide and 120 miles long. A U.S. Army Corps of Engineers' study later underscored the improbability of the rainfall amounts in Nelson County, Virginia, which totaled 27 inches within eight hours. The study concluded the probable maximum rainfall that was possible for the area was 28 inches in six hours and 31 inches in twelve hours. An unofficial 31-inch total that was recorded is believed by meteorologists to represent the probable maximum rainfall to be theoretically possible for Virginia during this period of the year.

As a measure of the storm's uniqueness, it is estimated that rainfalls of this magnitude occur only once every thousand years. Ironically, a severe drought had plagued Mississippi, Tennessee, and Kentucky for much of the summer before Camille's arrival, reducing soil moisture content far below normal levels. As a result, pasture conditions and crops were in poor shape, and though the rains alleviated some of the conditions, they were too late to overcome much of the drought damage.

Virginia experienced what many authorities considered was one of the worst natural disasters in the state's history. Thousands of families in the mountainous sections of west-central Virginia were left homeless by rains of 10 inches or more, as walls of water washed down mountain slopes and through countless homes, businesses, and industries located in valley communities. Many of the residents of the tiny mountain towns and hamlets were asleep when the floodwaters struck. The swollen streams and landslides precipitated by the torrential rains uprooted trees and hurled them down the mountainsides with enough force to smash houses and overturn automobiles. Entire families were swept away by the waters, while others climbed onto trees and roofs and waited until rescue helicopters could reach them.

In some areas whole sections of mountainside tumbled down like mudslides, dumping tons of silt on houses and their occupants. The entire downtown area of Glasgow, Virginia, was inundated by over 14 feet of water, which flooded nearly 75 percent of its homes. Among the hardest hit regions was Buena Vista, Virginia, located at the foot of the Blue Ridge Mountains, where some buildings stood 30 feet underwater. In Louisa County, an earthen dam broke, collapsing a 500-acre human-made lake.

Camille's remnants washed out close to 200 miles of primary and secondary roads and damaged or destroyed 133 bridges in Virginia, 92 of which were located in Nelson County. Route 29 between Amherst and Charlottesville suffered severe damage, with 5 major washouts and 30 landslides. At one point during the storm, only one highway crossing the state remained open for its entire length. The James River, a placid stream that normally runs 100 feet to a few hundred yards wide above Richmond, turned into a sprawling wet plain a mile wide in places. More than 80 bridges spanning major highways and secondary roads were washed away by the rampaging waters. Railroad routes throughout the state fared little better, as several railroad bridges were destroyed and long stretches of track put out of operation.

Camille regained tropical storm status when it crossed back into the North Atlantic but dissipated when it was absorbed by a cold front as it moved about 175 miles southeast of Cape Race, Newfoundland. Based on its path of destruction, Hurricane Camille ranks as one of the most devastating storms to strike the U.S. mainland in the twentieth century.

William Hoffman

FOR FURTHER INFORMATION:

Dikkers, R. D., and H. C. S. Thom. *Hurricane Camille—August 1969.* Washington, D.C.: U.S. Government Printing Office, National Bureau of Standards, 1971.

Hearn, Philip D. *Hurricane Camille: Monster Storm of the Gulf Coast.* Jackson: University Press of Mississippi, 2004.

"Hurricane Camille." *Weatherwise,* July/August, 1999, 28-31.

Longshore, David. *Encyclopedia of Hurricanes, Typhoons, and Cyclones.* New York: Checkmark Books, 2000.

Wilkinson, Kenneth P., and Peggy J. Ross. *Citizens' Responses to Warnings of Hurricane Camille.* State College: Mississippi State University, Social Science Research Center, 1970.

Zebrowski, Ernest, and Judith A. Howard. *Category 5: The Story of Camille, Lessons Unlearned from America's Most Violent Hurricane.* Ann Arbor: University of Michigan Press, 2005.

■ 1970: THE ANCASH EARTHQUAKE

EARTHQUAKE

DATE: May 31, 1970
PLACE: Northern Peru
MAGNITUDE: 7.7
RESULT: Approximately 70,000 dead, 140,000 injured, 500,000 homeless, 160,000 buildings destroyed or damaged

The scene of this disaster is known for its rugged beauty. Towering, snow-capped mountains with steep, rocky slopes overlook the valley of the Santa River, which flows to the north through the Department of Ancash and then turns west until it empties into the Pacific Ocean. This narrow valley—about 5 miles at its widest point—runs for 125 miles parallel to Peru's Pacific shore and is dotted by a series of towns and small cities. For example, Yungay, an old town with roots in the colonial era, was by the 1960's a forward-looking community with an interest in tourism.

One of the region's greatest assets is its physical environment. Looming 14,000 feet above the valley floor are the twin peaks of Mount Huascarán, which measure 22,190 and 21,860 feet above sea level. The peaks are prominent in a section of the Andes Mountains that also includes glaciers and, at lower altitudes, cold lakes drained by streams that feed the Santa River. The monumental Huascarán attracts mountain climbers from around the world because of the extraordinarily steep slopes that rise at angles of 45 to 90 degrees. At the base of these mountains are large boulders, evidence of the area's geological instability.

The Santa River Valley, also known as the Callejón de Huaylas, has a long record of human settlement. Archaeologists have found remains of the Chavin culture that date back as far as 800 B.C.E. The Inca Empire reached into the area in the 1460's, only to be superseded by the Spanish conquistadors in the 1530's. The Spanish controlled most of the agriculture in the valley during the colonial period (1530's-1820's), but the population became heavily mestizo—a mixture of Native Americans and Europeans.

The independence of Peru from Spain brought few changes in the society and the economy, with much of the best land in the valley in the hands of a few landowners well into the twentieth century. Yungay, an important political center, was also a leading market for the peasant farmers who bought and sold foodstuffs and textiles. By the 1960's, however, a new dynamism took hold in Yungay. A paved highway provided easy access to people and goods outside the region. Yungay had a dependable source of electricity, and plans were in place for the construction of a large hotel for visiting mountain climbers and tourists.

In spite of its location in the Andes, a mountain chain well known for earthquakes, the Callejón de Huaylas had experienced relatively few cataclysmic events before 1970. The three most serious events, however, did furnish forebodings of geological conditions that harbored the potential for a major disaster. The large avalanche of 1725 that destroyed the colonial city of Ancash was caused by the breaking of a high mountain glacier that sent tons of ice hurtling downward, picking up rocks and debris as it crashed into the unsuspecting city in the valley below. Another city, Huaraz, was inundated by the bitterly cold waters of a mountain lake that spilled into the valley in 1941. In 1962 another large avalanche overran the community of Ranrahirca. These events all involved loss of life, injuries, and property damage, but, in comparison with the earthquake of 1970, they also served as warnings of a disaster of much greater magnitude.

EARTHQUAKE AND AVALANCHE. The Sunday afternoon of May 31, 1970, was a time of relaxation for the people of the valley, with extended family visits, casual strolls through town plazas, and leisurely meals at local restaurants. This pleasant scene ended abruptly at 3:23 P.M. with the first rumblings in the ground. The Callejón de Huaylas and, indeed, all of Peru rests on or near the place in the earth's crust where two major tectonic plates come together. The Nazca Plate, gradually moving beneath the Pacific Ocean, tends to push under the South American Plate, causing the latter to rise. On May 31, the Nazca Plate's movement become sudden and intense, pushing the edge of the South American Plate upward. This extraordinary tectonic shift broke off a large section of Huascarán overlooking the Callejón de Huaylas—probably 0.5 mile wide and 0.75 mile long. The huge mass crashed down upon a glacier, adding large chunks of ice to the avalanche that, because of the steep slope, accelerated as it moved downward, reaching a speed of approximately 200 miles per hour. The rock and ice collided and shattered into smaller segments that, in spite of the fragmentation, weighed tons when they reached the valley floor.

Yungay was in the path of the avalanche. Within four minutes a great mass of rock, ice, soil, and water covered the 10 miles from Huascarán to the town. Eyewitnesses described the mass as being as high as a ten-story building as it roared across the valley floor to bury Yungay and nearby villages beneath a sea of mud and rock that, after settling for several days, was over 15 feet deep. Approximately 3,500 of Yungay's population perished beneath the huge avalanche. Only an estimated 200 survived.

A portion of the avalanche veered to the north along the Santa River, crushing virtually everything in its path. Included in the debris of this mass were bodies and houses from Yungay. Another section, or lobe, of the avalanche crossed the river bed and rolled about 200 feet up the mountain slope on the western side of the valley. As these lobes of the avalanche moved to the north and west, they carried boulders the size of automobiles and deposited them considerable distances from Huascarán, some reportedly as far north as the Cañón de Pato, approximately 25 miles from Yungay.

The earthquake that caused the avalanche also produced devastating results in areas not reached by the mass of rock, ice, and debris. For example, the city of Huaraz, about 35 miles south of Yungay, experienced the collapse of many of its structures, including portions of the cathedral on the main plaza and the homes of both rich and poor. All through the valley, walls made of adobe crumbled and roofs caved in. In Huaraz and other communities, some cemeteries were so severely shaken that monuments collapsed and tombs broke open. Recently built highways and bridges that linked towns and cities in the Santa River Valley were destroyed. The violent shaking of the earth also destroyed the region's electric-power grid, as well as water and sewer lines. Within a few minutes most of the human-made structures in the Callejón de Huaylas were in ruins or covered by thick layers of rock and mud. Surveys after the earthquake indicate that more than 160,000 buildings were destroyed or damaged—approximately 80 percent of the structures in the area. Although the impact of the earthquake was most intense in the Callejón de Huaylas, buildings collapsed throughout the Department of Ancash, including those in cities and villages along the Pacific coast.

AFTERMATH. Seismographic records made clear to the outside world that a powerful earthquake had struck the Callejón de Huaylas, but the survivors in the devastated valley had to struggle without external aid for four days. Airplanes and helicopters dispatched by the Peruvian government encountered billowing clouds of dust that extended as high as 18,000 feet, blocking visual observation of most of the valley. The destruction of telephone lines and highways prevented communication and the movement of people. Meanwhile, the survivors attempted to care for themselves. The only hospital in the valley was in the city of Huaraz, and it quickly became the gathering place for the injured. The hospital structure was damaged but remained standing as five doctors attended to a steady stream of hundreds of patients over the four-day period between the earthquake and the arrival of outside aid.

Finally, on June 5, the atmosphere cleared enough for pilots to find relatively clear drop zones and landing strips. The Peruvian air force dropped 70 tons of food and other supplies by parachute and transported over 400 injured residents to outside medical facilities by helicopter. Later on the same day, a landing field near Huaraz was sufficiently repaired to accommodate small transport planes. By June 9, Peruvian engineers had repaired highways into the valley, opening the way for emergency vehicles. On the same day, Peruvian president Juan Velasco Alvarado established the Committee for the Reconstruction and Rehabilitation of the Affected Zone (CRYRZA), a government agency that was responsible for supervision of efforts to supply material aid and the implementation of long-term plans for the rebuilding of communities. Soon military and other emergency aircraft from Argentina, Brazil, the United States, Canada, France, and the Soviet Union arrived not only with much-needed supplies but also with experienced crews who soon joined with the Peruvian air force to provide a continuous flow of relief and evacuation missions. Medical personnel, engineers, government officials, and volunteers worked with the survivors on the necessary tasks: the burial of the dead, the erection of shelters for the living, and the distribution of food and medicine throughout the valley.

RECOVERY. The reconstruction of communities began within weeks after the earthquake, but the complicated processes of reestablishing the physical infrastructure, such as roads, public buildings, private homes, and commercial establishments, as well as the institutions of local government and private businesses, required many months and, in some cases, years. For example, Yungay had virtually disappeared, buried beneath the avalanche, but, within a year, approximately 1,800 people had moved into its vicinity to build a new community with the same name. By the middle of 1971, Yungay had a functioning local government, primary and secondary schools, and a revived commercial sector. Huaraz also rebuilt quickly, highlighted by the construction of a modern airport with the capacity to handle small jet aircraft. By 1980, all the valley's cities were linked to a modern electric power grid and the new highway system that ran down the Santa River Valley to the Pacific coast.

This recovery, although impressive in many ways, was not free of acrimony and accusations. The distribution of aid was more prompt in some areas than in others, causing angry complaints from those who felt neglected. Some of the materials to be used in home construction were not suitable for the mountain environment. Finally, frustrated locals accused government officials of incompetence and corruption as some reconstruction projects dragged on for months and, in a few cases, years.

Much uncertainty remained about the future safety of the inhabitants of the valley. The geological conditions that had caused the disaster remained: an unstable land prone to earthquakes surrounded by steep-sided mountains with high-altitude glaciers and lakes. A key to the safety of the region was the Santa Corporation, a government agency charged with the responsibility of monitoring the buildup of ice and snow on the mountain summits and changes in the conditions of glaciers and lakes. The Santa Corporation was primarily responsible for avoiding another disaster soon after the events of May 31, 1970. The earthquake had thrust a large boulder into the stream that customarily drained Lake Orkococha, located on the flank on Mount Huascarán. As a result, the level of that lake was much higher than normal and threatened to spill over its banks, causing a flood on the valley floor. Working furiously, an international team of mountain climbers cut a new drainage channel for the lake by June 7, thereby averting a second disaster for the people of the valley. The Santa Corporation's duties were taken over by a new government agency called Ingeomin in 1977.

John A. Britton

FOR FURTHER INFORMATION:

Bode, Barbara. *No Bells to Toll: Destruction and Creation in the Andes.* New York: Scribner, 1989.

"Death by Glacier." *Scientific American* 223, no. 2 (August, 1970): 46.

Dorbath, L., A. Cisternas, and C. Dorbath. "Assessment of the Size of Large and Great Historical Earthquakes in Peru." *Bulletin of the Seismological Society of America* 80, no. 3 (June 1, 1990): 551-576.

Levy, Matthys, and Mario Salvador. *Why the Earth Quakes: The Story of Earthquakes and Volcanoes.* New York: W. W. Norton, 1995.

Lomnitz, C. "The Peru Earthquake of May 31, 1970: Some Preliminary Seismological Results." *Bulletin of the Seismological Society of America* 61, no. 3 (June, 1971): 535-542.

Machado, Jesús Ángel Chávez. "Remembering the Worst Earthquake in Latin America: The Day the Apus Turned Their Backs on Peru." *ISDR Informs—Latin America and the Caribbean,* no. 1 (2000).

Oliver-Smith, Anthony. *The Martyred City: Death and Rebirth in the Andes.* Albuquerque: University of New Mexico Press, 1986.

INDEXES

■ CATEGORY LIST

Category List

HURRICANES, TYPHOONS, AND CYCLONES
Hurricanes, Typhoons, and Cyclones (overview)
1900: The Galveston hurricane, Texas
1926: The Great Miami Hurricane
1928: The San Felipe hurricane, Florida and the Caribbean
1938: The Great New England Hurricane of 1938
1957: Hurricane Audrey
1969: Hurricane Camille
1970: The Bhola cyclone, East Pakistan
1989: Hurricane Hugo
1992: Hurricane Andrew
1998: Hurricane Mitch
2005: Hurricane Katrina

ICE STORMS. *See* BLIZZARDS, FREEZES, ICE STORMS, AND HAIL

ICEBERGS AND GLACIERS
Icebergs and Glaciers (overview)

LANDSLIDES, MUDSLIDES, AND ROCKSLIDES
Landslides, Mudslides, and Rockslides (overview)
1963: The Vaiont Dam Disaster, Italy
1966: The Aberfan Disaster, Wales
2006: The Leyte mudslide, Philippines

LIGHTNING STRIKES
Lightning Strikes (overview)

METEORITES AND COMETS
Meteorites and Comets (overview)
c. 65,000,000 B.C.E.: Yucatán crater, Atlantic Ocean
1908: The Tunguska event, Siberia

MUDSLIDES. *See* LANDSLIDES, MUDSLIDES, AND ROCKSLIDES

ROCKSLIDES. *See* LANDSLIDES, MUDSLIDES, AND ROCKSLIDES

SANDSTORMS. *See* DUST STORMS AND SANDSTORMS